Dream a little dream of me

Eddi Fiegel is a freelance writer and broadcaster. Her work has appeared in the *Sunday Times*, the *Guardian*, the *Independent on Sunday* and *Mojo* and she is a regular contributor to BBC 6 Music. She is well known for her interviews with artists across the musical spectrum from Paul McCartney to kd Lang, David Bowie and Ennio Morricone. She is the author of the highly acclaimed *John Barry: A Sixties Theme*. She lives in London.

Also by Eddi Fiegel

John Barry *A Sixties Theme*

Eddi Fiegel

Dream a little dream of me

the life of 'Mama' Cass Elliot

Pan Books

First published 2005 by Sidgwick & Jackson

This edition published 2013 by Pan Books
an imprint of Pan Macmillan, a division of Macmillan Publishers Limited
Pan Macmillan, 20 New Wharf Road, London N1 9RR
Basingstoke and Oxford
Associated companies throughout the world
www.panmacmillan.com

ISBN-13: 978-0-230-77241-0

Cass Elliot's sleeve notes for Denny Doherty's *Waiting for a Song*
reproduced by kind permission of TKO Licensing Ltd.
'Everybody's Been Talking' lyrics reproduced courtesy of Kim Fowley.

A CIP catalogue record for this book is available from
the British Library.

Typeset by SetSystems Ltd, Saffron Walden, Essex

Contents

Introduction

Writing *Dream a Little Dream of Me* has been little short of an epic adventure. Finding the reality behind the 'Mama' Cass myth led me on a search which spanned nearly four years and three continents. From Hollywood's leafy hills and the outer reaches of California, Florida, Tennessee, Arizona, Massachusetts and New York to downtown Johannesburg, South Africa and the more far-flung corners of England, it was a memorable trail. Cass's friends and acquaintances were never, by any stretch of the imagination, dull and my encounters often proved highly entertaining.

'I will give you a hundred dollars,' David Crosby told me, 'if you can find a single person who says they hated Cass.' It was not a challenge I actively sought to meet, but despite having spoken to over a hundred friends, colleagues and relatives, Crosby's dollars are still safe.

I soon found out that few who encountered Cass Elliot ever forgot her. Long before she was famous, she made an indelible impact on almost everyone she met. She had a talent for forging friendships and for making even the most casual acquaintance feel that they were a trusted confidante. In the notoriously shallow worlds of entertainment and showbiz, Cass stood out as a beacon of genuine warmth and inspired unparalleled affection.

Throughout my research I repeatedly found that those who had known her, whether they had been close friends or merely passing acquaintances, were almost without exception willing to sit down and take time out for no personal gain, to remember her, often simply for some small episode or act of kindness which she had once shown them over thirty years ago. Many also mentioned how glad they were that someone was finally according Cass's life, talent and personality the attention and respect they deserve.

I was too young to have known Cass myself but whilst still in my early teens, I was struck by the sound of her voice both on her solo recordings and those with the Mamas and the Papas and was intrigued to know more. Her story seemed immediately fascinating and later on, once I embarked on the writing of this book, it only became more so as my research progressed. Inevitably, however, ascertaining the truth behind many situations was far from straightforward as the past and its events are invariably elastic, particularly when going back three decades and more. Ask ten people about a single episode and you will often get ten different versions, particularly as Cass lived much of her life in an era when people's minds and memories were often clouded by stimulants of one kind or another. I therefore endeavoured to talk to as many people as I could in order to reach my own conclusions and come as close as possible to a true understanding of her experiences and examine her life and work accordingly.

My thanks must consequently go to all those who agreed to be interviewed. In particular, those who not only agreed to cast their minds back three and in some cases, four decades, but also to open their homes and address books to me: Denny Doherty, for a warm, hospitable and often wonderfully entertaining time in Canada as well as the many subsequent phone-calls, Michelle Phillips, for making long interviews seem like a fun afternoon's chat with one of my best friends, Leah Kunkel, for remembering her sister and family over a series of epic interviews, Owen Elliot Kugell, Henry Diltz, Nurit Wilde, Lou Adler, Roger McGuinn, Gary Burden, Hal Blaine, Carl Gottlieb and Allison Caine, George McGovern, Stephen Sanders, Cyrus Faryar, Chip Silverman, Ken Waissman, Shelley Spector Ipiotis, Jerry Cohen, Israel Young, Tom Smothers, Esther Samet, Diane Hamet, John E. Brown, Leon Bing, Keith Allison and Judy Henske, Walter Painter, Dougal Butler, Dot Hendler, Maggie Phillips, Richard Sparks, Don Levinson, Priscilla Lainoff Stein, Micki Leef Stout, Toby Kobren, Rose M. Andrews, Gina Gaspin and David Platt.

Two other close friends of Cass's, Tim Rose and Zal Yanovsky, were both tremendously enthusiastic about my project, but did not live to see its completion. Tim took time to reminisce at length on his days with Cass in the Triumvirate and the Big 3 whilst Zal similarly remembered back to his days in Greenwich Village and Washington, DC with the Mugwumps before contacting me the next day with suggestions for further people I could talk to.

Other interviewees (in alphabetical order) were: Eddie Abramson, Joanne Baretta, Barry Bethell, John Bettis, Caren Bohrman, Bob Bowers, Harvey Brooks, Rodney Burbeck, Bob Cavallo, Mike Clough, Laurence Cohen, Ray Cooper, Caroline Cox-Simon, David Crosby, Joe Croyle, Barry Dennen, Donovan, Appie Evintoff, Frank Evintoff, Paul Evintoff, Lil Finn, Ralfee Finn, Kim Fowley, Lois Ganna, John Gardner, Kay Garner, Terri Garr, Jill Gibson, Russell Gilliam, Nick Gravenites, Larry Hankin, Ramona Heinrich, the late David Hemmings, Jim Hendricks, Eric Hord, Bones Howe, Les Hurdle, Bob Ingram, Erik Jacobsen, Henry Jaglom, Bruce Johnston, John Keats, Lee Kiefer, Marijke Koger-Dunham, Paul Krassner, Pat LaCroix, Marvyn Laird, Fran Landesman, Sharon Paige Lisenbee, Dave Mason, Lee McBride, Spanky McFarlane, Barry McGuire, Lewis Merenstein, Barry Morgan, William Morgan, Paul Morrissey, Graham Nash, Del Newman, Joe Osborn, Van Dyke Parks, Shawn Phillips, Peter Pilafian, Alan Pollock, Mike Sarne, John Sebastian, John Simon, Bobby Simone, Marc Strange, Peter Tork, Donald von Wiedenman, John Wallowitch, Jan Walman, Miranda Ward, Vanessa Ware, Jimmy Webb, Paul Williams and Tyler York.

My research was also helped greatly by Richard Barton Campbell in Richmond, Virginia, co-creator of the official Cass Elliot website www.casselliot.com and keeper of the Cass archive, whose unfailing energy, friendship, assistance and advice often felt like a lifeline when the trail threatened to run dry.

During the course of nearly six weeks in LA during the summer of 2002, as well as my interviewees, there were several who helped with my search. Thanks therefore go to: Lisa Horowitz for providing hospitality and general LA know-how and Susan Compo for advice, assistance and friendship. Also to Scott Portnoy, Bronwen Garrity, Zeena Kapsoff and Stacey Morello for helping me negotiate the LA traffic system and brave the width and breadth of LA County and beyond. Thanks also to Bill Petrasich at 20th Century Fox Film Corporation and Josh Scherr at Candy Entertainment. Likewise, American Airlines, for assistance with the journey from London to LA and back.

Others who also offered invaluable assistance in America were: Marie Arana at the *Washington Post*, Deb Weiner at the Baltimore Jewish Museum, Sylvan O. Feit at the Baltimore Hebrew Congregation, Alexandra Brandon, Mark Turner, Wesley Stace, Frank and Estelle Horowitz, Ellen I. Goldberg, Marge at *Baltimore* magazine and Michael

Miller – historian at the Lyceum city history museum in Alexandria. Similarly, Dr E. Terry in Montreal, Canada.

In London, meanwhile, where the trail began and indeed, ended, the following people all helped progress my search: Alan Rowett, Katherine Campbell, Lynne Holden and Ed Stewart at BBC Radio 2, Judith King, Jemima Gibbons, the late Gus Dudgeon, Shaun Greenfield, Rob Haywood, Barney Hoskyns, Mark Ellen, Tony Calder, David Brolan, Benedict Johnson, Michael at the much-missed Helter Skelter bookshop, Mark Brend, Mick Rock, Norman Blake, Harry Shapiro, Pat Tynan, Keith Altham and Mark Fox at the London Palladium.

Also Lisa Darnell for early belief in *Dream a Little Dream of Me* and Gordon Wise, previously of Sidgwick and Jackson, for commissioning it, Ingrid Connell, my editor, for valuable suggestions and input, Louise Davies for painstaking copyediting and Penny Price for working so hard on the picture research.

Several others also played a vital part in the evolution and completion of this book and thanks in no small part are therefore due to: my parents, Jo Graham, for encouragement, conversation and a fellow-writer's empathy, Robyn Hitchcock and Michèle Noach, not least for helping provide much-needed bursts of air with memorable nights at the Feghorn and Henry Lopez-Real, whose friendship did so much to sustain me through the final months of writing.

Finally, special thanks must go to Lloyd Bradley, whose conversation, advice and belief were such a continued source of encouragement and, of course, to Cass Elliot for the voice and the life which inspired *Dream a Little Dream of Me*.

Prologue

Cass Elliot was determined that she would not die young. 'I don't want the stigma of the Judy Garland type,' she said in July 1974. 'I've lived the folk scene, the rock scene, the drugs, the booze and the men. And I've survived and I feel good about myself.' Cass had reason to feel good. At thirty-two, she had just fulfilled a lifelong ambition and opened a headlining show at the London Palladium. She had dreamed of playing there since she was a child and still felt a girlish thrill and euphoria at having been a success there. The audience clearly adored her and there was standing-room only. After the final Saturday night show she went to her friend Mick Jagger's birthday party in Chelsea. The festivities went on for most of the night and afterwards Cass then drifted on to two further parties before finally returning home early on Sunday evening.

When she arrived back at Harry Nilsson's luxurious, chrome-and-mirrored flat in Mayfair, Joe Croyle, one of the dancers in her show who was also staying there, was already at the flat. They talked for a while and Cass told Croyle that she was tired and wanted to take a bath. But, she told him, she was also slightly hungry and asked him to make her something to eat. 'I went into the kitchen,' Croyle remembers, 'and there wasn't a lot of stuff to cook, but I opened the refrigerator and there was some sliced ham and some bread so I made her a ham sandwich and I poured her a pitcher of Coca-Cola and put it by her bed.' Some time later, Cass emerged from the bathroom in her robe, her hair piled up in a towel.

She told Croyle she was going to relax and have an early night and he left to go out for the evening. By the time he got back to the flat, it was about one thirty in the morning and as he came in he heard the murmuring of Cass's television. He walked down the hallway and peeped through the bedroom door which had been left slightly ajar. He saw Cass lying naked on her bed with her head propped up, snoring. Croyle thought about going in to switch off the TV, but he was worried he might wake her. Instead he simply closed the bedroom door and went back to the living room where he fell asleep on the sofa.

When Cass's London PA, Dot McLeod, went into the bedroom to wake her the following day, she immediately sensed something was wrong and Cass's body was cold to the touch. At some point during the course of the night, Cass had died. Initial medical tests were inconclusive and the coroner's report stated that further investigations would be carried out. What was later determined was by no means unequivocal, but what was established, without doubt, was that she had not died from choking, either on a sandwich or anything else. Somehow, however, the notion that Cass Elliot, the star who was famous for her size as much as her voice, might have died whilst eating seems to have been, for many people, too convenient an explanation and, despite its untruth, the story has become unshakably lodged in rock mythology.

It seemed, on the surface at least, as though Cass Elliot had everything to live for. Her manager later said she had told him she felt better about the Palladium shows than anything she had ever done professionally and, in the light of her success, she had received dozens of offers for TV and film roles and was due to record a new solo album. She also prided herself on having survived the excesses of the sixties rock and roll lifestyle; she was now living a cleaner life and considering the future of her seven-year-old daughter Owen. 'I was the all-time Miss America pop star,' she told the *Daily Express*. 'I even had a waterfall running through my house with goldfish. But I overdid it – drugs, booze, the lot. Staying out all night, just being totally undisciplined. When you're on your own you're only responsible for yourself. [But] I'm not that self-destructive any more, because I have a lot of things to live for now.'

Almost everyone who saw her at the parties after the final show remembered that Cass seemed tired but unquestionably happy. But she usually seemed happy and this was one of the central paradoxes of her life. People who met her would invariably comment on the fact that she could light up a room and make everyone laugh the moment she walked in, but those closest to her knew that beneath the witty, jovial facade lay considerable unhappiness.

'I don't think Cass was ever happy,' says Cass's close friend, musician and songwriter David Crosby. 'She was a desperately unhappy person, I think. Most of the time. When she was performing she was happy or when she was with somebody that she had fun with and you were getting high and you were laughing and playing and it was good, *that* was when she was happy. The rest of the time, she had a *very* rough go,' he says sombrely. 'Because *inside* she was very beautiful but our society is built on surface not substance. And that's how all the programming was back then and it's worse now, so she had a rough go. She never talked about it or came out front, but she wanted to be beautiful! She wanted to be loved. I think that was probably the single greatest driving force in her character.'

The combination of outer bravado and inner sadness defined not only Cass's life but also her stage persona. Even though she rarely showed it in person, when she sang, alongside the smile in her voice, you could also hear the sadness and vulnerability which were such an integral part of who she was. '"Just hold me tight and tell me you'll miss me"' she sang in the lines which, although they could easily have been written for her, in fact weren't, '"While I'm alone and blue as can be / Dream a little dream of me."' Cass Elliot could be the ballsy burlesque Mama, but she was also a tender young woman who knew how it felt to be 'alone and blue as can be' and yearned for a different life. That unlikely combination was what made her 'Mama Cass'. But somewhere between the two extremes lay Ellen Naomi Cohen – the girl from Baltimore who knew she was different and dreamed of being a star.

1

A design for living

By the time Cass was four years old, she could speak five languages. She was a natural mimic and as a small child during the Second World War she would spend hours listening to the refugees her parents had taken in from Poland, Germany, Russia and Italy, imitating their speech and the folk songs they brought with them. Or so she said. Nobody in her family has any recollection of this happening and when a BBC interviewer later asked her whether she had retained much of this linguistic talent, she replied 'Not a drop! I barely have enough English to order coffee!'

It was probably just one of Cass's many attempts to reimagine her past as somewhat more colourful than it had originally been. But however many languages she may or may not have spoken, she was, without doubt, an unusually precocious child and her intelligence immediately set her apart. 'I've always been different,' said Cass in the early seventies. 'I've been fat since I was seven. Being fat sets you apart, but luckily I was bright with it; I had an IQ of 165. I got into the habit of being independent and the habit became a design for living.'

Cass's size meant she was already shut out from the carefree, playful world of most children her age, but Cass seemed to know almost immediately that if she couldn't find love and acceptance from those around her, she would find it elsewhere. 'I'm going to be the most famous fat girl who ever lived,' she would tell anyone who would listen. And she was just about right.

Being 'the famous fat girl' was nevertheless a staggering idea. Today, more than nine million Americans are at least seven stone overweight, whilst half the adult populations of England, Brazil, Finland and Russia are overweight or obese. When Cass was growing up in the forties and fifties, this was not the case. Being overweight was relatively rare and as a result, her size often made her the object of derision and abuse. For Cass therefore to even hope that she could become a star required a canyon-wide leap of the imagination. There had been popular jazz singers like Ella Fitzgerald and entertainers like Sophie Tucker, but never a mainstream white pop star who looked like Cass. Cass had to become a star on her own terms, but her size was her reality and as far as she was concerned, if necessary, she would forge a role for herself where none existed.

Despite the unhappiness her weight caused her, she refused to accept what many might have considered the limitations of her size by flaunting it and standing out as a beacon of non-conformity instead. She trailblazed her difference and refused to be ashamed of it. She wasn't going to let society's rigid expectations dictate what she could or couldn't do and by the age of seven, when she sang Cole Porter's 'Don't Fence Me In' at the Baltimore Hippodrome, the song's title couldn't have been more apt.

It was an unusual childhood. Not simply because of Cass's size and intelligence, but also due to her upbringing and personality. Later on, when Cass was a star, people would often comment on how her arrival at any event inevitably caused a stir, and as a small child the impression she made was no less memorable. 'She was the brightest child I've ever seen in my life,' remembers Cass's childhood neighbour Ramona Heinrich. 'She was very intelligent and a little bit feisty in her talk and if you said something that she disagreed with, she would, just with logic, bring you right around to her thinking. And all the time she'd have her hands on her hips, swinging back and forth. She had quite a personality.'

As well as using logic, by the time she was eight or nine, Cass also seemed to have developed a wisdom and maturity way beyond her years. While most children of her age would still have been content to concern themselves with toys and children's games, Cass had already developed a keen interest in politics and would regularly astound adults with the precocity of her questions. 'So tell me,' she asked a doctor friend of the family's, 'what's the world situation like?' 'It bowled him over I'll tell you that!' laughs Cass's ninety-four-year-old aunt Lil Finn, 'but we were always discussing politics in our house and she would listen in and she was a very astute little girl.'

It was an unusually stimulating environment for a bright child. Cass's maternal grandparents – Joseph and Chaya Levine – both held passionate political beliefs and these certainly influenced Cass's own political involvement later on in the early seventies. Joseph was a tailor who had come to America from Poland at the end of the nineteenth century, but in spite of being a recent immigrant and only speaking the most basic English, he almost immediately became an active trade unionist in the Amalgamated Clothing Workers' Union and was swiftly blacklisted by numerous employers. 'My parents were completely committed to social reform from A to Z!' remembers Lil of her parents. 'We all grew up like that. We were always involved in what was going on in politics and prior to World War Two my mother and father were anti-Hitler. They knew what was going on and so we were raised in a family along with Cass's mother knowing that there was a world out there and we better know what was going on.'

As an only child for the first eight years of her life, Cass had more time to absorb the conversations of the adults around her, but her parents Philip and Bess Cohen also always treated her and their subsequent children as adults, involving them in discussions at meal times and listening to their opinions. What was more, Cass was clearly not just a daughter but a friend and confidante to her mother Bess, from whom she inherited her forceful personality.

A robust, forthright young woman with tightly curled brown hair and twinkling blue eyes, Bess herself came from a line of strong women. Both Bess and her own mother Chaya refused to be constrained by the accepted gender roles of their time, holding political views, which in itself was considered unusual, and going out to work at a period when respectable women were actively discouraged from doing so.

Cass would also have seen in her mother a determination to live her life with the same passion and conviction that she brought to her political beliefs. Everything about Bess seemed to shout out to anyone who would listen that she was ready for more or less anything that life might throw at her, and indeed she was. The story goes that while training to be a nurse, the sparky young Bess Levine first met Cass's father Philip Cohen on a train, somewhere between Baltimore and Washington, DC. Bess was on her way to get married. To someone else. But within forty-five minutes of meeting the handsome, well-dressed and witty young Philip, she had decided not to marry her fiancé but to marry Philip instead. It was instant romance. They shared a sharp, irreverent sense of humour and a love of music which would become an important part of Cohen family life. Bess loved swing jazz and had briefly sung with the well-known swing band the Fred Waring Orchestra. Philip meanwhile, had a passion for opera which he had inherited from his father William.

William Cohen, like Bess's father Joseph Levine, had come to America from Eastern Europe, arriving from his native Russia when he was just eighteen in 1892, and like many other immigrants before and since, he saw America as a gleaming land of possibility and prosperity. Thousands arrived, famously, at New York's Ellis Island, but William, like many other Jews, arrived at America's eastern port of Baltimore. Situated at the mouth of the Patapsco River in Maryland, between Philadelphia and Washington, DC, Baltimore had been a busy ship-building centre since the eighteenth century and its wide, sprawling streets and imposing buildings reflected the pride and grandeur of the industrial age. There had been a Jewish community there for over a hundred years, consisting mainly of tradesmen, clothing manufacturers and grocery store keepers, but rather than setting himself up as just another shopkeeper and moving into the existing Jewish neighbourhood, William had looked around for a way to offer something slightly different and find a guaranteed clientele. He noticed that the crab and oyster fishermen who lived in houseboats off the eastern shore of Maryland regularly came up the river needing supplies, and sensed a gap in the market. He found commercial and residential premises in the Canton district close to the waterfront at 2300 Cambridge Street and promptly set up shop offering ship chandlery and groceries.

A few years after arriving in Baltimore, he married the well-educated Esther Rosenberg, whose family had also recently come over from Eastern Europe, and two years later their first son was born, followed by ten more children – five boys and five girls. In many ways William was typical of the Jewish immigrants who came over from the Old World. He worked long hours to provide as best he could for the family, and held education and study sacred for the children as the route to professional success and economic prosperity. Several of the Cohen children did in fact far exceed even the most moderately ambitious parent: Bernard became not only a cardiologist, but chief of cardiology at Johns Hopkins, Hilliard became chief of pathology at Menorah Medical Centre in Kansas City, Missouri, and Laurence an orthopaedic surgeon. 'It was the real American story,' says Cass's cousin Esther Samet, 'out of the grocery store would come the next generation and through education they would rise up the ladder.'

Philip, however, the second youngest of the Cohen children, always seemed different from his siblings. Although just as bright and unanimously adored for his happy disposition, wit and charm, he expressed no interest in the academic aspirations of his elder brothers. His mother Esther had died when he was only eight years old, leaving his elder siblings to raise him, and he was soon characterised as the dreamer of the family. As a child he had sat with his father every weekend enthralled by the weekly radio broadcast from the Metropolitan opera, and by his teens, instead of going to college, he had dreams of becoming an opera singer himself. Philip was known for having a good voice and, along with his brother Hilliard, had managed to win a spear-carrying part in *Aida* at the Lyric Opera in Baltimore, but the job, along with Philip's operatic ambitions, ended one night later. Feeling his operatic career was clearly destined to failure, Philip instead embarked on a series of jobs and entrepreneurial schemes in the catering industry.

Twelve months after Philip and Bess's wedding, their first child Ellen Naomi – as Cass was originally named, was born on 19 September 1941 and by the time she was two, she could talk. As a sensitive and unusually alert child, Ellen would also gradually have become aware of the conflict in the world around her. Eleven weeks after she was born, the Japanese had invaded Pearl Harbor and America joined World War Two, and over the next few years, even without overhearing the political discussions of parents and grandparents, few children could remain oblivious to the broader world situation. Philip himself was not drafted into the armed services because of an ulcer, but until the war's end in 1945, Bess, Philip and Ellen had, like everyone else, to live with food rationing, air-raid drills, blackouts and curfews.

When Cass was four years old, the atom bomb was dropped on Hiroshima, and although this event effectively ended the war, in the years that followed, the memory of such a global catastrophe still resonated, and with the rise of the Cold War people were encouraged to live in daily fear of a similar attack from the Soviet Union. 'I remember when I was ten years old,' Cass later told *Rolling Stone*, 'in Washington, DC and I lived with the fear of the atom bomb that would keep me awake nights and make me wake up screaming. I used to babysit for my younger brother and sister and I'd be terrified if I heard a siren, a police car or an ambulance. I'd say, "My god, what if this is it! How do I protect them?"'

Cass's childhood fear of the bomb was clearly as intense as most other children's, but the fact that on her mother's side Cass's own family were committed socialists meant that they went against the grain of mainstream American society with its phobic fear of anything remotely associated with communism. Cass's childhood friends did not know details of her family's political beliefs, but there were some suspicions and this served as something else that would, at some level, set Cass apart from her peers.

Financially Cass was also different from many of the other children around her. Although in the years after World War Two, everyone faced financial challenges as America slowly worked to regain economic stability, the Cohens' lives were perhaps more economically volatile than others. Throughout Cass's childhood, Philip conjured up one short-lived business scheme after another, and depending on the location of his latest venture, the family shuttled back and forth between Baltimore, Alexandria, Virginia and the various suburbs of Washington, DC. One project was a kosher catering service and function facility in a large ballroom above a Cadillac showroom in Alexandria, Virginia. Unfortunately, however, Alexandria only had a small Jewish community at the time and Philip was forced to close the business. His next idea was a deli opposite the Library of Congress in Washington, DC where the young John F. Kennedy would come in and pick pickles out of the barrel and John Phillips would later remember seeing Cass as a 'little, chubby girl, with the stained apron on behind the counter'. The deli closed after only a few months.

With each new restaurant, catering service or deli, Philip hoped that this latest idea might finally contain the magic ingredient for success. But this was not the case. Cass later recalled at least ten instances of bankruptcy during her formative years but, no doubt eager to present her childhood in as positive a light as possible, she also said she considered her lot infinitely preferable to that of her playmates, most of whose 'daddies were in the dreary old army and carried their lunches in brown bags to the Pentagon every morning'.

By the time Cass was about eight years old, the Cohens had settled in a medium-sized row house at 308 Allison Street – high up on a hill in one of the many leafy middle-class dormitory suburbs of Washington, DC where most people did indeed work at the Pentagon. So in contrast to these nine-to-five workers, Philip, with his dreams and schemes, must certainly have seemed a comparatively lively father.

Around this time, in 1948, Cass's sister Leah was born, followed by her brother Joseph three years later. This meant that Philip and Bess had to work even harder to stay afloat financially, and while Bess had a part-time job working for the railways to bring in extra income, their children were often left to fend for themselves. 'We were really truly latchkey kids before that term was coined,' remembers Cass's sister Leah Kunkel, who after years as a professional singer now runs her own law practice in Massachusetts. 'But we were pretty safe and we stayed at home in our front yards, we weren't wandering around.' Leah felt that their circumstances were not significantly different from other children's around them, but although life was economically fraught for most people, the fact that the Cohens were perhaps less financially secure than others was noticed. 'It seemed like Ellen was left on her own a lot more than other kids and left to her own devices,' remembers her friend Priscilla Lainoff Stein, who knew her through the local synagogue. 'I think her parents tried but they were always busy working and they worked hard.'

Like most parents, Bess and Philip wanted to provide the best for their children but at the same time, in many ways, they also took a much more laissez-faire attitude to parenting than many of their contemporaries. Whereas most of Cass's friends were used to being grounded almost as a matter of course, Cass and her sister and brother never knew the meaning of the term. All three children were allowed significantly more freedom than most children their age, and even when Bess would occasionally get angry and suggest to Philip that they be punished, his attitude was unusually enlightened for the time. 'Once when I must have been six or seven years old,' remembers Leah, 'and my brother and I had really driven my mom to the brink, she kept saying to us, "When your father gets home, I'm gonna tell him and you're gonna get a lickin'." And we never got hit so we were like, "Oh, my God, we're gonna get a lickin'. What does that *mean*?"' she laughs. 'We knew it was bad! So my dad came home and my mom just read him the riot act about how badly we had behaved and said, "You need to go punish them and give them a spanking." And my father said, "Right oh. Now you guys go right up to your rooms," and he came up the steps and said, "OK, well your mom says you have to get a spanking and so I'm gonna do it," and he starts to undo his belt and he kind of turned around and he had undone his pants too. So when he took his belt off, his trousers fell down – he was wearing his boxers and he was like, "Oh, I kind of need my belt to hold up my trousers." Well of course, we cracked up! And it turned into this big conspiracy like, "Tell your mom I gave you a spanking!"' she laughs again. 'And that was the end of *that*.'

The discrepancy between Philip and Bess's approach was indicative of their respective temperaments. Philip's blithe nature meant that although he always worked hard to make each business venture a success, he himself was not particularly materialistic and didn't consider the trappings of success in any way essential. Bess, meanwhile, was an altogether more dynamic character, and whilst their devotion to each other was never in question, Philip's unhurried approach seems to have brought some tensions to the marriage and although Cass was only a small child, particularly in the early years of their marriage, she would certainly have picked up on them. 'Basically Philip was a rather laid-back individual,' remembers Toby Kobren, a close (female) family friend who had known Bess and Philip before they were even married. 'Bess on the other hand was not. Bess was the steering wheel and Philip was one of the wheels on the car and she would prod him about different things. Bess had a lot of emotional energy and so I think that led to a bit of friction sometimes but they did love each other very deeply.'

Leah similarly remembers this fundamental difference in approach causing difficulties between her parents. 'My dad was incredibly easy-going,' remembers Leah 'and I can *never* remember my father yelling at us. Not once. But some of that wasn't great. I know that earlier on, when my mum and dad were first married and Cass was a baby, my dad had a bleeding ulcer. My mom was working for the railroads and my dad was pretty sick – apparently he almost died of this bleeding ulcer and so he came home one day and said, "The doctor told me I should go to Florida and really rest," and my mother who was at that time supporting the family with this little baby – my sister – said sarcastically to him something like, "Well, that sounds good, so why don't you take a vacation," and apparently she came home the next day from work and there was my sister in a crib and a note from my dad saying he'd gone to Florida! I think that at that point they went through some *very* tough times.'

*

By the time Cass was in her teens, her appearance singled her out more than anything else. As a small child, she had been as slim as most children, but by the age of eight, shortly after the birth of her sister Leah, she had begun to gain the extra pounds which she would retain for the rest of her life.

Just before Leah was born, Cass developed ringworm, and with contagious scaly, itching patches on her head, was forced to wear a tight bonnet which she would angrily pull off whenever it became too uncomfortable. Bess, meanwhile, was about to give birth to Leah and so it was decided that young Ellen should go to stay with her grandparents until she was better.

The birth of a second child after a gap of seven years will inevitably be an emotional upheaval in the life of an older child who has, up until that point, been the sole focus of their parents' attention. The addition of being sent away in this fashion would therefore be significant, and later on in her life, particularly as there were no other known cases of obesity in the family, Cass herself was aware of this. 'I was a thin child and a poor eater until my sister Leah was born when I was almost seven years old,' she told *Ladies' Home Journal* in 1969. 'I imagine that aroused some insecurities within me. At least so I've discovered through psychoanalysis. After Leah came along, I did the thing that was most acceptable to me – and what I thought would please my parents: eat. By the time I dropped out of high school, two weeks before graduation, I weighed 180 pounds.'

While Cass was with her grandparents, she not only wanted to eat, but was actively encouraged to do so, as her grandmother Chaya had, as Leah recalls, an 'almost pathological' need to feed people, having survived poverty in Poland and the Depression in America. 'And so I think, when Cass was with her,' says Leah, 'my grandmother was just spoiling her and feeding her and plying her with food.'

Overeating, it is now acknowledged, often occurs as a displacement activity for unexpressed anger and the fact that Cass mentions that prior to Leah's birth she had been a poor eater points to the existence of a deep-seated discontentment or problem from an earlier age, probably due to her parents' long working hours and frequent absence. 'As a child,' remembers Leah, 'I felt like I never *got* enough of my parents because they both worked all the time. They weren't available emotionally particularly and also they weren't *actually* available and I think that sometimes Cass felt as if she wasn't getting enough attention.'

Even when her parents were at home and she was still the only child, there were often times when Cass was clearly frustrated by her parents' lack of attention. 'When her father and mother wanted to have a little quiet time for themselves,' remembers Ramona Heinrich, 'they'd put her outside and she'd just tear the house apart. We would hear her banging on the door, crying and screaming and screaming that they didn't pay attention to her. They didn't really lock her out but she sure didn't like it and she wanted to get in the house, so we used to go down and get her and say, "Come on and play with us," and she'd say, "No, no," and scream for her mother. We didn't know what they were doing ourselves really but we could well imagine that it was private time for them.'

Cass may have yelled and screamed, but like many children of her generation, she was actively discouraged from expressing any discontentment she may have felt. For all Bess's willingness to speak her mind and voice her opinions, when it came to emotions, both she and Philip kept their own feelings firmly in check and, by example, clearly encouraged their children to do the same. 'You could tell my mom really *felt* love,' says Leah, 'and she definitely was somebody who had this huge, huge, huge heart, but she was a physically undemonstrative person. She just did not grow up in a generation that was huggy and kissy and touchy and feely. I think the unspoken message wasn't so much, "Oh, don't talk about bad things," it was more like, "Hey, you know, stiff upper lip, everybody's got their own road to hoe," or as Zal Yanovsky used to say, "Everybody's got their own crotch to bear," she laughs. 'So it was sort of that. We all knew that the idea was to work hard and do your best and sometimes you're not gonna *feel* great, sometimes you're gonna have hardship. But that's life – no one promised you a rose garden, kind of thing.'

With no opportunity to voice her discontent, eating provided an outlet for Cass's feelings. But apart from being a comfort mechanism, food also had other positive associations during Cass's childhood. As Philip and Bess worked long hours, when they arrived home in the evenings, mealtimes became the main time when the family would be together and when the children would receive their parents' full attention. 'I remember really looking forward to that evening meal because I saw my *parents* then,' says Leah. 'It wasn't about the eating. It was just, sort of, *that* was our time to be together as a family after not having been together all day and where the kids sort of recharged and got filled up on love and whatever else and got our tummies filled up at the same time.'

Whatever troubles the Cohens may have had, there was always one constant source of diversion and that was music. 'Music was our opiate,' says Leah, and although the family was far from wealthy, having a good quality gramophone was considered a necessity rather than a luxury; so whether it was Bess playing Frank Sinatra or *Theodore Bikel Sings Yiddish Love Songs* or Philip playing *La Bohême*, there was nearly always music of some kind. Bess would also often sing the soft-shoe-style songs of the thirties and other standards, accompanying herself on the piano from her collection of sheet music.

Harmony singing was similarly central to both Philip's and Bess's families. 'Cass's mother Bess and I and my other sisters,' remembers Lil Finn, 'would lay on the bed and sing the old tunes of those days from the thirties and forties and we would harmonise and Cass, who was maybe three or four years old, would sing along.' Bess's father Joseph had been a cantor as well as a tailor in his native Poland before coming to America, but Philip's side of the family were no less musical. Everyone played the piano, especially Cass's uncle Bernard who played by ear, and whenever everyone gathered together for holiday meals, grandfather William would divide the family into groups and teach them each a harmony part before conducting the entire family chorus.

It was hardly surprising therefore that Cass loved music and was captivated by it almost before she could talk. Philip's passion for operas such as *Rigoletto* and *Il Trovatore* and in particular tenors like Laurence Tippets and Caruso meant that she constantly heard the great opera classics on the radio or on record and, like her father, she was soon mesmerised by their drama and romance. One afternoon she was taken to a performance of *La Bohême* and was so transfixed and convinced of the reality of what she was seeing that in the final act, when Mimi is dying, she cried out, 'Won't somebody please call a doctor – she's really sick.' 'Everybody just lost it in the entire place,' says her cousin Ralfee Finn, 'because it was so real for her. There was no separation between the music and her. 'Cause she couldn't have understood a word, but she knew that Mimi was sick and that somebody had to call a doctor.'

*

By the time she was six years old, Cass was already showing signs that she not only appreciated music but clearly wanted to perform in some way herself, and would never miss an opportunity to sing or act for anyone who would listen. 'She was always acting,' remembers Lil Finn, 'she would recite and she would sing. You wanna sing a song – she was right there! She would perform to everybody. When she went to bed, she would stand on the landing step and say, "Goodnight, sweet Prince, and flights of angels sing thee to thy rest, " from *Hamlet* .'

Cass clearly had a gift for capturing people's attention, whether she was singing, acting or simply playing the clown. The ability to almost instantaneously drop in a perfect harmony would later prove significant in Cass's career, as would the love of Broadway musicals which she had also developed, but for the time being, Cass just knew she loved an audience. She also knew she was going to be famous. She just had to work out how.

2

A tight bottle

'Success is the best revenge' it has been said and it is an adage which Cass not only believed, but lived. Having grown up in a household which encouraged competition and the will to succeed, she had no shortage of drive and ambition, but if she needed any further motivation, her experiences at high school would provide fuel and determination in ample supply.

Cass clung to the notion of her own impending fame like a last stick of driftwood in a shipwreck. As far as she was concerned there was no question that she was going to be a star and she lost no time in telling anyone who would listen. 'I was active in the drama department,' remembers Broadway writer and producer Ken Waissman who was Cass's friend at the time, 'and a classmate called me over to meet Ellen because she wanted to get involved in dramatics. I was introduced to a large rotund overweight girl with braces on her teeth and part of her lunch stuck to them. One of her high socks was up, the other was down around her ankle. Yet when she looked at me and said with absolute total conviction, "I'm going to be a star," I found myself believing her.'

Despite the improbability of the suggestion, given Cass's unconventional appearance, Waissman was not the only one who believed her. But most thought that if she did become famous, it would not be as a singer. What impressed people about Cass was her caustic wit and the originality of her humour. 'The striking thing about her,' remembers school friend Shelley Spector Ipiotis, 'was her personality and her wit, her cleverness, her shtick. She was *very* bright and very funny and *different*, you know? A *different* kind of sense of humour. She had a very nice voice but I thought if she makes it, it's gonna be as a comedienne, as some sort of Carol Burnett type and famous more for her comedy and her wit.'

Cass's wit would become an integral part of her stage persona throughout her career as well as the public face she presented to all but her very closest friends. Humour had always been a strong part of Cohen family life but it was also something which Cass came to rely on during her teenage years as a survival tactic as much as anything else. In the face of almost unanimous rejection, humour was a much-needed crutch. As family friend Toby Kobren remembers, 'There was something about her at that particular time of her life that was lonely, that was needy and very sad and she told me that, because she was overweight, she relied on her sense of humour for her popularity. She said that none of the boys asked her for a date, so she was the class cut-up – the jokester, the funny girl, the one who would crack jokes all the time, and that was how she relied on the company of people in her class.'

An acerbic put-down was the perfect way of deflecting attention from her size, and Cass would continue to use humour in this way for the rest of her life, knowing that it was also the perfect ready-fire defence against potential attacks. 'I used to work in my father's deli,' she later told John Phillips, 'but I ate so much behind the counter that I got stuck and couldn't move.' Cass would also use humour and story telling throughout her life to try and recreate the world as she wanted it to be and if sometimes her versions of reality bore little resemblance to anyone else's, it was because she needed to live, even if only in her own mind, a life that was different and better than her own.

Being ostracised by the majority of her class mates did, however, lead Cass to forge particularly close relationships with the few friends she made. She had a talent for friendship which would feature throughout the rest of her life, but although she felt great affection from those close to her, Cass would never get over the rejections of her high school years and despite her phenomenal success later in life, they would continue to haunt her. 'Over the years, she would always come back home,' her friend Chip Silverman remembers, 'and all she ever harped on was how the girls treated her in school. They looked down on her, they wouldn't have nothing to do with her, and she just never could get away from that. Even in the early seventies, she was still repeating stories of things that had happened saying, "I'm gonna get back at them," and that just was somehow kind of tragic. That with all she had achieved, she should have just laughed at it – it shouldn't have mattered.'

*

By the time Cass was fifteen, she had enrolled at George Washington High School in Alexandria, but it was hard for her to make friends. Not only did she look different but, beyond that, her background was different. Cass's parents were not particularly orthodox in their religious beliefs but they observed Friday evening Sabbath dinners and major holidays and belonged to the local synagogue. Cass had therefore become part of the local Jewish community, regularly attending dances and bar mitzvahs with the other Jewish children of the congregation, but by the time she enrolled in high school, Jewish pupils were in the minority and although she never experienced any direct prejudice, being Jewish set her further apart.

The dating rituals which were such an important part of fifties high school life were similarly never likely to be easy for Cass, but double-dating was common, and as her best friend Priscilla was slim (she said that she and Cass together 'looked like Mutt and Jeff' – one slim, one heavy), Priscilla made sure that if she had a date, her boyfriends would bring a male friend along so that Cass would have one too. 'If boys wanted to go out with me enough,' says Priscilla, 'they would get someone. My boyfriends would give a groan, like, "*Uuugh!* Do we *have* to?" And I'd say, "Yes, because I'm spending the evening with Ellen and I'm not going to go out without her, so you have to find somebody!" And I could usually arrange something.'

Under such circumstances it was hardly surprising that these dates were rarely successful, but through her already engaging humour Cass was accepted as part of their regular social set. It was not to last long. Her father's peripatetic business schemes meant that the family was almost constantly on the move and Cass had already had to change schools several times, but it was now time for yet another move. They had briefly lived in Baltimore when Cass was a small girl but Philip's latest venture meant that although Cass was in the middle of her high school year, the family were now set to move back to Baltimore, some forty miles away.

Baltimore in the fifties was still widely perceived as a primarily blue collar, somewhat sleepy, upper-southern town which lived more or less in the shadow of its more sophisticated neighbours: Philadelphia and Washington, DC. The city's only claims to fame as far as the rest of America was concerned were the professional football Colts, baseball's

Orioles, steamed crabs and an infamous adult entertainment area known as the Block.

Forest Park High School, meanwhile, was a grand, impressive institution with an exceptionally high level of academic success. Situated on a tree-shaded street, its main building was the classic storybook American school – a lofty, ivy-covered red-brick monument to learning, surrounded by a sea of neatly trimmed lawns and immaculately cut hedges. Over 90 per cent of the students who graduated went on to four-year colleges – an extraordinarily high figure for the time – and apart from Cass, her class of 60/61 produced film director Barry Levinson, author Chip Silverman whose book *Diner Guys* was the basis of Levinson's film *Diner*, writers Ken Waissman and Maxine Fox – authors of the musical *Grease* which was based on life at Forest Park, as well as numerous others who became successful in film, television and theatre. 'It was amazing,' says Silverman, 'because this wasn't New York or Chicago or Los Angeles. This was *Baltimore*! So it's amazing when you look back on what these people achieved.'

Unlike Alexandria, where Jewish pupils were in a minority, at Forest Park the majority of the school's two thousand students were Jewish and middle class and the Jewish study ethic was therefore all-pervasive. Academic success was not just encouraged by parents but also considered hip amongst the Foresters – as Forest Park students were known. 'A girl with an A in trigonometry,' said Silverman, 'had as many dates as a girl who was top heavy.'

On this basis, a girl who was as bright as Cass should in theory have had a wide circle of friends, but being smart didn't always equate with popularity. Although Cass had by no means been particularly popular at George Washington High School, she was indisputably part of the social group that revolved around the synagogue community and included Priscilla and her other friends. Life at Forest Park would be considerably harder.

'It was a *very* cliquey school,' remembers Diane Hamet (née Schwartz) who was in Cass's year and who, like many of her schoolmates, still lives nearby, 'and Ellen didn't fit their cookie-cutter image as far as the girls were concerned. All the sorority girls were the popular, pretty girls that met one image and Ellen totally was not like it. If you didn't fit in, if you weren't a certain size, they didn't *wait* to get a person's personality, they judged you according to how you looked. And everybody had to wear the same thing. It was very, very cliquey, to the point where it really could have been upsetting. Today they call it peer pressure, but we didn't know the word then, that wasn't in the vocabulary.'

Although teenagers today face similar pressure, they also enjoy a choice of options in terms of choosing an identity, whereas for girls growing up in the fifties, the codes of dress were utterly rigid, requiring them to emulate film stars like Natalie Wood and Debbie Reynolds with the right sweaters and pedal pushers, the right twin sets and the right gloves, lipstick and hair.

America's obsession with conformity was a reaction to the fears and uncertainties of the war years and the country clung to its ideal of sanitised model family life as the ultimate goal. Appearance was therefore seen as crucial and at Forest Park, although the school emphasised academic achievement for girls as well as boys, few girls considered their studies as serving any real purpose. There was virtually no encouragement for girls to plan a career, as any jobs they might take following school or college were considered merely time-killing fillers until they married and left the workplace to raise a family and create a home. The most important aspect of a teenage girl's life was consequently her ability to attract a husband.

Any wilful discrepancy from accepted codes of appearance and behaviour was considered an act of defiance, so when Cass arrived at Forest Park, she seemed to be breaking every rule in the book. Cass in fact desperately wanted to fit in; she loved looking pretty and later in life did her best to look as feminine and glamorous as possible, but during her teens it was as though, once she realised she would not be accepted whatever she did, she refused to dress in the ways 'nice' girls were supposed to or pander to their rigid codes of behaviour.

Possibly in another attempt to deflect attention from her weight, Cass seemed to go out of her way to dress outlandishly, often wearing what were thought of as wild combinations of Bermuda shorts and high heels, with white gloves to cover her bitten-down nails. Cass in fact seemed to have a whole range of increasingly eccentric dress habits. She told the girls that she had 'some kind of sun allergy', which meant she had to protect her skin from the sun, and so in the summer, whilst other girls enjoyed the opportunity to wear short-sleeved blouses and sweaters, Cass would remain resolutely covered up. 'She was very bizarre-looking,' remembers Shelley Spector Ipiotis. 'Always, always, she was wearing heavy stockings, long sleeves – she was quite a sight.

And teenage girls want to be beautiful and admired and all of that, so it must have been very hard for her.' It was indeed hard and most of the pupils at Forest Park either routinely snubbed her or openly showed their irritation and dislike, throwing paperclips or anything else that came to hand whenever she started singing.

With such an outlandish image, Cass was never going to fit in and nor was she likely to be considered suitable material for one of the sororities which were at the time a crucial element of not only one's teenage years but one's entire life. 'If you didn't get into a good sorority, it was very serious stuff in those days,' explains school friend Sharon Paige Lisenbee, 'and devastating if you didn't get into one at all. It made your entire social life just a living hell. You were pariahs. You just were not acceptable at all and then the parents would become involved. It would be like their child was not acceptable in the society of the Baltimore Jewish community. It was a terrible way to do things – very superficial. But it was like a stepping stone because in those days, if you *didn't* get into a good sorority, your prospects of who you would marry would be limited. A guy from one of the better fraternities is not going to date someone from a lesser sorority – it just wouldn't happen.'

Cass, like every other teenager at the time, was well aware of this and had consequently arrived in Baltimore wearing a sorority pin, explaining that she had belonged to the Alexandria branch of Sigma Pi Sigma – one of the best Jewish sororities. This meant that she would automatically be granted entry into the Baltimore chapter as, according to sorority rules, once you were inducted into a society in one town, if you moved, your membership carried with you. With such a large proportion of Jewish students at the school, it should in theory have been easier for Cass to fit in socially in Baltimore, but the Forest Park sorority was, as Ken Waissman remembers, 'a far more stuck up and snooty group than their Washington, DC sisters', and Cass's appearance fell far short of their high standards.

'When she came to town it was like "No way!"' remembers Sharon, 'How is this possible? Because who would have recommended her? In order to get into a sorority, you have to be recommended by somebody. Otherwise you have to be cute *or* very, very personable and smart *or* from a very good family *or* all three. If you are not any of those things, you probably will not be recommended. It was kind of like you have to have *something* going for you. So when Ellen came to town, this fat girl with these weird clothes and slovenly and peculiar in every way, saying that she was a sorority sister, everybody was like, "Oh, my *God,*" because it would bring down the name of the sorority to have her in. She just didn't look like the rest of us. She looked nothing like what we thought a sorority sister would look like: the rest of us weren't fat and we tried to conform with whatever was appropriate. Also it was a very closed kind of society, a very fifties mentality where you always had your make-up on if you were out, you always dressed properly, you always had the right shoes, the right everything if you were going to be fitting in. And certainly if you were going to get into a sorority – and this was one of the top sororities.'

But even if you were asked to join, there was still a draconian trial period during which your suitability was assessed. 'I remember for me, it was traumatic,' says Sharon, 'they came to my house and my room was a mess. I had pen-pals and I had all these letters in boxes under my bed because I treasured them and they said, "This stuff has to go and if we come here again, we want to see all these drawers completely clean," so I just threw everything out because you were so pressured and I always resented that because I had all these pen-pals and I lost them all. I took the sorority girls so seriously.'

When it came to Cass, the sorority girls, apart from harbouring an innate snobbism, were also clearly terrified that their own prospects might be hampered by the admittance of someone who didn't fit their physical ideals, and were adamant that, regardless of the rules, she should not be allowed in. Sharon, however, persuaded them that she should. 'We're supposed to be a sorority,' she told them, 'and that means sisterhood and if she's really a sorority sister, I don't see how you can not let her in.' Cass was duly allowed to keep her sorority pin and reluctantly admitted to the Baltimore chapter.

But even once she was let in, her admittance still clearly remained an issue for some time, as Ken Waissman remembers: 'One day, Ellen was on her hands and knees crawling under the long cafeteria tables, desperately looking for her sorority pin. It had been on a sweater that she had left on a chair. She was sure it had fallen somewhere and I was tipped off that one of the sorority members had taken it. They were embarrassed to have her seen wearing it. I went over to their table and spoke to the sorority president, who I knew quite well, saying

I would expose them if it didn't materialize. The pin miraculously was later found. It was Ellen's only symbol of a status, a kind of acceptance.'

Cass was obviously not going to be fully accepted whether she belonged to a sorority or not, but hard as her life was, it would probably have been harder still without the all-important membership. Whether Cass had in fact ever belonged to an Alexandrian chapter is questionable at best; Priscilla Lainoff Stein has no recollection at all of her having belonged to a sorority in Alexandria and nobody in Baltimore ever phoned to check. Sharon believes Cass could easily have bought the pin from a pawn shop but if that was the case, it is also easy to understand why she might have been desperate to prove she belonged.

However much distress the sorority issue may initially have caused Cass, it did result in her friendship with Sharon and this would continue for the rest of her life. Years later, when asked how she had first got into show business, Cass would often explain that it was through her best friend at high school that she had first got a part in summer stock (the American tradition of summer season theatre companies). Some five decades on, after a career in theatre which similarly happened through Cass's encouragement, Sharon spent several hours on the phone to me from Brooklyn where she now lives, remembering her times with Cass. 'I remember one of the first days I ever saw her,' says Sharon, 'sitting in a classroom that I was in and I went up to her because I saw her sorority pin and I introduced myself and I said, "I'm your sorority sister," and I guess from that point on we became friends.'

Although Sharon was pretty, slim and funny, she, like Cass, didn't feel that she really fitted in with the other sorority girls, and unlike them, she was less inclined to judge by appearances alone. 'I always thought it was wrong if my parents or anybody would exclude people for reasons that they couldn't control. Somewhere along the line I had my own set of ethics and moral code and it didn't fit into the kind of societal thing that they were doing. And I thought it was wrong to not be accepting of her and so I guess from my heart I did what I felt was the right thing to do and I think she read that as a gesture that she accepted and we just became very close friends from that day on.' Cass and Sharon found in each other a deeper sense of individuality and alienation from the mainstream social scene around them. Although Cass realised the necessity of belonging to the sorority for social survival, the whole ethos of societies themselves and rigid codes of behaviour couldn't have been further from her natural inclinations, and in Sharon, she found someone who, although she outwardly conformed, was at heart an equally lone spirit.

'Ellen really could *see* me,' explains Sharon. 'I was kind of hiding in a sorority that *I* didn't belong in. I could[n't] care less about it, but the pressure was that you *better* care about it, 'cause that's gonna be your life. And of course I never wanted that for my life and she never wanted that for her life either so we were kindred spirits and it was obvious from the very beginning that that's who we were for each other.'

From Cass's point of view it was easy to see why she would have been thrilled to have Sharon as her friend. While most of the other girls shunned her, here was someone who embodied everything Cass aspired to and who wanted to be her friend. 'I was a cheerleader girl,' says Sharon, 'so I was everything probably that she would like to have been or she thought she would like to have been. And I was a dancer, I could sing, I was funny: I had all those qualities. And I was *little* – I wasn't fat, so I always felt that she admired me, that she loved me. And I loved her. So each of us probably fed each other something that we really needed – the missing link of each of our personalities.'

Cass's friendship with Sharon also gave her an escape route from the tyranny of fifties teenage dating rituals. By virtue of her unconventional appearance, Cass was way outside what was considered attractive in a date. In fact many boys were reluctant even to be seen with her, as Ken Waissman remembers, 'One afternoon a good buddy of mine who drove an old '53 Buick, called me to tell me there was a party that evening and he would pick me up. I informed him that we would have to drop Ellen and Sharon off on the way. He balked. Sharon was OK, he said, but Ellen was too fat. He was worried about what the guys would say if they happened to see her riding in his car. Ellen had been driving Sharon and me back and forth each day, but her car had broken down a few days before and we had been taking the bus. "I can't very well hop in a car and leave them to take the bus," I said. "OK, OK," he relented. Of course, for the last thirty-five years, he has "dined out" on how he once drove Mama Cass home.'

This attitude was typical of the teenage obsession with appearance.

Whilst the ultimate proof of a girl's attractiveness was her ability to get a date, the whole dating practice was as much about being seen to have a date as actually getting to know the person you were on the date with. As far as Cass and Sharon's peers were concerned, therefore, the only thing worse than not having a date on a Saturday night was being seen not to have a date. This was a situation of incomparable shame and humiliation.

'Saturday night in Baltimore was date night,' explains Sharon. 'Friday night you could go out with the girls but Saturday night if you didn't have a date, *forget* it – you couldn't be seen on the street. Well Ellen was never gonna get a date any which way and I was not that popular either, so we decided to hell with that, and she would pick me up in her father's old Chevy with the back window busted out and we would go to the drive-in movies on Saturday night. In the summertime it was OK; in the wintertime we froze to death. It was ridiculous! But we really broke the rules on those Saturday nights and those were big rules to break because for two girls to go out and be seen without a date on a Saturday night just wasn't heard of. It was really something. If you didn't have a date, you were supposed to stay in to make sure nobody *knew* you didn't have a date.'

And Cass and Sharon not only broke the rules but trumpeted their defiance. 'Sometimes we'd just put our overcoats on over our pyjamas and we'd be just *out there*. We would just try to break out and not do what we couldn't do anyway. I mean we weren't gonna be getting dates, so what the hell? What reason was there for sitting up in a house when we could be going out having fun? And in a way thumbing our nose at the whole society. We really just were so free with each other. We felt like we could get out of this tight bottle that we were forced to live in, that we didn't fit in properly. The environment was wrong for our personalities.'

As well as flouting conventional fashion, Cass's appearance at Forest Park was frequently considered different simply by falling short of the highly groomed standards demanded. Often her make-up would appear badly applied or her hair unkempt, but this was not necessarily due to laziness or slovenliness but more to the fact that throughout most of her time at Forest Park, before she went to school, Cass would get up at four in the morning to help her father with his latest business venture: providing meals for the construction workers building Baltimore's Mondawmin shopping centre.

This latest scheme of Philip's had started off as seemingly just another whim. 'My dad loved to go to auctions,' remembers Leah, 'and so one day he came back and told my mom that he had bought a bus. And my mom said, "What do you mean?" and my dad said, "Well, they were selling it for only a few hundred dollars." He then informed her that it didn't run anywhere, that it couldn't run, but that he had this idea for what he called "meals on wheels" and actually he was the first person – and I'll stand by this forever – who thought of the phrase.'

At this point in the late fifties, there was a building boom in America and the first malls were being built. Philip Cohen realised that thousands of construction workers would therefore be wanting fast, on-site food to eat in their breaks, and talked the managers of Mondawmin into letting him tow his bus onto the site. Providing a mobile food stall was Philip's golden idea and would be the great success of his life. Eventually, it was so successful that he bought two further buses and hired extra staff but at the beginning almost everyone in the family was roped into helping run the business.

As the oldest child, Cass was an obvious choice to help staff the wagon during the early morning rush, taking orders through the windows and handing workers their food, and so by the time she drove to school, she would have already done several hours' work, leaving her tired, dishevelled and regularly late for class.

Cass's lateness did nothing to help her academic record either – the one other factor, aside from appearance, which carried currency at Forest Park. Cass would later quote her IQ as being a staggering 165, but since arriving at Forest Park, her rejection by her fellow pupils coupled with her lateness meant her grades belied her intelligence and her school counsellor found her 'intelligent but academically unmotivated'.

Being seen to have low grades could potentially have aggravated Cass's popularity problems even further, but she soon managed to associate herself with a small group of likeminded – and like-graded – friends, all of whom realised that if they were not going to shine academically, the only protection from constant attack was humour. 'Basically what we all had in common,' remembers Chip Silverman, 'was we finished towards the bottom of the class. As it was, [Barry]

Levinson finished *last* in the class, but it was very competitive there and so you said, well, I can't do this, so I'll compete on an interpersonal level, you know? And so that's what a lot of these people did. There was a great pressure to be funny or witty. Without a sense of humour, Forest Park was a tough place to be. So you were forced to develop wit.'

Amongst her albeit very small circle of friends who, apart from Sharon, included Silverman, Ken Waissman, Levinson and Shelley Spector, Cass could beat anyone hands down in the battle for the most lethal one-liner or funniest anecdote. She had also, whilst serving the construction workers at Mondawmin, developed an ear for their saltier language and no doubt in an attempt to fuel her verbal defence ammunition, and probably bring an added frisson of shock, brought some of it with her to school. 'She cussed like a *sailor*!' remembers Silverman. 'I'm *sure* she picked it up from the construction crews at Mondawmin . . . no question about *that*, but I'll tell you what – to this day, I don't think I've ever met anybody that had as foul a mouth as her. And the fact that she was a girl and that it was the fifties – it was kind of shocking. Because you didn't get that from the other girls at school. I'd never really heard a woman talk that way – not a girl my age,' he laughs. 'You know what I mean? So it was kind of like, Wow! Did you hear what she *said*? Or sometimes it'd be, "What she *mean* by that?"'

Later on in Cass's life, whilst she was never slow to make a point and cut to the heart of an issue, her language rarely seemed any more risqué than anyone else's, but during her teens it was certainly just another ploy to gain attention for something other than her size.

It was obvious to everyone including Cass that her problems stemmed almost entirely from her weight, but she was clearly loath to address the issue too seriously. While she often claimed to be on a diet, even these seemed to work according to her own rather idiosyncratic rules, and whatever anxiety or unhappiness she may have felt about her weight, she clearly made a point of hiding it from her friends.

'She was just, like, this free spirit,' remembers Sharon. 'I remember one time we took a ride to Alexandria to meet her old friends from school and *nobody* drives to Virginia when you're sixteen years old! We were kids! I don't know *how* we got there and on the way back we decided that we would stop off at a doughnut shop. I think we must have wolfed down twenty-four – we were both sick as a dog! But she decided that she was going to lose weight and there was a place that the football star Alan Ameche opened which was one of the first drive-in hamburger places. We used to go there all the time and she would be so funny because she would get, like – I think they were called powerhouses – they were, like, *some* gezuntas! You would get three layers of hamburgers with all the sauces and stuff and she would get onion rings or French fries depending, but she wouldn't get the milkshake – she would get water. And that was her diet. That was as far as she got with her dieting. It was *great*!' she laughs.

At some perhaps unconscious level, Cass clearly needed to convince herself as well as others that she was in fact slim, rather than overweight. 'I do believe she created the world she wanted to live in,' says Sharon. 'She brought a picture one time of a tiny little skinny cheerleader with her legs behind her back, arms up in the air, with a little short skirt, skinny as could be, the face cut out and her face stuck in it. She carried it in her wallet, and she says, "This is when I was in Alexandria and I was cheerleader." You can *imagine*. Everyone would just look at it and no one would say anything. Because what could you say? We would just go, "OK." We were polite little girls, so we would never question it and I wouldn't want to hurt her feelings. I don't know *what* she thought, but it was so *obvious* – the fat face and the thin body – no *way*! And it wasn't the time of computers where you could really make it good. *No!* It was like a little Brownie photo with a cut-out of her face stuck on it. And this would go on *all* the time. But we just let it be. Because maybe even then, I realised that she needed to do that. It was something she needed to do to get by.'

The fact that someone of Cass's intelligence would go to such lengths to create a reality that was different from the one she lived in, simply confirms the depth of her unhappiness at the time, but for the other girls at school, this simply seemed another of Cass's fantasy tales. 'She was the most fantastic liar,' says Sharon. 'She would tell these tall tales of her acquisitions of men, fantastical stories, and we'd just say, "Well . . . that's what she does." We assumed that she kind of believed them or we didn't know *what* to think, but we didn't question it.' Cass eventually seems to have turned an innate talent for story telling into something of an art, as throughout the rest of her life, she would frequently find a way of embellishing the facts either to suit the requirements of the situation or often, simply for her own, as much as others', entertainment. But although, whilst at Forest Park, Cass clearly was not delusional as such, her tendency to stretch the truth far and beyond the confines of believability seemed just another symptom of her despondency.

Even though Cass may never have voiced this in so many words to her parents, they would almost certainly have become aware of it at some level. But they were themselves already concerned and were well aware that Cass's problems stemmed from her size. After she had initially gained weight around the time of Leah's birth, they, like many others, may have assumed that this was some kind of passing childhood phase which she would grow out of like any other. By the time she was in her early teens, however, this was clearly not the case.

Cass's parents had been understandably anxious about her weight since her early teens and their GP, Dr Abramson, had prescribed Dexedrine, a type of amphetamine or speed, which at the time was still routinely accepted as a diet pill for its function as an appetite suppressant. Much less was known about the drug at this point, and with the fifties belief in science's ability to solve the world's problems, this was accepted without question. 'It wasn't like you'd say to your doctor, "Well, what's in this medicine?"' explains Leah. 'Someone says, "She needs to lose weight. I'm gonna put her on this medication." But no one knew what it was. And my sister, at one point, said that it just was impossible for her to sit still during classes.'

Amphetamine in fact has a similar chemical structure to the body's natural adrenaline and consequently has a stimulant effect, heightening energy levels and sharpening the mind. During World War Two, it had been routinely supplied to American, British and German forces and continued to be standard US army issue throughout the Vietnam war, but the reality of the drug was that after a few weeks it lost its potency, and in order to boost the effect the dosage had to be continually increased. The drug's side effects, which included sleeplessness and anxiety, likewise rose in tandem with the increase in dose. But as these shortcomings had yet to be fully acknowledged, the medical profession continued to prescribe it.

The Dexedrine also certainly contributed to Cass's lack of concentration at school, but despite its side effects, by the time Cass was in her final year at Forest Park, it did not seem to have made any visible difference to her weight. Bess and Philip, therefore, aware of Cass's unhappiness and resulting social problems at school, sent Cass to a psychologist.

Today, teenagers and children are routinely sent for counselling on a variety of issues, but in the late fifties, this was far from the norm. 'In those days *nobody* went to a psychologist,' remembers Sharon. 'To most of the population in Baltimore, to go to a psychologist would have meant that something was really wrong with you. That you were nuts. So for her parents to be even with-it enough to try to get her help was saying a lot for them. But also they must have thought they had quite a problem with this girl, that there was a really big need for it because it was just not something that you did.'

Cass would inevitably have been aware of this stigma, but whatever her true feelings about going to the psychologist may have been, again, she appeared unconcerned about it to Sharon, and far from attempting to conceal her visits, she took her along in the car. 'It was just like, "Do you wanna go with me?"' says Sharon. 'And she probably lied her way through it. Knowing her, she probably told them any story they wanted to hear so that would have been a *real* waste of money! I can't imagine that she would open up but I don't know that she would have *known* to tell them the truth.'

The concept of discussing her real feelings would have been relatively alien to Cass as it had never been remotely encouraged at home, but whatever she may or may not have told the Baltimore psychologist, years later in 1967 when she was asked 'Why are you fat, Cass?', after initially saying, 'I don't know,' she eventually offered a plausible theory: 'Everyone has fears, I guess. In my mind, I've thought that my weight protects me. See, I'm a very gullible person. If you tell me anything seriously, I'll believe you. An attractive young girl in this world who is gullible can get herself into a lot of trouble and I find that ... It keeps the lechers away. Whatever psychological reason motivates me to stay heavy also motivates me to succeed ... eventually, I'll lose it all.'

The 'weight as protection' explanation is one now commonly recognised by psychologists as an often unconscious motivation for weight gain and a subsequent resistance to weight loss, but whether Cass truly believed this to be her case is debatable. Someone as bright as Cass could easily have been offering an easy text-book theory for something that was perhaps more complex and quite possibly less easily defined, even to herself. But whichever was the truth, it was clearly not a subject she felt comfortable discussing.

Cass's visits to the psychologist, whether they were constructive or not, in the end had no more effect on her weight than the Dexedrine. Cass's initiation into the drug world, meanwhile, would have repercussions throughout the rest of her life, but at the time, drugs of this kind were seen as a solution rather than an additional problem in themselves. Cass's introduction to Dexedrine by doctors as a teenager arguably precipitated her use of other drugs, but by the time Cass was in her late teens smoking marijuana was already prevalent amongst those with a taste for adventure and so it seems more than likely that Cass would have at least tried it, if not embraced it as an activity regardless. What seems without doubt, however, is that having been inducted into the regular use of pharmaceuticals at such an early age, later on in her life, it would prove doubly difficult to extricate herself from the cycle.

Whilst she was a teenager, though, Cass's prescribed drugs just served to further differentiate her from her peers, but during her final year at Forest Park, Cass would discover one area which did seem to make a difference to her life. Cass had never missed an opportunity to perform – indeed even by her teens it could be said that a large part of her life was already a performance, but finding a chance to take part in real theatre would prove of monumental importance to her life. For the first time it would give Cass the chance to do something in which she felt completely happy.

3

The Boyfriend

As classic musicals go, *The Boyfriend* was never the greatest show of its kind, but for Cass it would have life-changing importance. As a child, Cass had dreamed of Broadway, and throughout her solo career, after the Mamas and the Papas, almost everything she did would tread a fine line between rock and roll and a more old-fashioned style of showbiz glitz. Her first love remained the Broadway musicals of the thirties, forties and fifties and the song she would come to be most closely identified with, 'Dream a Little Dream of Me', was similarly an old tune from the songwriting traditions of the thirties. Musicals also seemed to offer the perfect outlet for her comedic talent, opening the door to her stage career and allowing her to leave Ellen Cohen behind and become Cass Elliot.

During Cass's high school years, rock and roll had erupted onto the music scene and Elvis and the artists who had come in his wake had transformed popular music irrevocably, suddenly bringing high-voltage sex into the previously staid pop world of romantic crooners and novelty acts. But although Cass loved Elvis and his fellow rockers, unlike many of her generation, for whom rock and roll would define their youth, it didn't affect her in the same way as the Broadway tunes she had always loved. Whilst rock and roll was determinedly earthy and inextricably linked with being young, sexy and above all alive in the here and now, Broadway musicals offered a different kind of glamour and magic that existed somewhere else, in another time and place that was far removed from the often less appealing realities of life as Ellen Cohen.

At Forest Park, apart from her friendship with Sharon, Cass felt even more alienated than she had in Alexandria, and so it is easy to see why this world of musicals and film would have provided a welcome escape. Day after day, Cass would spend hours in Sharon's basement, as the pair of them listened to musicals on the record player, singing along, acting and making up skits of their own. *Gypsy* was their favourite. They knew all the songs in their sleep and would recite whole swathes of dialogue back and forth for weeks on end.

Cass and Sharon were also both music majors and sang in the school choir but any ambitions either of them may have had to take music further were never voiced. When there was an opportunity to take part in a real theatre production, albeit local summer stock, Cass was surprisingly loath to put herself forward, but instead made sure Sharon auditioned. Perhaps she realised that, despite her announced intentions of being a star, given her size, her own chances of gaining a role were minimal, and so if Sharon could be accepted, she could in some way vicariously enjoy the experience too. 'One day, she came to my house in the afternoon,' says Sharon, 'and she said, "Get your leotard on," and I said, "What for?" She said, "You – not we, *you* are going to audition for a summer stock company." Summer stock was held at the Hilltop Theater at Owing Mills, just ten miles outside Baltimore, but at the time it was still considered quite far, certainly for two young girls to be travelling on their own, but Cass and Sharon nevertheless headed out in Philip's old Chevy and drove off out to the countryside.

Sharon passed the audition and was accepted for the entire summer season, starting with the first show – *Bells Are Ringing*. She has no recollection of Cass auditioning for a role herself, but she clearly wanted to be around the theatre very much, and as her friend was now in the show, as was Shelley Spector, Cass now had an excuse to hang around Hilltop and lost no time in making friends with virtually the entire cast. With the exception of a few other Foresters, such as Ken Waissman, the summer stock players mostly comprised professional young actors from New York, and unlike Cass's fellow pupils at Forest Park, they warmed to her immediately. Theatre culture, almost by definition, had always embraced the unconventional and welcomed those who didn't fit into so called 'polite' society, particularly someone as naturally outgoing, gregarious and entertaining as Cass.

Bells Are Ringing was eventually followed by *The Boyfriend* which was so successful that the producers decided to extend its run. It was a decision which would have monumental consequences for Cass. *The*

Boyfriend – a 1920s pastiche about a regional English theatre company putting on a musical – included the small part of a French maid. But in one of those accidents of fate on which many a career has been launched, the young girl who had been playing the part had another commitment and could not stay for the extension to the run. The producers were understandably loath to begin auditioning for such a small part, particularly as there was someone who assured them she was uniquely qualified for the part. Cass had by this time spent virtually the entire summer hanging around the Hilltop Theater and so, as she knew every song and every line of the show already, she was given the role.

The way Cass later told it in a radio interview, her landing of the albeit small part, was essentially down to Sharon. 'They were desperately looking around for somebody,' Cass said, 'and my girlfriend said, "Well, *she* sings." And I had braces on my teeth, and you know, just every other adolescent hang-up and the next thing I knew I was into the chorus, you know!' Years later she would tell *Esquire* magazine how she remembered singing 'It's Nicer, Much Nicer in Nice' – one of the show's big set numbers and still remembered the song. 'I was *very* good,' she told them, 'It was *so sophisticated*.'

Sharon, meanwhile, recalls her having slight difficulties attempting the maid's French accent. 'I remember rehearsing her,' says Sharon, 'and it was so funny because the maid was French and the first line was "*'Allo? 'Allo?*" and I was trying to tell her, "Try to do a French accent. Sound French!" And it kept on coming out Yiddish: "All*ooo*' All*ooo*,"' she says in faux Yiddish accent, 'and I was saying, "No! You can't do it like that." It was very funny! And in the end she did sound very Jewish!'

Accents aside, Cass nevertheless felt instantly at home onstage. 'Cass had just not *one shred* of nervousness or stage fright,' remembers Leah, 'not a shred! When she was up there dancing around and singing and looking right at the audience, she just looked like she was to the manor born. She was a complete natural. She just looked like she belonged up there from the first time I ever saw her in a musical. It looked like it was totally what she was supposed to be doing.'

The Boyfriend was followed by another show in September, *Prior to Broadway*, and this time Cass was given a part straight away. As a clown. Made-up and dressed in full clown regalia, Cass was required to come on in between scenes and put placards on an easel announcing the next scene, silent movie style. But although the clown role may only have been small, Cass was so thrilled to have finally been recognized with a specific part of her own, she made sure everyone at Forest Park knew about it by coming to school with dabs of clown-white make-up left in her ears or on the side of her face. It seemed to be her badge of honour and this way people would have no doubt that she was an actor at the theatre.

After performing in *The Boyfriend* and *Prior to Broadway*, there was absolutely no question in Cass's mind that the stage was where she belonged. 'I did the show for three weeks,' she told a radio interviewer for the United States Army Reserve in 1973, 'and then I went back to school, somehow school didn't seem the same to me. Just the idea of going on to become a doctor, just didn't seem like I, you know . . .'

School clearly didn't feel the same. As she had been unhappy at Forest Park for some time already and was eager to find herself a part in another theatre production, Cass decided to drop out just a few months before graduation. Meanwhile, the idea that Cass intended to be a doctor was of course immortalized in the Mamas and the Papas's 'Creeque Alley': 'When Cass was a sophomore, planned to go to Swarthmore; But she changed her mind one day . . .' but the extent of these medical ambitions is debatable, to say the least. As far as the song lyric is concerned, she had told John and Michelle Phillips that she planned to continue her education after high school at Goucher College near Baltimore and John had simply exchanged Swarthmore for Goucher as it fitted better in the song. But few who knew Cass at the time remember her having any medical aspirations or thoughts of going to college. 'I had never heard about her being a doctor,' says Sharon. 'I never heard this in my life! Be a doctor? Never a word! When I first heard the line about Swarthmore in the song, I went, "*Not on your life!*" So I'm coming from thinking, really, no way.'

None of Cass's other friends from Baltimore, or Alexandria for that matter, have any recollection of this being mentioned either. The only suggestion of any interest lies in the George Washington High School Yearbook, *Compass* from 1958, which shows Cass in the school's Caduceus club which was for students interested in medicine, and Leah vaguely recalls there being some talk of it, although she too concurs that any ideas Cass may have had never materialised into any concrete plans, '*Somehow* I remember her talking about stuff like that.

My mom wanted us to go to nursing school. Not to be doctors but she just thought, "Go be nurses or teachers – that's a great profession." But I don't remember that those ideas with Cass were anything more than a fantasy.'

The fact that Cass had dropped out of high school shortly before graduation meant that she would have lacked the necessary qualification to go straight to college immediately, even had she wanted to. But later on in her life, as she embarked on a career in the music industry, she would have found herself in an environment where women's intelligence and their capacity to hold a valuable opinion were routinely undermined. The college degree she lacked would have served as a kind of social badge of intelligence; with a degree people automatically assumed you were bright. For Cass, the 'I was going to be a doctor' tale would therefore have provided a reasonable substitute for a degree, saving her the frustration of constantly having to prove her intelligence.

But these issues were still a long way off. While performing in summer stock, Cass had begun to think about going to New York to pursue a career on the stage. New York was the home of theatre and of the Broadway musicals which she loved, and if she was going to stand any chance of becoming the star she had convinced everyone she would be, it was clear that that was where she would have to be. She had been there for a weekend and loved the turbo-charged animation of the city, and besides, Sharon and Shelley were both planning to go there for the same reason so it seemed the obvious thing to do. Cass's parents, however, were less convinced.

Eager for his daughter to avoid the precariousness of his own working life, Philip did indeed want Cass to attend Goucher College. Whether he had thoughts of her studying medicine or not, he and Bess had high aspirations for their intelligent daughter and therefore insisted that, rather than go to New York, she continue at night school in order to make up the half credit necessary to be accepted at college. With no money of her own, Cass had to reluctantly agree. But she would get her own way soon.

Whilst attending night school, Cass got a job working on reception at the *Baltimore Jewish Times* newspaper and was soon roped into writing obituaries, although she later admitted to copying most of these from the *New York Times*. In order to please her parents, and avoid working on the lunch wagons, this was followed by a brief stint at the *Baltimore Sun*, taking classified ads over the phone, but Cass hated this even more than the previous job and was eventually fired for clogging up the phone lines chatting to her friends all day on the 'out' line.

She knew she had to do something else, but while she worked out what that was, she continued to see some of the few friends she had from Forest Park. Sharon and Shelley had gone off to New York, but Chip Silverman and a few other friends were still in Baltimore, either at school or going to college.

On Cass's outings to the psychologist, she had discovered Baltimore's downtown area, which at the time was home to the city's bohemians, beatniks and misfits and was consequently considered decidedly louche by respectable society. Beatnik culture had emerged in the late fifties in the form of writers William Burroughs, Jack Kerouac and Allen Ginsberg and their rejection of the sanitised, straitjacketed ideals of mainstream America. As forerunners to the hippies that would follow later in the sixties, the beats were the original social rebels: jazz was their soundtrack and they championed a new, existentialist freedom in every aspect of their lives. So successful were they in creating this subversive image that J. Edgar Hoover promptly warned that 'beatniks are one of the three greatest threats to America'. Cass's attraction to the beatnik ethos, and the bars and clubs that embraced it, was almost inevitable.

Cass's natural curiosity and sense of adventure led her to explore the poetry readings, bookshops, artists' studios and cafes of the neighbourhood. 'That was a very "in" place when it was beatnik time,' remembers Sharon, 'and she was a kind of beatnik, so that would have been right up her alley and very much like her to have seen what's happening. We lived out in the suburbs where just suburban people lived and had very little understanding of anything subculture, because the Jewish community all lived in a ghetto; it was a very large ghetto but we all lived within a couple of square miles of each other. And the downtown area was definitely kind of verboten, you know? That was not for us. It was really not a place you went. If you went, you'd get quite a reputation and you couldn't chance that in Baltimore.'

'Nice' girls obviously had to worry about getting a 'reputation' as this would adversely affect their chances of making a good marriage, but although at some level Cass may have secretly yearned for such normality and respectability, that had never been in the script for her and she immediately gravitated towards downtown hang outs like Martick's – a smoky dive-type bar which had its own reputation as a magnet for mixed-race couples, gays, beatniks and anyone else shunned by supposedly respectable society – and the Peabody Bookstore, which, like City Lights in San Francisco, was also a gathering place for artists, intellectuals and anyone seeking something beyond mainstream culture. Another venue was the Checkmate coffee bar, and there Cass would often meet up with Chip Silverman and others, fast forming a kind of hip, underground group who would sit around exchanging gossip, attempting to dazzle each other with the most colourful story or the most caustic put–down. The rest of their time was spent going back to each other's houses to smoke hash or grass.

Cass's prescribed use of amphetamines had not put her off drug use, and for Cass and her friends, any new drug, apart from being fun, would have had the cachet of being considered subversive and rebellious. Marijuana had already long been in use by jazz musicians and beatniks, and Washington, DC and Baltimore were at the forefront of drug culture. But for Cass and her friends, smoking was nevertheless still a fairly covert activity. As far as most people, including most young people, were concerned, drug culture was still relatively uncharted territory. Apart from being illegal with a potentially severe prison sentence attached to even small-scale marijuana possession, all drugs were considered taboo and carried a powerful stigma in the wake of recent films like *The Man with the Golden Arm*. But whilst alcohol was associated with their parents, drugs seemed like Cass's own generation's discovery and would therefore be adopted by Cass and subsequently many others, just as rock and roll had, as a central, defining part of their identity.

Most of Cass's contemporaries in Baltimore by this time were either already attending college or planning to do so in the near future, and so, as the months went by, it became clear to Cass that she would have to make a decision as to what to do next. She had started taking singing lessons with Shirley Richmond, a local voice teacher who believed she had genuine talent and encouraged her to try her luck in New York. She was so impressed, Richmond would even lend her some money to get there.

Cass went back to Philip and Bess and pleaded with them to let her go. They still desperately wanted her to go to college but eventually she managed to persuade them. As she later explained: 'I talked it over with my parents. I said "Listen, I'd like to be in show business." And they laughed "ha ha" at that funny joke and they said, "Nobody's gonna pay you for that," and "Don't be silly," and, you know, "Go to college like you're supposed to." And I said, "Well, look, I'll make a deal with you. You let me have five years and I'll go to New York and try and make something of myself and if I don't make it in five years, I'll come back." And I went on September nineteenth and five years later on September fourth, 'California Dreamin'' was released. So, I really just made it under the wire!'

This is indeed not far from the truth. Bess and Philip were disappointed that by going to New York Cass would miss out on graduation. The idea of Cass pursuing a career in itself had never been in question. Unlike many parents of the time, Philip and Bess had no issue with the idea of a girl having professional ambitions – Bess was herself clearly a feminist before her time and Philip's family included several strong, independent women – it was more the uncertainty of the show business life which worried them. At the same time, however, they weren't entirely sure what else she could do. They knew that she hated working at Mondawmin and so that clearly would not work as even a short-term option, and given Cass's certainty about going to New York, in spite of their doubts, they finally agreed. 'Cass *hated* working for my dad,' remembers Leah. 'In fact I always suspected Cass ran away to New York so that she wouldn't have to work on the buses any more. But she seemed so *sure* that this was what she wanted to do. It was just, I *have* to do this, I *have* to go to New York. And I think my parents just thought, Well, we don't know if it's right but let her go, so they said "OK, go ahead." 'Cause I don't think they knew any other direction to point her in.'

If Cass was going to begin a new life, she would need a new name, she decided. That way, she felt she could magically erase Ellen Cohen and transform herself into someone else altogether. She had been given the nickname Cass by her father, because, she said, 'I was kind of loud and crazy and he used to say, "Ah, it's the mad Greek Cassandra!"' Or at least that was what she told one journalist. As would often prove the case throughout the rest of Cass's life, she would come to tell various versions of just how this had come about. Nobody she was at high school with, either in Alexandria or in Baltimore, has any recollection of her being called anything other than Ellen prior to this point, and the whole idea of changing names was only brought up in summer stock. 'She and I were sitting on the steps outside the stage door,' remembers Ken Waissman, 'when she told me what her stage name was going to be. "I'm going to take the 'C' from my last name 'Cohen' and the 'E' from my first name 'Ellen' and become 'Cass Elliot.'"'

The origin of Cass's new name may well have been as simple as that but it depends on who you talk to. A year or two later, she would tell Tim Rose, with whom she would form the folk trio the Big 3, that it was a combination of comedienne Cass Daley and T. S. Eliot. Ellen Cohen didn't have a ring to it, she told him.

The Cass Daley suggestion may well have more than an element of truth to it, as Cass certainly admired the vaudevillian comedienne and singer, and listening to her performances, there are clear comparisons between Daley's broad, sassy humour and the stage persona which Cass would later develop as Mama Cass. But as for any connections with T. S. Eliot, this seems to have been based on perhaps a momentary literary aspiration of Cass's as Sharon remembers a more prosaic version of events, which also backs up Waissman's recollection.

'It was around this time at summer stock that we were playing around with the stage names that we were gonna pick out. And Kay Kendall was very popular and Ellen thought she was maybe gonna name herself after her. I think it was gonna be Kendall Elliot. She got the name Elliot from Jesse Elliot – a jazz singer whose girlfriend had acted in *Prior to Broadway*. She was killed in a car accident in New York ultimately but Cass was gonna be Kendall Elliot and somehow after that it went to Cass. But that was the idea of how she was gonna get this and she was gonna somehow make it backwards, so she would have the E and the C of her name backwards – she was intent on that.'

Cass had had a fascination with spelling backwards for some time, as Priscilla Lainoff Stein remembers from their time in Alexandria. 'When we were kids we used to call each other by our names spelt backwards, so her name was Nelle Nehoc and mine was Allicsirp Ffonial. Years later when she came to Philadelphia to appear on the *Mike Douglas Show* after she had left the Mamas and Papas, I called her and she called me right back and she called me by my name backwards!' she laughs.

Whatever the origins of her new name, Ellen was now Cass Elliot. And she was going to New York.

Cass's Aunt Lil already lived in New York with her family and so Cass had somewhere to stay, but having grown up around Baltimore and Alexandria, some aspects of New York life came as rather a shock for Cass. Aunt Lil lived in what was at the time considered an undesirable neighbourhood on 125th Street and Riverside Drive. When Cass arrived from Baltimore, unused to the ways of the inner city, she left her belongings in the car which she parked outside her aunt's apartment. Unlocked. By the time she went back down, the car was empty. Cass was devastated. She had packed everything that was most important to her – her favourite clothes and possessions – and now she was faced with starting a new life in New York with nothing. Her aunt and uncle tried to deal with the situation as best they could and although Cass would later try to make light of the incident, describing herself as having been 'just a country bumpkin', it was nevertheless a traumatic start.

In some ways Cass may have had a lot to learn about life in a giant metropolis, but in others, Cass clearly took to New York life as if to the Apple born. Within weeks she had found herself a job working as a hat-check girl, first at the Duplex and then at the Showplace, both key venues on New York's thriving cabaret scene. Cass was thrilled. She told Michelle Phillips later that she hadn't even had to sleep with anyone to get the jobs. She said no one had asked her.

Apart from being the legendary home of Broadway, New York in the fifties was the epicentre of American show business, with the exception only of the film industry in Hollywood. Although music and television would move to Los Angeles in the decade to come, in the fifties, New York was the key city for music, television, comedy and of course theatre. Since the mid-forties, New York had also been home to what would come to be thought of as the 'golden age of cabaret' and, until the early sixties, it seemed like every other block in Manhattan was home to a small club cramming in audiences of anything between thirty to two hundred. At the top end of the cabaret scene there were the large famous clubs like the Copacabana with its ostrich-feathered chorus girls and elaborate stage designs or glitzy hotel supper clubs such as the Plaza's Persian Room, whilst at the other end, there were the many smaller, more intimate cabaret venues which flourished throughout the fifties. In the years following the end of World War Two, people suddenly also had more money and were keener to go out for the evening and spend it.

By the end of that decade, with the sudden arrival of television into millions of homes, New York's umpteen clubs, mostly kitted out in the forties and fifties all-black New York chic, quickly became a talent pool for the new variety shows and chat shows constantly on the lookout for new stars. Eartha Kitt was famously picked for TV stardom after appearing in a cabaret revue show, so opening the floodgates for thousands of stage-struck young singers, comedians and musicians to rush to the city from the furthest-flung corners of America.

As the fifties rolled into the sixties, Cass therefore suddenly found herself in the midst of a community of aspiring singers, comedians and actors where everybody felt they were going to be a star sometime very soon. Amongst the regular performers at the Duplex and the Showplace were upcoming comics Joan Rivers, Woody Allen and Robert Morse, singers like Joanne Beretta singing numbers from *West Side Story* plus aspiring actors/pianists George Segal and Warren Beatty, both of whom were noticed more for their looks than their piano playing.

The Showplace, which occupied two floors of a five-storey brownstone at 146 West 4th Street, in the heart of the West Village, was also fashionable with theatre stars such as the young Liza Minnelli and George Grizzard, and Cass would stare at the door eagerly awaiting Grizzard's next visit. 'When is George Grizzard coming in?' she would repeatedly ask. 'I've got such a crush on George Grizzard!'

With shows at nine and eleven o'clock, Cass would usually be taking hats till about 1 a.m. each night, but after the acts had finished and most of the audience had gone, people would drift in from other clubs to wind down after hours and invariably a small, informal party would evolve around the piano. And Cass would finally get her chance to sing.

She had been practising her singing at her aunt and uncle's apartment and had already developed the ability to belt out a song like she was singing for the back row of the gallery. 'I remember coming home from school one day,' says Cass's younger cousin Ralfee Finn, 'when she was with us in New York and it must have been early springtime because I could hear her singing all the way out on the street corner. She was in the apartment, ironing, just singing away and all the windows were open and you could hear her on the *corner*. I ran into the house and I was like, "They can hear you on the street!" I was *so* embarrassed and humiliated and her response was, "*Great!*" She was *thrilled*. I'll never forget that. I had never heard anything like that as a child – that you could be happy about that. That was amazing to me.'

Although Cass never sang officially at the Showplace, the club's manageress Jan Walman distinctly remembers the occasions at these informal gatherings when she did, 'She was *not* a pretty girl, and I'm a pretty good size myself!' she laughs. 'She had beautiful hair and lovely eyes but she was fat and kind of *floppy* and did not dress very well, but when she *sang*, she just turned on thousands of watts of talent.'

Comedian Larry Hankin was also working at the Showplace, opening for the still relatively unknown Woody Allen. Hankin never heard Cass sing, but the two of them became friends and her personality and unusual looks made a lasting impression on him. 'Cass stood out,' remembers Hankin, 'because she was weird-looking and she approached *me*. She'd say, "Hey, that was a good set." She would be checking coats and then me and her would go out for coffee. I guess she kind of liked me because I was funny, because I was up on the stage and she wasn't and she was just a fan. But she stood out. Even if she'd never become famous and you'd said, "Do you remember anybody from those days?" I would have said, "Yeah, the hat-check girl." And she always remained that in my mind.'

The same way Cass had initiated her friendship with Hankin, she similarly quickly developed an extensive network of new friends in New York. Unlike the suburban conformity of Baltimore, Cass fitted into the New York theatre scene instantly. So much so that most people around her didn't even realise she hadn't been born there. 'I was surprised she was from someplace else,' says Cass's friend songwriter and pianist John Wallowitch, who played regularly at the Showplace and Duplex. 'I thought she was a New York girl. I reckon, people with talent, after three months, they're native – they're New Yorkers.' The ability to make friends quicker than most people could blink was part of Cass's naturally gregarious nature, but it was also in her interest to do so as she only got paid in tips. But her success on the social front did not endear her to Jan Walman. Cass's friends would come up the main staircase from the street and then congregate around the coat-check counter in the foyer, creating a bottleneck and blocking the entrance to the club. With a whole crowd of them in for the evening, the sound of their chatting and laughter would also travel through to the club, and as Walman remembers 'it wasn't too good for the acoustic!' Cass's friends were also not generally paying customers of the club. As far as Walman was concerned, they were simply hanging out and clogging up her lobby. 'You *cannot* have all your friends come and visit you, Cass!' she told her night after night.

Cass's new friends were mostly other aspiring performers and Cass quickly keyed into the theatre circuit, beginning acting classes at a small theatre workshop, chatting up the agents that would often come into the clubs, getting pictures taken and attending auditions for parts in musicals. She used 'Glitter and Be Gay' from Leonard Bernstein's musical *Candide* as her audition piece and producers often loved her singing. The image, however, was another matter. 'Abe Burrows wouldn't even look at me,' Cass later remembered. And even when they would look at her, she was repeatedly turned down. 'There wasn't much call for a three-hundred pound ingénue,' she quipped.

Her greatest disappointment was losing the part of the secretary Miss Marmelstein in Harold Rome's *I Can Get It For You Wholesale*, a musical comedy set in New York's predominantly Jewish textile and clothing area. Cass seems to have come close to getting the part, but lost out in the final stages to the then relatively unknown Barbra Streisand. Or at least that is how Cass always told it.

Streisand, at the time, was not very much closer to stardom than Cass herself. She may have been performing in the clubs where Cass was still only the hat-check girl, but she was also still struggling to get noticed. 'I remember Streisand on the phone in the booth at the club all the time with the agents,' says John Wallowitch. 'The phone was still a nickel and she'd stand there with handfuls of nickels saying, "You gotta see me in . . ." some off-Broadway play. Nobody took her seriously. But she was *so* convinced that she was gonna be a giant star and that became the Streisand year – "Ugly girl makes good".'

The fact that Streisand was, in her own way, a similarly unlikely bet visually in terms of not conforming to accepted conventions of feminine beauty, and that the part of Miss Marmelstein would provide her first big break towards success, before Cass was anywhere close, obviously rankled with her, and over the years to come, she would wheel out the story of this near-miss in one version or another at every opportunity. As Sharon remembers hearing it, 'She went in with her hair piled up on her head and she put a hat on and when she got out in front of them, she pulled the hat off and all of her hair fell in front of her face and she sang that way.' If this was even half true, it seems hardly surprising that Cass didn't land the role.

Whatever the reasons, as Cass struggled on, doing the rounds of auditions, the daily rejections must have been hard to take, and when she went home, her uncle's criticism and snipes were often no more encouraging. 'What makes you think you're gonna get ahead?' he would ask repeatedly, before making disparaging remarks about her looks and potential.

Finally, against what by this time seemed considerable odds, Cass got a small part in a touring production of *The Music Man* with Forrest Tucker, but after a few months there was news from Alexandria – where the family was once again living – that her father had been in a car accident and sustained internal injuries. Bess was at the hospital with Philip and so Cass returned home straight away to take care of her young sister and brother.

A week later, in 1961, Philip Cohen died. He was forty-two. Cass, like her younger sister and brother had adored her father, and at his funeral, if they hadn't known before, they were left in no doubt as to how much affection his generosity and good nature had inspired in those around him. The chapel at the funeral home was vast but so many people arrived to attend that many were left outside unable to squeeze in the building. Throughout his life, particularly when he had been managing restaurants, Philip had made a habit of offering food to anyone who came asking. This was not particularly unusual in the restaurant business as homeless people and tramps often came begging, but as well as offering food to those less fortunate, Philip had similarly never missed an opportunity to help someone out if he could. The funeral chapel was therefore filled with friends from those closest to the family to tradesmen and those with only the slightest acquaintance, such as the driver who delivered bread to the Mondawmin buses, and almost all of them made a point of approaching Bess to tell her of some act of thoughtfulness, kindness or generosity that Philip had carried out on their behalf and how they had maintained their relationships with him over the years. Cass, Bess and the rest of the family had always known of Philip's good nature, but even they were stunned by the number of complete strangers arriving to pay their respects.

Cass would come to inspire similar affection in those who knew her, often with the humour she had inherited from her parents, and at her father's funeral, Cass was, as ever, the first to try and lighten the situation. 'We were in the limousine,' remembers Leah, 'and my dad was in the hearse in front of us and my dad had always really wanted to drive a new Cadillac – he thought they were the coolest cars, and we were in the back of this limo and Cass said, "Well at least Dad finally got to ride in the frigging Cadillac the same year," and I just remember us all cracking up and for a moment thinking, Is this OK? To be laughing while you're at your dad's funeral? I mean there's no question we were all bereft beyond belief but I remember saying something about it like, "Should we be laughing?" and my sister saying, "Daddy would want us to." And he would have. It's really true. He wouldn't have wanted us to sit around moping.'

Bess Cohen was, as ever, a model of self-control. 'My mum cried a little bit but not too much at the funeral,' remembers Leah who was only eleven at the time, 'and thereafter I never ever saw my mom cry about my dad. And I'm sure she must have, but I never saw it.'

After the funeral, as is the Jewish custom, a shiva was held – a kind of wake which begins the seven-day-long period of mourning during which people visit the relatives of the deceased to offer their condolences. For all Cass's show of humour earlier in the day, she clearly did not feel strong enough to brave the public grieving of the shiva and instead looked to family friend Toby Kobren. 'Cass did not want to go to the shiva,' remembers Toby, 'so we stayed at my house and we had one of those old-fashioned tape recorders – the ones on a flat surface with two large reels and you spoke or sang into it and so Cass stayed at my house and she just sang the most beautiful, plaintive songs into that tape recorder.'

Philip's death inevitably forced Cass to think about her plans for the future. So far her attempts at achieving Broadway stardom had not gone entirely to plan, and as her young sister and brother were not yet in their teens, it seemed right that she should come back from New York and stay closer to them. Besides, despite her part in *The Music Man*, offers were not exactly flooding in, and although Cass had not abandoned her dreams of a career in show business, she realised that she might have to try a different approach. What she could not of course have predicted, was that someone else would unexpectedly come into her life who would change the course of her entire career.

4

'A smooth-talkin' banjo player'

When did music come into your life, Cass?
'I always listened to music in our home, but I never thought about it until I was in college. I met a guy who said to me, "Hey, baby, ever think about singin'?" I went to Chicago with him and he made me a star!'

Cass Elliot, *Flip* magazine 1966

Cass Elliot never intended to be a pop star. She certainly never intended to be a rock star. When she was growing up such a concept did not exist, but even the idea of being a popular singer was never what she had in mind. Folk music changed that. The folk music boom of the early sixties would change the course of Cass's life and give her the entrée into showbiz that she had been looking for. It wasn't quite what she had imagined but it didn't matter. For the first time in her life, she would have someone leading the way. A smooth-talkin' banjo player.

After her father's death, having decided to stay closer to her family, Cass moved into the basement of the house Bess had bought for herself and the other two children at Crestview Drive, Alexandria. And just as her father had wanted, she decided to go back to college and attend American University in Washington, DC. But she was not going to study medicine, nor for that matter, music. Cass still wanted to be an actress – preferably on Broadway – and so she enrolled in the Speech Arts course which covered drama, radio and TV and was, at the time, the only degree course that covered theatre at all. Once she had a degree, she thought, she would go back to New York and attempt another assault on Broadway.

In spite of her lack of grades, American University accepted her on the basis of high test results and Cass immediately got involved in the college radio station. She made friends on campus, although as Cass was by now twenty-one, it felt strange being back in an educational establishment amongst teenagers who had never set foot on a professional stage, especially now that she had been away, fending for herself amidst the brittle frenzy of New York's theatreland. 'I'd been out in the world doing my thing,' Cass later told *Esquire* magazine, 'and here I was a freshman – a provisional one because I didn't have my high-school diploma – with all these seventeen year olds, all dewy-eyed about the theatre.'

The way things turned out, Cass would not spend that long at American University and, in the years to come, her most significant memory of her time there was of the Cuban Missile Crisis which, for a few days during October of 1962, had America on alert for nuclear attack. 'Remember the Cuban Missile Crisis?' Cass later asked *Esquire*. 'Well, I remember it mostly because American University is a very political school, and everybody was sitting around instead of going to classes. American University is kind of like Berkeley. It gets pretty radical there at times. So we were all sitting around wondering what was going to happen – whether we were going to get bombed or what was going to go down. That day when nobody knew what was going to happen.'

The 'crisis' was the discovery that Russia was using Cuba as a missile base; Cuba's close proximity to America and the fact that its leader, Fidel Castro, was a Communist ally of Russia, meant this was seen by Washington as an enormous threat and potentially the worst political catastrophe since World War Two. For thirteen days, before the situation was peacefully resolved, a fraught game of tactical politics ensued between the two superpowers whilst Americans hastily built makeshift bunkers and stocked up on food supplies amongst widespread fears that nuclear war could indeed be imminent.

But the crisis was short-lived and Cass was soon immersed in some of the required course activities. For the radio element of the course, students had to create programmes for WAMU-AM, American University's radio station, and as a natural talker with a solid knowledge of music, Cass immediately landed the job presenting a five-nights-a-week jazz show. 'Climb out of your fallout shelters,' she urged the campus listeners, 'and welcome to Ring-A-Ding-Dong School.' Cass would then introduce the show and announce the records, giving short explanations about the artists and the history of the music. She had discovered jazz whilst still at Forest Park and stunned Sharon with her knowledge of Dave Brubeck and Edie Gormé – both of whom were far from mainstream and considered almost beyond hip at the time – and she now impressed everyone at AU equally with the extent of what she knew and her natural on-air talent. 'She knew a *lot* about jazz history at that time,' remembers Alan Pollock who was producing the show. 'Cass was always just *so* professional and of course her natural ability to be funny and make outrageous comments meant she was entertaining. You'd put her in front of the microphone and put the on air light on and she just *comes alive*! It was clear that she was not long for college life. She was too talented and too restless. In front of the microphone she had a twinkle in her eye, this impish smile, and was in complete control of her audience.'

Cass and the attractive, broadly built Pollock shared a love of Dave Brubeck and many other jazz greats but Cass seemed to particularly identify with Billie Holliday and Ella Fitzgerald and whilst she was in the studio Pollock soon began to notice that Cass had another talent beyond her personality. 'When the record was playing,' he remembers, 'it was a treat for me to hear her just singing along by herself in the studio. And I said, "Wow! She can *really* sing!"'

Pollock, who would later go on to a highly successful career in TV as a news producer, became one of Cass's first boyfriends and remained one of her most trusted friends throughout her life. They were both Jewish and from the Baltimore/Washington, DC area and shared not only a love of jazz but an outlook on life which seemed to stem from the similarity of their upbringings, and Pollock still vividly remembers their first meeting at AU. 'A bunch of us were working in Clendenon Theater one afternoon and a small group of students were talking over in the corner. Laughter erupted, I looked over and in the middle of the group was this bolt of lightning talking a mile a minute and entertaining her friends with stories. Most people learned not to verbally mess around with Cass. If crossed, she could render you senseless with a quick blast of laser-guided words. But she never did that to me. We just always hit it off.'

At Forest Park, the likelihood of Cass having a boyfriend at all had always seemed remote but here at AU, just as in New York, she suddenly found herself surrounded by like-minded friends and was no less popular than any other girl her age. With Alan, therefore, she could now experience a normal boyfriend-type relationship. Cass and Alan would spend afternoons together strolling through the cobbled Georgetown streets looking at art or go out for the evening. On one occasion, Pollock took her to a major college dance and Cass finally had a chance to dress up 'corsage and all', as Pollock recalls, in a glamorous black evening dress which 'showed off her killer legs', and the pair spent the evening dancing, talking and laughing. Cass had always secretly wanted to wear beautiful clothes and be admired, just as any young woman would, and it was only the high school jeers which had previously pushed her into a corner of eccentricity, but those days were over now.

Often Cass would invite Alan back to her mother's for dinner, but in romantic terms, the early sixties were a still comparatively innocent age and the relationship was never considered by either of them as something particularly serious. As was common practice at the time, they both dated other people whilst seeing each other and the emphasis was more on friendship than anything else. 'We just enjoyed each other's company a lot,' says Pollock, 'and it was a time when neither of us were looking for any type of commitment, so we kind of floated in and out of each other's life depending on what was going on.'

Despite being at university, Cass had by no means forgotten her show business ambitions. Obviously Broadway was still a long way off in every sense, but there were, however, opportunities to perform closer to home. The clubs around Georgetown were now holding 'open mic' nights where anyone could come along and try their hand at singing or playing, but they were not playing jazz, standards or the pop hits of the day. Jazz had been the beatniks' music of choice and was still considered cool and underground as a hip alternative to the bland pop sounds of the day, but within the last year students had embraced a new style of music which had taken over from rock and roll as the ultimate badge of youthful dissent and rebellion: folk.

By the end of the fifties, rock and roll's initial impact had dissipated dramatically. The standard explanation for this is that its key players had for various reasons been removed from the arena: Elvis had been drafted into the army, Little Richard left the rock world in 1959 to serve the Lord, Jerry Lee Lewis was outcast following scandal in 1958 when he married his thirteen-year-old cousin, whilst Buddy Holly and Ritchie Valens were killed in a plane crash in 1959.

These were certainly factors in what has been seen by many as the castration of rock and roll, and certainly contributed to its loss of momentum, but to cite this as the sole reason for rock and roll's demise is an over-simplification of the facts. During his two years in the army, Elvis had fourteen records in the American top thirty, so although his creativity may have been thwarted, his stint in the services did nothing to keep him off the airwaves or out of the charts. Buddy Holly, meanwhile, had only one top thirty hit as a solo artist before his death and only became internationally famous afterwards. Other artists, however, such as the Drifters, Ben E. King, Sam Cooke, Dion, Roy Orbison, Del Shannon and Gene Pitney, as well as a slew of girl groups continued to have hits with dynamic, captivating records throughout the late fifties and early sixties. But these were not what America's students objected to. The object of their scorn was the proliferation of what was briefly known as 'Philadelphia rock', referring to the anodyne rock 'n' roll 'lite' crooners such as Frankie Avalon and Fabian who both hailed from that city.

Rock and roll had effectively become sanitized, marketed and most importantly of all, mainstream, and so almost inevitably teenagers and students alike again wanted something new of their own. The charts were also still choked with hits by the stars of their parents' generation: Dean Martin, Andy Williams and Frank Sinatra, and although Cass may personally have loved them, as far as America's youth were concerned, they reeked of conservative commerciality.

Folk music as popularised by Woody Guthrie and Pete Seeger on the other hand seemed to offer an entirely different perspective. It was acoustic and in contrast to the standard chart fare which inevitably consisted of boy/girl romance scenarios, its lyrics were almost undeniably earnest and therefore seen as 'authentic' and 'honest' – two words which would come to be synonymous with the entire folk movement. Folk's sense of political commitment was therefore perfect for the new generation of politically aware students and was soon embraced by campuses across America.

Folk was also effectively the punk rock of its day, both in its emphasis on honesty and authenticity but also, equally importantly, in its accessibility. Folk embraced the do it yourself ethos in the same way that punk would do some fifteen years later, albeit with perhaps a little less attitude. Just as skiffle was doing in Britain at around the same time, folk prided itself on the fact that it was taking music back from the songwriters, producers and arrangers, who were still responsible for most commercial pop, and creating music written and performed by ordinary people. The Beatles would eventually take this one step further by writing their own songs, but for the time being, folk's simple chords and easy-to-sing songs meant that literally anyone could pick up a guitar and launch themselves, often within minutes, as a folk singer. And many did.

By 1961 no less than three of the year's bestselling albums were by the Kingston Trio – three clean-cut looking young folksters from Palo Alto, California, who had scored an unlikely international hit with their folk harmony version of the traditional murder ballad 'Tom Dooley'. The folk craze continued to spread throughout cities and campuses across the country including Washington, DC, and the city would eventually produce several key musicians of the folk rock era.

But in spite of the folk boom, Cass herself was still steeped in the Broadway heritage of the Rodgers and Hammerstein musicals which she loved, and was essentially unimpressed by folk. At American University, however, particularly in the drama and entertainment department and in the radio station where she was working, she couldn't help but be aware that folk was what everyone wanted to hear. By Autumn of 1962, there wasn't a campus in America without its share of would-be folk musicians and singers, and within months of Cass's arrival at AU, Joan Baez – the goddess of the folk movement, was featured on the cover of *Time* magazine in November 1962. The folk craze was now official.

Cass may not have felt a particular inclination towards folk, but while she was in Washington, DC, if she wanted to sing and perform, it was clear she would have to do what every other wannabe performer was doing and sing folk. It was also a welcome distraction from the part-time job she had taken working in a local drugstore, so she began singing at local clubs on an ad hoc basis, performing a narrow repertoire of folk songs, loosely hoping that an opportunity might emerge to do something more official, although she was getting little encouragement. Just as there were few Broadway musical stars who looked like Cass, similarly, the heroines of the folk movement: Joan Baez and Mary Travers (of Peter, Paul and Mary) embodied the new ideal of the long-haired sylph-like waif. Cass would clearly have no trouble singing folk songs, but when it came to image, she faced the same problems as before.

By singing around the local clubs, Cass did, meanwhile, begin to meet and make friends with other aspiring musicians on the local scene, one of whom was a young solo singer, still in his senior year at Georgetown University, with the poetically fortuitous name of John Keats. Keats liked Cass and was impressed by her voice and decided she should meet an old school friend of his who was newly back in town and looking for a new act. His name was Tim Rose.

Rose was the man who Cass would later say 'made her a star', and he did. A somewhat stockily built twenty-three year old, with thick wavy brown hair and intense brown eyes, Rose had been brought up by his mother, at a time when single mothers were rare, in Arlington, not far from the Cohens, but due to the more strictly segregated atmosphere of the times, being Catholic, he had lived in different neighbourhoods and attended different schools.

Rose had taught Keats to play guitar while they were at school and the pair had briefly played together as teenagers in a band called the Singing Strings, alongside their fellow schoolmate Phil Blondheim – later known as Scott Mackenzie. The band played mostly rockabilly covers of early Elvis and Sun Records singles, but in their final year at school, as the music scene began to change, the pair decided to form a guitar and banjo duo, calling themselves the Kentucky Colonels, and became a regular fixture at school functions.

'We were more playing than singing,' remembers Keats, now a prominent DC lawyer whose past work includes both the Watergate and Iran/Contra cases. 'Timmy would play the five-string banjo and I backed him on guitar. But Timmy was a phenomenal musician. You could put strings on anything and Tim would play it. When we were in high school, I watched Timmy tune a guitar to a five-string banjo and teach himself to play it that way until he was able to afford to buy himself a real banjo. An amazing musician!'

In 1960, by the time Tim and Keats finished high school, the duo had broken up and Tim started playing occasionally in another local group called the Abstracts – a vocal harmony quartet which had been formed by a close school friend of Phil Blondheim's by the name of John Phillips. Rose, however, had already developed the gravelly vocal style which would become his trademark as a solo artist later in the sixties and this didn't suit the pure a capella harmonies Phillips was aiming for, and so although he played several gigs accompanying them, he was never officially part of the group. Seeing no future with the combo, Tim instead signed up for officer and pilot training in the air force.

On his return to DC, after a brief stint in a short-lived folk duo Mike and Timothy, Rose once again found himself without an act and started looking around for someone else to work with. Keats, meanwhile, was now firmly entrenched in the local music scene and knowing that his friend was looking for a new musical partner, he invited him to a party given by his Georgetown friends. 'There'll be a girl there who sings,' Keats told Rose. 'I'd like you to meet her.'

Some forty years on, in the summer of 2002, just over a year before his death from cancer, Rose and I met in a small local pub close to the central London home he had lived in since his brief period of solo success in the late 60s. Although he had been teetotal for the previous eight years, the now-portly, silver-haired Rose was still on friendly terms with the publican, and while he was clearly a man who didn't suffer fools, having decided you weren't one, Rose gave the impression that he would quite possibly be a friend for life. In person, he brought the same intensity to his opinions as to his combative guitar and singing style but his occasionally belligerent manner also clearly belied a great warmth, accompanied by a dry and sharp humour. Over two days he talked to me with a mixture of affection and frustration about his memories of Cass and the time they spent together. A day later, he sent me an email thanking me for allowing him to talk about what he said were some important times for him.

'There she is, sitting over there,' Keats told Rose, as he pointed Cass out across the room at the party in Georgetown in the late autumn of 1962. 'I looked over,' remembered Rose, 'and there was this *very huge* woman sitting there. And I turned to John and I said very unkindly, "Look, I don't care what she sings like, I envisaged something like Mary Travers. This is *not* what I imagined."'

'Well, *boy*, are *you* in for a surprise!' laughed Keats, knowing just how well Cass could sing. 'Just go talk to her, say hello – no guarantees – you don't have to do anything. Just talk to her,' he said. 'And so,' Tim explained, 'against my better judgement, I did.'

The conversation that ensued would effectively change Cass's life. Cass would certainly have been more than happy to chat to this attractive, charismatic young man who told her he was a musician and had a worldly air that seemed to suggest he would be unfazed by anything life might throw at him, and she could have had no idea that the next five minutes would have such an impact on her future. But people were invariably impressed by her personality and Tim was no exception. After only a few minutes, he was utterly captivated.

'I was *fascinated* with her,' he remembered animatedly. 'She was the *wittiest* woman I had ever met. She was pretty much the wittiest *person* I had ever met up to that point in my life. She was quick and grown up beyond her years – or at least she acted it. She had lived in New York and by then *I* had been around too. I had left Washington and done my little trip with the air force so we were kind of soulmates.'

In an age where marriage in your early twenties if not in your late teens was still commonplace, the fact that Cass, like Rose himself, was still single and didn't have a boyfriend also drew them together. 'Usually when you meet somebody the fourth or fifth word is "my boyfriend" or "my girlfriend" and so the identity thing comes in the pairness – it's "us", rather than "I" or "me". It was never like that with Cass. There was never an "us" with her and there was never an "us" with me and I thought, Well, she and I could be the "us". Not romantically, but in every other way. Body type she was not my type at all, and still isn't, but I felt that the other ways: musically, artistically, sensitivity-wise – we had the same sensitivities, manifested in different ways.'

With hindsight one could suggest that there was clearly more than a little ambiguity to Tim's feelings for Cass and this would indeed become an issue for her in the months that followed but for the time being, Cass was clearly as taken with the fast-talking Rose as he was with her. 'It turned out she lived two blocks from my house, so I took her home and I said, "Do you fancy a beer or a coffee?" She said, "Yeah, sure." I was living with my mother at the time, so I went down to my basement and I played her some blues – stuff like Jimmy Reed, Elmore James, Blind Lemon Jefferson and John Lee Hooker and she'd never heard any of that stuff. I said, "You never heard this stuff?" And she said, "Well, I've heard *of it*." Cass's love was Broadway: things like *South Pacific* and *The Sound of Music*. She could sing "Happy Happy Talk" from South Pacific and this didn't mean shit to me!

'"Have you heard of Richard Rogers?" she would ask, so I said, "Yeah, but that's not where it's at. Where it's at is the next step on

Peter, Paul and Mary. Elmore James is where it's at." It's simpler music than Rodgers and Hammerstein and Cole Porter and all that and so I played her some Jimmy Reed 'cause it's so *simple* in its form, not for the banjo playing, but for the three-part harmonies you get in bluegrass. That was where I saw it going – this kind of synthesis between the simplicity of the blues but with Cass's voice and my voice and a third.'

Despite his initial misgivings, Tim decided he had nothing to lose by listening to Cass sing. She may not have looked like Mary Travers, but he needed a female singer and in the absence of any Travers lookalikes, why not try Cass?

'I gave her some parts to sing,' continued Tim, 'and I'd play something and say, "Now you sing this," and she'd do it right away – I didn't have to tell her twice. With most singers who are not very good, when another person starts singing they will start drifting automatically to what the other person is singing – because they don't really know what they're doing. Cass didn't. I sang anything and she still stuck with it, so I thought, "She's a singer. She *knows* what it's about." She *was* a singer, she was a musician. There are people who play guitar and there are people who are musicians – they're not the same people. Same with singers – singers are musicians just like guitarists, pianists, violinists. Cass was a musician. Gabrielle's a singer. And that's what impressed me the most about her that evening. She could sing a C against a C sharp and *no* singers can do that hardly 'cause it's only half a step. But she could do it! She had such perfect pitch and it was like she had a little computer in her brain which could lock into perfect pitch. Most singers don't.'

But while Rose was enormously impressed with Cass as a singer and clearly liked her personally as well, Cass was also the owner of an old VW Beetle and as he at the time had no car and no foreseeable source of income, it soon became evident to him that Cass might indeed be just what he needed for that next step. All he needed to do was to convince Cass.

Rose asked her if she had any plans for the immediate future. Cass told him she was working part-time in a drugstore. 'That doesn't sound very exciting,' he told her. 'It's not,' she replied.

'Well, look,' Tim explained, 'I have a friend in Chicago who wants to put together a group. We can plug into that folk circuit there.'

Tim was suggesting that Cass leave Washington, DC and go to

Chicago with him and form the third part of a possible, vaguely discussed trio that he and another folk singer, John Brown, supposedly had in mind. It was hardly the most concrete of offers but Rose could always talk up a good argument, and years later Cass would refer to him as a 'smooth-talkin' banjo player'.

Prior to the emergence of Greenwich Village as the epicentre of the folk universe, Chicago was still a major musical centre. Chicago after all was the birthplace of the blues and a natural breeding ground for folk, and it was now home to the Chad Mitchell Trio, Ian and Sylvia, Buddy Travers and Bob Gibson – all already big names on the folk scene. Chicago therefore seemed like a great idea. Cass was charmed and enthralled all round, and so when Tim asked her, 'So what do you think?' there was clearly no doubt in her mind.

'When do you wanna leave?' came back her reply.

'Erm, well, day after tomorrow?'

'Fine,' said Cass.

'It was the greatest con job of my life!' laughed Tim. 'Let's take *your* car and *your* backing capital and go to Chicago and we'll do *this*. And she did! But that was her part of the investment in the group: I had the connections and knew the third member of the group – she didn't know any of this stuff! So her investment was financial and transport, mine was "I'll get us the work and get us off your ass." So that's a reasonable exchange. So she packed up, went home and told her mom she was going off to Chicago with this new guy she met and the next night we practised a little more at my house. The following day we packed into her old VW and headed off to Chicago.'

From Cass's point of view, she had nothing to lose. Although she had enjoyed presenting the radio show at AU, the prospect of continuing at college for another two years seemed far from appealing and she was hardly going to stay in Washington for a part-time job in a local drugstore. As far as leaving her mother and sister and brother were concerned, meanwhile, enough time had now passed since her father's death to mean that it was no longer essential for her to be at home.

What Rose was offering was an opportunity to sing and maybe become the star that she had promised her goading high school friends she would be. Admittedly, folk was a different route to the future she had originally hoped for on Broadway but here was somebody who was a serious musician, who seemed to know what he was talking about, and who was offering her a chance, at the very least. During her time in New York she had also discovered that in spite of her obvious talent, even aside from the problems caused by her size, compared with many of the thousands of other young hopefuls squeezing into every Broadway and off-Broadway audition, she lacked some of the requisite technical training. She was not a trained singer and could not read music and this had often proved a setback. The DIY approach of the folk scene on the other hand meant that her natural ability was more than enough and she, like everyone else, could learn as she went along. Tim's out-of-the-blue offer therefore seemed like a better chance than she could have hoped for and an adventure at the very least. It was a decision she would never regret.

5

A ruling body of three

Nothing in Cass's life was ever straightforward. Least of all her relationships. Tim Rose would provide Cass with an entrée into life as a successful working musician and so change her life fundamentally. But her relationship with him was complex from the start and its very complexity and ambiguity would become a blueprint for many of her future involvements. 'The emotional complications went *everywhere* with her,' remembers Denny Doherty. 'Wherever she went she would leave this trail of beaus, taffeta and shit flying around. And perfumes! This thing that was Cass! And Tim thought he was controlling it! Ha, ha, ha!'

In December of 1962, Cass and Tim set off on the five-hundred-mile drive to Chicago. The long journey in Cass's freezing, heaterless Beetle gave the two of them a chance to talk and get to know each other more, and Cass, certainly eager to impress him and nurture her image as an experienced woman of the world, duly regaled him with tales of her adventures in New York.

One in particular stuck in Tim's mind. 'She told me she was in a restaurant with this guy she was seeing in New York one night and they had had an argument so she was angry with him. He then began flirting with somebody else while they were sitting at the table and she purposely spilt a drink on him. He turned to her and said to her, "Oh, I'm sorry, excuse me. I'm sorry I spilt your drink," knowing full well that she had done it. And she thought that was the height of class! And that also struck me as being something beyond my concept of what sophistication was, beyond even what Cary Grant movies were in those days. That's how sophisticated this was. So Cass to me was a woman of the world. I did later wonder whether these stories were true or not, but the story itself was good so I never really cared one way or the other.'

Whether they were true or not, stories like these helped take their mind off the cold and eventually the pair of them arrived shivering on the doorstep of John Brown's second-floor flat in the hip Old Town area of Chicago.

'Come on in, what's happening?' said Brown, welcoming them in. Brown was a few years older than Tim, had a wife and three children and had recently given up a job on a suburban newspaper to pursue a career in folk. He had admired Tim's banjo playing as soon as he had heard him perform with Mike and Timothy and the pair had forged a rough plan to form a new act together, possibly another duo. Since then, however, Tim had only phoned him to tell him he was on his way and had made no mention of Cass, so as soon as the introductions were over, he took Brown to one side.

'I brought Cass along,' he told him, 'and I'd like to try us singing as a trio with her.' At this point Peter, Paul and Mary were already amongst the folk movement's biggest commercial stars and had recently played Chicago so the idea of a two boys and a girl trio was well established as a possible route to folk success. But Cass didn't look to Brown any more of a likely star than she had to Tim. 'I looked at this . . . *immense* girl,' remembers Brown, 'and I said, "Tim! This is not exactly Mary *Travers* you're talking about here!"

'Yes but she's got a great voice,' Tim told him. 'Just let's rehearse a little bit and see what you think about it and we'll take it from there.'

Although none of this was said to Cass's face, she would doubtless have been used to these kinds of reactions by this time, but this can't have made them any less painful. It did perhaps spur her on to sing even better than she might have done otherwise, determined to confound people's expectations and win them over with sheer talent. Whether it was conscious or not, it always seemed to work and Brown, like everyone else – before and after – soon changed his mind. Cass may not have looked like the waifish Mary Travers folk ideal, but the force of her voice and personality more than compensated.

Brown mentioned that he had already been booked to play a Christmas party for the Fred Niles Film studio – a small local firm that made ads and industrial films. They would be playing to around a hundred film business types and their families and Brown reckoned that the gig would be a good gauge of their potential.

Cass was thrilled. It appeared she had been right to put her faith in Tim and so far everything seemed to be going just as he had promised. With a definite goal to work towards, Cass and Tim found themselves lodging in what was known as an 'efficiency' apartment, meaning a cramped two-room flat consisting of one bedroom and a kitchen with a communal toilet and shower on the landing. Cass got the bedroom whilst Tim slept in the kitchen, although as this was the warmest room in the building, he was not too bothered. 'If you've never been to Chicago in winter, you don't know what cold is!' Tim recalled. 'You don't even know what the word *means* when you see it on the weather forecast. Compared with Chicago in mid-winter, Moscow seems warm, hun.' Cass would later remember the arctic conditions as 'a horrible, miserable, starving winter, singing, learning songs. Twenty-five below zero,' she said. 'It was one of the roughest winters they ever had in Chicago.'

When they were not rehearsing in the apartment and not at John Brown's, the obvious solution was to go out. And there was no shortage of options. Whatever type of music you were looking for, Chicago, at this point in the early sixties, offered a hotbed of performers who in years to come would become legends of every genre. Miles Davis was working regularly at the Sutherland Lounge, Willie Dixon and the Chicago Blues Allstars were at the Club Deliza, while Howlin' Wolf, Muddy Waters, Buddy Guy and Junior Wells were playing their blues at clubs around town. Meanwhile, Count Basie and vocal trio Lambert, Hendricks and Ross were playing the Tivoli and Regal Theatres, and on the folk front, there were clubs like Fickle Pickle, the Gate of Horn (where Joan Baez had already played), Old Town North, Mother Blues and the Quiet Knight, as well as a particularly hip club called the Bear where an unknown musician by the name of Bob Dylan was starting out.

For aspiring musicians like Cass and Tim, Chicago really did seem to be the centre of the musical universe and they lost no time in exploring it. Although they had both been out of Washington before, they were nevertheless thrilled to be in the musical melting pot that was Chicago, working towards a gig with their own new act by day, and discovering the clubs and bars of Chicago by night.

Brown, meanwhile, had lived in Chicago all his life and was more interested in concentrating on work and his family, so it usually fell to him to initiate rehearsals in the mornings. Bleary-eyed and hung-over from the night before, Cass and Tim would be woken by the sound of Brown at their door, shaking off the snow from his boots and guitar case and making coffee to get them up and ready to rehearse.

They only had ten days to get some material together before the Christmas party but, once they had started, rehearsals went reasonably smoothly. As Cass was a relative novice as far as folk was concerned, the choice of material was left to Tim and Brown. The folk ethos encompassed a conveniently broad range of music styles from bluegrass, work songs from the deep South and Negro spirituals to Appalachian mountain songs and Elizabethan courtly ballads. A standard repertoire of these songs was already being covered regularly by most artists on the circuit so, with little time to prepare, it made sense to opt for songs that they already knew with a few others that were chosen for impact. Tim and Brown between them also already knew many of what had by this time become folk standards, such as 'Delia', 'Pretty Little Horses' and 'I Know You Rider' – all three of which would eventually surface on Cass and Tim's two albums as the Big 3 – and so Tim arranged these for the trio, along with a few of the bluegrass songs which were his lifelong passion. Between them they soon found a common musical vocabulary and, as Cass had always been a fast learner, within no time at all, they had something resembling a repertoire. For the time being, Brown was also content to let Tim take overall charge, believing that as he was the more accomplished musician, it made sense for him to be musical director.

After days of intensive rehearsals, the trio decided to try things out prior to the Christmas party at one of the small folk clubs nearby and as Brown remembers it, 'the reception was good, our sound was good, Cass's shtick was good and Tim's banjo playing was flashy and showed promise'. Clearly a success. Now all they needed was a look. And a name. After some discussion Brown came up with a suggestion. 'I had a pretty good vocabulary,' says Brown, 'I had been to a technical high school in Detroit and I knew that a triumvirate was a ruling body of three, and at that point, nobody came up with anything better. So the Triumvirate it was.'

As far as an image was concerned, the hit folk combos invariably looked neat and clean-cut and so the newly named Triumvirate needed to work out some kind of formal dress wear. Conveniently, they discovered that Tim and Brown both owned green flannel blazers which were similar enough to look as if they matched when worn with black trousers. All they needed were matching ties which they duly went out and bought. Cass, meanwhile, had brought her one smart black dress with her, and suddenly they looked like an act. By the time it came to the night of the Fred Niles party, they were indeed an act in every respect complete with banter from Cass between songs. 'We did our seven best tunes,' remembers Brown, 'and Cass made up stuff to say while Tim and I tuned so we not only looked like an act, but we *sounded* like an act! They clapped for an encore and we did our last tune but then they just kept clapping. "Sorry, but that's all we know," we told them. Then someone asked "Well, how long you been together?" "Oh, about forty-five minutes," Cass quipped. And it was like: "No, no, how long you been together – a year?" It was *that* good. Right from the start.'

Within a fortnight, the Triumvirate were booked to play two weeks at the Old Town North in Chicago, one of the key folk venues on the circuit. The trio were suddenly at the heart of the city's folk scene and quickly got to know musicians playing the other clubs. As a group with a gig, they were also the target of aspiring songwriters who would often approach them with offers of material. These were usually handled – and summarily dismissed – by Tim, but one stuck in his mind. 'A guy came into our dressing room in Chicago once,' Tim remembered, 'and played us a song that I hated. I thought, Fucking awful, the guy can't sing! Who the fuck is this? Cass said I was wrong. I said, "No! The guy'll never make it." The kid's name was Bob Dylan and I think the song was "Don't Think Twice" or "Masters of War". So I was definitely wrong that time! But what did I know? That's not the point. It didn't matter whether *he* could sing or not. But I did have an ego the size of Huddersfield.'

Gradually, through the new contacts Tim was making in Chicago, and those Brown already had, the Triumvirate began to get more bookings, and the trio set off, cramming themselves, three suitcases, two guitars and a banjo into Cass's still heaterless rattling Beetle to criss-cross America's wintery north-east. In most towns it was a case of sleeping on folk friends' floors as the group was only earning fifty pounds a week between them. Cass would later look back on these days as the hard times they clearly were. 'The three of us in that *ancient* Volkswagen, I mean, *really* ancient, that was really something!' remembered Cass. 'We were really broke and we had so little money,' she said. 'I did all the cooking and I used a lot of tomato sauce. They used to call me the "Tomato Sauce Queen". If I had a can of tomato sauce and a cup of rice, I could feed about twenty people! A little bit of cheese, that was a treat!'

Hard as these times may have been, the three of them were also gaining valuable performing experience but whilst Rose was the unquestioned leader when it came to all things musical, in terms of life experience, in certain areas, Cass clearly had the upper hand.

The Triumvirate's first stop outside Chicago was Evanston, Illinois at what Tim remembered as 'a real Mafioso club'. The group had been booked for three days but things did not go smoothly from the start. 'We were in the club and I tried to pick up one of the waitresses, but *she* was flirting with *me*!' He laughed. 'And, well, OK, I was flirting back, but suddenly Cass pulled me aside and said, "That waitress is going with the guy who owns the club. He's called Nunzio and you don't fuck around with guys named Nunzio who own clubs, you know!" She was a little aware of these things and said, "He's one of *those* guys." But then Nunzio went over to Cass and said, "You guys better be out of here by the end of the night. And don't come back to finish your contract!" We hadn't actually *done* anything but Nunzio didn't see it like that. So that was it. We were fired after the first night!'

Back in Cass's Beetle, the trio headed back east, this time over to Cleveland to a club called La Cave. By the time they got there, despite only having been together a short time, tensions were already beginning to build between Tim and John Brown. From the start, Brown had deferred musical control to Tim as he was the more accomplished musician. Brown, however, was the more successful and established artist and was never going to kowtow completely as far as leadership of the group went. It was only a matter of time therefore before a power struggle escalated.

Whilst playing at La Cave, the band were booked onto a local daytime TV programme – the *One O'Clock Show*. The producer was clearly impressed by the two numbers they did and after the show, he approached the band with what Brown considered the big break of his life. 'The producer came over,' remembers Brown, 'and said, "Look, we'd like to book you to be on the show *five days a week*. You'll appear, you'll sit around and talk with the host and then you'll get up and do a song, every day. And we'll pay you . . . scale," which at that point was two hundred and fifty dollars per man for the five days. Now, at that point, I had been working solo in Chicago, five *nights* a week, for *one* hundred and fifty bucks and I was feeding my family on that!'

The offer also stipulated that once they had recorded their daily appearance on the show, they would be free to accept any other engagements in their own time, singing in clubs or anywhere else. But then again they were in Cleveland, which was hardly the epicentre of any kind of commercial universe. Whether the offer would have proved to be the band's passport to success is therefore debatable and Tim doubted it, but to Brown, it seemed like manna from heaven. He believed – as he still angrily does, more than forty years on – that the offer would have given them an opportunity to broaden their repertoire, and wardrobe, whilst earning good money and that they would have then emerged six months later with extensive TV experience into the bargain. He was therefore ready to uproot his family and move to Cleveland for the contract.

Tim, however, was far from keen on the idea of spending six months in Cleveland, TV show or not, as unlike Chicago, New York or even Washington, DC, Cleveland did not seem too bright a light in anyone's itinerary. The Cleveland issue therefore signalled the beginning of an unbridgeable chasm within the Triumvirate. Apart from differences of opinion over the band's bookings, friction had arisen between Tim and Brown as both considered themselves the band's natural leader. Both were strong personalities and both were insistent on their respective opinions as regarded the Cleveland booking. Which left Cass to decide. But whatever Cass's own views on the subject may have been, she had become used to deferring on such matters to Tim's judgement. She was also, by this time, no longer strictly impartial. Since meeting Tim, her feelings towards him had grown from their initial friendship into a deeper affection, and consequently, if there were disputes within the group, Cass nearly always sided with Tim.

'Cass always acquiesced to Tim's wishes because she had a crush on him,' says Brown, and it is not hard to see why Cass would have been immediately taken with her smooth-talkin' banjo player. From Cass's point of view, after more than a year attempting to break into show business in New York, this attractive, talented musician had come along, taken charge of the situation and whisked her off to Chicago and almost immediate success. For a girl who had spent her teenage years unable to get a date, it would almost have been more surprising if she hadn't developed a crush on him.

Rose later wondered himself whether Cass's affection did not in fact stem from her own need and from her admiration for his get-up-and-go dynamism. 'I don't know whether Cass was actually *in love* with me,' Rose told me, 'or whether she was just very needful of me for any number of reasons. Maybe because I was the leader of the group and the man in the group. I can only guess about this, but I think to her I represented the kind of man she'd like to be associated with.'

Whatever the origins of Cass's feelings for Tim, as with most of the men who would be significant in her life, her relationship with him was ambiguous from the start. While Cass certainly would have liked a romantic involvement, Tim made it clear that he only wanted friendship and had no interest in her sexually. But although Tim, even all these decades later, continued to insist on his romantic indifference towards Cass and physically their relationship certainly remained platonic, emotionally the situation doesn't appear to have been quite so straightforward.

By his own admission, Tim had been smitten with Cass's personality and talent straight away, and there had clearly been a mutual connection between them from the start. 'In the beginning Cass and I became best friends,' admitted Rose, 'I think one of the first things I sensed about her, that first time we met, was her sensitivity. And I sensed this woman who had a great passion for life and a great interest in life, a great curiosity. And I also sensed a very lonely person. It doesn't take a doctor's degree to realise that.' Although she may not have been aware of it at the time, at some level Cass had certainly picked up on the same inner loneliness within Tim and the two of them had quickly become close. 'We would talk to each other about things that weren't necessarily related to music,' continued Tim. 'We would talk about people. That's where she told me about the guy in New York and I would tell her about various women in my life. And I just remember having these wonderful conversations about life in general with Cass. Not with John Brown or anyone else, it was just Cass and I.'

The fact that they had both embarked on this Chicago adventure together certainly brought them closer still, and so from Cass's point of view, although they were not in a physical relationship, on an emotional and intellectual level, it is easy to see how she could have felt that her feelings for Tim were reciprocated. And similarly easy to see why the idea of their living together was doomed.

When they were rehearsing, performing or travelling together, Cass could let herself believe that there was some kind of romantic involvement between them, albeit a platonic one – maybe sex would come later, and having convinced herself, it was even simpler to convince her friends. The only problem arose when Tim started having real girlfriends of his own. In Chicago, as the Triumvirate became more recognised on the city's folk scene, this inevitably began to happen more and more frequently. 'Like any young guy,' remembered Tim, 'I was going out with women and all those things and suddenly in Chicago girls would start to come up to me at gigs saying, "Why do you treat Cass that way?" And I'd say, "What do you mean?"

'They'd say, "Why are you going out with all these women?"

'I said, "What business is it of yours?"

'And they'd say, "Well, it really hurts Cass."

'What? Nothing was going on between us but that's not what Cass's story was to these people. Years later, Denny (Doherty) told me: "Cass used to say you were shagging all these people *and* shagging her." I said, "Denny, I never . . ." He said, "*I* know you didn't. I *know*. But that's what all these people thought." When we first met, he thought *that* was the deal.'

In a situation of this kind, the fact that Cass and Tim weren't physically involved would easily have seemed irrelevant to her and so one can see how their emotional entanglement with each other would have made anything he did outside that feel like a betrayal. As far as Cass was concerned, in her mind, she and Tim were together. For Cass, therefore, the combination of living with someone who played up to her feelings for him but was sexually unavailable must have felt like a daily rejection.

Presumably fired by jealousy and anger at what she would have genuinely perceived as a kind of infidelity, Cass seems to have been determined to prove she could have her own romantic encounters. But from what Tim recalled, this was not always too successful.

'One night she picked up this gay guy and she was determined to help him go straight.' Tim laughed. 'They were in the bed and I could hear all this yanking and stuff going on and all of a sudden I hear this crack – *kaplong*! Oh, fuck! There's absolute silence for a minute, and then they both start laughing and laughing. So I go to the door and say, "Everybody all right in there?" And they say, "Don't come in yet." About five minutes later, they said, "Come on in," so I went in and they'd broken the bed! The frame was up here and the mattress was on the floor and all the slats had broken. And it was kind of funny, I have to say! There was Cass trying to get this gay man to . . . well, I'm not quite sure *what* they were doing, but one can guess. And it was a telling thing. I mean it didn't bother me. I didn't care if she had a group of midgets in there – you know, what do I care? As long as she sings well and gets onstage and just does her thing.' Both Cass and Tim agreed, however, that living together was clearly not proving a success and so, once they had left Chicago, it was not an arrangement they would ever repeat.

The tensions between Tim and John Brown were, meanwhile, not showing any signs of improvement and, according to Tim, the increasingly complex relationship between the three of them was further exacerbated by another problem with Brown. 'Every night,' claimed Tim, 'Johnny Brown was trying to get in Cass's knickers. And not because John was particularly in love with Cass, but because John just fucked everything – he really did. More than once *I* would get calls from his wife saying, "Where's my husband?" And I'd have to say, "*I* don't know where your husband is. What do you mean where's your husband?" "Well, weren't you playing a gig?" "Well, yes, but I don't know where your husband is!" And he was out shagging somebody. And when there was nobody else to shag, John started hitting on Cass. So then at 2 o'clock in the morning, I would get a phone call from Cass saying, "He's knocking on my door." "Who's knocking on your door?"

'"Johnny."

'"Well what does he want?"

'And then there'd be this pause and I'd say, "Oh, shit, *come on*. You know, Cass, I really don't want to get in the middle of this." So I'd go over there but by the time I'd got there and knocked on her door, he had already gone because she wouldn't let him in. So then I'd try to have a talk with John the next morning. You know, John, could you please maybe not . . . and he'd just say, "It's none of your business." And I looked at him and I said, "You're right. It really *isn't* any of my business, is it?" So I said, "I'll shut up and I'll see you at rehearsal." But when this first started happening, I knew that this was gonna be a trap.'

Brown, meanwhile, dismisses this entire suggestion. 'Is that what Tim said?' he laughs heartily. 'No, I was not attracted to Cass in a physical way. I admired her *mind*. She and I had connections on that level with little phrases and words we would make up and she could talk to me 'cause I was a little bit older, 'cause I had a wife and children. I had a little edge on her in life experience and I admired her quick wit and her voice and we had a connection that Tim was not part of. He probably was jealous of that because his relationship with Cass was much different, so that's Tim's imagination working overtime!'

Either way, the group dynamic was becoming increasingly strained, but Tim nevertheless got the group a booking in Omaha, Nebraska, where he had played previously with Mike and Timothy. On arrival in Omaha the Triumvirate found themselves preceded on the nightly bill by the house act – a solo singer by the portentous name of James Hendricks, not to be confused with his more famous namesake – Hendrix with an x.

Hendricks looked like the quintessential Ivy League golden prom dream, and had an angelically pure tenor voice to match. In fact Hendricks had grown up on a cattle ranch in Nebraska, in the heart of America's mid-west, and was at this point earning his living as a part-time school teacher. Cass found the whole package irresistible and was captivated the instant she laid eyes on him. 'I was totally infatuated with him,' Cass would later admit. 'I had never seen such a good-looking, clean-cut kid.'

Hendricks would eventually go on to write Johnny Rivers's 1967 million-seller 'Summer Rain', before moving to Nashville where he has lived since the eighties and where he is well-known in the contemporary Christian music field. But at that first meeting with Cass in Omaha, Jim was equally aware of Cass's interest. 'She would come and sit right down in front of me while I was singing,' he tells me in his mid-west drawl, 'and just *stare* at me and smile and do all kinds of funny faces and stuff. She could flirt with yours truly, you know what I'm saying?' he laughs knowingly. 'My first impression was, Wow! You know? Here's this girl with this huge body and she's acting like she's Miss America! It was such a strange thing but it was really amazing! *Boy*, she really blew my mind, 'cause I was this little mid-west country boy and I just didn't know what to make of her or *what* to think! All I knew was that when I got talkin' with her she was very funny, very sweet and it was really wild. I mean she had such a great personality that you just couldn't help but *love* her, you know? It was hard for me to categorise all that and find a place for it you know? But we did of course, and as time went on, we became really good friends.'

By the time Cass had discovered Jim, she and Tim had already discussed the idea that John Brown might not work out in the long term, and so once she saw Hendricks she immediately urged Tim, 'You *gotta* watch this guy.' Tim was equally impressed, as much by Hendricks's voice as by his obvious ability to win fans. 'There was Hendricks with this great chiselled face,' remembered Tim, 'and the girls just fell at his feet.'

Cass and Tim quickly discovered that Jim was just as easy to like in person and also, most importantly, found that their voices complemented each other perfectly. After the shows each night, the three of them would go and eat together and on their way home in the car afterwards, they would start singing a capella. Hendricks had spent four years learning harmony by this time and could drop in a third part without even pausing for thought. Suddenly their voices seemed to magically blend together.

The fact that the three of them had discovered a very definite sound of their own was particularly significant. Musically, obviously, this is always what anyone looks for, but at this time in the folk boom, as everyone was essentially covering the same songs, it was doubly important, and in fact necessary. Very few artists were writing original material, apart from Bob Dylan – who at this point was barely known outside Greenwich Village and certainly not beyond the confines of the folk scene itself, so the only thing that differentiated one act from another was the sound of the voices and the arrangements.

As far as Tim was concerned, Hendricks was therefore a more than suitable replacement for Brown for several reasons: firstly he recognised the commercial potential of having someone as physically attractive as this in the group, secondly his voice was superior to Brown's and harmonised beautifully with Cass's and Tim's. Thirdly, he had no family obligations and was therefore flexible, and finally – and perhaps just as significantly, he was a less wilful personality than Brown and so more likely to concede to Rose's leadership.

But they first had to see if Jim might be persuaded to join them. Faced with Tim and Cass's offer, Jim was initially keen and excited at the idea of working with two so clearly talented people, but he was nevertheless slightly hesitant about giving up the steady job and life he had in Nebraska to venture out into the unknown. So before agreeing, Jim sought advice from the club manager, Ray Valerio, who as Tim remembered was considered 'Mr Sophistication' in Omaha. Valerio – who Cass and Tim had nicknamed Ray Venerio – subsequently called Tim over and suggested they have a drink. He told him he had not only advised Jim to accept their offer but that he himself was impressed by the prospect of the three of them working together. 'I think you guys can go places,' he told him, 'and what's more if you're serious about this, I can finance a trip for the four of us to go to Florida so you can rehearse for a week, get some songs together and get started.'

Tim's natural scepticism immediately questioned Valerio's motives. 'Why?' he asked. 'Why would you do that?'

'Well, you guys are gonna need some place to rehearse,' Valerio replied, 'I need to go to Florida and I've got a little bit of money, so I'll finance it.'

'What do you want in return?' Tim asked him.

'Nothing. Jimmy's a friend. If I can help you guys get a leg-up, just come back and work the club for me.'

'OK,' said Tim, 'you got a deal.'

With Valerio's recommendation and backing, Hendricks thought he couldn't go too far wrong and accepted Cass and Tim's offer, thinking that at the very least he'd have some fun as they harmonised so well together. Cass, meanwhile, was more than delighted to suddenly find herself in a trio with someone as matinee-idol handsome as Hendricks.

Once the Omaha booking was finished, all that remained was for Cass and Tim to break the news to John Brown. Brown had put a lot of energy and expectation into the Triumvirate and the parting was never likely to be easy, but exactly how this episode panned out is another area in which Tim's and Brown's memories varied considerably. Tim claimed that when he and Cass told him that he was out of the band, he threw a tantrum and put his foot through Tim's guitar. Brown, meanwhile, denies this, saying he only threatened to do so and his lengthy and detailed recollections of the scenario carry on from there. Whatever the exact circumstances and reasons for Brown's dismissal, he and Cass cannot have parted with too much animosity, as they subsequently kept in touch throughout the rest of her life.

Years later, when Cass was performing in Miami as a solo artist in the early seventies, an incident caused Brown to remember their

Triumvirate days again. 'During that gig in Cleveland,' says Brown, 'she and I were out strolling one night and everybody was saying "Boss" – meaning great or wonderful. It was a kind of buzz word of the time like, "I gotta 'boss' guitar" or "this is boss". Then we walked by this hotel with a big red neon sign that said the Bass Hotel, and we remembered how the word "hep" turned into "hip" in the fifties, you know? And I said, "Wouldn't it be fun to just start saying 'bass' for 'boss' and everybody would look at us and they wouldn't know what we were talking about except that we would know. It would be our inside thing." And so we started to say "bass" for "boss". It was just one of those silly, stupid things, right? Fast forward to 1973 and Cass is onstage here in Miami doin' her act and I'm sitting in about row four out in front of the stage and she made some cute little remark that I felt needed a compliment. So from the audience I yelled, "Bass!" And quick as a wink, she said, "Ah! The voice of Christmas past!"'

The Triumvirate had only existed for a few months, but during their time together Cass had had her first opportunity to gain valuable experience singing and handling a live audience. It had also led her and Tim to find Jim Hendricks who would continue to be significant in Cass's life for some years to come. The addition of Jim to the group would also give them a new identity which would pave their way to success.

As would be the case in the years to come with the Mamas and Papas, on paper they were an unlikely combination: a rugged, bohemian-looking bluegrass enthusiast who'd been a pilot in the air force, a clean-cut ex-Sunday School teacher with the voice of a choirboy and, as Tim would later describe her, 'a sassy Jewish girl who loved Broadway'. But somehow it all worked and they had found their own sound. As with every act she sang with, it would be Cass's voice and stage presence which would inevitably dominate but as far as she was concerned, for the time being, this was even better than she had imagined. She was now the centre of a group flanked by two attractive men whom she liked and thought of as friends. There were certainly worse ways to make a living, and what was more, after the arctic winter of Chicago, they were going to Florida. What she didn't know was that Florida would be merely a stepping stone to a whole new life.

6

Wild women sing the blues

'They had such a *great* sound!' remembers Bob Bowers, the trio's musical director. 'Peter, Paul and Mary did not have a sound. They sounded like three people singing. *These* people sounded like a chorus and an orchestra – really just an overwhelming, overpowering sound. And it would pin you to the wall like Stan Kenton's Big Band or those sheets of sound from Coltrane and people like that. It was truly thrilling!'

The folk boom would provide a start for many of the biggest stars of Cass's generation but while many of them would later look back on their folk days with embarrassment, loath to expose the often tame tweeness of their musical beginnings, Cass's debut with Tim and Jim defied anyone not to sit up and listen right from the start. Compared with the edginess of much of the music that has followed, even their folk offerings may be comparatively innocent and gentle but, forty years on, the power and dynamic of their combined vocals have lost none of their punch.

Cass's time in the trio would provide her with the opportunity to sing live on a regular basis and, in particular, sing harmony. She would also gain invaluable experience in handling an audience, gauging their mood and honing her natural talent for spoken repartee – talents which would prove central to her subsequent success.

In the spring of 1963 Cass and Tim set off in the old VW on the long drive back to Chicago to close up the flat. Jim Hendricks, meanwhile, needed to hand in his notice at the local school in Iowa where he had been teaching, so the plan was for the three of them to meet a month later in Washington and then travel on together to meet Ray Valerio at Fort Lauderdale, 100 miles north of Miami, Florida.

The journey back to Chicago was not to prove as smooth as they had hoped, however. Cass and Tim had been driving all day when they approached the small, sleepy town of Newton, Iowa, some forty miles outside Iowa's capital – Des Moines. As the town came into view snow started to fall and soon a violent wind was sending large snowflakes swirling through the sky before settling thickly on the ground. Cass's rattling VW had already been stretched to breaking point by their extensive cross-country mileage and in the face of deep snow finally caved in under the strain. Stranded 'in the middle of fucking nowhere' as Tim later recalled, the two of them had no choice but to trudge through the snow in the dark till they found a phone and Tim called Newton's one and only local police car to come and take them to the town's one and only hotel.

Safely ensconced in the relative warmth of the old western-style, high-vaulted, wooden-frame hotel, Cass and Tim began to wonder what they were going to do. They only had twenty dollars between them, a car that had effectively died and they needed to get back to Chicago sometime, preferably soon. At least their huge room was comfortable though and in fact bigger than any apartment they'd ever stayed in, with both a bed for Cass and a couch for Tim to sleep on.

'Do you have any credit cards?' Cass asked Tim.

'No.'

'I don't either,' said Cass.

'Can your mom send us any money?' Tim asked, thinking this might be a solution.

'No,' said Cass, knowing that her mother was unlikely to have money to spare and not wanting to have to phone her to ask. 'So what the fuck are we gonna do?'

Finally Tim had an idea. 'Let's sell the car,' he suggested.

'But if we sell the car, how are we gonna get to Chicago?' asked Cass.

'Well, hey, we can't move the car anyway. We don't have any money to fix the thing. So what are we gonna do?'

'Yes, but how you gonna sell a car that doesn't run?' asked Cass logically.

'Well, I don't know, but it seems like a plan.'

By this time it was well into the early hours of the morning and Cass and Tim were both tired and more than ready for sleep. But before they slept, Tim thought he'd test the water on his plan's viability.

'I managed to call the all-night garage and explain the situation and they said, "Yes, we'll go round and pick up the car on the highway and take it back to the garage." Fine. So after that we went to sleep for a couple of hours. Eight o'clock in the morning I woke up, she wakes up. It's still snowing. I called the garage and said, "How's the car?"

'"Well we had a quick look and it looks like you've blown a piston out and we don't have any parts for this car. What is it? One of them *German* cars?"'

At this point Volkswagens were still relatively rare in America, but Tim replied that it was indeed a Volkswagen.

'"Hey, one of them Beetles. Well we'd have to go to Chicago to get parts and it might take a week and I don't even know what those parts are *called* here." So I said, "Well, look I'll get back to you, but do you think you might wanna buy it?" And he said, "Well, let me think about it." So I got the Yellow Pages and at eight thirty called another car dealer and said, "Look, Bob over at Benson's Car Garage just told me the car needs a little work and he's offered us $300 for it." He said, "A VW?" I said, "Yeah." He said, "You mean one of them *foreign* cars?" I said, "Yeah." He said, "We haven't had one of those here. What's your offer? Three hundred dollars? I can do better than that. Let me go and take a look at it." So then I did the same thing again. I called up the guy over at Upstairs Motors and said the guy down the road's offered me $400." And nobody's offered me shit so far, by the way. And Cass is sitting there open-mouthed. And then the first guy calls me back and he says, "Well, I'd be happy to give you three hundred and fifty dollars for this and we'll just fix it up." So I said, "Well, the guy at Upstairs Motors has already offered us seven hundred dollars." And of course he hasn't! So he said, "Well, I could go up to four fifty." Then the guy from Hedges Motors calls me back and says, "I hear you got quite a few offers for this." I said, "Yes, you can have the first VW and you can fix it up."

'So he gave us eight hundred dollars! Cass signs the pink slip, he gives us *eight hundred dollars!* Cass says, "This is fucking amazing! A car that didn't run for eight hundred dollars!"'

Using some of their newly earned dollars, Cass and Tim finally boarded a train back to Chicago. Cass by this time felt even more certain that she'd made the right move by deciding to take her chances with Tim. She had seen him for the smooth-talking salesman he was from the start and now, having watched him sell a car that didn't run for eight hundred dollars, she knew she could do worse than have someone like this taking charge of her career. They also still had fun together and, despite the complexity of their relationship, Tim similarly enjoyed her company on the long train journey back. 'Cass was good to travel with,' remembered Tim. 'She had travelled a bit before, during some off-Broadway theatre or something like that, so she had the advantage of having been on the road so she knew what to do on a bus or train to keep herself busy. She had all these survival techniques for travelling on the road which I still use. Cass was *very* good at this kind of shit. In fact I've not met many people who were this enjoyable to travel with. She was just like a little kid on the road.'

Once they got back to Chicago, Cass and Tim packed up the flat and took another train to Washington, DC. From there they called Jim Hendricks who drove down to meet them. 'We were flying on a wing and a fucking prayer!' remembered Tim, 'We had no idea *what* was goin' on!' Then, having linked up with Hendricks in Washington, the new trio set off in Hendricks's red convertible Tempest to Florida to meet Ray Valerio.

After the Chicago winter and snows of Nebraska, the Florida sunshine was a welcome change for all three of them. Every day they would get up and go out onto the beach at Fort Lauderdale, sitting in the sand with their guitars, practising and learning new material until their arrangements were perfectly honed.

After a week in the sun, they returned to Washington. It made most sense for them to use Washington as their base for the time being, as it was home for both Cass and Tim and had a rather more significant music scene than Omaha. Tim also had contacts there and had arranged for them to audition for Bob Cavallo at the Shadows, the key folk venue in town.

When the new trio arrived for their audition, they were understandably nervous. During the previous months with John Brown, the band had been aware of the need for management and auditioned for both Harold Levanthal who handled folk acts the Tarriers and Bob Gibson, and Albert Grossman who looked after Peter, Paul and Mary, Joan Baez and later, more famously, Bob Dylan. Neither manager had seen any future for the group. Even now, with Jim Hendricks, it was all very well having perfected their harmonies, but as far as the group's immediate future was concerned they had no bookings and no work, so they desperately needed the audition to be a success. 'There was no Plan B on this,' explained Tim. 'If the audition for Bob Cavallo at the Shadows didn't happen, I didn't know what we were gonna do. We had no agent, no manager; Jimmy had given up his life, Cass didn't have a job and I didn't have a job. What the hell were we gonna do? This kind of *had* to work.'

They sang 'I Know You Rider', a version of 'The Banjo Song', 'Pretty Little Horses' and Cass's showpiece 'Wild Women' – a bluesy tour de force which would become one of her early signature songs, but the pressure of the situation meant that they all sang badly. Cavallo hated it. Eventually Cavallo would become a big supporter of the group and of Cass in particular and they would later go on to play the Shadows extensively, but at the time, he just didn't see their potential, mainly because of Cass's appearance. In spite of her evident vocal talent, Cavallo still held the view that in order for an artist to be really successful, they needed to conform to a more conventional body image.

But Cavallo had not been the only one to hear them audition. At this point, the headlining act at the Shadows was a twenty-four-year-old, up-and-coming comedian by the name of Bill Cosby whose first album was just being released. His manager, a New York-based friend of Cavallo's called Roy Silver, also happened to be in the club at the time. Silver had previously worked as an agent alongside Albert Grossman and was now in partnership with Fred Weintraub, owner of the Bitter End, a central fixture on what had by this time become the thriving Greenwich Village folk circuit. Six foot tall and slim with horn-rimmed glasses and a slightly studious air, Silver was always immaculately dressed and perfectly groomed and had a reputation as 'a world-class hustler'. Unlike his friend Cavallo, Silver immediately saw the trio's potential and telephoned Tim the next day. He didn't like the name Triumvirate he told them and from now they were to be the Big 3. What was more, they were opening at the Bitter End. 'How soon can you be in New York?' he asked Tim.

'But we only know four songs!' Tim protested.

'Well, you'll know five by the time you get here,' replied Silver.

Cass and Tim had known Jim for barely six weeks at this point but now the newly named Big 3 were leaving behind the likes of Omaha, Nebraska, and heading off to New York. Their mood was understandably euphoric. They had all been reasonably excited about going to

Florida, but New York was in another league altogether. Cass had been there before alone but this was an entirely different scenario. This time their trip was being financed, they had a real New York music business manager and a booking. It was not a route that Cass could ever have predicted.

In the six months since Cass had first met Tim in Washington, the folk scene had continued to grow countrywide, with centres emerging in Los Angeles, San Francisco, Washington, DC, Boston, Chicago and New York. Of these, however, it was New York's Greenwich Village which, just as it had earlier been for cabaret, was now seen as the heart of the movement.

The Village was originally an Italian immigrant community, bordered by Chinatown on one side and the docks on the other. Populated by its own type of outsider, it had been a haven for non-conformity since World War One. By the fifties, therefore, it was almost no surprise that it had become a natural gathering point for beatniks, jazzniks, existentialists and bohemians of all description and once these gave way to the folk movement it was only a matter of time before Greenwich Village once again played host. Cass had felt instantly at home there whilst working at the Duplex and Showplace, and she was now more than happy to be going back.

For the disenfranchised post-war college generation, eager to find an identity of their own, the Village lived up to its name, and its narrow, leafy streets and low-rise brownstones offered a more down-to-earth, human environment than the polished steel and glass glamour of fashionable Fifth Avenue. Instead of the cocktails and the sparkling glitz of mainstream American culture, here was a bustling little corner of European culture where old-fashioned espresso bars still steamed and frothed with the sound of pre-war copper coffee machines.

Folk had originally started off in the Village in the mid-forties as the weekend hobby of a few hundred enthusiasts who would gather every Sunday with their guitars at the circular fountain in Washington Square Park. But its popularity had grown dramatically since then and by 1963 Sundays in the Park had become a major-league jam session for the entire musical community.

While Broadway had brought theatreland to one stretch of Manhattan, the Village now seemed to have evolved organically into a kind of free-range entertainment theme park, densely packed with a simmering mix of coffee houses, off-off-Broadway theatre, cabaret, comedy, poetry and jazz. On any given night you could see a remarkable array of as-yet undiscovered talent, from the Simon Sisters – Carly and Lucy, Judy Collins, Fred Neil, Tim Hardin to Phil Ochs, John Phillips (with the Journeymen), Denny Doherty (with the Halifax Three), John Sebastian, Roger McGuinn, David Crosby, Barry McGuire and Maria Muldaur, all of whom were just starting out.

That year there were no less than thirty-seven coffee houses crammed into the ten block loop from West Broadway and Bleecker to MacDougal Street west across Seventh Avenue. At the weekends the clubs were so popular that several streets were closed to traffic. Cars simply couldn't get through, and even walking it could take an hour to cover three blocks, elbowing your way through the lively mix of tourists, students, old Italians, drag queens, militant lesbians, old-time socialists, drifters, longshoremen and sailors on leave who comprised the Village audiences.

Folk's 'anyone-can-do-it' ethos also meant that the Village was teeming with so-called 'musicians', strolling through the Village in their regulation 'folkie' denim jackets, turtleneck sweaters, worn-in cowboy boots and wool caps, many of whom were now happily describing themselves as such in spite of the fact that they might only have the most passing acquaintanceship with a guitar.

Into the midst of this arrived the Big 3 and throughout the summer of 1963 they were the house act at the Bitter End, a small cellar-like, cabaret-style venue on Bleecker Street in the heart of the Village which was famous for having launched Peter, Paul and Mary a couple of years earlier and was still revelling in the association. With its unpainted brick walls, black ceiling and dark-wood plank floor, the club was the typical folk dive, regularly squeezing in up to a hundred and twenty people vying to see the small wooden stage from the black-painted wooden tables and plywood benches. As there were also rooms above the club, Roy Silver arranged for Cass to move into one whilst Tim and Jim moved into another.

As the house act, the Big 3 were required to play usually two if not three sets every night, opening for whoever the main attraction was. This could be either folk artists like Peter, Paul and Mary who, despite their new-found fame would still play there, and Fred Neil or any of the Village's other comedians or acts. The Big 3 now had the chance to develop both their repertoire and act, and the group was soon attracting its own fans. More specifically many were soon coming to hear Cass and listen to her stage routine. 'I was playing a twelve-string guitar one night,' remembered Tim, 'and Jimmy's ready to go and my guitar is so far out of tune that Cass is up there and she's mocking and finally she just looks at me and says, "I know there are twelve of them but can't you get *one* of them in tune!" The audience broke up and it completely broke the ice and gave me some more time.'

From their early gigs with John Brown, although Tim, as official leader of the group would often introduce songs, whenever he needed to change instruments or tune up, without a second's pause, Cass would immediately step up to the mike and hold the audience's attention by magically whisking up stories, seemingly out of nowhere. 'Once she made up this story,' remembers John Brown, 'about the guy who invented the banjo – a man named Irving Banjo – you pronounce it with a Spanish h – "Banho". The story went like this: Irving Banjo was an itinerant marijuana picker who had lost his job and he couldn't even collect compensation because his employment was illegal, so he said to himself, I think I'll invent the banho. And he did. And he strapped it to his back and he swam the Rio Grande only to discover that no one *wanted* a damn soggy banho. And at this point Tim would play out some points of interest on the banho and point to the neck of the instrument and we'd make a little game of it and by then we'd be ready to go into the next tune. But it all played so smooth! It was like an act that had been written out and rehearsed and it was just Cass improvising off the top of her head!'

Cass had a natural talent for impromptu repartee; she would often forget a lyric but, whereas many singers would freeze, she would just carry on regardless in her best Judy Garland style. She also had impeccable comic timing. 'Just watching her timing,' remembered Tim, 'it was like line, bing, *bang*! She knew exactly what most comedians never get. That's why they're not funny. *She* was funny. She knew *how* to be funny. And I could watch her – how she worked a room. I learned a lot from her 'cause performing-wise, she *had* studied Broadway and Broadway required that little bit more discipline than *I* had been used to and she had a sense of that.'

By the time Cass was at the Bitter End with the Big 3 she had also developed her audience technique to a fine art. 'She knew how to work an audience,' continued Tim. 'She knew how to manipulate people. But she also knew how to bring in an audience. She knew how to sing to this corner, to that corner and she knew how to talk to you as though she were talking to you one on one.'

While the Big 3 continued their residency at the Bitter End during the summer of 1963, folk continued unchallenged as the favourite pastime of the nation's youth. The record companies, as was their wont before and since, were eager to sign almost anyone that could hold half a tune – and quite a few that couldn't. More often than not, this translated as whoever most closely resembled whichever act was already selling large quantities of records i.e. the Kingston Trio, Joan Baez or Peter, Paul and Mary. Only too aware of this, Roy Silver had lost no time in trying to get a deal for the Big 3. The major labels, however, didn't appear to be interested – Warner Brothers already had Peter, Paul and Mary and CBS and all the others just said no. As a last resort Silver approached his friend Pete Kameron – an old-time music industry hustler who had managed the Weavers and now owned the small FM Records label. Kameron agreed to release a record by the Big 3 and explained that it would be distributed independently. Silver remained vague in his explanation of the deal to the group; all they knew was that they weren't going to get any money upfront and that Kameron was going to finance it. But as far as Cass and Jim were concerned, this side of things was always dealt with by Tim and what mattered at the time was that they were going to cut their first record – the logistics of what deals were done and with whom seemed unimportant.

'We were all excited, and Cass especially was,' remembers Hendricks. 'She really wanted to do her very best, singing-wise, and she did. She was very up for it and there's a lot of excitement about recording. The first time that you put it down in wax – it's a great feeling, and you kind of feel like it's another milestone that you've conquered.'

With Cass's stage wit and voice, and Tim and Jim's musicianship, the Big 3 were already enormously accomplished compared with many of the acts floating around the Village at the time, but their act, like so many of the others, still lacked polish musically. The Bitter End's owner Fred Weintraub felt that some of his acts would benefit from some musical supervision and the assistance of a more accomplished and experienced musician and so he brought in Bob Bowers, an ex-jazz musician who had played with Charlie Parker and Lester Young, as in-house bass player, arranger, coach and musical director.

As the Big 3 were the Bitter End's house act, Bowers began rehearsing with them daily, working on their sound, technique and repertoire and, used as he was to the frustration of working with frequently inept players, the Big 3 were a welcome surprise. 'Cass could sing very well and Tim was also a very good, accomplished guitar and banjo player – I mean we're not talking Andres Segovia, but for a folk guitar player he played *very* well.'

Within a few months of rehearsing with Bowers by day and playing between two and three sets a night, the group was certainly not short of songs, and they had all been road-tested on live audiences; all they needed to do was sit down with Roy Silver and choose the strongest ones for the album.

Since they had first rehearsed on the beach with Hendricks at Fort Lauderdale, their repertoire had grown considerably. Many of the songs had evolved from the Triumvirate days, Hendricks had brought some from his solo act, and a few had been added during their months in New York. They were mostly traditional folk ballads with lead vocals split between Cass, Tim and Jim. But in spite of the limitations of acoustic folk, Cass's numbers also gave her the opportunity to showcase her voice in a range of different styles.

There were haunting ballads such as 'Young Girl's Lament' which John Sebastian still remembers 'tearing him up' every time he heard her sing it, and raunchier numbers such as 'Wild Women' (which would later surface on the Big 3's second album), which showed the influence of the blues which she and Tim had seen first-hand in Chicago. Bringing a bluesy aplomb to the song, her voice laden with salty innuendo, Cass made it entirely her own. 'She didn't do it like Joplin,' remembered Tim, 'but when she did it, it was real tongue-in-cheek, with kind of this little wink in her eye. And then other times, she could also sing like a choirgirl from Cincinnati, which was beautiful!'

Cass was also constantly working at her singing and listening to other singers to learn from their technique. She especially admired Matt Monro for his use of vibrato and brought some of this to her interpretation of 'Wild Women'. 'Right after Tim's solo,' remembers Bowers, 'she comes in with that, "*Weeeelll, you never*",' he sings. 'That's the kind of thing she picked up from Matt.'

There was also the rousing crowd-pleasing 'I Know You Rider' – guaranteed to leave the audience cheering for more as a show closer, or more often to get them revved up as an opener. It was therefore an obvious choice for the opening track of their debut album's first side. 'We always got a *great* reaction with that,' remembers Hendricks. 'Everybody would just flip out because the song was *very* driving and full of excitement.'

Their first recording session was booked for the prestigious Music Makers – a hulking barn of a recording studio on Fifth Avenue. The recording process itself was relatively simple; stereo recordings had yet to be introduced and so compared with the months and sometimes years people now spend making rock and pop albums, everything was done very quickly. The days of overdubbing and multi-tracking were still a sound engineer's daydream, so for the Big 3, making an album consisted mainly of recording a live performance, very much as they would have played it at the Bitter End. This meant, however, that there was more pressure to produce a performance that would really capture the band at their best.

Although the Big 3 were essentially ready to record in terms of having perfected their act and having a repertoire, Silver nevertheless decided to flesh out their sound with the addition of Bowers' stand-up bass and drums and guitar from legendary session drummer Panama Francis and guitarist Carl Lynch respectively. But the band's nerves were apparent in their sound from the start. Not only were they faced with the daunting prospect of their recording debut, but they were also having to play with a drummer for the first time.

They started off with 'Rider', thinking that their crowd-pleaser might do for them what it normally did for their audiences and set them off on a roll. But their nerves seemed to be creating havoc with their harmonies and Bowers, as musical director, suggested they try some other songs first instead. A few hours later, none of the others were working any better. Cass had gone up to the control booth to listen back to what they had recorded so far with Roy Silver but as studio time was running out fast, everybody just seemed more and more frustrated and tense.

Silver called Bob Bowers up to the booth. 'It really isn't happening,' Silver told him.

'Well, no, it isn't man,' Bowers replied.

'Well, here, maybe this'll help,' suggested Silver.

Silver brought out a piece of hash and Cass proceeded to magically create a pipe – complete with bowl and stem, out of the foil inner lining which cigarette packets still contained at that time. 'We went back out,' remembers Bowers, 'and said, "Let's try 'Rider' again," and we did it in one take. Exactly what you hear on the record, right? Tim and Jim had gotten a contact high from being with someone who is high. They got into the same space as we were – which is to say *relaxed*!' he laughs. 'After that we basically *re*-recorded the whole album in about an hour and a half. And those are the takes you hear. Everything else was thrown out.'

The album – titled simply *The Big 3* was released in October of 1963 and featured what for the time was an avant-garde op art, Vasarely-style square mosaic image of the number three on the sleeve. 'The Banjo Song' (their reworking of the folk standard 'Oh Susanna'), which featured a rousing lead vocal from Tim and was one of the group's standout live tracks, was also released as a single.

Cass was now a recording artist with a record in the shops, and if that was not enough, in an effort to promote the album and single, Silver used his contacts to secure the group a slot on what was at the time America's most watched TV show – the *Tonight Show* with Johnny Carson. TV shows were still live at this point and Cass and the others were almost paralysed with nerves, but the performance went smoothly. Cass looked her most feminine in a knee-length black velvet dress with a white lace collar, handmade for her by Jim Hendricks's girlfriend Vanessa, while Tim and Jim seemed to gallantly flank her on either side in their sharply tailored suits. Their success should have been guaranteed, but in spite of the exposure, neither the album nor the single made any dent on the charts. Tim put this down to the fact that the record's distributor Veejay specialised in blues and had no track record with folk. Given the band's appearance on TV and the fact that they were certainly musically on a par with any of the other successful folk acts of the time, this would indeed seem to have been a contributing factor.

But although 'The Banjo Song' failed to make any impact on the record charts, the group themselves definitely did make an impression on the *Tonight Show* and were not only invited back but became regular fixtures. Carson thought Cass was tremendous and they also stood out from the run-of-the-mill Peter, Paul and Mary-style combos.

Cass's size had become their gimmick and made them instantly memorable. 'It wasn't because our records were selling,' believed Tim, 'or because these were particularly great songs. They just said, "They sing well, they look good and they have this girl." Everybody else was kind of the same and had more of a standard body shape, so we got away with it. And I guess for a while the industry was kind of mesmerised. Our agency was getting us on shows before people that looked a hell of a lot better than us and we were getting the *Tonight Show*. People with hit records weren't even getting the *Tonight Show*!'

There was also of course the fact that the Big 3 could actually play and sing in tune. Reasonable requirements one might think for appearing on national TV, but then, as now, not necessarily the norm. 'Most of the folk groups, they really couldn't sing or play well,' Bowers remembers. 'It's just that it was such a craze that anybody who owned a guitar and could play three chords and hung out in Washington Square Park could get a recording contract! And did!' The Big 3 were therefore a welcome change. 'The musicians on the *Tonight Show* told me often,' Bowers continues, "Hey, this group can really sing! In *tune*!" That was one of the brilliant things about them – that they could really sing in tune. Which was why they had such power! This stuff resonates when you get it in tune!'

In the six months since they had arrived in New York, the Big 3 had become an established act on the Village circuit, recorded an album and had appeared on the biggest TV show in America. In the wake of their TV appearance they had even been asked to record a radio jingle for Ballantine's Beer, and guitar manufacturers Guild were giving Tim and Jim free guitars. But even apart from these developments, all three of them had felt a musical spark from the combined power of their voices from the start and the thrill of hearing their sound improve day by day seemed even better.

The folk boom had given Cass the entrée into show business which had previously been denied her. On the boards of the folk coffee houses it didn't seem to matter what you looked like; there were plenty of people onstage with neither talent nor looks, and so in this context, it was only natural that Cass's gifts would be recognised and acknowledged immediately. She wasn't the star yet that she would later become, but she had always loved singing, and she now had the opportunity to do so every night and a platform on which to perform and excel. It was to be one of the most exciting times of Cass's life.

'She seemed to be *very* happy,' remembers Hendricks. 'I think musically she was very fulfilled because she wanted to do music that really was full of meat and I think that this group really provided a lot of that kind of thing for her.' In years to come all three would look back on these early times in the Big 3 with affection.

'We were just having a great adventure!' remembered Tim. 'We were living in New York City, we had this lovely guitar firm *giving* us guitars. Cass is wearing these handmade beautiful dresses, we're having our jackets tailor-made, our haircuts razored – we were having a *great* time. We were all as excited about it as each other. We just really enjoyed it. It was like every day we were saying, what's next?'

7

Hell on wheels

The Big 3's honeymoon period was not to last long. 'The first six months were fine,' remembered Tim, 'the second six months were hell on wheels,' and although this may perhaps have been a slight exaggeration, the truth was not that much better. Whilst the group now had a record deal and were fast becoming national TV stars, the dents in Cass and Tim's relationship were beginning to deepen, and over the coming months would grow increasingly difficult to ignore. For Cass, meanwhile, the early thrill of success would soon give way to some of the deeper issues and concerns which would dominate her life. On the surface she seemed to have turned her back on the unhappiness of her childhood and teenage years, but many of these residual feelings would continue to emerge over the coming years, often with considerable impact on her working life.

Following the success of the Big 3's appearance on the *Tonight Show*, the trio had become regular fixtures on some of the most-watched shows on TV from the *Danny Kaye Show* to Jack Linkletter's *Weekly Hootenanny Show* – the folk equivalent of *Top of the Pops*. By this stage the folk boom had reached its peak as a national craze and there were even '*Hootenanny*' candy and T-shirts, so the, albeit commercial, *Hootenanny* TV show was therefore obligatory must-see TV.

The original Hootenanny idea had started in 1940 when Pete Seeger and Woody Guthrie had performed at Democratic fund-raising events, but the concept had subsequently evolved and spread country-wide to mean an open-mic night in which new acts would perform for free, and so once the TV talent show proved a hit, the natural next step was to take Jack Linklater's *Hootenanny* out on the road.

In the autumn of 1963, the Big 3 set off to play thirty-one nights, travelling across America on the official *Hootenanny* bus alongside Les Baxter's Balladeers – featuring a young pre-Byrds David Crosby, folk/soul duo Joe and Eddie and ragtime guitarist Raun McKinnon. But whilst the group may have become TV stars, in terms of luxury travel arrangements, the Big 3 were not much better off than they had been in Cass's old Beetle.

'*Boy!* What a *horrible* tour!' remembers David Crosby who had met Cass in the Village and already become a close friend. 'Tour buses now have got bunks, galleys, a bathroom, satellite TV, video tapes, games – *everything*! Back then it was like a Greyhound bus – Trailways with seats in it. And there was only *one* place you could lie down which was the back seat and we used to give that to Cass. And even there you were listening to the engine – *really* loud. And it was bumpy too. I remember one time she hurt herself when the driver hit a big bump and it was so bad that it bounced her right off the rear seat and onto the floor.'

The bands already knew each other from the folk circuit either in New York, Chicago or Florida and while on a bus tour consisting of eight men and two women (Cass and Raun McKinnon), some less self-assured women may have gravitated towards the other woman, Cass felt a much closer affinity with her friend Crosby and his fellow Balladeers: Bob Ingram and Mike Clough. They were also more fun than Mackinnon who, according to Clough, was 'more of a Joan Baez-type, the real hard-core folkie'. As far as Cass was concerned, if she was going to be stuck on an uncomfortable bus for days and nights on end, she would make sure she had some fun along the way and she and her friends soon developed a reputation for 'bad behaviour'.

'We were having fun,' says Clough, ''cause we were on the top of the world! We were the bad kids and the ones that were smoking dope and all of these other things,' he laughs. 'But we had the world by the tail and we had everything going for us.'

Cass had been smoking pot since her post-Forest Park days in downtown Baltimore, but at this point, even in Greenwich Village, it was still far from ubiquitous. 'This was the *very* first edge of it,' remembers Cass's friend, producer Erik Jacobsen. 'To buy pot then in the Village you had to go to a junkie, to a dealer. John (Sebastian) and I went many times to some incredible tenement building on the Lower East Side which was like dead people on the street. There were junkies, but there were no white potheads – *very* few. It was before that all happened.'

This, of course, only reinforced the sense of superiority and hipness of those who were initiated into the dope-smoking culture. 'Everybody *else* seemed so *stupid*!' says Jacobsen, laughing. 'And immature and just no taste and blind and I guess our attitude was a little arch in those days: you were young and you were hip and you were happening and getting high and laughing at everybody and they were laughing at *you* but you didn't care! That was the exuberance of youth gone kind of amok there for the first time.'

On the *Hootenanny* Tour, the rest of the Big 3 meanwhile, were less interested in 'being bad kids' and seemed to have their own respective agendas. Jim would be hard at work either buried in a book or honing his guitar skills with scales and exercises on the bus while Tim was taking his leadership role seriously and seemed more concerned about the health of his singer. Cass's smoking was beginning to take its toll on her voice as she already sang hard every night during their shows and was prone to bronchitis. Her vulnerability to throat problems would become a recurring issue, not just within the Big 3 but later in her career, but for the time being Cass was doing her best to enjoy the tour. 'Cass was a *wild* woman,' laughs Bob Ingram, 'a maniac. And *really* kind of at the top of her game comedically. I remember one night we were driving through the wilds of West Virginia and Cass was on the back seat of the bus and we had stretched a blanket that we stole from a hotel across the back and made like a private area for her. The bus was almost empty apart from us because it was near the end of the tour and David (Crosby) had left the tour because he had a credit card his dad gave him, so he could jump on planes and fly to the next stop and some other people had flown ahead too, so it was basically Mike and I and Cass and a few other people like Raun. So there we were driving through the mountains in this empty bus and Clough was in the back, acting like he was a barker at a carnival and Cass was behind the curtain doing a bogus striptease and unbeknownst to them, the bus driver stopped to pick up this family whose car had broken down and give them a ride to the next town to find a tow truck or something. But we barely even noticed that the bus had stopped and Clough is doing this carnie barking thing and Cass is behind this curtain and she's like sticking an arm out and putting a naked shoulder out and doing all this provocative stuff and of course with a woman four hundred pounds, or whatever she weighed, it's pretty silly and these poor hillbillies in the front of the bus, they couldn't *wait* to get off. They *knew* they'd joined a tour of lunatics, you know!'

Anything that would liven up the seemingly interminable hours on the uncomfortable bus was welcome as, more often than not, they would pull into a town, play the local college campus or venue and then get straight back on the bus, driving through the night to the next town. As the tour progressed through America's South, bigger issues began to come into play, as the groups came face to face with the realities of life outside the cosmopolitan, liberal confines of Greenwich Village. Although President Kennedy had passed a mild bill in 1960 outlawing segregation in public places in the South, three years later it was still being routinely ignored and hotels would frequently suggest that duo Joe and Eddie, who were black, should stay in a separate hotel to the other groups. Only a few months before their tour had started, Dr Martin Luther King had led 250,000 marchers to Washington in what had culminated in his historic 'I Have a Dream' speech, but the final Civil Rights Bill would not be passed until the following year in 1964 and what Cass and the others on the tour were experiencing were the still deeply prejudiced beliefs of the old South. 'Everyone reacted to it,' remembers Mike Clough. 'We were probably the most progressive of any of the people on the tour, because to us there was no race or no colour. There were people and there was talent.'

While this view today might seem self-evident and not in any way radical, in 1963 it was seen as liberal and progressive and was still quite some way from being adopted by the American population as a whole. Cass had not got involved in folk music because of deeply held political beliefs but at the same time, she and her friends were nevertheless aware enough to be concerned about what was going on around them. Both Baltimore and Washington, DC, where Cass had grown up, had diverse racial groups co-existing alongside each other in relative harmony and compared with the rest of the country were relatively liberal in their outlook, so the realities of life in America's deep South would have been new to her. Cass was, as David Crosby remembers, 'a dyed in the wool liberal from the beginning' and 'totally for civil rights'. But civil rights was not to be the only political issue that would encroach on the *Hootenanny* Tour.

As the bus started working its way back east on the last leg of the tour, on 22 November news broke from Dallas, Texas that President Kennedy had been assassinated as his presidential motorcade drove through the city. The impact of his murder left not only America, but the world, stunned.

Cass lay on the long bench seat at the back of the bus and cried all the way back to New York. It was as though, for Cass, as was the case for many, thirty-four years later after the death of Princess Diana, Kennedy's assassination had brought out the pent-up tears and emotion that she had previously been unable to express, in particular for her own father's death. 'She really took that hard,' remembers Bob Ingram. 'I remember her just crying, crying, crying and obviously she was crying for Kennedy but I never could figure out the extent of her love for him that would cause that extreme reaction.'

Whatever the underlying reasons may have been, Cass was not alone in this outpouring of grief. As the bus drove on, they saw women everywhere crying in the streets and wherever they stopped, the mood was unflinchingly solemn. As much as Cass and her fellow folk musicians may have embraced an anti-establishment stance and a general spirit of non-conformity, Kennedy was nevertheless seen as a pioneering force for good in the establishment, and the embodiment of a younger, more dynamic, optimistic and liberal style of leadership. It was also a more innocent age when the assassination of presidents was, as yet, relatively unheard of. 'The country just wasn't ready for it,' recalls Ingram. 'The country was less sophisticated and more naive than it is now. We hadn't gone through the introspection and divisiveness and pain that Vietnam cost us. We hadn't been disillusioned the way we are now, so the people, from top to bottom, were just in shock.'

Despite the widespread mourning, Jack Linklater, as manager of the *Hootenanny* tour, was determined that the show would go on. Cass, meanwhile, and indeed everyone else on the tour thought differently. 'We said, "*You* play it, Jack. We're not playing tonight!"' remembers David Crosby laughing. 'And he couldn't believe it! Everybody said, "No, no, no – you're crazy. Nobody's gonna come." And there was quite a little battle about that, but Cass was *absolutely* not going to and I sided with her and that was pretty much that.'

Although Cass's reaction to Kennedy's death may have seemed extreme even compared with the widespread grief felt by much of the

American people, it was not only connected with her own father's death but also with a deep-rooted unhappiness which, despite the Big 3's success, had continued to surface in the form of regular depressions.

'She was very moody,' remembers Mike Clough, 'and sometimes she was very depressed. She would be emotional about different little things, which at the time didn't bother us at all, but they did her. But if she was in a bad mood everybody just kind of left her alone. Everybody except David. David was the one that would try and talk her out of it and cheer her up. If she was depressed or moody or something, she and David would go off together after the show or on days in between concerts and the rest of us could go to hell.'

Cass would remain prone to depression throughout her life and this was only aggravated by the post-high slumps caused by marijuana, diet pills or most other drugs, but depression was also something which was in her family history and which she had inherited from both her parents. 'My mom, I think, lived her whole life fighting an un-named depression,' believes Leah. 'Not just after my dad died, but before too. And I *know* that it made all three of us suffer from depression because you learn depressed behaviour like you learn any other behaviour.'

The situation was certainly not helped by the family's reluctance to discuss emotional issues but this was common at the time, and with the Cohens, as with many Jewish families, this silence often masked the traumas of their parents' generation which were often too great to fully acknowledge. Cass's maternal grandmother Chaya had been one of only three members of her entire family to survive the Holocaust. Much later in life, she would show Leah a photograph taken when she was a small child of the twenty-seven members of her original family, almost all of whom, including her parents, grandparents, aunts, uncles and siblings had been forced by the Germans to dig a mass grave in their Russian shtetl before being pushed into it and buried alive.

The cumulative effect of this family history seems to have been inherited by Bess, although it was never acknowledged as such, and in spite of the upbeat persona which Bess and indeed Cass adopted, Cass would nevertheless also have absorbed her mother's underlying depression. Similarly, in spite of Philip's humour and easygoing nature, she would also, at some level, have picked up on his equally deep-seated sense of frustration with his life. 'If I'm so smart, why ain't I rich?' he once remarked to Toby Kobren, the exhaustion and despondency evident in his voice. He had also had to contend with his own parents' lack of approval and this no doubt aggravated his sense of failure further. 'They just thought he was a disappointment really,' remembers Leah, 'as he was almost the only male sibling in his family who didn't go to college and then he wanted to be in the restaurant business which they just thought was so *déclassé. Oh my God!* And then, furthermore, he was a failure at it for year after year after year.'

Although Cass's depressions would be evident to several who knew her throughout her life, there were few whom she trusted enough to fully confide in. David Crosby, however, was someone whom, from the earliest days of their friendship, she felt close enough to trust. Cass immediately sensed in Crosby an impish wit and sharp intelligence which matched her own, as well as a deeper emotional kinship, and later on in Cass's life her friendship with him would be enormously significant.

Crosby himself, meanwhile, like so many others, was simply captivated by Cass, and her humour in particular. 'She was tremendously smart and certainly one of the funniest people I *ever* met in my life. She made me laugh so hard my sides hurt and it was intelligent humour – she didn't have to sit there and recite jokes to you that she'd heard some place. Her take on things was funny and she was quite the wonderful girl. She was a fascinating human being. And I loved her.'

In a second bid for chart success, the Big 3 released another single from the album in December of 1963: 'Come Away, Melinda' – a melancholy anti-war ballad which they had first heard sung by Harry Belafonte in the fifties. Four years later Tim would re-record the song himself in a highly dramatic, almost Gothic solo rendition which many consider to be the definitive version of the song, but back in 1963, the Big 3's arrangement was an altogether gentler affair featuring Cass singing lead. The Big 3 had generally steered away from anti-war songs as Tim felt strongly that that direction was not suitable for the group's talents and in spite of Cass's liberal attitudes, she was similarly unmotivated to use music as a vehicle for social concern. But this song was an exception.

The single fitted in with the anti-war songs prevalent at the time, but in the light of Kennedy's death, it was deemed too sombre for the nation's mood and consequently received virtually no airplay. For the same reason, the group was not allowed to perform it on the *Danny Kaye Show* nor their subsequent appearances on the *Tonight Show*.

But the question of which song they performed would turn out to be the least of their problems once they arrived at the TV studios. After the initial euphoria of their first *Tonight Show*, Cass had started to develop a pattern of nervousness before the shows which would invariably affect her voice, causing laryngitis or even bronchitis to immediately resurface. Within hours of a TV performance, Cass would suddenly become hoarse and the band would be thrown into potential crisis by the possibility that she might not be able to sing. 'She would get hoarse and she'd sound *terrible*,' remembers Jim Hendricks, 'like she could hardly talk but we kind of kept pushing her, because it seemed like, unless it was *really*, really bad, when it came to it – she would always be able to sing. Once she got there she would always somehow manage to pull it off.'

Cass claimed that her weight meant she was more vulnerable to laryngitis and that this was aggravated by nerves but Tim did not believe a word of it. He was convinced it was all merely a cry for attention and became incensed every time the problem occurred. 'It was a ploy, a sympathy vote,' Tim told me. '"*I can't!*" he mimicked in a hoarse whisper. 'You can't yell at a fat girl! You can't say, get off your arse and get your shit together – people won't *say* that to a fat girl. They'll let her do it, so the more they let her do it, the more she did it. It was her way of manipulating – she was in control. But it was a negative kind of control – of course if she couldn't sing, we couldn't go on, so everyone was making a fuss of her. After about the third or fourth time she did that, I just didn't have the patience any more.'

Even Jim agreed with Tim's reading of the situation but soon Cass's illnesses were not the only thing she and Tim were arguing over and suddenly they seemed to be bickering over everything from who was singing what and when to Cass's shoddy treatment of the expensive handmade dresses the three of them had jointly paid for. These surface wrangles were symptomatic of a steady decline in their relationship. Despite Jim's arrival into the group, during their first few months in New York, the ambiguity of their relationship had by no means dissipated and to many it seemed that Cass's confusion was not necessarily only the result of wishful thinking. When they were rehearsing and singing, some remember Tim pandering to Cass's affection and at the very least making her feel that it was reciprocated, possibly for the good of the group. The fact was, meanwhile, that Tim was in love with a young comedienne named Mory Haden and had been seeing her for some time, and so, although Cass would soon transfer her affection elsewhere, it was only a matter of time before the residue of their complex relationship became an increasing strain within the group.

There was now also the added issue that although Tim was the trio's undisputed leader, Cass had become the star of the group and this clearly rankled with him. Cass's voice and stage presence unsurprisingly made her the natural focus of attention in the group. It was to be expected: if you had an unusually large, charismatic woman with a voice that could stop traffic, flanked by two albeit attractive, fine musicians in suits, there wasn't much doubt as to who was going to stand out in people's minds.

'She didn't have to do much to wipe you right off the stage,' remembered Zal Yanovsky who would work with her later. 'So if you had an ego, it would be pretty hard – you'd have to be bigger than life. I don't think Jim had that problem but I think Tim did. He was a very good musician and a songwriter, but ultimately she could dominate without seemingly much effort. And I think it came very natural to her to be the centre.'

Tim did find it difficult to deal with and admitted as much himself. 'Cass became like the clearing house for the groups. They all came to see Cass which didn't thrill *me* a lot because I *also* was onstage with her and I used to think, "Well, what about me?" 'Cause I was doing the arrangements and most of the writing. My little ego unfortunately got in the way because I wasn't always comfortable with her being the centre of attention. After all, I'm an only child and I have *my* demands. So that was *my* animal to deal with.'

Perhaps as a defence mechanism against his seemingly threatened position as the group's focus, Tim also seemed to be taking his role as leader ever more seriously and as a result grew increasingly alienated from Cass and Jim. 'Tim was just an *unusual* character,' says Jim. 'He was the leader of the group, so he kind of kept himself aloof from us, you know? That was his attitude. He was the boss and he kept himself apart. He didn't socialise with us as we had in the beginning. When we first got together, everything was like . . . very equal, you know? But as time went on it was like he became an elitist, or whatever, and Cass and I were, like, on the lower totem pole.'

All these factors combined meant that by the end of the year, the initial excitement and camaraderie that the three of them had shared seemed to have evaporated. Tim's attitude inevitably drew Cass closer to Jim and the two of them grew complicit as schoolchildren desperate to escape their overbearing schoolmaster colleague.

By the end of 1963 the growing antagonism between Cass and Tim was not the only issue threatening the future of the group. In the year since the Cuban Missile Crisis, the fear which had spread across America had not abated and a further political crisis was looming. In the summer, the North Vietnamese had attacked an American Navy ship in the Gulf of Tonkin and America's new President – Lyndon B. Johnson, was beginning to usher the country into the start of an undeclared war in south-east Asia. The threat of the draft therefore began to dangle ominously overhead in the life of anybody who was male and under the age of twenty-four.

Tim was exempt because he had already served in the air force before meeting Cass, but Jim was not. At that time, unless you had already served or been deemed for some reason unfit, you could be exempt only if you were either married or held a job such as teaching, which was considered essential to the community. Jim's teaching job had consequently worked in his favour back in Omaha, but now that he was with the Big 3, he was once again fit for service and the draft board duly sent him notice to report for a physical.

The Big 3 may not at this point have had chart success, but they had become regulars on national TV and were certainly stars within the Greenwich Village folk scene. For the three of them, having worked so hard to achieve this, the idea of losing it all by having to send Jim off to fight was inconceivable. To Cass, the solution was obvious. 'Well, let's go get married!' she told Jim. Roy Silver likewise saw the scheme as the perfect solution and Jim agreed. His girlfriend Vanessa also readily accepted the situation as she was a close friend of Cass's and was glad that Jim could avoid being drafted. Cass couldn't believe her luck. It was the wildest, most fun idea she had ever had. As far as she was concerned it didn't matter that the marriage wasn't genuine in the romantic sense; she was getting married to someone who was way beyond any boyfriend she had ever hoped for and, even if only in her head, it was just another two fingers in the face of those sorority sisters who had jeered at Ellen Naomi. It was also, at some level, a way of getting back at Tim, a payback for the hurt his rejection had caused her. This time, Tim would be the one left out as, given the sensitivity of the political situation, it was decided that Cass and Jim should keep their marriage a secret from almost everyone, including Tim. But the decision to exclude Tim was not entirely personal. Cass told neither her mother nor her sister till quite some time after the wedding as, given the less than legitimate reasons for the marriage, the consequences of being found out by the authorities were no small matter. 'At the time, this was nothing to bandy about,' remembers Cass's friend John Sebastian, who had found someone to marry him for exactly the same reason, and amongst their circle, faced with the alternative, marriages of this kind were not uncommon. 'If you did something like this, you couldn't smirk about it among your friends because the repercussions were tremendous and you wanted to appear as un-noticeable as possible. I think it would be several years before we could joke about those kind of things. It was a very tough period.'

Despite the secrecy, Cass put all her energy into arranging the wedding – a small, discreet ceremony held at the home of a judge in Arlington towards the end of 1963. As her friendship with Tim had gradually deteriorated, Cass had begun to transfer her affection to Jim, and when they had first arrived in New York she had done her best to help him acclimatise to life in the city. 'I had never seen a building taller than three or four stories,' remembers Jim. 'So, of course, I walked around there staring up and Cass was always so sweet to me. She'd say things like, "Don't keep looking up all the time, people are gonna know you're not *from* here!" And I'd say, "I can't help it. I've never seen anything like this before!"'

Cass also enjoyed helping Jim choose clothes. Unlike Tim, who tended to sport the more bohemian Dylan-style cap with a bandana tied round his neck, Jim liked to wear well-cut suits and this was something else that Cass adored. She liked her men to be well dressed and would spend hours accompanying Jim to the tailors, choosing the best cloth and the best Italian cut. She also did her best to look as smart as was possible herself given that she could rarely find off-the-peg clothes and Jim remembers her as being 'a real Brooks Brothers kind of girl, a real collegiate Georgetown type'. It was as if with the right clothes and the right man on her arm, despite the fact that Jim had a girlfriend, she could really live out the fantasy that she and Jim were in fact a couple. 'A lot of times we would be going somewhere,' continues Jim, 'we would take two or three days off and get a room together somewhere in a hotel and we would go out and she was always *buying* stuff for me – clothes and stuff, she was the sweetest thing in the world. She really was and we had fun with it, acting like married people sometimes. Even though we never consummated the marriage.'

Cass had long had a tendency to see things the way she wanted them to be, rather than the way they actually were. It would soon recur again in her next significant relationship.

For the time being, however, Cass and Jim's marriage inevitably drew them closer and increasingly further from Tim, who would not find out about it until some years later. His aloofness, meanwhile, seemed to only escalate as the months passed. 'We shared our lives with each other,' says Jim, 'and Tim did not come in on that. He didn't want to be part of that 'cause of his personality. I can't really say why. The only thing I can think of is that he wanted to be a little bit above everything – being the boss, being the one that made the decisions and that kind of thing.'

By the end of the year, their relationship with Tim had disintegrated so far that Cass and Jim decided to take some time out to go to Toronto and visit two new Canadian friends they had recently met: guitarist Zal Yanovsky and a dangerously charming Irish Canadian named Denny Doherty.

8

Love, love me do

> '*We* never thought life in the Village was anything out of the ordinary until years later you look back on it and you think, *Holy Shit* – wasn't that some kind of maelstrom to walk through! All that *energy*! And Cass was right in the middle of it, when *I* arrived. She was *creating* it. Wooooh! I just wanted to get some of *that*.'
>
> Denny Doherty

As much as the music, the social side of life around folk had become a vital part of the scene and nowhere more so than in the Village. When groups finished their own sets onstage, most nights they would wander along the street to one of the other umpteen venues where some of their friends were performing and invariably some sort of impromptu party would evolve.

If they hadn't met in the Village itself, most musicians had got to know each other whilst playing in the same clubs across the country. 'In folk music,' Cass later explained, 'when you travelled around, everybody sort of came together. When you'd go into a strange town you'd find out who was playing and, whether you knew them or not, you struck up a friendship, because there wasn't anybody else there that you could talk to, you didn't know the people who were in the town you were working in.'

It was an extraordinarily fertile period and on any given night in the Village, aside from the comedians like Woody Allen and Bill Cosby, if you stumbled into a bar you would most likely have run into at least a handful of musicians who would go on to become major stars. But although nobody of course knew exactly what the future would hold, there was nevertheless a feverish rush of creative adrenalin surging through the Village's narrow streets. 'The whole atmosphere was one of excitement,' remembers Jim Hendricks. 'It was just in the air and there was a lot of anticipation about things that were gonna happen. Everybody who was in the entertainment business felt that they had a real shot at being a star!'

The openness and do-it-yourself spirit of the folk scene also gave everyone an extraordinary feeling of optimism, and whilst there was a healthy spirit of competition, on the whole, the atmosphere was one of unusual camaraderie and respect for each other's talent. 'It was an unusual period of time when everybody loved everybody else!' laughs ex-Modern Folk Quartet member Cyrus Faryar. 'We were all of a mind to admire one another in those days – there was very little in the way of competition or petty jealousies and each of us was amazed at the other person and happy to hear them sing! Each person had in his act new songs that you didn't know, so a lot of time was spent learning songs from one another or stealing songs, but it was a very likeable atmosphere and that made it a wonderful time to be involved.'

Cass adored the constant party ethos of life in the Village, and as acceptance there was based on talent and personality, she was almost immediately recognised as a central figure in Village life. Her wit and gregariousness had gained her instant popularity, but as the unquestioned star of the Big 3, her talent had also earned her unequivocal musical respect. 'I think everybody that heard her thought, Oh, *God*! That's a *really* great voice. *Immediately*,' says David Crosby. 'She had an incredible voice and she was already a pretty polished singer.'

Cass got a reaction from everybody who heard her, not least from Dennis Stephen Doherty, the man who, years later in 1972, she would say she had been 'in love with for the last nine years'. Cass was clearly thinking back to 1963 when the Canadian Doherty had arrived in the Village alongside fellow guitarist Zal Yanovsky and the other members of his group the Halifax Three.

Tall and auburn-haired with mischievous blue eyes, the twenty-three-year-old Doherty had the mercurial charm of Errol Flynn tempered with the unflinching masculinity of Robert Mitchum. He had grown up at the rough end of Halifax, the small coastal town on the far eastern shores of Novia Scotia, and at sixteen, as a dare, he had taken the stage at a local dancehall to sing 'Love Letters in the Sand'. Denny was clearly a natural singer and the bandleader was so impressed he invited him back.

Then rock and roll and Elvis had arrived and over the next three years, while working first as a lingerie salesman and then as a pawnbroker, he started singing with local rock and roll group the Hepsters. Denny's father, however, was unimpressed by his son's musical ambitions and expected him to follow him into a steady job in the dockyards. He himself had had his own dance band and played in The Princess Louise Fusiliers marching band, but, unable to make enough money to support his family, had become a plumber and marine pipe fitter in Halifax's docklands. 'Singin'!' he railed, 'You get yourself a goddamn trade, son. Something you can put in your arse pocket and rely on.'

But Denny had other ideas, and at a New Year's Eve party in Halifax in 1960 he joined forces with Pat La Croix and Richard Byrne singing a mix of Kingston Trio covers and traditional songs they had learnt from their families. Eventually, like everyone else on the folk scene, they arrived in New York and were promptly offered a record deal with Columbia's Epic Records and rechristened the Halifax Three. Doherty would later go on to sing alongside Cass, first in the Mugwumps and then in the Mamas and the Papas, but equally significantly, he would become, and remain, probably the most important man in her adult life.

In spite of the fact that he sang lead on many of the Mamas and the Papas' most well-known hits, historically his role in the group has been slightly obscured by the long shadow cast by John Phillips's songwriting, Michelle Phillips's looks and Cass's voice and personality. Meeting Denny all these years on, however, in person he is much sharper, funnier and talented than he is often given credit for.

In the years since the Mamas and the Papas' demise, he has had a successful career as an actor and TV star in his native Canada, where he now lives with his two grown-up children in a large, rustic house overlooking the woods around Lake Ontario. The tranquillity of the setting is a long way from the twenty-four-hour party life he lived during his time with the Mamas and the Papas and reflects the fact that Denny has not drunk alcohol for twenty years. But his years with Cass and the group are still vivid in his mind (he has recently starred in his own one-man show 'California Dreamin' – The Rise and Fall (and Music) of the Mamas and the Papas') and, over the course of several afternoons in Canada, he regales me with what feels like an enormously entertaining private performance of the Tales of Doherty. No tale is complete without accompanying voices and expressions and the pace only lets up for the brief moments when the story is more tragic than comic.

But Denny's first encounter with Cass certainly features more of the comedy. One night walking along Bleecker Street, Denny was stopped in his tracks by the sound of a woman's booming, tender voice belting 'Rider', and singing, for all the world, like her life depended on it. 'I *heard* her,' he tells me. 'Every time someone would come out of the club, they would lift up this curtain and you could hear this ... *sound*. And I just wanted to hear more. So I stuck my head under the black curtain and Cass was onstage in some blue satin or taffeta thing with the white lace collar. And she took full focus. It was like: *Jesus!* What the hell? *Ohhhh!* There's other people onstage with her too!' he laughs. 'And there's a bass player too! Because she was like wow, goddamn, look at *that*! And *listen* to that!'

Just as it was impossible to be around the Village for too long without chancing upon Cass, Denny was soon noticed as the handsome guy with the golden voice. And no one noticed sooner than Cass, who lost no time in making sure they got acquainted one night at the Dugout, the spit and sawdust bar which had become the unofficial green room for the Village's musicians. 'Cass just came over,' remembers Denny, 'and sat down. "Hi! I saw you singing ... and I *like* the way your group sounds. You guys sing really good ... blah, blah, blah. How *are* you?"' he says in mock Cass-style voice. 'And we started drinking and I said, "Well, I'd like a Canadian Club – CC and ginger." And she goes, "Jack Daniels. Green label. Straight up." I was a drinker – I drank more than my share, so I'm like ... ho ho ho *Okaaay*! So she gets her Jack Daniels straight up and, blap,' he says, making a gulping sound, 'down that goes. About an hour or so later, we've blap, blap, blapped a couple of shots each and she says, "We're gonna drink each other under the table, aren't we?"' he says in drunken-style slurred speech. '"I've an idea," she says. "Why don't we just get under the table and drink? Come *on*!" So by this time, we're under the table – and the Dugout had an old marble terrazzo floor with sawdust – and we get down under the chequered tablecloths, and the Chianti bottle with all the wax all over it, and the waiter would bring our drinks and put them on the chairs. And we sat under the table for the rest of the night watching people's feet going around! That's all I remember. The next thing it's the next day! Hello, Cass! I got her home, I guess.'

Cass was instantly smitten with Denny. Aside from being handsome, charming and entertaining, he gave the impression, just as Tim had done before, that here was someone who could handle anything life threw at him and for all Cass's outer confidence and bravado, this was something that she found deeply reassuring. But unlike Tim, Denny was relaxed, easy-going and had a devilish wit to match her own. She was spellbound. Denny, meanwhile, just like Tim before him, was similarly enthralled by her personality. 'There's a segment in the front of the *Reader's Digest* that I'd read as a kid,' he tells me, 'which was just like four paragraphs of somebody talking about "the most unforgettable character that I've ever met". And it could be a fighter pilot, it could be *anybody*, but you *know* them when you meet them. And sure enough, you know them for all of your life. There's only a handful but they're *Reader's Digest* people. "*The most unforgettable character I've ever met!*" And that was my initial thought with Cass – that this was a lot of fun.'

But although their night at the Dugout would mark the beginning of an intense friendship, Denny did not feel the same romantic attraction. He had a girlfriend at the time, and no shortage of female admirers, and besides, as far as he could see, Cass was not free herself. Their meeting at the Dugout had happened shortly after the Big 3 had first arrived in New York, and so Cass and Tim were still the close-knit team they had started out as. Denny, like many others, had therefore assumed that Cass and Tim were involved with each other romantically, as well as musically. 'I thought they were married,' remembers Denny, 'or at least lovers, a couple. Nothing was ever said but it was gleaned, you know? Jim had girls around but Tim never did and Cass never had guys around. Tim and Cass were always out together so everyone *assumed* that they were together, and had been together all the way from Washington. I presumed Tim saw what everybody else saw and went, "Oh *ho*, let's hook onto this one, we're going to the top." That was *my* perception. That this is her boyfriend, her Svengali. This is Rasputin here.'

As Cass and Denny gradually became closer friends, he would begin to see the truth of the situation but it still made no difference to his feelings. As far as Cass was concerned, however, this didn't matter. This, she felt, was something worth waiting for.

After their initial meeting, Denny and Cass inevitably ran into each other at the Dugout or elsewhere in the social melée that was life in the Village, and on Cass's part what may have started out as a crush soon developed considerably. 'She was madly in love with him,' remembers Mike Clough. 'That was kind of obvious. She didn't go around *broadcasting* it to everyone, but it was pretty much common knowledge, I guess.' Cass had first met Denny shortly before the *Hootenanny* bus tour, but had managed to find ways to keep in touch with him while she was away although he himself was on a parallel tour with the Halifax Three, along with fellow folk group the Journeymen featuring John and Michelle Phillips. Somehow, whilst stopping at motels or gas stations, Cass would use the time to find a phone booth and track down Denny, usually at a motel himself somewhere several thousand miles across the country. 'She would find ways to reach,' remembers Denny, 'and I was baffled then and I'm baffled now. How does she get someone to *find* you? Has she got someone at the CIA or the FBI? Someone in Washington she's not talking about? Well, it's easy I guess: call the agency and say, "Where are they?" Or have her manager "find him" and track us down from our itinerary. She was wily. If she really wanted to get hold of you, she knew how. I remember standing in phone booths having long conversations but I never put the thing together. She would always be talking about being on the road or what she did that day or who's doing what on the bus, gossipy kind of stuff. But it never got personal. They weren't love phone calls or anything, she was just keeping track of her boys. Keeping all of her people in line.'

But it was not only Cass who was clearly keen to keep in touch. Cass would often leave the motel bar early saying that she had to be back in her room at a certain time because Denny was due to call or else she would find little handwritten notes saying 'Thinking of you' which Denny had left in dressing rooms if the Halifax Three had played the same college towns the night before.

This, Cass believed, was clearly a romance that she hoped would develop, and during the Christmas break of 1963, she and Jim flew to Toronto to visit Denny and Zal, who had briefly returned home.

After the strain of the last few months with Tim, being in Canada felt like a huge relief and any afternoon or evening would usually involve someone picking up a guitar whilst whoever was around sang or harmonised with them. Cass and Jim soon found that Denny's warm, mellifluous tenor harmonised beautifully with their voices, and as it was by this time becoming clear in both their minds that their relationship with Tim could not continue much longer, and Denny was also looking for an alternative to the Halifax Three, he seemed an ideal replacement for Tim. Denny was also a much more laid-back personality than Tim, and it seemed to Cass and Jim that with him in the band, they could be a group again rather than a duo with a leader. 'Denny blended with us well in so many ways,' says Jim, 'personality-wise, vocally and everything that we were doing. He was right down there *with* us, being *part* of it, not trying to be like Tim was.'

There was also the question of musical direction as musically their sound had evolved since Tim had first whisked Cass off to Chicago. Suddenly, there was a new English group who people in Canada were calling the most exciting thing since Elvis. They had apparently already caused hysteria in Britain and, although they had yet to erupt into America, most musicians who had heard them realised how significant they would be.

Forty years on since the Beatles captivated the world, it is often hard to fully appreciate the enormity of their initial impact, both musically and socially. While folk had remained the dominant music of choice for discerning teenagers, particularly in America, the major stars of the folk movement such as Peter, Paul and Mary and Joan Baez, whilst being vastly successful commercially, lacked the charismatic sexuality which differentiates the celebrity from the superstar. Whilst Joan Baez may have symbolised the protest movement, and so in theory carried the subversive charge of dissent, her virginal, holier-than-thou image meant that it was essentially a virtuous dissent and lacked the charge to capture the imagination of a nation in the way that Elvis had. The Beatles on the other hand not only sang infectious pop songs which daringly introduced electric instruments and a back-beat to what were still essentially folk and blues harmonies, but performed them with such unrestrained euphoria and energy that by the end of 1964 there were few in the Western world who were not, at the very least, aware of the Beatle phenomenon.

Their personal demeanour was also completely at odds with the way showbiz personalities were expected to behave. They were cheeky, irreverent, witty and relaxed, and although they had a manager, it was clear that these were strong-minded individuals with opinions of their own, who would not only speak their mind, but wrote their own songs. And it was this last aspect, more than anything else, which would have the most dramatic and lasting effect on the music industry as a whole.

When Cass heard the sounds of 'Love Me Do' and 'Please Please Me' bursting out of the Toronto jukeboxes, she thought they were quite simply the most exciting thing she had ever heard. 'Cass really had a good ear for anything: literature as well as films,' Zal Yanovsky told me over a delightful and hilarious lunch at his Kingston restaurant Chez Piggy only a few days before he died of a heart attack in December 2002. 'She was a smart woman! So when she saw the Beatles she sort of took it all in and said, "These aren't just four little guys in suits – they look cute but these lyrics are good and *boy* you can dance to it! It's not moon, June, spoon – there's something going *on* here."'

For Cass, the Beatles also had the added attraction of hailing from her favourite country. 'Cass was a big Anglophile,' remembers Denny. 'Dunhill and the *Queen*,' he says in mock English accent, laughing, 'and all of that sort of thing! She loved all that. She could *relate*. And I'm a Canadian. So when Cass first met me it was, "Oooh! Where from?" "Halifax, Nova Scotia." "*Ooooh*, it's close to England! It's in the Commonwealth!"' he laughs.

Englishness aside, Cass and Jim were also both struck by this stunningly new sound of electrified instruments and recognised the importance of what would evolve into folk rock. It seemed obvious to the two of them therefore that this was the direction they needed to go in. Denny and Zal meanwhile, felt the same and, as Yanovsky had already discovered his way round an electric guitar, gradually the idea developed of involving not only Denny but Zal into a new, extended and indeed amplified Big 3.

By the time Cass and Jim arrived back home in New York from Toronto, the seeds of Beatle fever were beginning to be sown in America as news broke of the group's imminent arrival in the US. On 8 February 1964 the band landed at the newly named Kennedy airport amid the now legendary scenes of screaming hysteria from what appeared to be half the female teenage population of New York. The band were scheduled to appear on the *Ed Sullivan Show* the following night.

The Beatles would in fact become an enormous influence on Cass and the others' musical direction, while John Lennon would become one of the enduring minor obsessions of Cass's life, but for the time being, the Big 3 in their existing incarnation featuring Tim were very much ongoing and, as well as a steady stream of concert bookings and TV appearances, there was also the prospect of recording a second album.

By the spring of 1964, when the Big 3 went into New York's Gotham Studios to record a new album, the atmosphere was fraught at best. Having mastered the basic three-part harmony arrangements of their by now extensive folk repertoire, Cass and Tim were eager to branch out and progress musically. Folk was still the predominant popular style, so, as far as Cass was concerned, the only way to work within it was to experiment with the time signatures and explore more complex harmony structures and arrangements. 'How about a little five/four?' she would suggest to Tim and Jim, trying to edge things into a jazzier direction, and the harmonies on tracks like 'Down in the Valley' and 'Ana Fia (Feher)', although not jazz as such, had more dissonance and stronger intervals and were clearly heading in that direction.

Ironically Tim was equally keen to progress, but disagreed when it came to the details of how. Both he and Cass knew that they needed to involve a more dynamic, percussive sound but while Tim veered towards the bluesier style which he would later explore in his own solo work, Cass was more interested in a Beatles-style hybrid of pop and folk. The result was a constant tug of war with Tim saying 'I wanna do it this way', while Cass insisted that she wanted to do it '*that* way' and it went downhill from there.

Cass, meanwhile, also found other ways to express her discontentment with the situation. 'Cass was a *great* talent and I *loved* her singing,' says Bob Bowers, 'but her attitude could be *very* unprofessional. She was just difficult to deal with. Like being late *all* the time. If rehearsal was at ten o'clock in the morning, she might show up at eleven or eleven thirty. They always started two or three hours late because Cass would show up late and then she couldn't sing because she hadn't eaten, so she would order a half dozen hamburgers and a few shakes and several orders of French fries and proceed to eat *very* quickly. And then of course she couldn't sing because she was so full. So then we would sit around and wait till she felt she could sing. And then they would do a take and she'd start whining saying, "I can't sing today, my voice hurts, I've got to go to Chicago and have nodes removed from my vocal chords." That was a very popular thing at the time and a lot of the girl singers were always doing that, but with her it came from being tense and insecure. She was just an *enormously* insecure human being and she made up for it by being arrogant and belligerent and egocentric. So I would say, "Cass, we've got the studio booked. We're here. You've *got to* sing." So eventually it got done and she did manage to find ways to make it work. But it was that sort of thing. And *constantly. All* the time.'

Despite these problems the album was eventually finished, and alongside their debut, *The Big 3 – Live at the Recording Studio*, does exactly what good albums of that era generally do, which is to provide an aural snapshot of the Big 3 at their performance best. The album includes the single 'Come Away Melinda' and is the standard folk blend of traditional ballads – some better known than others – and more bluesy numbers such as 'Wild Women'. As with the previous album, they were augmented by Bob Bowers on stand-up bass as well as drums and electric guitar and their rocking version of 'Grandfather's Clock' hints at the more driven sound that, within a year, everyone would be adopting in the wake of the Beatles. At the time, however, as the album had ended up as such a compromise of ideas, neither Cass, Tim or Jim were too pleased with the result.

When the new record was released in June 1964, as with the first album, it suffered from poor distribution and, as it turned out, the first earnings any of them would see would not appear till some forty years later when Cass's by this time adult daughter pursued the record label for back earnings. But at the time, the Big 3's lack of chart success seemed proof of the necessity for the band to move on musically. Cass and Jim knew exactly the direction they wanted to go in and, since their trip to Canada, knew who they wanted to do it with. Denny and Zal were keen to join them and try something new and Roy Silver fully supported the idea of this new combo and so had agreed to continue managing Cass and Jim on that basis. Relations with Tim, meanwhile, had by this time crumbled to the extent that it seemed clear to all of them that the Big 3, as they stood, had very little future. As Jim remembers it, 'Cass and I had a desire to go on and do something else and Tim was really getting worse and worse and bucking it and finally it got to the point where Cass and I just quit. We said to Tim, "This is not working out and we want out."'

The Big 3 played their final gig in late April at a large auditorium at

Fall River State College, Massachusetts. They had always drawn good audiences at college shows and this was no exception, but after the show Tim walked into the dressing room, seemingly aware that their days together were over. 'Well, that's it,' he said. 'Yeah,' said Cass and Jim, 'let's call it a day.' And with that, the Big 3, as it had been, officially came to an end.

Cass's time with the Big 3 had lasted little more than eighteen months in all, but it had transformed her life altogether. The group may never have achieved the commercial success they had hoped for, but their brief time together had launched Cass's musical career and gained her access to a community which, both musically and personally, would remain central to her life.

9

It's got a backbeat, you can't lose it

'We were all in love with Cass at one time or another,' says John Sebastian. 'Cass had a wonderful kind of funny, savoir faire quality about her mixed in with a kind of snugly friendliness that was *contagious*. Her warmth came through for us and we all cared *very much* for her, whether we would simply pantomime it for other people or for jokes or whether it was private – we all felt it and we were all under her spell. Zally in particular. Zally and Cass were always like climbing on each other and it was sort of more silliness with them than actual amorous chemistry. They had another kind of chemistry. But nobody was immune to Cass's charms.'

Cass's capacity to inspire this kind of devotion would prove to be one of the central ironies of her life; whilst she yearned for conventional romantic love from a boyfriend or lover, she was probably much more genuinely loved by the men closest to her than many of the more traditionally attractive and sexually desirable women she envied. Within a year of arriving in Greenwich Village, she had come to occupy a unique position in the heart of many of the most sought-after men in folk, and the close friendships she had developed with Sebastian and Zal Yanovsky, like her relationship with David Crosby, would continue through most of her life. But rather than just revelling in her friends' affection, Cass played an active role in creating the situations and relationships around her. She had an uncanny ability to bring like-minded friends together and she would play a major role in the formation of not one but two major groups of the sixties. It was little surprise she was called 'the Gertrude Stein of her generation'.

*

Cass had first met John Sebastian when he was a roving guitarist accompanying Valentine Pringle – a calypso-singing protégé of Harry Belafonte's who had often been on the same bill as the Big 3. He, like almost everyone else, had been immediately impressed by Cass's wit and talent and Cass was likewise charmed by this attractive, intelligent and charismatic young New Yorker. They became immediate friends and close confidants, but as with David Crosby and several of the other important male friendships of her life, their relationship similarly crossed into that often magical but nameless land of eternal possibility which hovers somewhere between friendship and romance.

Decades on, Sebastian is still recording and touring as a solo artist but on a sweltering July afternoon, in shorts and loose polo shirt, he met me at the Village Green in Woodstock and drove us back to his rambling home, nestled in a clearing amongst the lush surrounding forestland. For the next few hours as we sat amongst the casually strewn guitars and bean bags sipping iced water, Sebastian talked with a mixture of protectiveness, insight and love about his memories of Cass and her unique role in Village life.

'She had what I would consider to be a bit of a salon – a really cool drawing room of the sixties,' he remembers. 'Because whether she was living in a rented funny space somewhere or the more opulent digs of the later days when pop stardom afforded her a nice house on the side of a hill, there were always amazing catalytical things happening in her living room or swimming pool.'

Cass's insightful introductions would eventually lead Sebastian and Yanovsky to their next project the following year. 'The Lovin' Spoonful grew out of a meeting which Cass very much arranged at the apartment she had in New York. She said, "Now, John, I want *you* to come and watch the Beatles on Ed Sullivan with *me*." I said, "Fine." She said, "And by the way – Ringo will be there." I said, "*Ringo*?" She said "Yeah." I said, "OK." Because when Cass said those things I frequently believed her because somehow or another she would probably pull this off. So she opened the door a few nights later and sure enough there was a very Ringo-like fellow with a prominent nose and a *lot* of hair, except that he was *very tall*. And we sat around and got acquainted and it was Zal Yanovsky and we had actually met once before, but what was important was that Cass really provided us with a very low-key setting in which what happened was, "Oh, somebody left a guitar here. John – here play this," and suddenly there were two guitars out and Zally and I were able to play together and discover that there was a tremendous affinity.'

The apartment Sebastian remembers was a small but comfortable townhouse flat on Irving Place near Gramercy Park, which Roy Silver had rented for her, and compared with the mostly cockroach-ridden hotel rooms which the majority of Village musicians were living in, it was positively palatial. The flat looked out onto a private garden square which Cass loved and would often spend time walking in as, being a resident, she was entitled to her own key. Although only sparsely furnished with a bed, on which people would lie to watch TV, and very little else, the apartment was nevertheless good for entertaining, but as with most other aspects of her life, Cass was not a typical hostess. She had never been keen on housework and the atmosphere wherever she lived was generally one of barely organised chaos with a guaranteed pile-up of dirty dishes in the sink. But that never really seemed to matter. 'It was pretty funky,' remembered Yanovsky. 'Cass was really messy, so there were always bits of food and beer bottles all around, but she was a *wonderful* hostess and incredibly generous. There was always food and drink and you could crash there and it was right by Gristede's – a great deli in New York. Cass loved to eat and so did I, so that was another thing that sort of drew us together and we always used to get smoked turkey legs which are really good if you're stoned!' he laughed.

The turkey legs and food also came in handy for Cass and Zal's relentless games. 'We were very physical together,' remembered Zal affectionately. 'Kind of like demented siblings I would say. I didn't want to go to bed with her or anything and I don't think she wanted to go to bed with me necessarily. It was very brotherly sisterly – but more so. Slightly incestuous brothers and sisters in a way! She was a very, very pretty woman slash girl and she had *beautiful*, long auburny hair and we used to play 'Captive Hair' where I used to close it in the windows of cars and hang mustard jars or chicken bones or little bits of food in it and sort of fool around. I had quite a hair fetish! And she was very happy to participate. She was just great!'

Over the next year, both Yanovsky and Sebastian would, along with Denny and Jim Hendricks, become not only Cass's closest friends but also her working colleagues and the coming months would be some of Cass's most fulfilled.

*

The Beatles' debut performance on the *Ed Sullivan Show* was watched by an estimated 73 million viewers and statistics later showed that during the group's time on screen not one single crime was committed by a teenager throughout America. The Beatles subsequently proceeded to ambush the American charts to such an extent that almost every American musician was left quivering in their wake.

During April of 1964 every one of the top five positions in the singles charts was held by the Beatles, and in the album charts their presence was no less evident. By the end of May, the group's first American albums *Meet the Beatles* and *Introducing the Beatles* had held the number one and number two spots for no less than nine weeks, only to be overtaken by *The Beatles Second Album*, which by the time it was released had amassed over two million advance orders.

It was a staggering coup for a British group and it is easy to see why the wave of British bands who followed them into the American charts over the next few months came to be known as the 'British Invasion'. As far as Americans were concerned, they had invented rock and roll. It had grown out of American rhythm and blues, had been made universally popular by Elvis - an American - and all over the world, musicians from Cliff Richard to Johnny Halliday had become stars by imitating him. The very idea of a British band forging ahead therefore and taking this essentially American genre by the scruff of its neck and moulding it into something new was, in every sense of the word, revolutionary.

As a result it was soon obvious to most that folk, as it had been, was on its way out, and suddenly the Village was filled with musicians looking for ways to update and, literally, electrify their sound. 'Things changed because of the Beatles,' remembers Denny. 'Suddenly it was, "We gotta do this English thing. This thing is coming, it's gonna overtake everybody and we gotta get ready."'

Most people were not quite sure how they were going to do it, however, and Cass and Jim initially started rehearsing with Zal and Denny to adapt the Big 3's existing act to become Cass Elliot and the Big 3. Since first hearing the Beatles, Cass had wanted to 'go electric' and so the plan was therefore to work out fuller, more up-tempo arrangements driven by Denny's newly acquired electric bass. Cass had also roped in John Sebastian to play harmonica, as at this point he was only a floating accompanist without a regular group. In terms of songs though, their starting point was still the folk-based material that they all already knew, but gradually they started introducing newer, edgier songs by friends such as Felix Pappalardi and Fred Neil whose 'Tear Down the Walls' soon became a staple of their repertoire.

As rehearsals progressed, the new group became more polished and they played a couple of gigs at the Bitter End, but audiences expecting to see more or less the same Big 3 act as before were surprised to find a new set, complete with electric bass, which, regardless of the Beatles, was still, as far as the Village folk audiences were concerned, sacrilege.

Roy Silver, on the other hand, who was still managing Cass and Jim, felt differently. He believed in what they were doing and suggested they go see his partner, Bob Cavallo, the owner of the Shadows for whom Cass and Jim had unsuccessfully auditioned the previous year as the Big 3. Situated on M Street in the heart of Georgetown's cobbled streets and colonial eighteenth-century mansions, the Shadows had by this time become a beacon in the folk community and a kind of central casting pool for talent. Everyone seemed to have played there at some point, and John and Michelle Phillips would even hold their wedding reception there, so this was potentially an important step for the new group. Cavallo could now see Cass and the new group's potential and he immediately offered to hire them for the rest of the summer. What was more he would put them up in an apartment hotel and give them a weekly salary as well as a 1961 Buick Le Sabre to get around in. How much better could things get?

Cass's kudos in the Village, meanwhile, meant that various managers aside from Silver would have been more than happy to take her on, and so, clearly wanting to keep her happy, Silver paid for her to have new chiffon gowns and her hair professionally coiffed while the rest of the group received new guitars, amps and suits.

As the band now had a new booking and a new sound, it seemed only fitting that they should also have a new name. In the wake of the Beatles, all the old Big 3 and Halifax Three-type names were beginning to seem like yesterday's news, and one evening as the group was rehearsing, their friend Erik Jacobsen happened to remark, 'You guys sound like a bunch of thundering Mugwumps.' It sounded like the perfect new Beatles-type name and so the Mugwumps they became. The name was also apposite in terms of the band's hybrid folk rock style as it originally dated from the American Revolution and referred to someone whose allegiance was divided between the new state and

King George, thereby having their 'mug' on one side of the fence and their 'wump' on the other. The band themselves were unaware of this but the name sounded great and that was all that mattered. 'We were the Mugwumps,' says Denny, 'and as far as Cass was concerned, she was from somewhere near London.'

And so Cass packed up her things from Gramercy Park, and in the summer of 1964 the newly named Mugwumps headed off for Washington, DC.

Finding themselves with a new nightly slot to fill, the Mugwumps now needed to expand their repertoire and gradually they began to introduce blues numbers like Bo Diddley's 'You Can't Judge a Book By Its Cover' as well as songs like 'Silver Threads, Golden Needles' by Britain's own pop-folk hybrid the Springfields, featuring Cass's heroine Dusty Springfield. Cass rightly considered herself on par with Dusty Springfield vocally, and in many ways they had much in common; their voices both combined that rare blend of strength and power with vulnerability and heart, and yet whilst they were contemporaries (Dusty was only two years older than Cass), their careers took very different routes. But at this early point, Dusty was already a star and Cass clearly saw her as a rival.

With the Mugwumps, unlike the Big 3, Cass now found herself with an open platform for her musical ideas and gravitated towards a role as the group's natural musical leader. 'We'd sit and bang out arrangements with Jim playing the guitar and Cass would come up with notes for people to sing, because nobody knew about [reading] *music*,' remembers Denny. 'So there were these rehearsals that went on and on and on and then we'd go down to the club and pick up the instruments and work on the material.'

Although technically untrained, they were nevertheless all experienced musicians by this time, and Cass and Jim, inspired by the Beatles' ability to pen their own hits, decided to try writing themselves. 'We heard that stuff the Beatles were doing,' explains Jim, 'and we said, "*We* can do that," and started fooling around with it and it came very quickly and very easily really.' Jim would generally work out the music while Cass wrote the lyrics but essentially it was a collaborative effort, and in under an hour the pair of them had come up with their first song – 'Everybody's Been Talking'. This and another song – 'Here It Is

Another Day' both appeared on the Mugwumps' only album – *The Mugwumps: An Historic Recording* and both would sit perfectly on any Merseybeat album of the time, if not one of the Beatles' own.

A mid-tempo ballad with backbeat, 'Everybody's Been Talking' sounds like typical early Beatles and the lyrics also stand comparison with any similar song of the time. They tell the tale of someone who's been rejected by a lover whom friends disapprove of but who remains doggedly determined to win back the lover's affection regardless. Whether Cass was thinking of herself is uncertain and Jim believes the lyrics were invented purely for the purpose of the song, but if the scenario was not based on experiences Cass had already had, it was certainly prophetic of ones she would have in the future.

Everybody's been talking / You don't love me no more
I don't wanna believe them / I've heard that before

My friends just ignore me / They laugh and call me the fool
I smile and say they're all mistaken / You couldn't be so cruel

'Here It Is Another Day', meanwhile, another gentle Beatle-ish ballad, described the temporary loss of a lover who has gone away. The scenario itself was far from groundbreaking but although the song was sung primarily by Jim and Denny and referred to a female lover, it was also almost certainly something Cass herself related to: '"Here it is another day,"' they sang. '"I feel like running away / Can't remember when I felt so sad ... She's been gone so long / Since she's gone everything's wrong / Now I've lost the only love I had."'

Musically the Beatles' influence was equally clear. Having seen the newly released film *Hard Day's Night*, the band had persuaded Roy Silver to buy Zal a gleaming new twelve-string guitar – the origin of George Harrison's twang on both the title song and the rest of the Beatles' accompanying album. This was the sound which would also be famously adopted by the Byrds, but it was similarly evident in the Mugwumps' songs, particularly the guitar break in the middle of 'Everybody's Been Talking'. The final requirement for the Beatles sound, meanwhile, was, of course, a backbeat and so the Mugwumps had acquired a drummer.

In folk circles the very idea of having a drummer was still considered virtually blasphemous so, unsurprisingly, when it came to finding one, Cass was the only one in the band who even knew a drummer. With her knowledge of the Village's jazz haunts, Cass had come across Art Stokes, the nephew of jazz supremo Art Blakey, and persuaded him to come along to Washington, DC with the Mugwumps.

The addition of Stokes as well as John Sebastian on harmonica now brought the band total to six, and so in an attempt to somehow convince the public that the Mugwumps were in fact a Beatles-style four-piece, Cavallo insisted that Cass, Denny, Zal and Jim appear centre stage, while, bizarrely, Sebastian and Art Stokes sit behind them in opposite back corners of the stage. With hindsight, the positioning of Stokes, who was black, could be viewed in a racial context on the basis that racially mixed groups were still virtually unheard of at that time, but given that Sebastian was similarly set aside, this doesn't seem to have been the major factor. But regardless of their rather incongruous stage grouping, the band's new repertoire and stage patter made them an immediate hit with the Shadows' audiences.

Leads on songs were generally taken either by Cass or Denny or shared between them and Jim, with Zal adding backing and harmonies. With her adored friends Denny, Zal and Sebastian now in her group as well as Jim, the friendship and humour amongst them was similarly evident in their act. Particularly with Denny. 'They could have been just Cass and Denny,' remembered Zal. 'It would have been quite mind-blowing really without everybody else. Because they were just very *similar* onstage in that they didn't have to *do* anything except just open their mouths and sing. And quip, very easy, relaxed. I remember once we played the Buffalo War Memorial Auditorium and they were just spieling and schmoozing onstage and Denny said, "Do you know which war this would be dedicated to?" and she said, "Oh. The war on poverty." It was just *boom* and it took off! They were sort of like George Burns and Gracie Allen. Very, very funny.'

Tales of the Shadows' new resident band spread quickly through Georgetown and the group soon had a small army of fans not only inside the club but outside too. As the club sold alcohol many were too young to be allowed in and Cass had noticed a bevy of young girls who would regularly sit outside the club, squeezing their faces up against the window. She therefore suggested to Cavallo that the group play Saturday mornings as a special teenagers' show serving only soft drinks and that afterwards they go up to the lounge and offer them an autograph-signing 'meet the band' session. Cavallo agreed.

The Mugwumps' new fans had also noticed them on the streets of

Georgetown as much for their appearance as anything else. Over the previous few months, Denny, Zal, Jim and John had all grown their hair in the style of the Beatles, which was still considered extravagantly long, and hence controversial, and the combination of these avant-garde looking musicians with a large, flamboyant female singer and a black drummer was considered unusual to say the least. 'It was like, "Who are these freaks with the long hair and this big fat woman?" says Denny. 'And Zal looked like Ringo so Cass was telling everybody, "I have *Ringo*." And they're going, "Really? What's he doing with *you*?" And then chasing after Zal, running down the streets like something from *A Hard Day's Night*. It was *crazy*!'

Cass christened the band's new fans 'teenyboppers' – a term which John Sebastian believes Cass invented, but making up words and phrases had by this time become part of everyday Mugwump life. Cass and Zal had heard blues musicians like Sonny Terry and Brownie McGhee use the black vernacular which had grown out of the Mississippi delta and, along with their friend Bill Cosby, had evolved their own comic version into a whole new Mugwump language of their own. Even shopping lists were written in Mugwump and eggs consequently became 'ebth', while the other items on the list were similarly renamed. 'It was *relentless*,' says Sebastian. 'You couldn't *escape* it. Cass would be running this *all day* and after thirty times of somebody being asked, "Wod you 'ave any doe?" You start to say: "I wasn't avin havin any doe," and so you just kind of pick up on it in a *joking* way and that was always her way *to* you. Through jokes.'

Cass and Denny would continue to use Mugwump speak with each other throughout Cass's life as a kind of private, shared code. Some of it even survives on the end of 'Dancing in the Street', on the Mamas and the Papas' second album *Cass, John, Michelle, Dennie* (Denny's name was accidentally misspelt), and you can hear just how much fun they're having.

Cass and Denny had also recently discovered another source of fun. It was called LSD. Lysergic acid diethylamide, or acid as it became popularly known, had been discovered by Swiss scientist Albert Hoffman in the forties and now, following extensive research by the CIA, was being championed by Harvard professors Timothy Leary and Richard Alpert. The pair were both evangelical about the drug as a shortcut to enlightenment for the individual and a conduit for positive change in society as a whole, and Leary would go on to become the unofficial High Priest of acid and the hippie generation with his credo to 'Turn on, Tune in and Drop out' but at the start of the decade, acid was still a relatively well-kept secret.

Few people knew about it at this point in 1964, apart from those well-connected enough to know Leary and be invited to the research centre he had set up at Millbrook, a turreted mansion in upstate New York where the professor was gradually 'turning on' a succession of key figures in the New York arts world. Allen Ginsberg was one of the first to be inducted, and through his close friendships within the jazz world, it was in fact jazz musicians Thelonious Monk, Dizzy Gillespie and John Coltrane rather than rock or folk musicians who were the first to try LSD.

But Cass, ever at the forefront of any new development, knew Leary too and, even more usefully perhaps, someone that worked in his laboratory, and so had access to a ready supply of the purest acid. The Mugwumps had, like most of their friends, long been using diet pills and amyl nitrate to keep awake for the long hours of daily practice sessions followed by nightly gigs and the inevitable round of parties and drinks, but this was something new and seemingly much more exciting. With the exception of Jim Hendricks who kept resolutely straight as a dye, the rest of the group took every opportunity they could to experiment with the fantastically colourful, kaleidoscopic hallucinatory visions induced by this new drug. But before too long it was noticed that Cass in particular seemed to be having just a little too much fun.

During a particularly vivid acid 'trip' Cass decided that a jar of mustard was just what she needed to do some hand paintings on the walls of the Arlington Park Towers apartment Silver had rented for her. Soon the walls of not only the bathroom and kitchen but the living room and hall were covered with clouds, birds and trees all colourfully painted in vivid mustard yellow and this would certainly have proved highly decorative had the landlords not arrived the following day and promptly evicted Cass for what they termed 'slovenly living'.

But for Cass, finding somewhere else to live in DC was not a problem and years later she and Denny would come to look back on these times as some of the happiest of both their lives. 'We were like a bunch of otters,' says Denny, having a great time sliding down through the water and thrashing with each other and leaping and bounding about. Laughing and playing and running about like a bunch of puppies. All except Jim who was like the big brown owl, sitting up in the branch watching us and going, "Oh, Jees!"' he laughs.

For Cass, being a successful, professional singer had brought with it many of the things she had always wanted: pretty clothes, respect and, perhaps most importantly, love and affection from the type of men who, in her earlier life, she would rarely have had the chance to come close to. Cass had always loved the company of attractive men but had previously had little opportunity to enjoy it. This was now something else which her new career and life had made possible. 'Cass and I talked about this a lot,' remembers folk singer Judy Henske, 'because it was apparent, I think, to both of us that the only freedom you could have as a woman would be as a girl singer, because we both saw the movies a lot and at that time there was always like Claire Trevor or Peggy Lee playing a girl singer on the screen, who was usually alcoholic, right? But you didn't think of ending up like that ever and this was the *only* woman in the movie that anyone ever paid attention to! And the only one that ever got to wear cute clothes!' she laughs. 'And it was *obviously* a way to get men! It was a role model for hell-cat women, women who didn't want to toe the line and the hell-cat women all became girl singers.'

Cass would have several close female friendships throughout her life, but they were intermittent, and during the coming years, her closest companions were generally male. It was natural for Cass to enjoy being surrounded by men but there were also other reasons why she preferred their company. 'Men are much more honest than women,' she told the *Daily Express* in 1974. 'Most women like to have me around because it makes them feel attractive.' With Cass's male friends, it would be them who made her feel attractive.

Although, for the time being, she was back in Washington, DC, this new life she was living was as far as it was possible to get from her old high school life as the ostracised outsider. The genuine love and affection Cass felt from Sebastian, Zal, Denny and Jim was like a warm blanket, protecting her from the sneering hostility that she had so often felt in the past. It also, albeit temporarily, muffled her insecurity and made her feel that if she was going to become a real star, as she had always believed she could, she would no longer have to do it alone. She could now do it with the support of what felt like her new family. As the sixties progressed more and more young people would similarly embrace this idea of creating an alternative 'family' of one's choice, moving away from the traditional social norms of the forties and fifties in which the transition between the parental home and the creation of one's own family had been almost uninterrupted. In this, as with so many aspects of her life, Cass was once again ahead of her time.

But for all her new-found contentment there were still moments when her old insecurities would inevitably return and when, for all the affection she was receiving, the lack of romantic attention, particularly from Denny, would rankle. It was almost no surprise therefore that her thoughts soon returned to a friend of Zal's, a tall, good-looking young actor cum blues singer whom she had met in Toronto, called Marc Strange.

Strange, who Zal remembered as 'a big, powerful hunk who looked kind of like Duane Eddy on steroids', like most other people, could hardly fail to notice Cass. He was clearly taken with her in every way. Strange would later go on to write the hit Canadian TV series *The Beachcombers* and still vividly remembers that first meeting with Cass. 'The first time I met her,' Strange tells me, 'she'd just had a bath and was wrapped in towels and, *gee* – she had wonderful hair! My first recollection is watching her comb out this incredible long, thick auburn hair and you got the impression she was maybe a little vain about it but I remember she was drying it with a towel, lovingly. And I liked her straight away. First of all she was incredibly bright and funny and she had a lot of presence. Also she and Zal obviously loved each other and could banter rather nicely so it was very entertaining to be in their company and she made a big impression.'

A few months after this first meeting, Strange had come to stay with Zal in New York and had clearly not forgotten Cass. 'By that time I was really quite taken with her,' continues Strange. 'So I made a pass at her, which I think she appreciated. She liked attention and she enjoyed that, so we started hanging out and she and I had a little love affair.'

Cass did indeed appreciate the attention and was thrilled to have a boyfriend who was not only attractive but who genuinely admired her in every way. 'I always thought she was *quite* beautiful,' says Strange. 'She always struck me . . . I don't know how to phrase this right but there was something like a big baby about her because she was kind of dewy: her hands and her feet and her lips especially. She had this wonderful cupid's bow mouth and beautiful, very pink, very clear skin and very smooth and lovely thick hair.'

Cass was also no less attracted to Strange herself. Although she was still unashamedly in love with Denny, she thought Marc was quite wonderful, and friends immediately noticed that Strange was clearly her latest crush. While it was fun to be surrounded by friends like Zal, Denny and Jim, with Marc she now had a real boyfriend of her own, not to mention a handsome beau to escort her around Greenwich Village. 'Cass liked to promenade,' remembers Strange, 'to walk through the Village, and she was somewhat regal in the way she moved, quite queenly. She adopted a kind of Mae West, grande dame manner in public.'

Being with Strange had given Cass a new lease of confidence. He had courted her, romanced her and told her she was pretty, and Cass was now basking in his attentions. She had always loved dressing up and although her flat may have generally appeared far from immaculate, when it came to clothes, Cass was always impeccably dressed and irrepressibly feminine. 'She liked to be pretty,' recalls Strange, 'and wear nice clothes and to show them off. She'd spend a long time getting ready and she liked to wear slightly over-the-top but very pretty stuff – big hats and pretty scarves and silk and flouncy things. In other words, she didn't wear things to hide her weight. Given her shape, obviously a lot of the clothes she wore had that severe A-line from the neck down but she would top them off with Easter bonnets and shawls and belts and fringes and very lovely boots. I suppose to a certain extent she was also showing me off; I was a good-looking young man in those days, so I imagine there was *some* of that.'

Cass certainly relished every moment that she could parade her handsome new lover through the Village, but she also wanted time with him alone. One particular, rainy New York weekend, Cass made sure they were left to themselves and dragged Strange off to her apartment. 'It was like, "Let's get out of here." Strange laughs. 'And I remember the apartment because it had a lovely, fancy bed, which she plonked dead square in the middle of the living room. She said the only reason she had the apartment in the first place was to sleep there so she might as well have the bed front and centre in the best room in the place!'

When it came to sex, Cass made no less of an impression on the comparatively gauche Strange than she had done in every other department. 'She was very open,' says Strange. 'Being a bit of a country boy at the time I recall being taken aback by her frankness about sex, about romance and relationships. Cass had the first vibrator I'd ever seen.' He laughs. '"What the *hell* is that thing?" I said. "What about *me*?" "Don't worry about it!" she said. "It's the lesbian's best friend!" She also told me she'd had a couple of affairs with women; she wasn't a lesbian but she was definitely,' he pauses, '. . . intrigued by *relationships*, by romance and she was very open and unafraid to express herself. So that was new to me, that I'd be talking to a woman about these things.'

It's possible that Cass may have explored her sexuality with women earlier on in her life and she certainly had several gay friends of both sexes, but given Cass's love of telling a good yarn and even greater love of getting a reaction, it seems equally likely that she was being deliberately provocative with Strange.

The lesbian tales would have been a perfect ruse to avoid someone jumping to the conclusion that a vibrator was perhaps the ideal substitute for an overweight young woman with a shortage of boyfriends. Someone who clearly had a very healthy sexual interest in men but had experimented with bisexuality was, on the other hand, certainly at that time, fascinating, exciting and risqué. This after all was still several years before the hippie ethos of free love and a decade before David Bowie made bisexuality momentarily fashionable. Cass would have known that with a man such as Strange, coming from a small town in 1964, the idea of a woman even having done such things, let alone openly discussing them, was obviously going to trigger a reaction. It would likewise consequently have presented a level of risk; some men in that situation might simply have found it all too much and walked out.

It may also have been an unconscious attempt to sabotage her own fleeting happiness. At this point in her life, Cass had not exactly been inundated with handsome suitors queuing up at her door. She may have recently found several who wanted to be her friends, but not to be her lovers. Here, in contrast, was someone who was perfectly attractive himself but was also attracted to her and liked her for who she was. For someone such as Cass, who beneath the bonnets, shawls and bravado suffered from chronically low self-worth, this may well have provoked feelings of deep unease. In such situations, the underlying fear would have been that she was unworthy of such attention and so she may have been prompted to avert it.

These revelations were also a means of maintaining what was clearly her position of power within the relationship. As the star and the New York sophisticate allied to the small-town ingénue, at some level Cass was certainly also enjoying having the emotional upper hand; it would have been a sharp contrast to the rejections she had felt at Forest Park, which she still resented bitterly, and also more recently the situations with Tim and Denny in which the power balance clearly lay with them rather than her. Later on in her life, Cass would have several other relationships where, as with Strange, she was similarly in control and this would form a pattern over the coming years, but for the time being, shocked though he may have been, Strange was broad-minded enough to stay.

When Strange did subsequently return to Toronto, Cass kept in touch with him and a few months later, when she was playing the Shadows, she called him and invited him to Washington. As Strange's acting work was proving elusive, she said she would even send him a ticket. When Strange arrived, however, he spent more time catching up with his old friend Zal, and it seemed to Cass that perhaps Strange was going to prove as unreliable as so many other men she had known. She was understandably riled but nevertheless whisked him away to Arlington to the self-contained basement of her mother's house where she was now living.

Cass enjoyed Strange's company, but as much as anything else his appeal seemed to lie in the fact that for the first time she had the type of boyfriend who throughout her teenage years she had only ever dreamed of and who had seemed entirely beyond her reach. It was as if, although she was now in her early twenties, she still needed to live out the romantic fantasies of her teens, and just like the high school prom queen she had never been, she took great glee in giving Strange her high school ring – a classic fifties symbol of affection. She seemed as much smitten with the trappings of romance as with love itself and for years afterwards kept a lone cigarette butt that Strange had left in an ashtray.

Inevitably Strange eventually had to go back to Toronto, but their time together had clearly meant a lot to Cass and they stayed friends for the rest of her life. 'We were close enough that we could speak on the phone whenever,' explains Strange. 'There was never any rancour – never any bad feelings or, "You broke my heart," or any of that. We had a fling but out of the fling was a genuine friendship.'

Although Cass would confide in friends like Sebastian and Crosby over the years to come, at this point, perhaps it was because Strange was not part of her regular life and social circle that she could really talk to him about the more personal issues which she did her best to hide from most who knew her. 'We seemed to spend a lot of our time talking,' says Strange. 'Obviously there was some sex involved but we were also very comfortable in each other's company and there were a lot of intimate conversations. I got the feeling that in some ways I let her talk about things that she didn't talk about in the music business so much or in the middle of all the other stuff that was going on – personal stuff: what she thought about being fat, what she thought about her yearnings for Denny Doherty which were unfulfilled. He wouldn't give her the time of day . . . well, he *liked* her a lot but she always yearned for Denny. I was an interlude but I don't think I was really her ideal. There was something about Denny that just made her blossom.'

Being in a group with her closest friends, the Mugwumps brought Cass an environment of support and fun which had long been missing amidst the constant disputes and wrangles with Tim. Cass had built herself a unique and prominent role within the Village, but now the admiration and respect she felt socially had been carried through to her working life. And it felt wonderful. It had also given her the confidence to start writing her own songs with Jim, and although their compositions were more than proficient, with a brief exception much later on in her career, she would never again have the courage to do so and these would be the only songs she would ever write. But this was just further testimony to the support she felt from her fellow Mugwumps. 'The acceptance that Cass had within this community of singers and songwriters,' says John Sebastian, 'was so unconditional that I think that was one of the things that made it her family. There wasn't going to be anybody going, "Hey, fat Ellen Cohen," in this setting – because here this was a safe place.'

This was indeed a safe place, but as the Mugwumps' career progressed, some of the old issues would soon, inevitably, resurface.

10

'I don't go out with freaks'

'I want to look like everybody else and feel like other people,' Cass once told *Ladies Home Journal*, and despite the acceptance and recognition Cass had found from the folk community and the friends around her, her weight was still nevertheless an issue.

Throughout her life people who met her were invariably struck by the fact that, despite her size, Cass was irrepressibly feminine and everything about the way she dressed and behaved seemed to be an expression of the glamorous diva she wanted to be. Cass had always idolised movie stars of the thirties and forties like Vivien Leigh and Greta Garbo, and her continuing tendency to develop crushes on good-looking and frequently unavailable men all seemed part of the romantic dreams and girlishness she had been unable to express as a teenager. 'Cass was like a kid!' remembers her great friend Vanessa Ware (who was Jim Hendricks's girlfriend and later wife and made many of Cass's clothes during her time with the Big 3). 'She loved to play dress-up, she *loved* clothes, shopping, hair and make-up and she was very attracted to things that were edgy rather than punky. That's where that lace collar comes from,' she says, referring to the frills Cass can be seen wearing on the cover of the Big 3's second album. 'She had a huge passion for movie-star stuff like batting of eyelids – she used to do that all the time and her eyes would look up at you in this *innocence* that only Cass could do. And it was all part of this little girl and this desire to be accepted by men as a feminine, beautiful woman. She wanted that acceptance.'

To Cass, it seemed as though an accident of fate had trapped her in an oversize body, and over the next few months, she would once again be inescapably confronted with her weight and the impact it seemed to have on every aspect of her life.

*

In spite of Cass's affair with Marc Strange, her feelings for Denny, far from dwindling, had simply escalated, and it seemed obvious to most who knew her that she was, as Zal put it, 'madly in love with him'. It wasn't that she articulated her feelings as such, it was just something in her manner towards him that people invariably picked up on. 'Cass was so bright, so quick and so funny,' remembers Nurit Wilde, a friend of Zal's from Toronto who had similarly moved to New York and become ensconced in the folk scene, 'but when it came to Denny – she didn't clam up around him or anything like that, that wasn't her style, but there was just a *difference*. Sometimes she'd even put him down a little bit – but you could see that she really cared about him. And Denny was sort of a laid-back, nice guy who would always try to put it off with a little bit of humour.'

It seemed just as obvious why Cass should be in love with Denny. He had by this time grown a short goatee and, as Zal put it, 'was just drop-dead handsome. He looked like D'Artagnan or some sort of swashbuckler guy with a golden voice.' But it was also clear that whilst Denny liked Cass very much, when it came to romance, her weight was a major obstacle. He also had a somewhat hectic social schedule which, whilst it included a variety of women, did not involve Cass. 'Denny was a bit of a rake and a rambling boy,' remembers Marc Strange, 'and so there was always a lot of romance going on and girlfriends popping in and popping out and all kinds of recreational drugs and booze going on, piling into cars in the middle of the night and running into the White Castle for sacks of hamburgers and then onto this thing and that thing. Indefatigable old Denny Doherty!' he adds in mock-Irish accent. 'Always *something* going on!'

Cass was well aware of all this, and indeed his very waywardness was probably part of the appeal, but whilst Denny may have been spending his nights with a variety of other women, his feelings for Cass clearly ran beyond conventional friendship. Just as with Tim beforehand, the intimacy between them often convinced many observers that they were not just friends but lovers. 'There were situations where Cass and Denny were musical partners,' says Sebastian, 'and then all of a sudden they were . . . an item.' But unlike the earlier scenario with Tim, where Cass seemed to have been doing her best to convince people that they were together, in this instance Sebastian's, and no doubt other people's, impressions were as much from Denny as Cass. 'I always felt that this really was a great love for Denny,' explains

Sebastian, 'and I think that other people than me would have assumed it too. Their relationship was starting to overlap into,' he pauses, 'well, you know, there's a certain rhythm that husbands and wives or people that have been together for a long time have. There's just an intimacy of speech and things. It's everything from compliments to criticisms. It's easier to criticise somebody that you love a lot – they know that it comes from a place of love, so she'd be on at him about not getting too drunk or it'd be kind of jocular stuff about clothes between them: "Are you really gonna *wear* that?" or complicity about, "You have to help me meet John Lennon," he says, 'A *recurring* theme!'

But whilst their relationship may have appeared ambiguous to many, including Cass, as far as Denny was concerned the situation was plain. Some months earlier, before they had left for Washington, Denny had visited Cass at the Gramercy Park apartment one evening and Cass had done her best to move the relationship forward, whilst treading a fine line to maintain her dignity and avoid risking their friendship. Denny had arrived in the midst of a snowstorm and Cass, immediately recognising the romance of the eerie twilight sky and snow, suggested they take some acid and go up on the roof. There, amidst the galaxy of the New York skyline, she dragged up her old brown leatherette portable record player and put on the theme tune from *Peyton Place*. It was a scene straight out of one of the Hollywood movies she adored. Or at least so she thought.

'We sit there holding hands in the snowstorm,' remembers Denny, 'and she's telling me this is her favourite piece of music and all she wants,' he says in mock tearful, female sobbing voice, 'is a little Cape Cod house and some kids and the picket fence and the whole thing, and I'm going, "Oh,"' he says in a casual, only vaguely interested, polite-conversation voice, '"I hope you get it. It'd be good for you, Cass." And I'm *so* thick, I'm sitting there going, "Oh, that'd be nice," thinking, What would *I* like to have? Oh . . . a car, a Cadillac convertible or something! That's all that I remember, but it's only in looking back at it now that I see how hard it must have been *for* her to do that. And she did it more than once with me when I look back at it. That was just *one* time. 'Cause she was my *buddy*. We had great *fun* together. But fucking? It never entered my head!'

Denny now concedes that, even on acid, holding Cass's hand in such an obviously romantic situation would almost certainly be seen by her, at some level, as an encouragement to intimacy, 'Mmmmyuh,' he says tentatively, 'but then you have to go the other step, don't you? Who took whose hand when? *I* wouldn't have gone up on the fucking roof by myself! I didn't take her up onto the roof, she took *me* up onto the roof. She was being romantic. She was doing her thing. She had no compunctions about dragging someone up on the roof in a snowstorm and grabbing them by the hand. It was another one of those moments where you get right up to the wire with someone, or *she* was getting right up to the wire with someone, and trying to make something happen that wasn't about to. That was as close as it got.'

Having played the Shadows throughout the summer of 1964, it soon became obvious to the Mugwumps and Bob Cavallo that if they wanted to progress they would need to return to New York. In between their Shadows gigs, they had played occasional support slots opening for America's latest teen idols the Beach Boys and got a taste of playing baseball stadia, complete with the ear-piercing screams of thousands of teenage girls. But if they wanted more than a taste of such fan worship, they clearly needed to look beyond Washington, DC. Cavallo had by this time parted company with Roy Silver and it had been decided that whilst Silver would take Bill Cosby, Cavallo would continue to manage the Mugwumps. By the late autumn Cavallo had therefore got the group a booking back in New York at the prestigious, upmarket Peppermint Lounge.

The Peppermint Lounge was in a different league to the Bitter End and the other dive-like venues on the folk circuit, and the group felt that this was really a step-up in terms of gaining more widespread recognition. Piling their belongings into the Buick, they headed back to New York, this time to the Albert Hotel, one of the most widely used rock 'n' roll lodgings at the time. Situated just off Washington Square in the heart of the Village, the Albert was an old grande dame of a fin de siècle building, complete with ballroom and grand staircase, which had now become somewhat grouchy with old age. In contrast to the earlier comfort of her apartment in Gramercy Park, Cass now had to make do, like the rest of the band, with the less salubrious cockroach-ridden faded grandeur of the Albert. But down at heel as it may have been, the hotel was not without its own charm and came complete with its own cast of eccentrics including Hallelujah, the bellboy and resident artist Noel, who lived on the ground floor and tried to sell his dubious landscapes by hanging them out of the window on the wrought-iron railing around the building.

The group settled into the Albert for the winter and started rehearsals for the Peppermint Lounge. What the group wasn't prepared for, however, was the fact that this audience would have different demands to their Washington, DC counterparts and, after the familiarity of the student-filled Shadows, this was going to be quite a change. The Peppermint Lounge was at this point one of New York's hotter nightspots and the audience was a mix of cool hipsters, celebrities and Upper West siders slumming it in a bid to appear momentarily hip. The music they had been used to was the frenetic Italian rock and roll of the long-since-forgotten Joey Dee and the Starlighters which was designed purely for dancing rather than listening. The arrival therefore of the Mugwumps with their charming but still essentially gentle vocal harmonies was doomed from the start. But, as it turned out, the Peppermint Lounge closed the night after the Mugwumps played there anyway, leaving the group in New York without a gig and no prospect of getting one anytime soon. 'They came back from that Peppermint Lounge gig looking like somebody had gotten killed,' says Sebastian, 'and I spent several days pretty much at the hotel because everybody was going, "Make sure Cass is OK," "Make sure Denny's OK," "Denny's going into a depression." Suddenly we were like making sure that Denny was "aired" once a day because he'd sit up in this room and let the temperature get up to about eighty-five.'

Sebastian himself was no longer in the group by this time, having been fired by Cavallo for being what he considered 'a disruptive influence'. Sebastian and Zal had become inseparable, and according to Cavallo he 'kept instigating Zally to change the music to be really bluesy which I *loved* but wasn't appropriate for Cass and Denny. John was the sideman on harmonica and guitar but he would tell Zal, "That song sucks or *whatever*." So eventually I fired him.'

Cavallo had, meanwhile, been trying to get the group a record deal for some time and a few months earlier had paid for them to go into a New York studio and record some demo tracks for him to take to the record companies. These would eventually be pulled together to form the Mugwumps' one and only album, although it would only be released in 1967 once Cass and Denny had parted company with Zal and Sebastian and found fame in the Mamas and the Papas and the Lovin' Spoonful respectively.

The album is typical of its time and combines the twanging mix of blues, rock and roll and harmony ballads which the Beatles, Stones and Animals and many others were playing at the time. But it also reflects the transitional stage which music was at – these are the teething problems of folk rock captured in time, and the album's occasional rawness also reflects the circumstances in which it was recorded.

The sessions had been squeezed in amongst their nightly sets at the Shadows and hurriedly recorded between the long drive to and from New York. 'We had played five sets the night before in a club,' Cass later explained, 'and then driven two hundred miles, made the demonstration tape and turned straight away round and came back to do a gig. So it wasn't the best quality and we didn't get to double track and do a lot of things that we would have done. But we wrote all our own songs.'

The Mugwumps hadn't in fact 'written all their own songs'. The truth was that although Cass and Jim had written a couple of songs together, these by no means formed the bulk of their repertoire and this was, in the end, a major part of the band's problem. The most ground-breaking aspect of the Beatles was the fact that they wrote their own material, and in their aftermath every record company was looking for groups who could do the same.

Aside from their lack of original material, however, the other main problem with the Mugwumps was that in pop terms they were too late, in folk terms too early and in image terms, just misunderstood. The band weren't rock 'n' rollers – what they were trying to do was their own attempt at what would become American folk rock but they were ahead of their time. The Byrds at this point had yet to release a record, the Lovin' Spoonful were merely an idea in Sebastian and Zal's heads and Bob Dylan wouldn't go 'electric' till the following year.

Their image, meanwhile, seemed equally incomprehensible. 'By the time we got to New York,' remembers Denny, 'it was like: "What are *you* people trying to do here? With the black drummer and the fat broad?" We have this three-hundred pound woman out front and then these freaks with the haircuts. What the fuck is this? People couldn't get their head past the *image*, never mind what the music was!'

The image question had been one of the main concerns for Warner Brothers Records who had initially expressed interest in the group and signed them up for one single. In an attempt to mould the band into what they considered a more palatable image, they therefore suggested to Cavallo that perhaps if the female vocalist lost some weight the band might have more chance of success – and indeed an album deal. 'That was what was holding Warner Brothers back,' remembers Jim, 'just the fact that they loved our sound but they didn't like the way we looked, because of Cass. And they eventually told us so. Nobody wanted to see a fat girl with three young boys.'

According to Tim Rose, who was still in touch with both Cass and Cavallo at this point, Cavallo told him that he had offered to pay for Cass to visit a health clinic to lose weight. 'It was a thirty-day programme,' Tim remembered, 'and it cost seven thousand dollars back then, so for a stranger, I mean somebody who wasn't named your father, to pay for that, that was quite something!' Four decades on, Cavallo is now chairman of Disney's Buena Vista Music Group, having since managed Earth, Wind and Fire, Prince and Alanis Morissette. As we sit in his expansive office at Disney's Los Angeles HQ, Cavallo has only a blurred recollection of this but admits it's certainly possible. 'I wouldn't put it past me at that time, at that age,' he tells me, 'to believe that that was something I could have said because I was developing as a manager. With Cass that was a serious problem for her and it probably shouldn't have been brought up. I don't like that I did it, if I did it. It sounds familiar, though, I have to tell you. It does sound familiar.'

Cass, however, refused the offer and was fully supported by the rest of the band who loved her as she was and quite rightly believed that she should be accepted as such. 'Art Stokes should have been sent somewhere to get fattened up!' laughed Zal. 'He was really skinny! Maybe if they would have fattened us all up, Cass wouldn't have looked so fat! That would have been an easier way of doing it and that would have made more sense!' Sebastian, meanwhile, was equally supportive but Cass tended to dismiss his opinion on the subject. '*Jesus*, don't ask *him*,' Cass would laugh, ''Cause *his* preferences are different.' 'I was a kid in post-war Italy,' explains Sebastian, 'where great big women were a sign of affluence and that you had *everything*, so it was a desirable thing to be. It was admired rather than, "Oh, isn't

Courtesy of Don Levinson

Ellen (second from left), aged fourteen at a friend's bar mitzvah in Alexandria, Virginia.

The Triumvirate. Left to right: Tim Rose, Cass, John Brown.

Courtesy of John Brown

Courtesy of Richard Barton Campbell Collection

Cass taking centre stage with The Big 3.
Left to right: Tim Rose, Cass, Jim Hendricks.

The Mugwumps. Left to right: Zal Yanovsky, Jim Hendricks, Cass and Denny Doherty.

Courtesy of Richard Barton Campbell Collection

Working those harmonies in the studio at Western Recorders.

Author's private collection / Courtesy of Universal

That bathtub shot for the cover of *If You Can Believe Your Eyes and Ears*.

Cass, John, Michelle, Dennie (sic) – the second album with Michelle reinstated in the window after the Jill Gibson episode.

Author's private collection / Courtesy of Universal

Cass settles into her hammock at Summit Ridge.

Author's private collection

'California Dreamin''. The Mamas and the Papas on TV, 1967.

Globe Photos Inc

With Lee Kiefer in London at the
How I Won the War premiere, 1967.

Getty Images

Smiles for the camera as Cass emerges, with Scott Mackenzie, jubilant from her London trial.

A moment's respite from the rock 'n' roll merry-go-round.

Redferns Music Picture Library Ltd

so and so *fat*!" So they'd try to get me out of the *room* about that because my thing was always, "You look *fantastic*! Go put on that silly fucking muumuu again and let's go do a show!"'

But regardless of the support she had amongst her friends, the self-assurance Cass generally displayed was part of the star persona she had created and was only heartfelt when bolstered by the presence and attention of those who she knew genuinely cared for her. Beneath the facade, Cass was clearly conflicted about her weight, and the fact that her size had also been at least partly responsible for the Mugwumps' failure to secure an album deal certainly did not help. Bob Bowers, the Big 3's musical arranger, remembers overhearing a conversation in the Village between Cass and a William Morris agent named Sherman Tenkel which seems indicative of how Cass really felt. 'Sherman was as big as Cass only taller,' says Bowers, 'I mean just a gigantic fat man – a very sweet, nice Jewish boy. And I remember I was coming to work one night at the Bitter End and Cass and Sherman were there and evidently he had just asked Cass to go out on a date. I caught the conversation in passing and she said, "Sherman, if you take me out on a date you're gonna wanna *fuck* me. And anybody who'd wanna fuck me is a freak. And I don't go out with freaks."'

Given that Cass's taste in men invariably tended towards the handsome (and arguably, by definition, slim) types, on this occasion her own size may have provided a convenient get-out clause. However, the intensity of her own self-deprecation suggests that the reality was at least partly also connected to her own low self-worth. In psychotherapist Susie Orbach's landmark work *Fat is a Feminist Issue* (written in 1978 and therefore particularly pertinent to Cass's generation), Orbach details one of the most common aspects of the overweight woman's self-image: 'Responses include . . . feeling like a freak, an outsider, a blob or assuming that whomever one had contact with was doing so out of pity or was also a freak.' This close mirroring of Cass's own words only confirms the distress and sense of alienation her weight clearly caused her. At this point in the early sixties, the whole issue of eating patterns and weight loss was still comparatively unexplored, and for anyone attempting to deal with the matter there was a chronic lack of information. 'Even if I lost all this weight, what would I do with all this skin?' Cass would say to friends, expressing what seemed like a genuine fear. Unsurprisingly perhaps, Cass's diets were therefore nearly always short-lived and after a few weeks, frustrated at the lack of dramatic visible effect, she would simply give up and return to her favourite staples of fried chicken and pizza.

When pressed to discuss the issue, Cass also seems to have had a range of different arguments, one of which she had earlier explained to Tim Rose. 'I want people to love me because they love me and not because I look good,' she had told him. Tim told her he agreed and saw her point but suggested that some men might be put off by her size. 'If you would lose the weight,' he suggested, 'you'd still be the same person, so why don't you do that?' But Cass replied, 'No, I wouldn't be.' The thinking behind this, she explained, was that she thought 'skinny, good-looking people were vacuous, and people like her were not'. Ergo, if she got skinny, she would be vacuous. But Cass was far too intelligent to really believe this. 'The kicker in Cass's life,' believed Tim, 'was that she was so smart that she understood that that thinking was wrong. She was way too smart to believe that. But emotionally she was locked into it.'

With no prospect of an album deal, and no gigs lined up either, the Mugwumps' career seemed well and truly over and in the absence of any new alternatives, Cass, like the others, had no choice but to bide her time at the Albert Hotel and hope that something else would turn up soon.

Without any money to pay the rent, Denny was regularly sent downstairs to see the hotel manageress to offer her payment in kind, but despite their lack of money, there was nevertheless an almost constant party scene at the hotel. Cass, Zal, Denny and Jim and his girlfriend Vanessa were all officially living in the apartment's three bedrooms but guests would regularly include any number of fellow Village folkies such as Tim Hardin, Sebastian, Peter Tork, Barry McGuire and Jerry Yester, any or all of whom would often end up crashed on mattresses on the floor after a night's smoking and singing. 'It was nuts being around them,' Jerry Yester later remembered. 'It was like the "Mad Tea Party". Lots of noise; Cass baking weird and wonderful-smelling illegal baked goods and Zally with no shirt, running around the place joking, playing pranks.'

Parties inevitably evolved into jam sessions and as one of their friends Erik Jacobsen was starting out as a producer and was eager to record anything he could, a few tracks were recorded featuring Cass,

Zal and Jim with Henry Diltz (later renowned as an LA rock photographer) and Jerry Yester – both of the Modern Folk Quartet. Jacobsen had already started producing Tim Hardin and would later produce the Lovin' Spoonful but at the time was ready to prove himself by working on a purely ad hoc basis with whoever happened to be at hand on any given day. The result was a handful of tracks including 'Oh Susanna (The Banjo Song)', which Cass and Jim had earlier recorded in the Big 3, 'Alley Oop' (a Coasters-style hit for the Hollywood Argyles in 1960) and the Kingston Trio's hit 'Tom Dooley' which would eventually surface on the 1999 compilation CD 'The Magic Circle', alongside early Big 3 and Halifax Three tracks. As with the Mugwumps material of the time, in the gutsy treatment of folk standards you can hear the occasionally creaking transition from folk into what would eventually become folk rock. 'Cass sang a couple of songs that I wrote which were just *atrocious*.' Jacobsen laughs. 'But she brought a vim and vigour to it, I'll tell you that! There was one of my songs called "Fun" and I remember she shouted out at the beginning of it, 'Mom, leave us alone, we're trying to have a good *time*!'

Eventually almost everyone involved started developing more serious projects of their own. Sebastian and Zal would soon form the Lovin' Spoonful but at this point, nobody, especially Cass, knew exactly what they were going to do next. Then Denny got an unexpected call from John Phillips.

Cass and Denny knew Phillips from the folk circuit and Cass also knew him as another local Alexandria kid made good. Although six years older than Cass, John, who died in 2001 of heart failure, had also attended George Washington High School and was known locally as leader of the successful folk combo the Journeymen. After a troubled childhood, dominated by an alcoholic naval officer father, Phillips had formed the Journeymen whilst still in his late teens. The group had originally been a trio, comprising Phillips, vocalist Phil Blondheim (later Scott Mackenzie) and a banjo player. Since Blondheim had left, however, John had replaced him with his gorgeous seventeen-year-old wife Michelle, a Californian model. John had previously been married and had two small children but, after being pursued by Michelle, had left his family, married her and, regardless of the fact that she had no previous experience as a singer and no particularly remarkable vocal talent, incorporated her into the group. And so the New Journeymen were born. But despite the addition of Michelle, when John got a two-week booking in DC opening for Bill Cosby, he realised that he still needed a tenor to replace Blondheim. He and Michelle had got to know Denny on the *Hootenanny* Tour when Denny was still in the Halifax Three and knowing he was now effectively without a gig, he seemed the perfect choice.

From Cass's point of view, in the light of the Mugwumps' communal poverty at the Albert Hotel, the prospect of paid work for even one of them was a godsend and so Denny was duly despatched to the Phillipses. As she would later explain, 'The Mugwumps were hungry and we heard that John needed a tenor for his group. Our group was breaking up, so we got Denny all cleaned up and sent him over to John's house.'

Denny got the job and after a marathon three-day rehearsal session fuelled by copious quantities of Eskatrol diet pills, Denny, John and Michelle had rehearsed the entire New Journeymen repertoire ready for the dates the following weekend.

Cass's time with the Mugwumps had given her the opportunity to combine the two things she loved most: singing and being with her friends but her weight had once again become a problem and would continue to be an issue, both on a professional and romantic level. Musically, meanwhile, the group's core mix of Cass and Denny's voices had already proved a powerful combination but the formula was not yet right. Cass had no idea just how significant Denny's new job would prove for her, as well as him, but in the meantime, she would soon find herself taking a different direction altogether. For the time being at least.

11

Sing for your supper

As first meetings go, Cass's initial encounter with John and Michelle Phillips was memorable in every respect. John and Michelle, like everyone else on the folk circuit, knew of Cass's reputation as 'the girl with the wonderful voice' and Michelle would later remember that she was often talked about 'with affection and some awe'. Denny had also talked to them about his 'best friend Cass' and during their short tour, seemed to be forever rushing off to phone booths to call her. Cass naturally wanted to meet Denny's new-found friends and colleagues and, as far as she was concerned, if these people were now friends of Denny's, as well as musical partners, she wanted to get to know them, particularly if they included an attractive young woman. So one evening Denny invited her round to John and Michelle's Lower East Side 'palace in the slums' apartment.

That particular night, John and Michelle had bought some LSD for the first time from their local dope dealer – as they, unlike Cass and Denny, had not yet taken it. Eager to try out something new, they took some with Denny just before Cass arrived. Michelle was to remember the experience for the rest of her life. 'There was a knock on the door,' she recalls, 'and at the very moment the acid began to take effect, Cass appeared in their doorway. I saw her standing there in a pleated skirt and a pink Angora sweater with great big eyelashes on and her hair in a flip and I just remember thinking, "This is *quite* a drug!"'

The four of them chatted and swapped gossip about mutual friends in the Village and John would later recall Cass as 'a brassy, self-mocking riot', telling them that she wanted to break out of folk and go into musicals, 'but Barbra Streisand's getting all my parts instead'. Cass clearly made an impression on John, and like almost everyone else was similarly charmed by him straight away. Michelle, meanwhile, seemed fun, and instead of being the vacuous beauty which Cass had theorised went hand in hand with slim good looks, was in fact bright, and the two of them liked each other from the start. Although only just out of her teens, Michelle had also already lived an interesting and varied life. Her mother had died while she was still a small child and she had been brought up by her handsome bohemian father and a succession of stepmothers in a nomadic and constantly changing existence between Los Angeles, New York and Mexico, which was not so unlike Cass's early years. She spoke fluent Spanish and whilst presenting a girlish exterior, had a streetwise toughness and feisty resilience which was probably, in fact, much more real than Cass's.

After the Mamas and the Papas, Michelle would go on to have a successful career as an actress and gain a new generation of fans for her role in the American TV serial *Knots Landing*. Although in her late fifties, Michelle is still girlishly slim and even without make-up, wearing only a simple vest and shorts, she is radiantly beautiful with a smile that could power the national grid. We talked over a glass of wine in her exquisitely decorated, charming Los Angeles home and Michelle cast her mind back to 1964 and that first meeting with Cass in New York.

'Cass captivated me,' says Michelle. 'I remember being carried away with the expressiveness of her face and the way she told these fabulous stories. She was streetwise and she seemed to know an awful lot and I envied her her freedom. Here was a fun-loving, intelligent woman and it seemed like everything she did was because she wanted to do it. She was just so completely independent and I admired that and was quite in awe of her.'

As the acid kicked in they decided to play a game and having placed a candle in a birdcage in the middle of the floor, huddled around it. Using the exaggerated shadows on the wall, Cass, Denny and Michelle then became birds in the cage and John was the cat coming to get them. You probably had to be there, but on acid it was quite something and the four of them found themselves squealing with laughter. Afterwards John and Denny disappeared into the kitchen and Cass proceeded to regale Michelle with a long and dramatic tale of one of her own earlier adventures. 'She told me this horrifying story,' remembers Michelle, 'about being raped in Florida. She had been sleeping and when she woke up, this big black man was holding a knife to her throat. He had come in through a window and next thing she knew, he was telling her to be quiet, he was gonna fuck her and that was that. And I remember saying, "Well, what did you do?" And she said, "Well, what *could* I do? I let him ball me!" And I said, "And *then* what happened?" She said, "Well, then he had a heart attack and died on top of me. I was too much for him." And honestly,' she laughs, 'I don't know if you've ever taken a drug, but I swear, I was so *confused*! And then she started to laugh hysterically. To this day, I do not know if the rape story was true, or if she just tried to put a spin on it that she could live with, you know? That he died. That she was too much *woman* for him! I've always suspected that she was just fucking with my head.'

History would certainly seem to suggest that Cass was indeed 'fucking with Michelle's head', particularly given her earlier episodes at Forest Park. A genuine rape at knifepoint would obviously have been traumatic and the likelihood of anyone retelling the incident with such gusto only a few years later seems minimal to say the least. Also, the only time Cass would have been in Florida up until this point in her life would have been with the Big 3 and neither Jim Hendricks nor Tim Rose had any recollection of Cass having been raped.

But the rape tale was not the only episode Cass confided to Michelle. As they exchanged secrets, Cass also told her of her feelings for Denny, detailing in great depth almost every aspect of his looks, personality and talent. Michelle had herself known Denny for some months by this time, having sung with him in the group, but had never thought of him in that way. By the time Cass had finished, she was beginning to see what Cass meant, but she also saw that as far as Cass was concerned, despite her evidently close friendship with Denny, any hope of romance seemed highly unlikely. 'It was almost like they were an old married couple,' remembers Michelle. 'They would sit around together all day long, drinking beers and smoking pot and singing together and she'd have her feet up on his lap and they'd be laughing hysterically. But it just seemed like a hopeless situation to me. Here was this absolutely gorgeous young, great tenor, as cute as can be. He was just so adorable, so funny, so talented and yet the relationship that Cass could have with him was being his best friend.'

Cass had not resigned herself to this idea at all, but this first meeting between the four of them would prove more auspicious for Cass than she could ever have imagined.

*

Despite the Mugwumps' lack of success, Bob Cavallo still believed in Cass's potential, but it also seemed obvious that, in the wake of the Beatles, she was unlikely to have a solo career in pop. The British Invasion was in full swing and the American charts were now dominated by British groups like the Dave Clark Five, Gerry and the Pacemakers and Billy J. Kramer and the Dakotas. Cavallo therefore saw a different route for Cass. Knowing her love of Broadway and jazz, he got her a booking back at the Shadows, this time singing standards accompanied by a pianist and a stand-up bass. It was a radical departure from what she had been doing with the Mugwumps, but Cass had always loved this kind of material and it seemed like the best route to take. 'Cass had this sort of legit voice,' says Cavallo, 'more like a cabaret singer, and she loved Cole Porter songs and all the great, traditional songwriters, so we thought that she could become like a Barbra Streisand with humour because she was *very* funny. I was thinking, "Cass is my ticket," because the Spoonful were going to take time to develop, and I had some money, so I put together a band for her.'

Because of Cass's natural leaning towards jazz and cabaret, and the vogue for bands rather than solo performers in the pop charts, neither Cavallo nor anyone else seems to have considered the possibility that Cass could have been nurtured as a female solo singer in the same way that her British contemporaries Dusty Springfield, Cilla Black and Lulu were at the time. Dusty Springfield in particular bears comparison, as she, more so than Lulu or Cilla, arguably fell slightly outside the conventional requirements of feminine glamour in a similar way to Cass. Had Cass had the guiding hand of a talented A&R man sourcing powerful new material for her from the best songwriters of the day, many of whom were close at hand in New York's Brill Building, she would surely have had similar success. But at the time Cass's main concern was that she needed work. Denny's gigs with the New Journeymen had paid the rent at the Albert Hotel but she hadn't had any paid work herself since the Mugwumps, so although singing standards at the Shadows wasn't necessarily what she had envisaged herself doing, it was nevertheless a welcome opportunity.

Once again she was leaving New York and having moved back into her mother's Arlington basement, she returned to the Shadows, not just as a singer, but also as an assistant in the club's offices during the day, doing the payroll, answering the phones and taking reservations for the shows. It was all quite a radical departure from life in the Mugwumps both socially and musically. On the same stage where only a few months earlier she had sung 'Silver Threads and Golden Needles' and 'Searchin'', she was now doing her best to look elegant singing 'Night and Day' and the spotlight was suddenly on her alone. After the camaraderie of working within a group, the responsibility of carrying this new show single-handed was a much lonelier prospect. But Washington was her home town and Cass had her own network of friends for support.

A few years earlier, whilst taking theatre classes at American University, Cass had met a charismatic young student named Pic Dawson who would later have a major impact on her life. An aspiring actor, Dawson had a mercurial air that led people to remark that he could just as easily have been named Puck. Despite pitted skin as a result of teenage acne, Dawson's immediately engaging brown eyes and floppy longish brown hair won him instant attention, and all these years on, Dawson, who died in the early eighties of a heroin overdose, is remembered by almost every woman who knew him as 'damn cute'.

He was born Harris Pickins Dawson III in 1942, the scion of a wealthy Southern land-owning family. His father was an eminent economist who had been sent to Germany after World War Two to help rebuild the economy and had subsequently gone into the American diplomatic corps. Dawson had therefore been groomed to follow his father's illustrious footsteps into government and had been sent to a succession of private schools, only to be expelled from one after the other for displaying what had already been diagnosed as a wayward nature.

Whether it was this very waywardness or the fact that he had great personal charm and a sophisticated, cultured intelligence or most likely a combination of all three, Cass had been immediately won over. He, like everyone else, was similarly impressed by her talent and wit and they had become friends straight away. They had subsequently stayed in touch and by the time Cass was back singing at the Shadows, Dawson was also in DC taking acting lessons. They resumed their friendship and, as it developed into an affair, Dawson moved into Cass's basement.

Cass was of course by this time much more established in her career, but Dawson's youthful aspirations and potential seemed to bring out Cass's maternal instinct. 'Cass really supported his acting with all of her being and she encouraged him greatly,' remembers Caroline Cox-Simon, a young student who had become friends with Cass over a shared love of music and getting high. 'She championed him as I did. He was an interesting guy and he had a *lot* of potential. He was very turned on and would quote Beckett or things like that. He was also cute and full of the Jimmy Dean angst and that kind of thing and wanted to find a vehicle for this expression, but he was very innocent when we first met him and he wiggled his way into all of our hearts.'

But as had happened in the past and would again in the future, Cass's relationship with Dawson failed to develop in the way she would have liked. In contrast to the earlier situation with Tim and Denny, there was sex and romance, but whilst Cass wanted this to evolve into a normal ongoing relationship, commitment was not something which appealed to Dawson. 'When I first met him and he was staying with her,' says Caroline, 'I think that sometimes they would, as we used to say in the old days – "ball". But it wasn't like a 'you're my partner' kind of relationship. It was more like friends, and I think Cass always wanted more than that but he was not willing to commit. I think she was in love with him off and on for*ever*. Their relationship went on for years and years and I think he loved her and had a lot of respect for her but not really in a physical, romantic way. And that was very difficult for Cass.'

Their relationship would indeed continue on and off for the rest of Cass's life, but, from the start, the loose parameters he had set were inevitably hurtful to her. 'He was a charmer,' says Caroline, 'and the girlfriend that I was hanging out with and he became sweethearts almost immediately. Which kind of put a bump in the relationship with Cass because Cass really *loved* him.'

With both Dawson and Denny, Cass believed, as ever, that it was her weight which was the real issue preventing them from loving her the way she wanted, and at various points this idea was reinforced by them both either directly or indirectly. Whatever arguments she may have put forward to the contrary, she knew Tim Rose's advice was valid; she could see his theory in action with both Dawson and Denny, but the task of losing so much weight seemed insurmountable and her dreams of romantic love from the men she wanted consequently impossible. 'She was very open about feeling bad about her weight,' remembers Caroline. 'She was always struggling with it, feeling that guys would feel differently if she lost weight. We were at an age where how men saw us was a big part of who we were so we would talk about these things and she would say how hard it was for her being appreciated for who she was and not just being thought of as the funny one or as the good chick singer. She wanted to be a love object too, and that was hard. And she always despaired that it would really happen with the guy that she really wanted it to happen with. There would be these guys that would come along who would be really turned on by her weight and her size and she would have flings with them but it seemed like her thing was always, "But the guy that I really want in that kind of long-term relationship way, because of this [meaning her weight], I can't have."'

Cass's self-consciousness about her weight was not helped by the arrival in Washington of Denny with John and Michelle. Whilst Cass had been singing at the Shadows, the New Journeymen had found themselves in New York with no further bookings and so had used the group's American Express card to take them off to St John in the Virgin Islands for a holiday. The tropical lifestyle had proved so much fun that on their return, with no further gigs lined up, they had decided to round up a posse of friends and simply take everyone back to the islands. Cass, however, was still booked at the Shadows and was understandably not entirely thrilled at the idea of Denny and the lissom Michelle discovering the delights of island life without her.

What was more, John was also planning to redevelop the New Journeymen into a new act, with Michelle taking centre stage and this, despite Cass's friendship with her, pleased Cass even less. Before heading back out to the islands, John, Denny and Michelle came over to Cass's apartment one evening armed with a thermos of liquid LSD, which only seemed to magnify the tensions already there. 'There were *very* uncomfortable feelings in the room about Michelle,' remembers Caroline, 'because Cass didn't know *what* was happening with Denny and Michelle. All of a sudden here was this *really* beautiful young woman who was thin, and they're saying, "We want her to dress up the group, be the front woman, be the pretty one out front. We want her in because she *looks* so good." Ouch! That had to hurt.'

Apart from the hurt of hearing of these new plans, there was also another reason why they would have frustrated Cass enormously. Since she had sung with Denny in the Mugwumps, Cass had realised how well their voices complemented each other and after the band had split up, she had begun to think they might form a musical partnership.

Never one to be easily defeated, and still in the hope that something might develop between her and Denny romantically, Cass started thinking about following them out to the Virgin Islands. But there was nothing she could do about it for the time being. She had a day and night job at the Shadows and another engagement already on the horizon.

After a few months singing at the Shadows, Bob Cavallo decided it was time to introduce Cass to a wider audience. She should play New York, he thought, so he got her a booking for one night at the Bon Soir – a well-known cellar-venue on the Village's cabaret circuit.

The Bon Soir had been established since the fifties, along with clubs like the Blue Angel and Le Ruban Bleu and was most famous for having launched that old thorn in Cass's side – Barbra Streisand. New York was also, of course, the traditional home of cabaret and torch singing and Cavallo, aware that this was potentially an important opportunity for Cass, made sure that every influential journalist in New York, as well as a major booking agent, was invited. It was crucial that the evening went well and so in order to try and make sure that it did, Cavallo decided to send Cass to a famous New York voice coach to help her prepare.

Cass was happy to go along, but even whilst trying to hone her vocal technique, her weight seemed an inescapable hindrance as the coach's studio was lined with mirrors on every wall. When Cass was singing it was usually one of the few times when she could forget her weight and just enjoy herself and the audience, but in this studio it was impossible to ignore. Cass found it excruciating and did not return. But her vocal performance was not really her main concern. Singing to a few dozen people late at night at the Shadows was one thing but playing to a roomful of the most influential decision-makers in New York showbiz was an entirely different matter. She loved the material and she sang everything beautifully in rehearsal, but the fact that so much of her future was riding on this one performance soon began to play on her nerves.

When it came to the night, Cass did her best and went out of her way to look pretty in a voluminous pink satin dress with puffed sleeves, but she was chronically nervous and her nerves soon spread to her voice. 'It was a terrible evening!' remembers Cavallo, 'Cass had all this patter worked out, all this very funny stuff and she was charming and funny and great, but she sang every song horribly out of tune from beginning to end.'

Cass had desperately wanted the night to be a success but she was experienced enough as a performer to realise how badly it had gone. 'She was devastated,' remembers Cavallo, 'but we both lied about how the evening was and we didn't put it on the table. I don't think she enjoyed it. I think she had a terrible time. She didn't like the kind of audience that worked in a place like that. These weren't the students at the Shadows but she knew it wasn't good though and she knew she didn't want to do it again. I think also she was just terrified to be onstage alone. In later years she did do it, but at that time, how can one explain the insecurities? Also, maybe it was bad management. Maybe she should have played more dates in front of people out of town, you know? And *then* had the big debut in New York. I don't really know. All I know is that it was enough for me to be relieved when she said, "Maybe I should go to the islands." I said, "Yeah. Go."'

As her big solo break had proved far from successful, Cass immediately thought back to her original plan of singing with Denny. The Shadows was by now in the process of closing due to financial problems and so working back there was not an option even had she wanted to. Also, after the fraught preparation for the Bon Soir gig, the idea of some respite on a tropical island was not exactly unwelcome either. The only question now was how she was going to get there.

Cass went home to Washington to try and find an answer and a plane ticket. She talked to her friend Stephen Sanders, an AU dropout who had been running the Shadows office, having recently bought a share of the club with the inheritance left to him by his banker grandfather. Sanders would eventually go on to be the Mamas and Papas' road and tour manager but at the time he was simply a good friend to Cass.

'If I could just *get* there,' Cass told Sanders. 'How about a one-way ticket?'

'"Well, I think you need a two-way," said Sanders, "just in case something happens and you need to get back."' Sanders duly gave her the money for a return ticket, and about two hundred dollars spending money, which, in the Virgin Islands, at the time, or indeed anywhere else, would have been enough to live on for at least a month.

It was an extraordinarily generous act and was testament to the affection and confidence that Cass so often inspired, but Sanders would also go on to become a lifelong friend and he would come to share many important times in her life. At the time, though, Cass, no doubt grateful and pleased to have a way out of Washington, booked herself on the first plane to the Virgin Islands.

12

Creeque Alley

St Thomas, The Virgin Islands

One afternoon, Denny, John, Michelle and their friends were sitting on the beach wondering what to do about their dwindling stash of drugs when someone spotted the speck of a pale, wide human being far in the distance walking towards them. '*It's Cass!*' shouted Denny, shading his eyes from the sun. Carrying her shoes in her hands, Cass duly arrived replete with dramatic tales of having her pockets picked on the journey and her money stolen. It didn't matter that much though as there was already somewhere for her to stay.

By this time the others had settled into a large boarding house on Creeque Alley, one of the island's narrow winding hilly streets. John had persuaded its owner, a local bar owner named Duffy, that he should turn the hotel into a club and that, in return for accommodation, the New Journeymen would help refurbish it and also provide the musical entertainment once it was ready. Cass had a room of her own and the blow of having her money stolen was softened as she settled into island life. It was more than a welcome change from the hard graft of the Shadows and her ordeal in New York.

As soon as you got off the plane, the heat almost hit you in the face and you could feel the pace of life dwindle instantly. Little had changed on the islands since the forties; there were still corrugated iron huts near the beach and old planes left over from World War Two and if New York was life at 45 rpm, St Thomas was cranked down to at least 33. There were peacocks squawking around the hilly, winding streets of the small island town, burying their noses in the bougainvillaea and tropical vegetation and, with perfect beaches only a short motorcycle ride away, Cass loved it immediately. She had also not arrived entirely empty-handed. Whilst her money may have gone, what she did still have was a vial of pure Sandoz liquid LSD, and acid soon became part of the daily island ritual. 'Wakey wakey!' she'd tell Denny every morning as she went over to his bed and released a small drop of acid onto his tongue. 'It was like communion,' says Denny. 'Wake up! Another day in paradise!'

Island life did indeed feel like a kind of paradise. During the day they'd go to the beach and snorkel in the reef, staring in acid-fuelled wonder at the exotic fish and the gorgeous scenery around them. Cass loved swimming and with a long muumuu over her underwear, would wade out into the crystal-clear turquoise water and just stay there for hours on end, floating and snorkelling and taking it all in.

The natural beauty of the Caribbean was considerably heightened and twisted by the addition of large quantities of acid, but one morning, as Cass was preparing her daily communion ritual, the acid bottle seemed to have finally run dry. Fearing a day devoid of psychedelic hallucinations, Cass went into the kitchen and filled the small brown bottle with water, shook it up and gave Denny half to drink before swallowing the rest herself. 'Good morning,' said Denny, yawning. 'What do you wanna do today?'

They soon had an idea and hauled themselves into the old ruggedly painted green Volkswagen that Duffy had given them and, with Cass in the driving seat, set out for Magen's Bay – an exquisite small beach on the far side of the island. It was a spectacular drive over the island's mountainous hills tottering above precipices and cliffs below, but as they approached the beach, the acid began to kick in. 'By the time we get down onto the beach,' remembers Denny, 'we are both *so* fucked up, we can't even see the dashboard. One drop of acid is like two hundred and fifty micrograms, so we probably had like six hits each!

'The front tyres of the Volkswagen stall the car in the sand and the doors swing open. I fall out one side, Cass falls out of the driver seat and we crawl on our hands and knees down the beach and out into the water, just up to our necks, floating and holding onto each other going, "Oooh, what are we going to do now? I can't *walk*! We can't come out of the water. How are we gonna get *home*?" So we stayed there watching the beach fill up with fucking tourists! *Oh my God!* Now we really can't come out! And then there must have been six or seven butterflies came out and all of a sudden there's eight million fucking butterflies and Cass is trying to catch them and she's got on a pair of like fireman's or farmer's overalls – dungarees, but they're cut off at the knees, and a T-shirt, I've got my bathing suit on and we're both in the water, staring at the beach slowly filling up with masses of humanity and butterflies and the car is sitting up there and the door is open. It must have been two or three hours we were down there floating around till we could finally crawl out of the fucking water, shoulders and arms all burnt, and get back in the car and drive home.'

Before the acid ran out, the evenings had been no less eventful. Leaving the lights on outside the house, they would darken the living room and perform sketches and tableaux in silhouettes against the light. There was also no shortage of cast members as alongside Denny, John, Michelle and Cass, there was also the original party of friends which included Michelle's sister Russell and her boyfriend Peter Pilafian, Eric 'the Doctor' Hord and his girlfriend as well as John's five-year-old daughter Laura (later Mackenzie Phillips). Usually people would group in twos or threes and do scenes pretending to be on a tightrope or doing some kind of pantomime and Cass was in her element. 'Cass was good,' Denny remembers, 'she did some very nice pieces with costumes and lights, crazy stuff and people in the living room would clap and cheer.' The intense brightness of the full moons were also another event in themselves and each month, Cass, Denny, Michelle and John would rent a seagoing Trimaran, drop acid and go out into the Caribbean for hours at a time, hanging onto the boat's nets, slung between the hulls, with nobody but themselves and the crew amidst the sea.

It was in many ways a carefree existence but Cass, as she had sensed back in Washington, had reason to be concerned. When Michelle had first met Denny in the Halifax Three, she had never thought of him as anything more than a fun and friendly fellow musician with a beautiful voice. That had changed, however, the night she met Cass, and after hearing her friend ardently describe every inch of Denny's appeal she had begun to notice it for herself and a dizzying flirtation had consequently started up between them. 'By the time Cass came down,' says Michelle, 'Denny and I were practically sitting on top of each other all the time. Nothing really had happened, except you know when there's a flirtation going on, you become very conscious of every piece of body language and if we were rehearsing and say . . . our feet were this far apart from each other,' she says, placing her feet a few inches away from mine, 'there was like an electrical current going through us, you know? And then it went from that ... to *this*,' she says, now gently, flirtatiously, brushing her feet against mine without taking her eyes off me for an instant. 'And we'd be talking with Cass but this footsy thing started very early on and we were doing that with each other for months! It was a very sensual experience being on the island, lying on the sand and we were always in each other's arms and it felt really good.'

Although Cass would certainly have sensed Denny's growing frisson with Michelle, she never discussed it with him. 'We never talked about what was going on with her emotionally,' says Denny. 'Was she down there chasing me around? Did she want me to marry her and move into the thatched roof and have the children *right then*? It never dawned on me!' But whatever Cass may have instinctively felt, the relaxed and sensuous island lifestyle made it easy to dismiss. 'You know what?' explains Michelle. 'If John walked into a room and I was lying in Denny's *arms* laughing, he wouldn't have thought anything of it and neither would Cass! Because that's the kind of environment it was – lying around the beach, taking acid and snorkelling. Even when we were back in LA, the bathtub picture (on the cover of the Mamas and Papas' first album *If You Can Believe Your Eyes and Ears*) is an interesting picture because this is before Denny and I got caught. You can see that I'm laying back into Denny's arms and I'm practically making out with him, but this was so *typical* of the way we behaved. And nobody was looking at us or thinking there was anything odd about it.'

John in fact was clearly determined to ignore even the slightest suggestion that anything might be brewing between his wife and his new best friend. When Michelle, having recently kissed Denny for the first time after an acid-powered night on the boats, suggested that it might be better if they all stopped sharing a house, he asked, 'Why?' Michelle then explained that she was beginning to find herself 'very attracted to Denny sexually', but John simply ridiculed the suggestion. 'Oh! I wouldn't worry about that, Mitch. Denny has no interest in you,' he assured her, displaying what was, even in the context of the relaxed island lifestyle, a spectacularly blinkered view of the situation. 'I mean here we are,' says Michelle, 'practically making out twenty-four hours a day, playing footsy under the table all the time. Denny and I were always the first ones awake and Denny would invariably be rolling a joint – seven o'clock in the morning. I'd pop open a couple of beers and we'd sit around and talk and then they'd wander in. So it was funny when he said that Denny had no interest in me. It was such an *insult* to me, especially when I was trying to be a good wife and saying, "Look, I see a problem developing here and I wanna nip it in the bud." So for John to just say, "I wouldn't worry about that, Mitch," I just thought, "Oh, *really*?"'

John's nonchalance at the situation would unwittingly give his wife a new incentive to prove him wrong, all of which would eventually have considerable consequences for Cass.

As John had convinced Duffy to hire the New Journeymen to play at his hotel, the three of them had begun rehearsals. Cass would sit with them as they warmed themselves around a bonfire in the evenings practising John's new harmonies and arrangements, but although she was immediately desperate to join in, John refused and so the songs were still three-part harmonies rather than four. This didn't stop Cass offering her opinions on his arrangements, however, and even though she wasn't officially allowed to sing with them, these sessions and the songs she would learn from them on the beach would prove significant to Cass later on.

Mostly they sang the same old folk standards they had been singing before, as well as a few new Dylan songs like 'Mr Tambourine Man' which were already being similarly adopted into every other folk group's repertoire. But John had also written a few new songs himself. During the course of the previous year, no doubt high on the guilt-charged thrill of his new marriage and new life, John had found a renewed surge of creativity and was writing songs at a phenomenally prolific rate. Some of these would later become some of the Mamas and the Papas' best and most enduring hits, although at the time, it was hard to know quite what category they might fall into. 'John had written a new kind of music that he couldn't identify,' Cass later told an interviewer. 'He had no frame of reference for it. We didn't either. He had written "California Dreamin'", and a few others. He knew they weren't folk songs but he didn't know what they were.'

The story has often been told of how John and Michelle – the archetypal California girl – had gone out for a walk one freezing winter's day in New York. Unused to the cold, Michelle had been shivering desperately and so they had gone into a church to warm up. It was Michelle's first experience of cold weather and, with no warm clothes, she was missing the sunshine and warmth of her native climate. That same night, John had woken Michelle, begging her to get out of bed and write down the words of the song he was busy writing, insisting that if she did he would give her half the songwriting credit. Michelle would later claim these to be the most profitable twenty minutes of her life and eventually the song would bring all four of them the success and fame they had all been working towards for so long. Listening to the Mamas and the Papas singing 'California Dreamin'' nearly forty years later, it's hard to imagine the song without Cass's distinctive voice so powerfully carrying the responses to Denny's lead, but when John first rehearsed it in the Virgin Islands, the song was still in a raw, acoustic form, arranged for Denny, himself and Michelle only. '"California Dreamin'" was just sung like a ballad,' remembers Denny, 'and it was done for three voices and it didn't have any balls. '"*All . . . the . . . Leaves . . . Are . . . Brown*",' he sings lamely at about a third of the speed of the recording. 'When we were rehearsing in the islands, there was no band and no backbeat, it was still just a three-part folk harmony thing.'

John didn't believe that folk was really finished. Whilst Cass and Denny had realised this long ago, John continued to insist stubbornly that, 'Folk music is gonna come back.' Denny had done his best to persuade him by playing a copy of the Beatles' latest album but John had taken one look at the gory 'butcher' cover (as the sleeve was subsequently nicknamed before being swiftly withdrawn by the record company) and dismissed it as 'fucking disgusting', refusing to listen to its contents. 'It's too simple!' he told Denny. 'It's just three chords! It's "Guantanamera" with a beat.' He said it was beneath him and that he was a folk artist and had been doing very well at it, thank you very much. But eventually, after the group failed an audition at the St Thomas Hilton, he conceded that 'going electric' was in fact clearly the way forward. Guitarist Eric Hord was therefore duly sent out to scour the hillsides of St Thomas for electric instruments and a drum kit which, against considerable odds, he found. With the backing of Denny on bass, the Doctor on guitar and Peter Pilafian – a trained violinist, on drums, the New Journeymen extended the old repertoire to incorporate Beatles numbers like 'Twist and Shout', 'Yes it Is', and 'Ticket To Ride', as well as instrumentals like the Ventures' 'Walk Don't Run'.

The band was a long way short of ideal, but it was a step forward from the purely folk-style Journeymen and Cass now wanted to join the group even more. Michelle still maintains to this day that John wanted her in the group but that it was Cass herself who refused because of her own fear of the inevitable comparisons that would be made between her appearance and Michelle's, but this is adamantly refuted by everyone else who was there, including John.

Cass had in fact been angling to be let in the group since she arrived on the island, but it was John's group and, as far as he was concerned, Cass definitely didn't fit the image he wanted. In years to come, both Cass and John would go to extraordinary lengths to rewrite this episode in the group's history. John would produce various excuses, maintaining Cass's vocal range didn't fit the group's material – it was too low, he claimed, as well as admitting that he didn't think her look was quite right. 'Mitch, Denny and I were three string-beans and she was huge. The sound was off and the look didn't fit either. So I kept her out,' he said. Denny, meanwhile, remembers there being no doubt as to why he wouldn't let her in. 'She was too fat! His ideal woman, he had: Michelle. This is it – I left my wife and children! I found *this*! This is the ultimate! *That?* [i.e. Cass] I swear to God at one point he took me aside and said, "Dennis, her eyes are too close together." "What?" "Her eyes are too close together and she smells." Gonna have a little trouble getting past *that* to the voice, aren't we, John?'

Michelle's sister Russell Gilliam, meanwhile, remembers John being straightforward with Cass and telling her the truth straight out. 'John wanted to have a Peter, Paul and Mary rock and roll group and he had no compunction of saying, "Sorry, Cass, but you're too fat," right to her face. But not in a *mean* way. He'd just say "Cass, I'm *sorry* – you're too fat."'

Once the Mamas and the Papas became famous, it is easy to see why Cass would have been as keen as John to gloss over some of these original facts. Rather than have to admit that her size had prevented John from letting her in the group, John's original yarn about Cass not having the right vocal range was reinstated and when journalists naturally wanted to know how she had miraculously gained the necessary notes, the well-worn, but frankly ludicrous 'pipe incident' story came to the rescue, and was vigorously defended by Cass as much as John. 'It's true,' she later insisted to *Rolling Stone*. 'I did get hit on the head by a pipe that fell down and my range was increased by three notes. Workmen dropped a thin metal plumbing pipe and it hit me on the head and knocked me to the ground. I had a concussion and went to the hospital. I had a bad headache for about two weeks and all of a sudden I was singing higher. It's true. Honest to god.'

How many people ever believed this is questionable and others who were there at the time dismiss the tale as the travesty it clearly was. 'All of that was *such* baloney!' says Russell. 'Cass was following them around like a little puppy. Just everywhere they went, Cass popped up asking to sing with the group and John wouldn't let her.' Nevertheless, once they were famous, everyone in the band seemed happy to go along with this revisionist version of events without so much as a passing glance back to the slightly more awkward truth.

But in the Virgin Islands at the time, Cass would hardly have been surprised that her weight was an issue. Obesity was still beyond many people's day-to-day experience, as Russell points out, '*Now* she just would have been accepted, because everybody's fat now. I'm in Chicago and there are *enormous* people around, but it didn't used to be that way. Believe me, she was really like an elephant in our society at that time. In fact Cass was the first fat person I ever knew because back then it was really *very*, very uncommon.'

But even apart from her size, John also admitted that they were 'two duelling Virgos' and his intrinsic antipathy towards Cass seems to have stemmed not solely from her appearance but also from the fact that she was a strong character whose very presence challenged his role as undisputed leader. More to the point, she was a woman with ideas of her own, who in contrast to what John and many others would have expected, refused to play the shrinking violet and retreat in what they felt should have been shame at her size. Cass had a mind and opinions and was not afraid to make them known and it was this that seemed to rile John still further, beginning the power struggle which would gradually escalate between the two of them over the years to come. 'Cass was an assertive woman,' says Denny, 'If she had looked like Michelle and been that assertive, God – she would have been the first woman president! But she was packaged the way she was packaged and John just couldn't handle it.'

It is arguable whether, had Cass 'looked like Michelle', her difficulties with John, or indeed anyone else, would have been solved. Women who were both sexually attractive and highly intelligent were, and often still are, frequently considered more, rather than less of a threat to the men around them, but John also seemed to resent Cass's generally easy-going nature and saw her consequent popularity as a threat. Cass in turn, no doubt irked by his need for control, seems to have enjoyed baiting him still further. 'One night Cass came up,' remembers Denny, 'and was saying, "Look at the sunset over the harbour, it's so *beautiful!*"' he says in an animated, highly excited voice, 'and John wouldn't look at it. Why? What's the matter, John? "I *know* it's there," says John. "It makes you stronger, if you *know* it's there and you *don't* look." Huh? It's a beautiful sunset. "Yes, I know, and I hope it's the most beautiful sunset there'll probably ever be, in the world, and I won't look at it. I'll just know it's there." Ok*aay*. She wouldn't let him get away with it though. *She'd* go look at it and take everybody *with* her, so John'd be left alone, not looking at the sunset and everyone was down the waterfront with Cass instead of staying, staring at the wall with *him* and that'd make him *really* pissed off! It was more fun to go with Cass. She'd always find a way to make him even *madder* about whatever she'd be doing! So there was always one-upmanship.'

Whatever friction there may have been between her and John, Cass had learnt to ignore it. That didn't necessarily mean it didn't affect her, but most of the time, if it did, she wouldn't let it show. The same applied to the offensive remarks she soon had to deal with at the restaurant where she and Russell had found waitressing jobs in order to earn some much-needed cash. As St Thomas was a stop-over for American marines, Cass was forced to endure nightly abuse from the sailors, eager to get a laugh at anyone's expense. 'Hey, fatty! You forgot our orders – or did you eat them all yourself?' they would call out and John later remembered her withstanding 'more humiliation in a week than a human deserved in a lifetime'. But Cass remained unflinchingly stoical. Although the sailors' jibes must surely have been hurtful, Cass would never let her feelings show, as this would be tantamount to defeat and so instead, she would let their taunts wash over her and pretend she didn't care. 'I was *constantly* protecting her,' remembers Russell. 'I was furious with these little nineteen-year-olds and whenever any of the sailors would disparagingly speak to her, I would run over and say, "Don't you speak to her that way," because it was just unbearable. But you know, Cass never complained. And this was what I found so shocking. That she never told the sailors to stop, and just *took* it and I think it was just because she was so used to it.'

Things looked set to improve, however, when the New Journeymen finally opened at Duffy's newly refurbished nightclub and Cass managed to get a job waitressing there instead. She might not have been up on the stage but nothing was going to stop her adding in fourth-part harmonies from the floor as she delivered the customers' drinks. Unsurprisingly perhaps, given the power of her voice, she could still be heard above the group, even with their newly amplified set-up and was consequently an instant hit with the customers. '*We* were on stage and people were applauding *her*!' remembers Denny. 'John's going *crazy* and she's out there getting adulation! She had a great time!'

Cass's success with the club's audience might in theory have given her further ammunition to persuade John to let her join the group officially, but before she could do so, the New Journeymen's run at Duffy's was cut short. The group had laboriously decorated the club with sack-cloth and candles to create a suitably intimate and convivial atmosphere, but the local fire marshall had been less impressed and after five minutes surveying the scene, promptly ordered the club be closed on the spot. Which left both Cass and the group once again without a job.

To make matters worse, John's credit card had been confiscated and Michelle had been arrested, first for driving her moped without licence plates and secondly for disturbing the peace after wailing and howling as they tried to arrest her. They also owed money to a seemingly endless list of locals including Duffy, the grocery store, the pharmacy and a local seamstress. John realised the only solution was to return to New York.

For Cass, even though she was still not technically part of the group, her fortune was nevertheless inevitably linked to theirs. Over the last few months, despite the rifts between her and John, the four of them had become very much a unit and it seemed only a matter of time before she convinced John to let her sing with them. Nor had she given up on the idea that there might still be hope for romance between her and Denny. They were as close as ever and, ironically, the islands seemed to Cass the perfect setting for romance. The news that they had to leave came as a shock and Cass's reaction was uncharacteristically extreme. 'When we told Cass,' remembers Michelle, 'she put her hand right through the window. She was *so* upset, and we had to take her to the hospital. I don't know if she had to have stitches, but she'd bloodied her hand. I think *she* thought we were gonna live in this tropical paradise for the rest of our lives. It was extremely upsetting. It was kind of the end of the dream because it was a very dream-like quality living there. It was *beautiful*. The weather was beautiful, it was *fun*, it was very care*free* and it was just this shock of reality that hit. And as extreme as it was to do that, I really understood her feelings. It was really kind of out of character though, but at this point, she was still working on Denny and now it was gonna screw up all of her plans because I think she felt that she was maybe wearing him down a little bit. Now this was back to the grind and she was gonna have to pick up *her* career, do all that and support herself. It was terrible – the idea of having to leave all this fun behind and face reality.'

Cass was distraught at the thought of leaving, but however reluctant she may have been, thanks to Stephen Sanders's foresight and generosity, Cass, unlike the others who were effectively stranded with no money and no airfare, still had her return ticket, so once it was clear that they all had to leave, she said goodbye and got on a plane back to New York. No plans were made between the four of them to reconvene either in New York or anywhere else, as nobody knew quite what they were going to do or where they were going to go, but the route Cass would take would affect them all.

Although John had refused to let Cass in the group, her knowledge of the new songs they had been working on would have a major impact on her life in the months to come. Her main spur for going to the Virgin Islands had been Denny, but by allying herself with him, and therefore John and Michelle by default, she had unwittingly paved the way towards her future success.

13

California Dreamin'

One afternoon in June of 1965, whilst still in the islands, Cass and the others had heard the unmistakable twang of a twelve-string guitar wafting hesitantly from a radio across the street. It was accompanied by harmonies not unlike their own: '"Take me for a trip upon your magic swirling ship ... all my senses have been stripped ..."' They knew the song – they had been playing Dylan's 'Mr Tambourine Man' themselves, but they had never heard it sound like this before.

While Cass was away changes had been happening, both on the folk scene and in the music industry as a whole. Suddenly, in addition to the British beat bands, there were new sounds flooding the airwaves and they were the sounds of Cass's friends. David Crosby and Roger McGuinn had joined forces with fellow musicians Gene Clark and Chris Hillman to form the Byrds and moved back to Crosby's native Los Angeles. There they had suddenly scored a huge hit with their blissfully harmonised, electrified version of 'Mr Tambourine Man', and although the song's author may have originally hailed from Hibbing, Minnesota, once embellished with the Byrds' inimitably gentle harmonies and the chiming twang of McGuinn's twelve-string Rickenbacker guitar, Dylan's jingle-jangle morning sounded like it could only ever have happened in the blue-skied warmth of California.

People's attention had gradually been turning towards the West Coast since the emergence of the surf craze a year or two earlier and the Beach Boys as America's biggest teen sensation. The music business had for years centred around New York, but the industry soon noticed that not only were these new artists Californian, but their records were also made there and released by West Coast labels. In the summer of '65, West Coasters Sonny and Cher had gone global with 'I Got You, Babe', whilst some months later, Cass and Denny's erstwhile fellow Mugwumps Zal Yanovsky and John Sebastian had teamed up with fellow folkies Joe Butler and Steve Boone to form the Lovin' Spoonful and decamped to LA, bursting into the charts with their debut single 'Do You Believe in Magic?' Just as the Beatles had fused pop, folk and rock and roll into something their own, the Byrds and the Lovin' Spoonful had now found their own ways to combine their influences into something similarly new and contemporary, but also unmistakably American. And just as Crosby, McGuinn, Sebastian and Yanovsky had done, John Phillips would soon find his own way and this time, it would include Cass.

This new amplified, electrified version of what was still essentially folk, was now labelled 'folk rock' and was soon being hailed as the latest musical sensation. That same summer Dylan himself had 'gone electric' at the Newport Folk Festival and in August, *Billboard* ran a headline proclaiming 'Folk + Rock = Profits'. By September, both *Newsweek* and *Time* magazines had run major features on the 'folk rock' phenomenon.

Suddenly LA had taken over from New York as the new centre of musical innovation and there were few in folk who had failed to notice. By the end of the year it was as though almost the entire Greenwich Village community had decamped en masse to LA, followed by virtually every record company executive in town, in a kind of laid-back, musical gold rush. Accordingly, Dick Clark, host of *American Bandstand*, the foremost TV pop showcase of the day, shifted the recording of his show from New York to the West Coast and subsequently launched a new show *Where The Action Is*, claiming that LA 'is now the most youth-oriented city in the nation'.

Returning home from the Virgin Islands in the summer of 1965, Cass therefore found Greenwich Village almost deserted. Where the streets and clubs before had been filled with musicians basking in the spotlight of folk fever, suddenly everyone, or at least all of Cass's friends, seemed to have left the party and all that was left were a few lone stragglers, dancing in a corner. Denny, Michelle and John were still stuck in the Virgin Islands while David Crosby, John Sebastian, Zal Yanovsky and Bob Cavallo were all already on the West Coast.

LA therefore seemed the obvious place to go. Jim Hendricks, who was still technically Cass's husband, had also long since gone West with his girlfriend Vanessa, and so Cass knew that, at the very least, she'd have a floor to sleep on. She had no particular idea of exactly what she was going to do in LA, but she had established herself as a successful player on the Greenwich Village scene, so it seemed reasonable to expect that she could do the same somewhere else.

Once she arrived she set about trying to network and get a foothold in the local music scene. Jim and Vanessa had by this time formed a Sonny and Cher-type duo and signed a publishing deal with music-biz hustler-about-town Kim Fowley, later to become legendary as a producer, publisher and manager and one of music's all-time great eccentrics. Via his connections to Jim and Vanessa, Fowley was a regular visitor to the apartment and Cass lost no time in taking advantage of his experience and local knowledge. She may have tasted success in New York, but she had the sense to realise that LA was a different matter. 'She was looking for an angle,' remembers the six-foot-tall Fowley (who describes their encounters as 'Frankenstein meeting Sophie Tucker'). 'I remember her staying on the floor and ironing and washing clothes, and she was saying, "I need to know how this place *works*, what's going on in the street, in the clubs, in the business, in publishing." She had the big grocery list and wanted to know about *everything*.'

Whatever she may have gleaned from Fowley's tales and advice, a couple of months later, Cass was no closer to getting herself a record deal and Fowley, although impressed by her singing and drive, was not offering any concrete help. He had recognised her talent immediately and explains, 'I *knew* she was *magical*, and she sang all the time so I knew she had a great voice,' but he had sensed a neediness and obsession with success in her which had made him wary of working with her himself. For Cass, there was consequently little prospect of a deal or even a gig. But she was about to be surprised. One afternoon there was a knock on the door of Jim and Vanessa's apartment and Cass opened it to find Denny, John and Michelle standing on the doorstep, hot, tired and desperate for somewhere to stay. They had driven cross-country all the way from New York and found themselves caught up in LA's Watts Riots along the way. Like Cass and everyone else, they had realised as soon as they got back to New York that as far as making it in the music business was concerned, the circus had left town and LA was where they needed to be. Besides, Michelle was eager to go home to her native California, and the prospect of another winter in New York wasn't particularly appealing to anyone. The folk grapevine being what it was, they had soon heard that Cass had somewhere to stay and had promptly tracked her down.

By this time, however, there was a bailiff's eviction notice pasted onto the door of the apartment for rent arrears. The one-bedroom apartment was already verging on the crowded with Cass, Jim and Vanessa, but with six of them now sleeping on dismantled mattresses on the floor and the utilities disconnected by the bailiffs, living conditions in the LA heat were far from luxurious. 'We were all stuck in the apartment like roaches,' remembers Denny, 'no water, no gas, no lights.' But the food crisis at least was salvaged by Denny's winning way with a bathroom heater. 'In California,' he explains, 'they have these heaters in the bathrooms called wall thermidors with screws on the top and bottom holding it in, so I took the screws out and I took the heater off the wall, set it on the toilet next to the tub and turned it on and it worked as a hotplate! So we're cooking beans and Wieners on the thermidor on the toilet and that was the kitchen!'

While John and Denny took to stealing cuts of meat from supermarkets during the day so there'd be something to eat for dinner, there was nothing to do in the evenings as they had no money with which to go anywhere or do anything. All that was left was to sit around the flat by candlelight and sing. John, Denny and Michelle would often also sing during the day, as much out of boredom as anything else and Cass inevitably joined in. She knew all the songs from hearing them rehearse in the Virgin Islands, but whereas there John had always been able to simply walk away, insisting that she couldn't be in the group, once they were all staying in the same confined space, in her friends' apartment, there was little he could do about it. 'She'd just start singing,' remembers Denny, 'whether it was right or wrong and finally after a couple of weeks of her singing along, John just couldn't deny his ears and so he just went "Don't sing that, sing *this*." And Cass was like, "*Sure! Gotchaa!*"'

With hindsight it was inevitable that by just being present and singing along, John's resistance to Cass would eventually cave in. However determined he may have been in his ambitions for the image of his group, his passion and talent for harmony arranging was always greater. John had been fascinated by vocal harmony and combinations of voices since he was a teenager. 'I've always liked the sound of men and women singing together,' John later said. 'I always thought that very moving and that's been very important to me. I don't know where it came from – church, people singing together, men and women in a choir – that kind of thing has always been the most beautiful thing I've ever heard and it's very integral to my life. I really admired the Hi-Lo's' harmony and the Four Freshmen's harmony and Modernaires, people like that, but never wanted a group with just all guys or all women. I wanted to mix it together. So that's what I got.' This was the Achilles heel through which Cass would finally win, as the temptation of not just a fourth voice, but a voice as emotive as Cass's proved too hard for John to resist. 'We'd be doing an arrangement and then *he* would find a place for her,' says Denny. 'I saw his eyes light up. It would be, "Oh, *yeah, OK*, Cass you sing that. Michelle – can you sing that octave with her? Sing the octave unison! And Michelle goes, "What's the octave unison?" "Well, sing what Cass is singing, only sing it up as high as you can!" And then he and I could be free to do things arrangement-wise that were not available to do with only three. And that only happened at Cass's apartment.'

With the addition of Cass's voice, the group's sound took on a whole new dimension and this was as plain to John as it was to everyone else. Neither John nor Michelle had naturally strong voices themselves – as far as the New Journeymen were concerned, it was Denny's voice which really carried the group, but with the addition of Cass and the combination of her and Denny's voices, complimented by John's arrangements for the four of them, the effect was compelling. 'When I heard us sing together for the first time,' Cass later told *Rolling Stone*, 'we knew, we *knew* . . . This is it.'

The sound was unmistakably magical and although John himself later claimed that he agreed to let her in the group as soon as he heard her sing with them in LA, others remember his reluctance continuing right up until the four of them, rather than three, were offered a record deal.

Cass had an innate talent for bringing people together and, throughout her life, she invariably used her contacts to help her friends in any way she could. In the same way, after hearing the group's newly polished harmonies, she thought that even if she couldn't join them, she would help them find a deal. Cass phoned Kim Fowley and asked him to listen to them sing. It may have been an entirely selfless plan, but she may have also intended to subtly bring herself in on any record deal which might be offered. What Fowley heard, however, was only

Denny, John and Michelle singing down the phone but he was sufficiently impressed to arrange an audition for them with his friend Nik Venet at Mira Records. Cass went along with them, as their driver, but as soon as Venet saw their striking image as a foursome, he – no doubt to Cass's delight – made a provisional offer to sign either the four of them or not at all, on the basis that a final audition for his boss would clinch the deal.

In the intervening hours before this second audition, Cass picked up the phone again, this time to call her old friend, fellow folkie Barry McGuire to get some grass to calm their nerves. She had met McGuire while she was still in the Big 3 and he was singing with the New Christy Minstrels and they had immediately become friends. Since arriving in LA, McGuire had signed to the small but successful Dunhill label and had soon been catapulted to global fame with the pop protest anthem 'Eve of Destruction'. Consequently, apart from being a source of good grass, McGuire was not a bad person for a bunch of aspiring pop stars to know. McGuire went round to the apartment and as they sat on the floor rolling joints, the four of them started to sing. McGuire was just as impressed as Venet. 'Man, this is awesome!' he told them and immediately offered to introduce them to his Dunhill producer Lou Adler. Thinking that perhaps the four of them could at least earn some money singing backing vocals on his album, he duly took them along to Western Recorders Studios where he was recording. Again, Cass went along with the group, although she was still not officially a member and the reasons for her presence remain the subject of some debate.

Some have suggested that John wanted Cass to sing with them at the audition solely to help Michelle sound better on the day. McGuire, meanwhile, points out that as he was primarily Cass's friend, rather than anyone else's, John decided that although she wasn't in the group, they ought to bring her along so that she appeared to be involved. Given John's long-standing reluctance to let Cass join the group, clinging as he was to his idea of a svelte, conventionally attractive, hipper version of Peter, Paul and Mary, the truth probably lies somewhere between the two. But in spite of these tales, and in keeping with Cass and everyone else's attempts at rewriting the early history of the group, Lou Adler, conveniently perhaps, has no recollection of Cass's involvement ever being in question. 'I wasn't aware that she wasn't in the group or that she was doing this just to get them through the audition,' says Adler. 'I just looked at them as a group and I didn't hear that story until recently.'

Whether as an official unit or not, the four of them went along to the studios. Even as backing singers, they needed to audition, and so Adler took the four of them to a huge empty studio where, accompanied only by John's twelve-string guitar, they sang 'California Dreamin'', 'Monday, Monday', 'Go Where You Wanna Go', 'Got a Feelin'' and 'Straight Shooter'. 'What do you think?' Adler asked engineer Bones Howe. 'Well, if you don't take 'em, I *will*,' replied Howe.

The twenty-nine-year-old Adler was already a successful producer, songwriter and all-round entrepreneur and would go on to play a significant role in the group's career, often being referred to as the 'Fifth Mama'. After growing up in the mixed Mexican and Jewish neighbourhood of Boyle Heights in LA, he had befriended an aspiring trumpet player by the name of Herb Alpert and the pair started writing songs together, one of which – 'What a Wonderful World' – became an international hit for Sam Cooke. He had then gone on to 'discover' volleyball players Jan and Dean and produced many of their surf hits, before moving to Dunhill where he signed Johnny Rivers and McGuire. Later on in the sixties and seventies he would launch comedy act Cheech and Chong, produce Carole King's million-selling *Tapestry* album and bring *The Rocky Horror Picture Show* to America, but his reputation was already firmly established by the time he met McGuire and his singing friends.

The band were immediately impressed by his success and laid-back personal style, not to mention the Cadillac he had parked outside the studio. 'He was rich, wore interesting hats, and didn't give a lot of clues as to his innermost being,' Michelle later recalled.

All these years on, Adler's style is no less casual. Still sporting the sinewy rabbinical beard he has worn since the sixties he remembers the group's initial impact as we sit in his spacious, but decidedly laid-back Malibu offices, perched high on a cliff top above the shimmering Pacific. 'It pretty much comes down to the title of the first album – *If You Can Believe Your Eyes and Ears*,' he explains in his soft-spoken, supremely unflappable-sounding, Californian drawl, 'because what I tried to do in those days is not look at the act while they were auditioning, I was just interested in the sound and not how they looked, both positive or negative. Because it wasn't the world of videos that we're dealing in now, I just wanted to perceive them as a sound coming off a record and they went through four or five songs and when I opened my eyes after hearing this incredible sound, taking a good look at who was singing it, it was like . . . they were as ragged as you could possibly be – Denny was wearing black leather, Cass looked like the mother of mankind and the *whole group* was just *not* to be believed. From as big as Cass was to as beautiful as Michelle was and as tall as John was . . . just an *amazing* collection – a *visual* that was unbelievable. And then the sound that was just acoustic guitar and their four voices was one of the most amazing things I had heard up until that time – I couldn't believe that anything that good had just walked in off the street, and so *If You Could Believe Your Eyes and Ears* . . . became the title of the first album.'

To Adler, they did indeed look like a bunch of hippies off Sunset Strip. Which of course was more or less what they were, although hippies had yet to be labelled as such by the media. Neither Cass nor Michelle wore any make-up and both Denny and John had what was still considered long hair. Also, after months on the Virgin Islands, and several more sleeping on Jim Hendricks's floor, grooming was the last thing on anybody's mind, nor did they have the money for it even if they had thought of it. This was in stark contrast to most of the aspiring acts who Adler would have seen up until that time who generally either conformed to the black-suits-and-thin-tie look of artists like Sam Cooke, the outdoor sportiness of the surf acts or the freshly scrubbed prettiness of the teen idols. In comparison, Adler found this foursome 'pretty amazing!' he laughs.

But as different as they looked, it was the sound of their voices that cut through the California haze like a tropical storm. There had obviously been vocal harmony groups before, from John's heroes the Hi-Lo's and the Four Freshmen to the 'barbershop' style of groups such as the Ink Spots and later the Orioles, and most recently the Beach Boys, but whereas most vocal harmony groups tended to be made up of voices which naturally complemented each other, the comparatively haphazard formation of the Mamas and the Papas had resulted in not only an unlikely visual combination, but most importantly an unlikely vocal one. Whilst the majority of vocal groups aimed for a grouping of equal vocal talents and perhaps included one obvious lead vocalist per group, the Mamas and the Papas had two clear leads in the form of Cass and Denny, highlighting the originality of John's vocal arrangements and the voices of the leads.

The other factor which differentiated them from many of their peers was that they also had their own songs. It was still only a year since the Beatles had introduced the idea of a band writing for themselves and groups who could do so were still a relatively new and rare phenomenon. 'In the Sam Cooke days,' remembers Adler, 'you were recording your vocalist coming out of the gospel field and even a few years later, you'd find someone that looked pretty good, had a pretty good voice, you had a song from Aldon Music and you thought about making a record like that. With the Mamas and Papas, John Phillips's songs were just *amazing* songs. It's a whole different ballgame, so you weren't looking at the artist thinking, How can I record him, what kind of song can I get for him? George Martin had already experienced it with the Beatles and I was experiencing it with the Mamas and the Papas.'

But however impressed Adler may have been, he certainly wasn't one to let his enthusiasm show, and when he offered the group a recording contract the next day, they couldn't have been more surprised. 'We didn't trust him,' remembers Michelle. 'We thought there was something very suspicious about him. He was just a little too quiet. We couldn't really put our finger on what it was that we didn't trust about it, but then the next day when he had all the contracts down on the floor, I said, "Oh, the guy loved us and he didn't want to show his hand," and that's pretty much what it was. He's a very slick businessman and he was Mr Cool! We loved Lou instantly once we got to know him.'

'I'll give you whatever you want,' Adler eventually told them, 'just don't go see anybody else,' to which John, without missing a beat, replied, 'What we want is a steady stream of money from your office to our house.' Adler's offer was unquestionably for the four of them rather than three and once the contracts were laid out, there was no longer the remotest doubt that Cass was part of the group. This was what Cass had wanted all along, and from John's point of view, if Dunhill Records were offering them a record deal as a quartet, then a quartet they would be.

Dunhill were in fact so impressed that they were not just offering the group one album, but a deal in which they would record two albums a year for the next five years. They would also be signing themselves to Dunhill's management and music publishing divisions so in effect they were all but signing their lives over to the label, but at this point nobody was too concerned with the small print. The idea of a record deal at all, plus professional management and publishing and indeed up-front money seemed too good to be true.

The following day, in December 1965, all four of them signed the contracts and John, being the smooth-talking salesman that he was, insisted that not only should the group be given five thousand dollars, but also a car. And not just any car. Adler arranged for a blue Buick convertible no less – subsequently nicknamed Howard the Bleak.

Having signed as a group, they now needed a name. On meeting Adler they had originally decided to call themselves the Magic Circle, as 'magic' was the new buzzword on the street and all-round adjective for anything good (as exemplified by the Lovin' Spoonful's hit 'Do you Believe in Magic?'). But Dunhill had also assigned the group a manager in the form of Bobby Roberts, an ex-tap dancer who was one of the Dunhill staff. Roberts was as impressed with the group as Adler but didn't feel the name Magic Circle would be well received by promoters and so another name had to be found. The now famous story goes that that same evening the group happened to be watching TV when a documentary came on about Hell's Angels. 'What do you call your women?' the TV reporter asked the Angels. 'Well, some call 'em cheap,' they replied, 'but *we* call 'em Mamas.' They went on to explain that the men called each other Papas, and Cass immediately latched onto the idea's potential as it seemed to hark back to their time in the islands. 'We wanted a name,' she later explained, 'that would indicate that there were both men and women in the group, because it was the first group that actually was sexually integrated – so you might speak,' (no doubt savouring what may not have been an entirely accidental allusion). She went on to further explain that since they had been in the Virgin Islands, they had been sharing a 'communal-type existence' where she had been 'kind of keeping house and doing the cooking', so, she said, 'it was sort of like if the ladies would cook the dinners, the men would take out the garbage and that kind of stuff . . . And so it became a gag: "Well, if the Mamas'll cook the dinner, the Papas'll go out and get the cat food," and it became the Mamas and the Papas.'

*

The next day the newly named group cleared their minimal belongings out of Jim and Vanessa's apartment and moved into the relative luxury of the Landmark, an old-school Hollywood, Hawaiian-themed apartment hotel on Franklin Avenue with its own pool. As 19 September was Cass's twenty-fourth birthday, they decided to celebrate both the day and their new Dunhill deal with a dinner in the apartment. Cass cooked her speciality: duck à l'orange, John provided ample supplies of Seconals (a type of barbiturate) and it was all washed down with copious quantities of brandy. By four in the morning, Cass and John were slumped over the table asleep alongside a parade of empty bottles glinting in the candlelight.

While Cass and John dozed away, Michelle and Denny were still wide awake. The flirtation which had begun in the Virgin Islands, far from having dwindled, had in fact escalated in the months since, and the rush of anticipation and sexual tension could have kept them awake for a week. Seeing the others asleep, Denny silently beckoned to Michelle and the two of them sneaked over to the glass sliding door that led out of the room. As they kissed on the balcony outside, Denny leaned back and a door fell open to the empty apartment next door. 'We went in there,' remembers Michelle, 'and we made love on the wall-to-wall. And honest to God, I think that's the only time it happened. I believe Denny and I slept together *once* – that's all. What was more important was what led up to it! But it was the *hottest* affair I've ever had. For one little roll in the hay, it was really hot!'

From Cass's point of view, for the last few months her main concern had been finding work in LA and getting a record deal; she had stopped worrying about what may or may not have been happening between Denny and Michelle as they were all just thrilled to have a recording contract, and so the next day Cass, and indeed John, unaware of what had happened, continued life as normal. The Landmark had only ever been a temporary situation, so they began looking in the paper for a house and it was taken for granted that they would rent somewhere together. They eventually found a classic, stucco-fronted, southern Californian three-bedroom house on Flores Street, just below Sunset Boulevard. It was painted dark olive green with light green trim and, as Denny recalls, 'looked like the Addams house with a weird fountain on the front lawn that sort of spit a little water out'. Life now really seemed to be improving for the Mamas and Papas:

they had a record deal, a Buick and a new Hollywood home, complete with its own sauna. This was certainly a change from searching for floor space at Jim and Vanessa's, and Denny and Michelle made the most of it, playing footsie while the four of them were in the sauna or sneaking off to the kitchen to canoodle while Cass and John were in the next room watching TV.

Unaware of what was going on almost under her nose, Cass, like John, thought life was just great and it seemed to be getting better by the minute. One morning there was a knock on the door and Cass went to answer it. There, standing on the doorstep, was none other than Liberace, suitably bedecked in furs and a blinding array of gold and sparkling gems. The Flores Street building had been advertised for sale and so, although there was as yet no sale and so no need for them to move, the entertainer had come to look around. Cass had been excited about being in Hollywood before, but this just seemed too fabulous. 'Cass was in fucking heaven!' says Denny. 'She's showing Liberace around the house – he doesn't give a shit about the house, he's gonna level the place and build an apartment block, but she's just *gushing, floating* and showing him the backyard, going, "We have *side* showers in all of the showers . . ." It was *crazy*! It's fucking *Liberace*! What's going on? *"Hollywood . . ."*,' he sings, '*"da da da da da, Hollywood."* Things like *that* happen.'

Things like that did happen in Hollywood, and compared with the relatively sedate confines of Alexandria and Baltimore, for Cass, stardom finally did seem within reach, but it was only a matter of time before this newly found Hollywood idyll would come to an abrupt end. In the meantime, however, they had a record deal and were about to record their debut album.

14

'Harvey'

As soon as Lou Adler had heard 'California Dreamin'', he knew it was a hit, but as the group had originally auditioned to sing backing vocals on Barry McGuire's album, he had suggested McGuire record it as his follow-up to 'Eve of Destruction', with the group on backing. This had happened before they signed their own deal and so John had agreed. Although with hindsight it might seem strange that John was willing to give up what he, like Adler, must certainly have realised was the obvious jewel in his songwriting crown, at the time, whilst John sensed it was a hit, nobody knew for certain and if there was money to be made in the here and now, that was all he had really cared about. 'It was like, "Sure, fine, great! Buy a hamburger or something,"' explains Denny. 'If *anybody* wanted to buy material, John as the songwriter would say, "Great – how much? Five grand? *Sold.*" It didn't matter *what* it was – it could have been the star spangled fucking banner at that point 'cause we were stone broke. He would have sold it to anybody.'

There was no question that the group was going to record an album in their own right, but they were also still committed to singing with McGuire, and the group therefore returned to Western Recorders, the studios which would later become the LA equivalent of Abbey Road, legendary as the home of the Beach Boys' most famous recordings and indeed, the Mamas and the Papas'. There they recorded several songs with McGuire, including 'California Dreamin''. These would eventually surface on his *This Precious Time* album, but having finished with McGuire, the group was now ready to record their own debut LP and explore their own sound.

The addition of Cass's voice into the group had provided John with the opportunity to explore harmonies and song structures which would have been impossible without her, pushing him into ever more daring arrangements. 'John Phillips's brilliance at songwriting and most especially vocal arranging was exceptional,' says lyricist John Bettis who would later write many of the Carpenters' hits as well as songs for Cass's final album. 'He is *as* important a vocal arranger as Brian Wilson or Richard Carpenter, but it was such an oddball way to arrange that no one could ever use it besides them. 'Monday, Monday' is a *loopy* vocal arrangement. Had he not had someone as musically powerful as Cass in that group who could literally sing anything from low contralto all the way up to second soprano and double Michelle and also double Denny, he'd never have gotten away with it! Never in a *million* years. You can't take four people unless you've got a Cass Elliot in the band and have 'em sing that. It's *not* possible! And you know he took *that* and he just turned it to ten.'

But aside from the quality of her singing, the addition of Cass also brought John another new element to the dynamic of the group's voices. Listening to the group's records, it's difficult not to notice the almost conversational way in which Cass and Denny volley off each other musically, particularly in John's often call-and-response style arrangements. In Cass, John had now gained someone with whom Denny, his star tenor, already had a long-established friendship and musical spontaneity. It would prove not only a gift but undoubtedly an inspiration for John's future writing and the sound of the Mamas and the Papas.

Although the group had been surprised at the impact of their combined voices when they had first sung together, once they were in the studio, they seemed to create something still more magical. 'When we were singing really well,' explains Denny, 'this phantom overtone voice would show up on top of everything else. It was a "fifth" voice and we used to call it "Harvey". It wasn't really there. We'd be singing, really close with our heads together trying to work on a part and suddenly we'd hear him – "Harvey's here!" Then it was like, "OK we can do it now. We found him!" When Harvey would appear, the arrangement would usually gel.'

The combination of Cass and Denny's voices had immediately given the group an acoustic power and edge which needed no amplification as all four of them were by this time used to projecting and singing live. The recording process, meanwhile, had barely changed since Cass had last been in a studio with the Mugwumps and was still effectively geared towards recording vocal performances as live. Artists of the time were therefore by necessity required to have reached a certain musical standard in order to even qualify for a record deal, unlike the current situation where technological wizardry can be used to create something at least passable from the most negligible of musical talents. At the time a studio's capabilities were far more limited, but with the Mamas and the Papas, engineer Bones Howe found that his raw material had given him a head start. 'They were really *good* live!' remembers Howe, 'The four of them with a guitar could make a *big* sound and if you stood in the room with them, you'd have no trouble hearing them! It was a group that was made up of making music *before* they got to the studio, not just in the studio. And they sang well and sang in tune and they were used to singing, hearing each other side by side.'

The only challenge for Howe, therefore, was to capture the balance and nuances of their harmonies on record. Using his background as a jazz drummer, Howe realised that the best way to do this was to physically position them in the studio the way they would sing live. Howe arranged Cass and Michelle around one microphone with John and Denny opposite them around another, so that they could face each other and hear one another while they sang. These were also the days before artists used headphones in the studio or recorded their vocals in individual booths. Just as they would at home or anywhere else, the four of them sat close and just listened to each other live in the room. It was something which Howe believed was central to the spontaneity of the performance. 'I believe that in order to make good music,' says Howe, 'people have to be breathing the same air at the same time and that kind of comes from playing live first. I knew that people always play better when they're close together and so I worked out ways to place the microphones in such a way that the most important thing was putting everybody together and then getting the sound of each individual instrument separated from the others enough so that you could somehow balance the sound.'

Although Cass's voice was clearly much stronger than Michelle's she had already worked out how to balance it and control it, but if any problems occurred in the studio, they could all amend their voices as they went along. The others had similarly got used to singing louder, stronger and better just to keep up with her. 'They'd come and listen to the playback,' says Howe, 'and you'd go, "You're too loud, Cass, soften up," or whatever, so they would do all that adjusting live, just like a brass section would. Which is much better, because this way, *they* make the performance, instead of *me* making the performance, which is the way it's supposed to be.'

John's finely honed arrangements didn't necessarily come easily, however, and sometimes, after a particularly epic session in the studio, Cass would simply faint with giddiness and exhaustion and collapse on the floor. They had rehearsed nearly all the arrangements beforehand, but once they were in the studio, problems would occasionally emerge and, while Cass and the others kept having to repeat individual phrases, it would sometimes take John hours to readjust and solve just one arrangement. 'They would sing these long passages,' explains Howe, 'and what happens when you store up that much air and you have to let it all out, you get depleted of oxygen, so you literally see stars! Denny would say, "I'm flashing!" And you do! It's like getting hit on the head, because the oxygen all goes.'

In terms of the album's material, seven out of the twelve songs were John's own compositions but John wasn't required to write an entire album's worth. The music industry was still dominated by the singles market and so it was standard practice for albums to be merely a collection of singles strung together and padded out with cover versions of other hit songs of the time. This was therefore what the Mamas and the Papas did and when it came to choosing which other songs to record, everyone brought in their own ideas, including Cass. Two favourites of hers at the time were 'The In Crowd', which had already been a hit for both Dobie Gray and the Ramsey Lewis Trio and the Beatles' 'I Call your Name', as performed (and written) by her very own John Lennon. Both songs featured a strong vocal lead and so, as they were Cass's choices, there was little question that she would carry them more or less alone. The results could very easily have been released as solo singles by Cass. Although the rest of the group featured strongly as backing singers with John's distinctive harmonies on both tracks, backing was essentially all they were. And even here, via double tracking, Cass's voice was audible singing backing to herself with the other three. But whilst Cass's version of 'The In Crowd' was very much a carbon copy of the song's previous versions, 'I Call Your Name' was cleverly arranged as a slow-shuffle ballad and adapted as a kind of duet between Cass and Denny with her taking the lead until the final bars which featured the four of them in John's unique harmonies. The song also married session keyboardist Larry Knechtel's honky-tonk piano to Cass's voice – a combination which would become a distinctive feature of many of her future lead vocals. The other most memorable aspect of Cass's 'I Call Your Name' was her whispering of the name 'John' over the instrumental break in the middle of the song. The 'John' in question referred to Lennon rather than Phillips and, given Cass's infatuation, people naturally assumed that it had been her idea. The initiative had in fact been John's, however, and Cass, far from liking the idea, had initially refused. She was so enamoured of the acerbic Beatle that she was far too embarrassed to do such a thing and she told John, 'No, I can't do that!' 'Go out there and whisper the name,' John told her. 'Go ahead, Cass, it'll be great. He'll love it,' said John, refusing to take no for an answer. But still Cass insisted that she couldn't do it. 'OK, Mitch, *you* go do it,' John said finally, at which point Cass shouted out 'No, no, no, no. *I'll* do it.' And a whisper was born.

But although Cass may have had a rather more intense interest in John Lennon than anyone else in the group, she was far from alone in her appreciation of the Beatles' music. Denny and Lou Adler had always loved them and John had by now realised their importance. From John's distinctive 'Day Tripper'-style twelve-string intro to 'Straight Shooter' to the flute solo on 'California Dreamin'' with its echoes of 'You've Got to Hide Your Love Away', their influence could be heard, not just in John's songwriting, but throughout the album.

But while John played guitar, the group obviously needed a proper instrumental band to pad out their vocal sound and Adler had duly assembled his usual crew of seasoned session musicians, the rhythm core of whom would collectively become known as the Wrecking Crew and would play on many of the most famous records of the sixties: Larry Knechtel (later of Bread) on keyboards, Hal Blaine on drums and percussion and Joe Osborn on bass. Guitarist and writer of 'Eve of Destruction' Phil 'P. F.' Sloan was also brought in on guitar, but the final touch came in the form of the 'sweetening' – the name given to the expansive, lush strings added to many of the tracks which brought breadth and fullness to their sound, particularly on songs such as 'Go Where You Wanna Go', with its cello intro and high strings punctuating the rest of the song. With the addition of the Motown-style tambourine beat to the strings, the songs took on the epic quality of Phil Spector-style mini pop symphonies and it was this, combined with John's spectacular vocal harmonies, which would become the musical signature of the group at its best. But what came through above all was the unique combination of their voices, which seemed to reinforce the idea of the band as four free-thinking, free-living individuals who had come together in a way which was harmonious in every sense of the word.

If the band sounded natural on record, they looked at least as much so on what would become the album's landmark sleeve featuring the four of them lolling in each others' arms, fully dressed, in a bathtub. Up until that time, bands invariably posed in their smartest clothes, or if not, at least stood solemnly in group formation. Even the Rolling Stones, who were still seen as pop's subversive bêtes noires, had done so, albeit sullenly, for their debut. Here for the first time were a group of seemingly raggle taggle hippies cavorting waywardly in a bathtub.

But what the public was seeing was only the reality of the group's daily life, because whereas most artists today would be inundated with stylists, managers and marketing gurus masterminding what they should wear and what pose they should strike, the record industry at that time – and certainly the relatively small Dunhill label – was a comparatively simple operation. 'Because we were so poor, we had no money,' explains Michelle. 'When we first came to Los Angeles, we were *broke*. We didn't *have* clothes. We had a couple of pairs of jeans and some T-shirts and that was it. And so that first picture of us in the bathtub, what we were wearing was really what we wore all the time. We didn't get dressed up for this photo shoot.'

In the original shot, a toilet could be seen next to the bath but as this was considered one indecency too far, propriety demanded it be blocked out with a sticker-like box listing some of the tracks included on the album. Cass had once again, albeit unwittingly, been the instigator of the picture's unorthodox location. Photographer Guy Webster had arrived at Flores Street to take the group's picture and was wandering around the house's backyard looking for them when Cass decided to liven things up. '"Let's go hide on him," whispered Cass, "Come on!" So we're running around different rooms of the house,' remembers Denny, 'and we can hear him coming in and she says, "Let's all go hide in the bath and be quiet. It's the one place he's not looking." So we're all sitting in the bathtub when he opens the door and goes "click".'

The bathtub shot seemed to capture a vision of familial harmony which would become central to the band's popularity, but was in fact, almost over before the album was released.

To celebrate the recording of *If You Can Believe Your Eyes and Ears* – as the album was eventually named – in January 1966 the four of them decided to take a short trip to Mexico. The plan was for them to relax after their long hours in the studio and have some time off, drink some Mexican beer and go horse riding on the beach. But things didn't quite work out that way. They drove down to Tijuana in 'Harold the Bleak' and on their first night, after numerous rounds of Dos Equis, they decided to explore a place called the Chicago Club, which as Michelle remembers, turned out to be 'a strip joint full of marines and sailors. We were all *very*, very drunk and Cass and I went to the bathroom to throw up and when I came back out, this stripper had Denny by the ears and was grinding herself up against him. It was the most disgusting thing. I went back to the bathroom and threw up *again*!'

Cass would certainly not have been too thrilled at the sight either and the next day things didn't exactly improve when, still hung-over, Denny went for a swim and came back to shore covered in blood with a broken Coke bottle wedged into his chest. He had to be rushed to hospital for stitches, but if things looked bad at this point, they were not going to get any better for Cass.

The four of them had checked into a local hotel with only the most basic of sleeping arrangements. Whilst Cass and Denny had rooms of their own, as did John and Michelle, the dividing walls between them were more like partitioning screens and the acoustics were consequently rather more open plan than they might have wished. 'We could hear . . . *everything* that's going on,' remembers Denny, 'so John and Michelle are . . . well the love of my life is in the next room with her *husband* copulating, and listening to them . . . I can't *handle* it.' Denny decided to get up and go for a drive, but hearing him stir, Cass, who was similarly awake, suggested she go with him. They had all been out drinking earlier in the evening and were still, as Denny recalls, 'half-shot'. Feeling more than a little drunk and no less distressed over the night's events, Denny did what seemed most natural. With a drink-fuelled need to talk and a similarly drink-fuelled lack of thought at the consequences, Denny told his best friend what was wrong. 'The scene back at the hotel was just too much and I'm going on and blah, blah . . . and *I love her*! *I* don't know how it came out, but that's the moment I chose to tell Cass that I'm having an affair with Michelle.'

With hindsight it seems hard to imagine Cass had not seen this coming, but it can sometimes be easy to avoid seeing things that you'd rather ignore, even when they're right in front of you. It had also never occurred to Cass, even if she had been aware of the flirtation, that anything would ever actually happen between them as Michelle was married to Denny's best friend. 'She didn't even see it coming,' says Denny, 'because *I* would never do that. I'm a nice boy from Canada. I would never have touched someone else's wife – I'm not *like* that. I was raised very *properly*,' he laughs.

When the reality then came flying hard in Cass's face, her reaction was no surprise. 'Stop the car!' she told Denny. 'She's crying and all she wanted to do was get out of the fucking car. At a hundred miles an hour!' remembers Denny heavy-heartedly. 'The top [of the car] was down and she was trying to get out. No one was wearing seat belts. And she's doing a Jackie Kennedy on me . . . over the back seat. So she's trying to climb out and I'm slamming on the brakes and the fucking thing stops in the middle of the highway. She said, "Michelle's never gonna leave John for *you*. Are you *crazy*? Poor, pathetic thing. You and Michelle? Take me home, shithead. Dumbass. I can't handle this – you're *pitiful*."' Despite her emotions, Cass was still clear-headed enough to grasp the reality of the situation and having spelt it out to Denny, there was nothing left to say. The two of them drove back to the hotel in silence.

The realisation that Denny was in love with someone else, and of all people, the woman who was not just her singing partner but her friend, must have been devastating. Whilst Cass knew that Michelle may have been much more conventionally attractive, she had always consoled herself with the fact that although her friend was by no means stupid, Cass was nevertheless sharper and wittier, and when it came to singing, there was really no contest at all. But it had never occurred to her that she would ever have to try and compete with her for a man, least of all the man she so wanted. But then again, she had never thought she would have to. Michelle was married to John and whilst she may have had to contest with any number of other women where Denny was concerned, up until this point, she still hadn't entirely given up hope. She knew that her friendship with Denny was much more important to them both than most of his romantic liaisons and she could invariably dismiss whichever woman happened to be around as a meaningless diversion, and frequently did. But to hear that he was in love with someone else, knowing that that someone was not only beautiful but fun and, most significantly, her own friend, clearly signalled the end of any hopes she could have had. Cass had been knocked back in the past, but this time, it seemed like the situation with Denny really was futile. However close she may have been to him, she would never be able to compete with someone like Michelle for his affection.

Whatever she may have been feeling, she didn't say anything to John. As far as she was concerned, the situation would either blow over or blow up in everyone's face and she didn't have to wait long to find out which it was to be.

A few days later, when they were back at Flores Street, John walked out onto the back porch where Denny was sleeping, to find Michelle getting to know Denny rather more intimately than inter-band friendliness strictly required. Michelle ran off as soon as she saw him, leaving Denny convinced that this was likely to signal a punch-up. But no. 'If I'd known this was going on,' mumbled John, 'I'd never have signed them goddamn contracts.' And with that, he walked back upstairs. A few hours later, he and Michelle moved out of the house.

Cass had been sleeping while the morning's drama had unfolded and so when she finally came downstairs, Denny explained. Cass realised immediately the potential consequences this could have for the group. 'Cass just turned to me,' remembers Denny, 'and said, "*Shit*," looking at me like, "You're not worth my time. How could you do this?"'

Now that the situation was out in the open, Cass could also confront Michelle and she lost no time in doing so. The way she saw it, when it came to culpability, she could hardly blame Denny for being attracted to Michelle. Besides, she had been in love with him for far too long for anything to really change that. Michelle on the other hand was her friend and knew how much Denny meant to her. 'How could you do this to me?' she demanded. 'You can have any man you want. Why the one that *I* wanted?'

Less than two months had passed since the Mamas and the Papas had signed the contract with Dunhill and they had yet to release their first single.

Lou Adler had decided that 'Go Where You Wanna Go' should be the band's debut single. John had originally written the song about an affair Michelle was having back in New York, but the irony when it came to recording the track, as would prove the case so often in the future, was that it was Cass's distinctive voice pleading, '"You don't understand / that a girl like me can't love just one man,"' when this was clearly John articulating Michelle's point of view. Cass herself would certainly have empathised with the lyric's sentiment later on in her life, but at the time would probably have been pleased to have been involved with even one man, let alone two.

Dunhill shipped the record out in December of '65, but almost as soon as it had been released, Adler changed his mind. 'California Dreamin'' was clearly a hit and seemed obviously to belong to the band, so he decided that Denny should re-record McGuire's lead vocal and that the song, rather than being given to McGuire, should launch the Mamas and the Papas instead. As McGuire and the band were friends, this was not a problem. John took him out to the hallway of Western Recorders. 'Look, we'd like to do "California Dreamin'" as our first single,' he told him. 'Sure, man,' replied McGuire, 'That's great. Then *you* can buy the grass next month.'

While initially recording the song with McGuire, the track had gained its distinctive opening acoustic guitar line from Phil Sloan. But in place of the flute that would become such a pointed feature of the Mamas and the Papas' version, the McGuire recording featured a harmonica solo. When it came to re-recording the song with Denny, Adler decided he'd like to do something different and as they only had four tracks to work with rather than the extensive options open to musicians working today, choices had to be made on the spot. 'You had to make your decisions *in the room*,' explains Bones Howe. 'Lou and all of us that made records at that time had to decide at that moment if we liked it or we didn't. Does the tambourine work or not? Does acoustic guitar work or shall we have electric guitar? Because there *weren't* a thousand tracks – you couldn't take 'em away later! You were *stuck* with whatever you did. So you'd get excited about whatever you did – that *works*! And you'd do it. And then you'd go onto whatever the next thing was and soon it would be in the layers. It was very spontaneous and you were constantly improvising. So with "California Dreamin'", Lou just said to me, "I'd love to have something besides a guitar solo. I'd like to have a *flute*."'

As it so happened, that day jazz flautist Bud Shank was recording in another studio along the hall, and as Howe had worked with him in the past, he asked him if he had a few minutes to spare. 'When you're done,' Howe told him, 'come down the hall to studio three, I got a fast overdub for you.' And he duly did. 'That's just the way records were made,' says Howe, clicking his fingers. 'Have an alto flute!' Backed by a steady tambourine beat and the Wrecking Crew's rhythm section, Shank's flute perfectly complemented the autumnal romance of John's lyrics and the result is probably one of the most instantly recognisable flute solos in rock history.

'California Dreamin'' has since become one of the great pop classics. Almost forty years since it was first released, it continues to top the charts and has been covered by countless artists from the Four Tops to José Feliciano and Bobby Womack. Like the standards of the thirties or the best known songs by Lennon, McCartney or Bacharach and David, it seems indestructible and can withstand almost any treatment. The Mamas and the Papas' original remains the definitive version, however, and although it was Denny's voice at its most soulful, passionately leading the song, it was Cass's voice so prominently carrying the response that would herald her future fame.

The single was released in December 1965 with another of John's songs, the raunchy 'Somebody Groovy', on the B-side. Featuring Cass on lead vocal, the song could almost have been written with her in mind: 'I need somebody groovy / Someone who's able to move me, yeah / they gotta move me like they should, and when I find somebody, yeah, I'm gonna treat 'em good.' It would be a little while before Cass had somebody groovy of her own but in the meantime her new group's single, 'California Dreamin'', began slowly but surely climbing the charts.

Just as Cass's voice had already become an inspiration for John, prompting him to try ever more daring harmonies, his songwriting was no less vital to Cass. Like so many debut albums, the Mamas and the Papas' first album represented one of the most productive periods in John's songwriting life. Michelle was the inspiration for his best material and, viewed as a whole, the lyrics to John's key songs can be read almost as a week-by-week diary of his relationship with her, from 'Straight Shooter''s 'Baby are you holdin'? holdin' anything but me?' to 'Got a feelin' that I'm wasting time on you, babe / got a feelin' that you've been untrue' in 'Got a Feelin''. As time passed, his new songs would continue to reflect every drama and crisis that happened between them, and there would be quite a few. Consequently, although Michelle and Denny's betrayal would be traumatic for Cass on a personal level, professionally, the stimulus it would bring to John's songwriting would provide her with the perfect vehicle for her voice and thereby launch the persona which would become 'Mama' Cass.

15

'Two duelling virgos'

In 1966, after five years of struggle, Cass became an overnight success. In early January 'California Dreamin'' entered the lower regions of the *Billboard* charts and began a torturously slow crawl upwards. Cass and the others watched and waited eagerly, checking the charts each week to see if it had gone down or simply disappeared, but it kept going up. Then, one day in early March they were all sitting in Harold the Bleak with the radio on, when suddenly they heard the opening strains of that distinctive Spanish guitar intro. They turned up the dial and there it was – 'California Dreamin'' blasting out of their own car radio. In spite of the strain between them, all four of them felt an incredible rush of excitement and the euphoric certainty that they were going to have a hit. The following week, on 12 March 1966, 'California Dreamin'' peaked at number four in the *Billboard* charts.

'California Dreamin'' was a bigger hit than anyone had ever imagined it could be – in Boston it was the biggest record since 'White Christmas' – and its follow-up 'Monday, Monday', went straight to number one. The singles also made the top ten in Britain, France, Germany, Greece, Spain, Italy and Australia. Suddenly, the Mamas and the Papas were stars, not just in their own country, but on a global scale, and Cass was, without question, the superstar of the group.

Just as Cass's voice was the dominant response to Denny's lead on 'California Dreamin'', when it came to 'Monday, Monday', her voice and the emotion it brought to the record was just as prominent. When this combined with her unconventional but phenomenally charismatic presence and stage wit, it was no surprise that fans adored her. 'Cass was without question the most popular person in the group,' says Michelle. 'We got more fan mail for her than anybody else. It was like

Cass here,' she says, pitching her hand at shoulder level, 'then John,' at waist level, 'then me,' somewhere near her knee, 'and then Denny here,' around ankle level, '*Denny* – who sang all the leads!'

With the Mamas and the Papas, Cass finally found herself in a grouping that worked on every level. She may not have been the front person or official lead vocalist, but she would make the role her own and become the undisputed star of the group nevertheless. Just as she had done when she first met Tim Rose in Washington, DC, she had confounded John's beliefs about what could and couldn't work as a commercial visual image and to his constant irritation, captivated the public's imagination against all odds.

Cass had never looked like anyone's idea of a star and the juxtaposition of a brunette woman of her size in psychedelic velvet pinafores and go-go boots next to Michelle's lithe, barefoot, blonde flower child seemed unorthodox to say the least. Throw into the mix a good-looking mop-topped male singer and a tall, thin eccentric-looking guy in a hat and it's not hard to see why the group had such an impact. You couldn't have dreamt it up.

To the group's audiences, meanwhile, the four of them, but particularly Cass, seemed to symbolise a new way of living and a freedom which was entirely fresh and contemporary. Everything about them seemed to trumpet the message of nonconformity, from Cass's size and Michelle's bare feet to Denny and John's 'long' hair. These were clearly liberated people with bohemian lifestyles and the informality of the group's pose and attitude seemed, just like their sound, not only new and different, but also spectacularly in tune with the change in mood that was happening across America.

The transition from folk into rock had gone in tandem with the emergence of what would come to be known as the counterculture or the hippy movement. This picked up where the beat and folk movements had left off, drawing on their liberal political ideals and sexual freedom and taking them to their logical conclusion. The rigid constraints of class and social obligation were rejected in favour of a freer and often communal style of living. Within a few months the media would home in on San Francisco's Haight Ashbury area as one of the major centres of the movement with its experimental poets, artists and musicians, psychedelic light shows and all-round embrace of non-conformity, unconstrained living and freedom of speech. Central to the hippie ethos was also the widespread use of LSD (and indeed marijuana), which were no longer confined to the hip, urbane circles in which Cass and Denny had discovered them. Suddenly everyone young, hip – or ideally both, was eager to explore LSD's mind-expanding possibilities or simply try the latest new fad. Gradually these ideas, or at least news of them, were beginning to spread across America, and the Mamas and the Papas seemed to be a living manifestation of what large swathes of the nation's youth aspired to, but were often either too young or too scared to try for themselves.

The cover of *If You Can Believe Your Eyes and Ears* seemed to sum up the group's relaxed image, and although innocuous by today's standards, caused an instant furore as soon as it appeared. The intimacy the 'bath' pose evoked, seemed to make just enough of a mark to be suggestive, without going so far as to offend; by flaunting their informality, the Mamas and Papas were inadvertently trailblazing the mood of the time and riding the zeitgeist for all it was worth.

What was more, the very idea of a quartet of mixed males and females seemed outlandish to start with. Folk groups like Peter, Paul and Mary and the Serendipity Singers had featured mixed gender singers, but since the arrival of the Beatles and the British Invasion, most people seemed convinced that whatever type of music bands were playing, they should be all male and playing it with electric guitars. Female singers were almost entirely restricted to performing as solo artists, so the idea therefore that two female singers could co-exist with two male singers on an entirely equal footing in a group seemed quite unheard of. Similarly, the very idea that a married couple and another unmarried couple might live together in the same house seemed utterly modern. And yet at the same time, nothing about their appearance seemed too threatening or dangerous. It made them the ultimate commercial package, whilst at the same time retaining their credibility.

If You Can Believe Your Eyes and Ears went straight to number one. It would stay in the album charts for more than two years, well into the beginning of 1968. With 'Monday, Monday', John had said he wanted to write a song with 'international appeal', and a theme that 'everyone can relate to', but both Cass and Michelle thought it the most contrived, pretentious thing they had ever heard, and Denny wasn't much more enthusiastic. It was 'a stupid little song about a day of the week', they told him and were convinced it spelt doom on the charts. The lyrics may indeed not have won any prizes for their deep profundity – 'Monday Monday can't trust that day / ... Monday Monday, it's here to stay' – but despite their reservations, once the song was recorded, John's infectious melody, combined with the group's soaring, multilayered harmonies and Denny's mellifluous lead, made for three minutes of perfect pop. Fortunately, in this particular instance, Lou Adler thought so too and told the group, 'You do the singing, I'll do the releasing.' The record sold 160,000 copies on the day it was released before going on to number one and receiving no less than four Grammy nominations, one of which they won.

But as their fame grew, so did the lie they were portraying. The group who had become symbols of Californian love and peace were, with the exception of Michelle, not in fact from California, and relations amongst them, particularly between Cass and John, were becoming increasingly strained.

If the success of 'California Dreamin'' had been exciting, having a number one record with 'Monday, Monday' catapulted the Mamas and the Papas into an entirely different league. 'Suddenly we had money for all the toys in the world ... the more extravagant the better,' said Cass. Money just seemed to flood in virtually overnight, and in a matter of weeks, they went from being too poor to pay the utility bills to having more money than they had ever dreamed of. 'It was like winning the lottery,' says Michelle.

Cass suddenly found herself with enough pocket money to indulge a passion for fast cars and went straight to the nearest car dealer. But her size and her 'hippy' appearance was not quite how the dealers imagined their prospective clientele to look. When Cass sauntered in and enquired about the gleaming yellow Aston Martin in the showroom, she was curtly informed that it was 'appointments only'. 'I'd like to see the guy who owns this place,' replied Cass. Half an hour later she had paid cash and was driving her new Aston Martin home. Over the next few years, her car collection would come to include a Porsche, an Eldorado Cadillac, a Citroën deux chevaux, a Mini Cooper and a Morris Minor – the latter two of which were chosen primarily for their Englishness. She also adored jewellery and the staff at Tiffany's Beverley Hills showroom soon got to know her. Cass had become particularly fixated with an enormous yellow diamond which she could not yet afford, but the assistants would let her take it out of its glass display case and parade around the store trying it on.

Even before she had had money, Cass's friends had always noticed her generosity and now that she was rich, she wanted to share her new-found wealth. She adored buying presents and bought several of her less-successful folkie friends colour televisions – still a state-of-the-art novelty at the time. She could also now indulge her love of clothes – if not on herself, then on others, and would often take her sister Leah, who was still only in her late teens and fashionably slim, on lavish shopping trips, kitting her out in designer clothes from Rudy Gernreich.

As well as the money, the group's new-found success also brought with it a newly hectic schedule. Suddenly, their days were filled with an endless round of TV shows: *Shindig*, *Hollywood Palace*, *American Bandstand*, *Hollywood A Go Go* and *The Ed Sullivan Show*, on which they duly performed their singles and answered the hosts' invariably inane questions. They also started playing live shows. Although they had never performed live since Cass had joined the group, with two top ten hits behind them, they suddenly found themselves playing their first gig, opening for Sonny and Cher at the Hollywood Bowl. The sun was just beginning to set as the group ran out onstage and, as John later remembered, the eight-thousand strong crowd went 'beserk'. Although the piercing of the fans' screams meant that the group could hardly hear themselves singing, the show was nevertheless a huge success. One critic commented that they were creating 'the most inventive vocals since the Beatles'.

The Mamas and the Papas were soon booked to headline a string of major venues and stadia. This meant that Cass finally had an audience for her easy wit and repartee and gradually her stage persona began to evolve into the uniquely sassy, hippy Mae West character that would become her trademark. 'Cass used to *encourage* people in the audience to talk to her!' remembers Michelle. 'People would call out from the front rows and there was this wonderful night when a guy shouted, "Caaaaasss – I luuuuuuve yoooou!" Cass said, "Dynamite! Where you staying?" And the audience just went crazy. They just *loved* her.'

For Cass, it was as though these hours in front of an audience seemed to make up for all the years of insults and rejection. Here, finally, onstage, she was queen and she played it for all it was worth. 'Cass just loved communicating with complete strangers,' says Michelle, 'and the more there were, the happier she was. She was mercilessly flirtatious and entertaining and funny and she would just carry on with the audience and make jokes with them and talk to them like they were long-lost friends. Sometimes, when it came to her solos, she would sit down on the apron of the stage and everybody would think she was singing just for them. She really was wonderful and people adored her.'

Fans would scream out 'Cass! Cass! Cass!' as she danced around the stage and everything about her seemed to confirm to the band's fans that while Cass was quite the coolest thing they had ever seen, the Mamas and the Papas were similarly the most jovial, free-spirited band in town. But it wasn't only Cass's wit which endeared her to her fans. Just as the group represented a lifestyle, Cass was also redefining the concept of beauty and how a female star could look. As *New York* magazine commented in 1967, 'She has broken the strongest barrier for an aspiring star. In America, the most weight-conscious nation in the world, she has become a glamour girl. She is a star, not despite her weight or because of it, but beyond it. Cass is a horizon.'

At every appearance the group made, young girls would seek Cass out, asking advice, sitting adoringly at her feet as she talked about her own life. Even in 1966, if you were a teenage girl, the pressures Cass had experienced at high school were still very much in evidence, and so for every girl who didn't fit in with the high school Prom ideal, Cass became their patron saint. She represented them and she gave them a voice. It had always been obvious that someone who looked like Michelle could become a star, but here for the first time was someone proving that you could do it on your own terms, whatever you looked like. As *Esquire* later commented, 'What Streisand did for Jewish girls in Brooklyn, Cass Elliot was doing for fat girls everywhere.'

Cass seemed to defy conventional expectations of what a woman of her size could or couldn't do. When you watched Cass onstage, you were left in no doubt that she was loving every instant of her performance as much as her audience and while Michelle often nodded and swayed along to the music nervously, Cass had mastered the Tina Turner running-on-the-spot dance to perfection and would nimbly shimmy her way through the show as if she were a go-go dancer on *American Bandstand*.

The scenes of fan hysteria which greeted them were now more worthy of The Beatles at Shea Stadium than *A Hard Day's Night*. As soon as the doors opened, thousands of fans would stampede the venues, carrying placards and banners declaring 'WE LOVE CASS' or 'DENNY FOREVER', but there were usually most for Cass. At the front of the stage rows of uniformed police sat squatting, facing out to the audience, ready to defend the group from fan frenzy, whilst their burly colleagues patrolled the aisles, brandishing torches in an attempt to keep some semblance of order. But this was nothing compared with the task of getting the group off the premises without having their clothes ripped to shreds. This required an operation of military precision in which the group's limousine would emerge onto the streets escorted by a formation of police bikes, in an attempt to fend off the swarms of teenage girls who rushed the car, pressing their faces against the windows.

Cass loved the fans because they loved her and were the source of the fame and adulation she had craved for so long, but she also hadn't forgotten what it was like to be a fan herself. After a stadium gig one night in San Francisco, as the four of them peered out from the limo at the clamouring fans, Cass noticed a girl with freckles holding a shirt cardboard with 'DENNY' written on it in lipstick. She was trying to break through the police line.

'Denny, wave to that chick,' said Cass. Denny waved. 'Made her day,' said Cass.

Given the level of their new-found fame, it wasn't long before a feeling of omnipotence also began to blind them to the more mundane realities of touring. Such as showing up to the gig. 'We cancelled a lot of shows,' remembers Michelle, 'and we were very cavalier about that whole aspect of the career. It was like, "Oh, let's not play Cleveland, fuck Cleveland, why don't we just go onto Detroit you know?"' Somehow or other, in contrast to the legal ramifications a band attempting such a course would face today, the group seem to have got away with it and just kept on going.

But the vision of internal group harmony on which the group's popularity was founded, was already well into decline. Their sudden success and superstardom may have taken the edge off the gloom created by the recent crisis between them, but it still wasn't enough to ease tensions completely. By the time their album was released, although in public they maintained an appearance of hippy togetherness, in private, the four of them were not only living separately but much of the time barely speaking to each other.

*

By this time, they had all moved out of Flores Street. Cass had gone to a temporary house off Kirkwood Drive in Stanley Hills, whilst John and Michelle, having discussed their relationship, were attempting a kind of trial separation and therefore living apart. John subsequently moved into bachelor rock-star pad bliss on Woods Drive with Denny, believing that if they were living in the same house, he could minimise the likelihood of an affair continuing between Denny and his wife, or at least if it did, he would know about it. John's attitude seemed to be that if Michelle was going to be unfaithful that was bad enough, but under no circumstances could she do so with Denny. 'You can do a lot of things to me, Mitch,' John yelled at her during one argument, 'but you don't fuck my tenor!'

Michelle, meanwhile, lost no time enjoying her own new-found freedom. John had been serially unfaithful to both her and his previous wife Suzy, so as far as she was concerned, she wasn't doing anything that John hadn't done already. But this proved more than John had bargained for. Although he himself was happy to play the field, and wasted no time in doing so, hearing of Michelle's various liaisons was too much to deal with. In a radical U-turn of thought, John now decided that if his wife was going to be romantically involved with someone other than him, then it ought to be Denny, rather than anyone else.

This was of course far from what Cass would have wished, but from John's point of view, there was, it seems, a certain logic to this notion, as his major concern was keeping the group together. He therefore decided to resolve the situation once and for all and force Michelle to decide between the two of them. When Michelle arrived for rehearsal the next day, John and Denny told her they wanted to have a heart-to-heart talk and confronted her. 'Now, Michelle – you've got to choose. Which one of us do you want?' they asked. Michelle looked at them in bewilderment and ran out of the house crying. Just at the moment Cass arrived.

'What's going on?' asked Cass. 'What's happening?' Denny explained and Cass, once again, looked at him witheringly with suitable disdain. '*Fuck* you, people,' she told him, 'you're too fucking civilised. I can't take this any more. You're just twisted. It's *sick*. It's like *bartering*. None of you should be respected.' She turned towards the door before looking back at Denny, 'It's just not gonna work. You're gonna be doing this for the rest of your lives,' she told him, displaying immense foresight, before adding, 'I can't handle this,' and walked out of the house.

For Cass, it had been bad enough discovering Michelle's betrayal and the fact that the man she loved was in love with someone else. Now she had to contend with the unavoidable fact that the two most important men in her life – the friend she was in love with and the leader of her group, were both battling for the love of her colleague and friend.

With both the Big 3 and the Mugwumps, Cass had got used to being the only woman, the star surrounded by adoring men. Suddenly, she found herself in a very different situation. Although the audiences adored her, when it came to the people she spent her time with and those whose affection she wanted the most, she had effectively lost out to the woman she had thought of as her friend. More poignantly still, she also, unlike Denny, realised the futility of his hopes. All these decades on, I ask Michelle if she ever seriously thought she and Denny might have a future together. '*No!*' she replies emphatically, without an instant's hesitation, before admitting that, 'It sounds so cold and horrible, thirty-five years later'.

By April 1966, despite their showdown, nothing had been resolved between John and Michelle and the group was due at Western Recorders to start their second album. Given the recent traumas between them, the idea of going back into the studio and being confined together for hours on end didn't particularly appeal to any of them. The friendships between them had been shattered so fundamentally that it was bound to affect the recording process and the atmosphere in the studio was decidedly acidic. As a result, it was hardly surprising that they were all often rather more keen to enjoy their new wealth and fame than to put in an appearance at the studio, so the task of recording the all-important but much-dreaded second album consequently became a challenge of logistics in getting all four of them to come to the studio at the same time. 'Sometimes somebody wouldn't show up,' remembers engineer Bones Howe, 'or they *all* wouldn't show up and Lou would order food in and he and I would eat dinner off the recording desk and then we'd go home – there was just nobody there.'

Even on the occasions when they all convened at the same time, they didn't always manage to get much work done. 'You never knew what kind of frame of mind people were going to be in,' says Howe. 'You didn't know whether Cass was gonna be happy or angry, you didn't know how much Denny was going to bring to drink – you know, the Crown Royal (whisky) bottles piled up on the ledge in front of the glass. It was like making the record was a secondary thing to just having a good time.' Sessions were booked from four in the afternoon till midnight and on a good night, they'd work through till six in the morning, but often, they'd just be starting to make progress with a track when one of them would announce they had to leave, effectively closing the session for the night.

But the group's lack of enthusiasm was not solely due to their recent dramas. In contrast to their debut album, the recording process itself had now become much more long-winded. Whereas with the earlier record most of the arrangements had been worked out long before they reached the studio, this time, with the four of them rarely in the same space other than for public appearances, virtually all the arrangements needed to be worked out on the spot. 'The second album was uncomfortable,' remembers Howe, 'and it took a long time to do. John literally taught them the vocal parts while we were there in the studio and the difficult thing was that John had much more trouble making up his mind on that album and each of them wanted to have more to say about the songs they were gonna sing.'

Cass in particular had gained confidence from knowing that she was the most popular member of the group. She was now the star she had always believed she would become and, understandably, she felt that there was no longer any reason to allow John to belittle her ideas or put her down. She also felt that her new-found status could give her the chance to start singing the way she wanted to, rather than as John directed. 'Cass had her own idea about the way she wanted to sing as a lead singer,' explains Howe, 'and I think that John had *his* ideas about the way she ought to sing, with the phrasing and so on, and I think that that was part of the problem. By the time we got to the second record, she was a *persona* and there was a lot of her coming into the studio saying, "You know this is uncomfortable to sing, John. Maybe we ought to just change such and such . . ." and "Is this the right key or not the right key?" or "I don't like this background part." Cass was particularly upset with some things that John wanted her to do, so there was friction in the studio a lot of the time. When we made the first album, John did a lot of coaching with Cass – he would say try this phrasing, or try that, but by the time we got to the second album, she wasn't listening to *anybody* tell her how to phrase anything.'

In terms of vocal technique, Cass certainly hadn't needed coaching, even on their first album, but almost from the start, John was keen for her to sing harder than she wanted. John had finally come to terms with rock and roll – albeit somewhat after the event, and was therefore keen for some of his songs to reflect that. He had managed it with 'Straight Shooter' and 'Somebody Groovy' on their debut and he wanted the new album to be equally balanced between the group's trademark ballads and songs which rocked out a little harder.

John later made no secret of the fact that he had had to persuade Cass to sing stronger. In contrast to the way she was often perceived, John explained, 'Cass is not a red hot Mama by any sense of the imagination! She's a *real* lady, and you have to really push her to sing hard. She won't sing hard naturally.' But Cass felt that her forte was singing in the more traditional torch-song style she had worked in as a solo artist at the Shadows. 'That was always a fight,' remembers Lou Adler, 'because John was learning rock and roll and he had two singers – Denny and Cass, who primarily were not rock and roll singers. Denny's got a big Western-style voice and Cass is Broadway. So her natural instincts were to sing it in a *different* way, to sing it a little broader than the records we were after and John was not content at meeting in the middle. He wanted it a certain way. And also, to her power she *could* sing it in a different way, obviously very good. When John was arranging the leads, he also had backgrounds in mind and knew at what point those background voices were gonna hit, so he's phrasing it in order to get those in, to get that four-part Mamas and Papas sound.'

But these were just the songs where Cass disagreed with John over phrasing. There were others that she just didn't want to sing at all. One of these was 'Words of Love', which would become one of Cass's two lead vocals on the album. Like virtually every other new song John had written, the lyrics documented his frustration at being unable to maintain a monopoly on Michelle's affections, but musically John envisaged the song as a strident ballsy lesson in love rather than a love-struck ballad and Cass therefore had the perfect voice to carry it.

Cass, however, refused. 'I think that she thought that it was so tongue in cheek,' says Michelle, 'and I think the honky-tonk piano thing kind of bothered her. Also she knew it was a song written for me, about me and I think she wanted me to sing lead on it and I just said, "No *way*." I was too afraid to sing leads! I just didn't want to do that. And then she said, "Well, let Denny sing it." And he said, "No, Cass. *You* sing it." And I remember there being this big ... well, it wasn't a fight, but finally she's out there in the studio and she's singing it, but she's not *really* singing it. And John says, "Cass, get on top of the piano." She says, "Why?" He says, "Just get up on the piano." So she climbs up on top of this baby grand and he goes out and gives her the mike and he says, "Now sing the *shit* out of this song!" And she does.' Having sung the final 'anymooooore...' of the song, Cass collapsed and passed out.

But Cass's exhaustion was not simply from the exertion of singing so forcefully. By this time, John had forced her to do take after take after take, for no apparent reason. After twenty-seven takes, Cass had begun to hyperventilate, but again John would simply say, 'Do it again, Cass.' 'Why?' she would ask. 'What was wrong with that take?' But John would never say why. If pressed, he'd simply say, 'We're just trying to do something in here.' 'What does that *mean*?' Cass would ask, knowing that she had just sung yet another perfect take. 'Just do it again,' would come back John's reply. 'He'd do it on purpose to drive her fucking crazy,' says Denny. 'The takes were *great*, but he'd just tell her to do it again. And she'd do it. You're not gonna beat me. Roll it. And she did it till she passed out.'

Whilst Cass and John's disputes were often due to a difference in musical taste or vision, there was also more than an element of power play, particularly on John's part. Cass's popularity had always irritated him, but now, although he was the leader of the group and author of their hits, the fact that Cass was seen as the figurehead and darling of their fans galled him immeasurably. John was also clearly frustrated that however much Cass's presence annoyed him, at the same time, although he would never have admitted it, he couldn't help but acknowledge her importance to the group. 'He couldn't live without her!' says Denny. 'Not in his world! But he didn't want her in. She was *creating* his world for him, but *still* not. He fought her on *every* angle because everything that she tried to do he would see as an effort to usurp his authority.'

Had it not been for this long-standing antagonism between them, the personal crises between the four of them might have drawn Cass and John closer to each other, sharing as they did the role of wronged party, but John had never made any secret of his personal antipathy towards Cass's very presence and recent events only seemed to heighten his taunts. 'Aaah! She who makes the earth move when she walks,' he would say as a greeting when she arrived at the studio. He also took to sending her trayfuls of the very finest Beluga caviar, knowing that although she loved it, she was also seriously allergic to it and risked death at the smallest mouthful.

But if Cass was hurt by John's comments or actions, she would never give him the satisfaction of letting him know. His obsession with control riled her immensely and she instinctively reacted against the idea of any man trying to forcibly govern her and put her down. But she had been enduring verbal abuse since her early teens, so although his jibes were certainly hurtful, she was also well practised at hiding and burying her feelings. 'She could detach herself emotionally,' says Denny, 'and she just wouldn't let it get to her 'cause that's what he wanted. She knew that if she showed a chink in the armour, he'd put the wedge in and tear it apart if he *could*. Because John *loved* arguing, loved to tear you to shreds. He could make you *cry*. And she wouldn't let him. And that made him even crazier.'

Apart from the friction it caused in the studio, the power struggle between Cass and John would also have another result which would have a much greater impact on Cass's life. For all his megalomania in terms of leadership, when it came to songwriting, John was in fact an effective and often generous collaborator. He had credited Michelle as co-songwriter on 'California Dreamin'' and given her half the publishing, mainly because she'd agreed to get out of bed in the middle of the night and write it down. He had also co-written several songs with Denny, such as 'I Saw Her Again'. But with Cass it was another matter. Cass had as much musical experience as Denny and, what was more, she had proved herself a more than competent writer on the songs she had written for the Mugwumps with Jim Hendricks, but although in theory Cass would have relished the opportunity to write with John, the reality was somehow never an option. Despite having written before, she knew she was nowhere near as experienced a songwriter as John, so given the arguments between them in the studio and the jibes and jeers he had long taunted her with, the idea of putting herself in the line of fire for further potential abuse as an unequal collaborator was unthinkable. At the same time, John would never have dreamt of inviting her to do so.

This issue would come to be a serious source of grievance to Cass for two reasons: firstly because she enjoyed songwriting and felt creatively frustrated at the lack of opportunity to do so, and secondly because of the growing discrepancy between her income and John, Michelle's and Denny's. Whilst the other three, particularly John and Michelle, reaped the considerable financial benefits of having written the songs on their million-selling records, Cass's income was restricted to record royalties alone and the earnings they made from touring. As time went on, she would come to feel the difference severely.

Meanwhile, in the studio, it was not only Cass who was not enjoying the sessions. If the tension between her and John was palpable, the atmosphere was hardly much more fun for anyone else. Denny, by his own admission, 'just stayed shit-faced the whole time', and the situation was no more exciting for Michelle, Adler or Bones Howe. Whilst John and Cass argued, Adler would sit in the corner of the control room with his hat pulled over his face and his arms folded, waiting till they might finally be able to proceed, and soon he and Howe developed a fatalistic attitude towards the whole project. 'You get to the point,' says Howe, 'where you go: I've just got to get this record made. There's a demand out there for a new record, there's a record company that wants it, there's a fan club that wants it and we just got to get it done. So you try to make the best record you can, but at some point you slip over the hump of making a great record to just getting a record made.'

But however fraught the sessions may have been, they did yield some memorable results for Cass and the others. The crisis in John's marriage may have destroyed the group's unity and friendship, but it had also inspired John to write a slew of new material. The new songs often reflected John's melancholy state of mind, but they also featured the same spectacular group harmonies as before and the result was a juxtaposition of poignancy on the one hand with a boundless buoyancy on the other which would become the hallmark of John's writing for the group. It would also be this contrast which would be central to their enduring success.

A case in point was the track chosen to be the group's next single – 'I Saw Her Again', which was released a couple of months ahead of the new album in June 1966. The song was in fact a collaboration between John and Denny as Denny had written the melody, but on the basis of recent events, John had written the lyrics knowing that it would be Denny who would be forced to sing it. 'I saw her again last night / and I know that I shouldn't . . .' ran the verse, although it would be both Denny and John singing 'Every time I see that girl, you know I wanna lay down and die' in the middle eight, backed by human beat-box style rhythmic staccato harmony 'do do do's at various speeds in one of John's most dynamic arrangements. As with their earlier singles, it was Denny who carried the song but it was once again Cass's voice dominating the response to Denny's lead in what was another epic wall of backbeat-fuelled harmonies and strings.

Between recording sessions, the band was also booked on a short tour and one of the gigs they were scheduled to play was at Melodyland, the theatre in the round at Anaheim, California. By the time it came to the gig, bad feelings were running so high, particularly between John and Michelle, that it was almost inevitable that sooner or later someone was bound to reach breaking point. Michelle had by this time embarked on a new affair, but this time Cass was almost supportive. There had been moments when Cass would occasionally vent her anger with Michelle onstage – one evening she had told an audience, 'Michelle won't be saying anything tonight because I didn't programme her before the show,' but however betrayed Cass had felt by Michelle, she still had to work with her, and although their friendship would take a long time to recover fully, on a day to day basis Cass generally remained as cordial as possible. She was also more than a little pleased to see Michelle asserting herself and emerging from the shadow of John's control. 'She was always pushing for my independence,' remembers Michelle, 'and she was *clearly* full of glee when I left him,' she laughs. 'She thought that was the best thing I had ever done!' In theory Cass would probably have been glad to see Michelle involved with anyone other than Denny, but her latest paramour was Denny-look-alike Gene Clark of the Byrds, who Cass herself had similarly admired. But whatever she may have been feeling personally, Cass was keen to avoid further friction in the group, and so when she saw Clark sitting in the front row with a red shirt on, she immediately went directly in front of him to prevent John noticing. 'We hadn't decided where we were gonna position ourselves onstage,' explains Michelle, 'we just went out and wherever we stood, we stood, so Cass kind of grabbed me and positioned me so that we were in front of Gene so that John and Denny couldn't be. She knew that if John saw him, he would freak.'

John, in fact had a girlfriend of his own at the gig, but as far as he was concerned, that was different. 'Halfway through the concert,' continues Michelle, 'we started to relax a little bit and Cass and I were playing to Gene and singing to Gene,' she laughs. 'And the next thing I know I hear John say, "Get the *fuck* over here!" As soon as he saw Gene, he said it right into his mike. Then Cass and I switched places with Denny and John and there was quite an astounded audience wondering what the hell's going on? What was *that* about?' But the show was not quite over. After the gig, as the fans streamed out of the auditorium, they were amazed to see John running out to the car park after Michelle. 'You're *fired*,' he shouted.

The next day John told Dunhill. 'Either *she* goes or *I* go', and as far as the record label were concerned, there was no question which it was to be. Clearly from their point of view, given the choice between losing the group's leader and songwriter and the group's weakest singer, albeit the most attractive one, there was no contest. Conveniently, Adler's girlfriend of the moment, Jill Gibson – an attractive blonde sometime singer and ex-girlfriend of Jan Berry of Jan and Dean fame – was proposed as Michelle's replacement. Dunhill duly produced a letter to Michelle for the other three to sign, officially firing her.

Although this may have seemed drastic, as far as Cass and Denny were concerned, if it meant an end to the ongoing hysteria and provided a way for them to get on with the business of being pop stars, then so be it. 'Cass was just sick up to here with everything,' recalls Michelle, 'with me, with Denny, with John. She was *so* fed up with the drama. Everything was one drama after the next and the firing was horrible. It was hard for her too. But John said to her, "You wanna go sing with her? Go sing with her. But *I'm* not gonna work with her. So you wanna stay with me? We'll replace her." So she just said, "Fine, I'll sign the letter."' There was also undoubtedly a slight element of revenge in Cass's quickness to make the decision. 'She was probably the first one to whip that pen out as fast as can be,' concedes Michelle, 'just to show me that she could hurt me, like I had hurt her. Now it was her turn.'

But apart from any questions of loyalty or indeed revenge the reality was that the group was only halfway through recording their second album and needed to finish it. They also had a promotional trip planned to London. As far as Cass, the lifelong Anglophile was concerned, given the option of leaving the group or firing Michelle, there was in fact, very little contest. 'It was just sign the fuck and get her out,' says Denny.

Whilst the firing of Michelle would inevitably have an impact on the group's future, from Cass's point of view, it was the deepening conflict between her and John which would have greater and more lasting significance for her personally.

But in the meantime, John's song arrangements had given her the final launching pad for success, and despite the internal problems the group was still facing, fame for Cass and the rest of the group was about to get even better.

16

Baby you can drive my car

> 'Tell me about the Mamas and Papas, Bob,' John Lennon asked Bob Dylan as the two of them sat chatting in the back of a limo in May 1966. 'I believe you're backing them very bigly, and they're great.'
>
> 'No,' Dylan replied, 'you're just interested in the big one, the big chick, right? She's got a hold of you too! You know, she's gotten hold of everybody I know. Everybody asks me the same thing.'
>
> *Eat the Document*, 1966

When Cass had told her high school friends that she was going to be a star, she had never imagined just how much of a star she might really become. By the summer of 1966 the Mamas and the Papas had had three top ten hit singles and had reached an even greater level of global fame than they had ever thought possible. The group, and therefore Cass, was now as famous as major Hollywood stars like Elizabeth Taylor and Richard Burton and they were accordingly treated with the same kind of awe and reverence. It was also an era in which relatively few people ever attained these levels of stardom. In the twenty-first century, Andy Warhol's maxim that everybody will be famous for fifteen minutes has been twisted to mean that almost anybody, however talentless or unremarkable, can have some kind of fame, even for fifteen seconds. But fame was very different in 1966. It was a great deal more elusive, and indeed, exclusive. 'The Mamas and Papas were, excuse me, *fucking* famous!' laughs songwriter John Bettis. 'Fame is dime a dozen now – there's a whole *lot* more famous people, or at least what we *call* famous, but I'm not sure famous even has the meaning it once did. Fame is different now than it was then and it's hard for people to remember. It's lost a lot of its specialness, but in Cass's day, the Mamas and Papas were *fucking* famous and not many people got to that level.'

If you had achieved this über-level of fame, apart from allowing you a spectacularly luxurious and often decadent lifestyle, it also, significantly for Cass, allowed you access to the small but international world of the celebrity elite. Cass now had the opportunity to meet some of the world's most famous stars on an equal footing. And she lost little time in doing so.

Having fired Michelle from the Mamas and Papas, the group had an album to finish, but although they had eliminated the person they saw as the root of their problems, there were now other issues to contend with. Whilst they had hoped Jill Gibson would provide a perfect solution, they hadn't counted on the strain of bringing someone new into such a closely entwined group. Whatever tensions Michelle's presence may have caused, the four of them still had an extremely close four-way alliance and even Cass and John, despite their constant warring, maintained a relationship that was intense in its swings between affectionate camaraderie and hate. However much they antagonised each other, Cass respected John's indisputable genius at songwriting and arranging, and he in turn couldn't help but admire and respect her voice.

Against the odds, John and Denny had if anything become closer since Michelle's affair, sharing their bachelor pad and enjoying its opportunities to the full. It would also take more than an affair to dent the deep feelings Cass and Denny still held for each other. The arrival of a relative stranger into the mix was therefore going to be difficult, both personally and musically.

Despite Michelle's lack of vocal skill compared with Cass, she had by this time got used to singing alongside her and also understood John's way of working. Jill's arrival meant that Cass now had to start afresh and help her adjust to the group's singing style and she and Denny would exchange sceptical glances across the studio, wondering how long Gibson would take. It wasn't that Gibson couldn't sing – her voice was perfectly adequate, it was simply that substituting one voice in a group where John had balanced all four to within an inch of their lives set his musical house of cards tumbling. 'If you take one voice away,' explains Bones Howe, 'you change the sound of the group. You have to be very very careful how you do it. Whatever it is about all those voices, together they make a sound and if you change one, particularly when there's only four of them, it's a problem.'

On a personal level, Gibson was also a very different character to Michelle, and, for that matter, the rest of the group. Like most bands who have spent time together before they become successful, the four of them could almost second guess each other's responses to any situation and shared a relaxed and light-hearted approach. In the early days, they had always had fun together and since Michelle's departure it was as though Cass, John and Denny had heightened their playful banter and humour to help them all somehow believe the recent ruptions had never happened. This was no doubt eased by the prodigious quantities of pot, pills and whisky which the three of them consumed both at gigs and in the studio, spurred on by John who undoubtedly led the group in his enthusiasm for mind-altering substances of all descriptions. But Gibson, unlike Michelle, was less keen to partake and her reluctance to get stoned did nothing to help her integration into the group.

But the band needed Jill – for the time being at least, and they all tried hard to be at least cordial. Cass, as her fellow female vocalist in the studio, often had the closest dealings with her and did her best to be accommodating. 'I did feel somewhat bonded with Cass,' remembers Gibson. 'I really did. I felt that she was trying to be helpful to me, but it was always under the business aspect, not personal. There was sort of like a line in the sand and they were on one side and I was on the other and a lot of that had to do with the allegiances.'

The situation was as difficult for Cass as the others. Although she was still angry with Michelle, she also felt guilty for having agreed to fire her. Then there was the complex question of loyalty to John. Whilst it had been John's idea to fire Michelle, his anger at her affair with Gene Clark was also indicative of the strength of his feelings, and so although bringing in Gibson in her stead may have seemed like a one-stroke solution to the group's problems, once it came to putting the idea into practice, John found himself missing his wife more than he had predicted. And his feelings in turn influenced Cass and Denny. From Cass's point of view, therefore, to be seen to be overly friendly with Gibson, even if she had wanted to, would have risked being seen as disloyal to Michelle. John's visible suffering in the light of his separation from Michelle had also inspired Cass's sympathy and somehow, seeing him so dejected, brought out her affection for him. 'She *liked* John,' says Denny. 'In spite of the negative input she got from him, she liked him. And she respected the fact that he knew what he was doing about music insofar as the group was concerned and then, when he and Michelle started falling apart, there was a bit of compassion on her part towards John. Like, poor sonofabitch.'

Nevertheless, as far as the public was concerned, Jill was the new fourth member of the group, and although the photographs for the group's second album cover had already been taken out in the desert beyond LA with the four of them sitting in a window frame, a shot of Gibson was superimposed over Michelle's image and the record company hoped no one would notice the difference.

Meanwhile, the Mamas and Papas had a short national tour scheduled and John decided that the group's stellar status demanded travel arrangements to match. Rather than suffer the inconvenience of travelling on ordinary commercial passenger planes, John felt that hiring the group its own private Lear Jet would offer the perfect respite from the stress of touring. Particularly since John had recently brought back a hookah pipe with four stems from a holiday in Morocco and decided to try it out on the plane. The words 'flying' and 'high' suddenly took on a whole new meaning and Cass savoured the situation as much as the others, but things were about to get better still. The jet's pilot was eager to tell the group about the model of the plane and how fast it could go. 'You know if I was to take this aircraft up above commercial traffic,' he explained, 'and hit the apex at 70,000 feet and go over the other side, you'd be weightless over there.' Cass was suddenly interested. 'Huh? *Weightless?*' she asked incredulously, 'How do you mean? Could we *do* that? That would be so much fun!' And so the pilot did. It was a technique usually reserved for trainee astronauts on larger aircraft, but in such a small space, the hookah pipe, drinks and everything else went tumbling. Cass, however, simply unfastened her seat belt and let weightlessness ensue. 'Heeeeeeey!' she beamed as she floated around the plane until a few moments later when she, and everything else, came crashing down with a resounding thud.

The irony and humour of the situation was far from lost on Cass. For someone whose weight had defined her entire adult life, the notion of becoming weightless even for a few minutes was unimaginably exciting. But the illusion and indeed the group's tour didn't last long, and after a few more gigs on the East Coast, the Mamas and the Papas had a longer journey to think about. They were due to go to London for a promotional trip as both 'California Dreamin'' and 'Monday, Monday' had already been hits in the UK and the British public were eager to see the new hippie superstars. None of them had ever been to London, so they were all excited, but Cass, the lifelong Anglophile, was almost sleepless with anticipation.

England and all-things-English had been an obsession with Cass for years, almost equalling her fixation on John Lennon, so the idea of finally going to the country that she had fantasised about for so long seemed better than it was possible to imagine. She adored Britishness of every description from King Arthur and the Round Table to Dunhill cigarettes and tea and crumpets.

Part of Cass's fascination stemmed from an interest in history and a love of all things old. 'You come from North America and everything's like two hundred years old, three hundred tops,' says Denny, 'but there, you look at a building and it's been there for six hundred years. That's what she liked – that solidity.' Cass's interest also extended to antiques and almost anything to do with English history whether it was the Tudors or America's British past. 'We played Boston,' remembers Denny, 'and Cass wanted to go over to the bridge conquered in Massachusetts with a shot heard round the world. This was the first shot that was fired in the American revolution. No one knows who fired the shot but a British soldier was killed. Some American in the woods took a redcoat and that started the whole thing, so she said, "I wanna go there." And we went and we stood on the Concorde bridge. She said, "This is it – this is where it all started. You can see them all coming out of the woods, can't you?" I said, "Which woods?" She wanted to see the redcoats coming! She would have loved it if the Brits had won the revolutionary war and it was all English. *Yes*!' he says. 'She could have been Dame Cass!'

When Cass finally did come to visit London, she couldn't have timed it better. By the summer of '66, London had taken over from Rome, Paris or New York as the world's hippest metropolis. Suddenly the most exciting developments in virtually every field seemed to be coming out of London. It was now home to the Beatles and the Stones; Mary Quant, Vidal Sassoon and David Bailey were trailblazing a revolution in women's style and photography whilst a new generation of London-born actors such as Michael Caine and Terence Stamp were breaking new ground in British films. The world's celebrities were now flocking to London, and on any given evening at one of the capital's fashionable niteries, you could stumble across a gathering of assorted Beatles, Hollywood stars, showbiz legends and bright young meteors revelling in the sheer thrill of it all.

This was what Cass, Denny, John, Lou Adler and Jill Gibson were about to discover, and on arrival in London, they were promptly installed in a magnificent town house apartment on Berkeley Square, one of central London's grandest and most prestigious garden squares. With floor to ceiling windows opening out onto the square below, the flat was furnished with antiques and the living room featured a grand piano, an extensive library and an original Regency fireplace. Cass had a room at the top with spectacular views across London, and she couldn't have been happier. What was more, within a few days of their arrival, the group discovered that Mick Jagger and his girlfriend, Chrissie Shrimpton, were living in the apartment below.

For Cass this was a truly English heaven. Not only was the very experience of being in London itself thrilling, but everywhere she went, she caused a stir. Whereas in LA it was commonplace to see major stars in the street or in the shops, in London, it was much more unusual to see someone like Cass who was now internationally famous, and people constantly stopped in the street to whisper and point her out. Cass loved every minute of it.

With her extensive knowledge of all things English Cass was also well-placed to make the most of London's cutting-edge fashions and had planned shopping trips on a grand scale. Within hours of arriving she had made appointments to have boots made at Anello and Davide, makers of the by-now world-famous 'Beatle' boots. Carnaby Street was also obviously a priority destination and London's famous tailoring was not left off the agenda either. While Cass's irregular size often made it difficult for her to buy clothes off the peg for herself, she still adored shopping and loved expertly picking out items for her friends, particularly the men around her. 'We had a *great* time,' remembers Denny, 'Buying everything in the world! Buy! Buy! Big bags of everything. Then we'd go to Abercrombie and Fitch and she insisted I try on this wolverine coat – eight wolverines. "Oh, you'd look *marvellous* in this! Put it on!" "It's a thousand dollar coat." "It'll look *lovely*," she says. 'Then of course John goes, "It looks really good," so he pulls out a big wolf one, puts the wolf coat on. I still have mine.'

But if shopping in London was a thrill, this was nothing compared with the idea of staying in the same town as the Beatles. When it came to finally being in London, the home of her idols, it hadn't occurred to Cass or the rest of the group that they might in fact come to meet them and Cass dismissed the notion as a virtual impossibility. 'I'm a teeny-bopper in many respects,' she later admitted to *New York* magazine. 'The Beatles overawed me tremendously. When we were in England, I saw Ringo sitting in a bar, and I didn't even speak to him I was so amazed. "Monday, Monday" was an enormous hit already, and he went back and told the rest of the Beatles that the Mamas and the Papas were snobs. But, I mean, what do you say: "Hi, you don't know me but I'm Cass and you're Ringo"?'

But Cass would indeed meet her Beatles, although not quite under the circumstances she may have wished. Within a few days of arriving in London, Cass had developed a severe cold and was forced to stay in bed one evening while the others went out on the town. The group's British record company RCA had put their names on the door of one of London's most exclusive and fashionable members' clubs – Dolly's, described in a guidebook of the time as 'a zingy and ear-shattering place' full of 'gyrating dollies and their guys'. Located in a basement in St James's, Dolly's was a regular haunt of the stars of the day and so was the obvious place for the group to visit on a night out. As it turned out, that particular evening, John Lennon had had the same idea. Sitting in one of the booths alongside the club's decorative mannequins in beads and sunglasses, Denny was the first to notice. Just around the same time that John Lennon noticed him. 'It's dark and I'm looking around and I see John Lennon looking at me going, "I *know* you. Aren't you . . .?" and I did the same thing to him! "Aren't you?" "We are, aren't we?" he says in a Lennon-style Scouse accent, "Yeah we are!"' they both said in a manner straight out of *A Hard Day's Night*. 'I asked him if he had any grass,' says Denny, ''cause we were hitting the whisky pretty good, but there was no grass in England; there was a lot of hash but it's harsh on your throat and I don't wanna smoke hash. So I said, "Has anybody got any *plant*? Any *weed* around?" Lennon says, "Oh, just a minute. Paulie's got some," and calls the studio and Paul McCartney showed up at Dolly's with a bag of weed and we all went back to the house to smoke it!'

In the limo on the way back to Berkeley Square, Denny thought of Cass lolling in her sick bed and told Lennon, 'There's somebody back at the house you gotta meet. She's not gonna believe this. Cass just *loves* you.' Lennon was intrigued. 'On that song that I wrote, which of the girls is whispering "John"?' he asked Denny. 'Cass,' Denny told him. 'The *big* woman?' asked Lennon. 'Yes,' said Denny, 'the big woman.' 'Oh,' Lennon replied, sounding disappointed. 'Pity.' But he was nevertheless keen to meet her.

As soon as they got back to the apartment, Denny went to see Cass, who was upstairs, moaning to herself at the injustice of being stuck in bed with a cold while the others hit the town in groovy London. 'John Lennon's downstairs,' Denny told her. This was not Cass's idea of a joke. 'Fuck off and leave me alone!' she told him. 'I don't *feel* good. Sonofabitch! Don't *do* that.'

'*No! No* ... John Lennon and Paul McCartney are in the living room!' Denny insisted.

'*Dennis!*' she shouted.

'I swear on my mother's life,' Denny protested. 'I swear to die!'

Paul McCartney was by this time attempting to play the grand piano downstairs only to find that the keys didn't work. Determined to get a tune out of it one way or another he decided to get inside the piano and pluck away at the strings instead. Cass heard strains of McCartney's plucking wafting upstairs and surmised that someone was clearly downstairs. 'I'm *telling* you,' said Denny. Finally Cass relented and agreed to come down and see for herself.

Meeting one's idols can be daunting and Cass had been besotted with John Lennon since she had first 'discovered' the Beatles in 1963. She had fantasised about meeting the god-like one endlessly, and when the time finally came, she was not disappointed. 'Hello, Beautiful,' said Lennon as she came down the stairs, and within minutes the two of them were getting comfortable by the fireplace, with Cass in rapt wonder. 'I have this image engraved on my mind,' remembers Denny, 'of the two of them looking at each other in the firelight and she's like – *gone*. The look on her face is just *adulation* – "*Oh My Goooood!* I've died and gone to heaven!" They just sat there and talked and babbled. And I didn't intrude. *Nobody* could. That was it!'

As dawn broke, they eventually said goodbye and watched from the balcony as Lennon drove off in his Paisley Rolls-Royce. Just how much better could life get? As far as Cass was concerned, meeting John Lennon was just about the pinnacle of her life so far and meeting McCartney was hardly worse. She would later describe McCartney as one of the great rock 'n' roll singers of all time and when she was invited to choose her favourite twelve records on a BBC radio show, no less than four of her choices were either by the Beatles, solo Beatles or were Beatle-covers. Cass would eventually become friends with the entire group and this would happen sooner than she had thought.

John Lennon and Paul McCartney had told George Harrison of their meeting with the group and Harrison was now similarly keen to meet them himself. He was also interested to hear tapes of their new album. The Beatles were, at this point, in a transitional stage between the collarless-suited mop tops they had once been and the moustachioed tripsters they would become the following year, and musically, there was a sense of open competition and mutual respect between them and their American peers. They were all eager to explore how they could develop and were almost as keen to hear what the Mamas and Papas were doing as the group was to hear their idols. Harrison duly invited them over to his house in Esher for dinner. The excitement in the group was immense.

'This was one of the Beatles inviting us for dinner!' remembers Denny, 'and we were all a tremble!' Harrison sent his limousine to drive them out to Esher and once they arrived, he was, as Denny recalls, 'sweet – very nice and down to earth' and tried to put them at their ease. They sat around on the floor, listening to records and passing joints. 'It was great!' says Denny. 'It was like everybody gets a joint. You just start rolling and by the time you've finished everybody in the room is passing and it's just going round and round. My *God*! There were no dull moments.'

When it came to listening to the group's new demos, Harrison lived up to his reputation as the silent Beatle and was quietly noncommittal. 'He just listened intently, and wouldn't say anything,' says Denny. 'It was all very tenuous.' But then, almost as if on cue, Paul McCartney arrived. 'I think he was coming by to see George about something, but we just happened to be there and he listened to the tapes too. He wanted to hear what was going on in America and Hollywood.' McCartney listened to 'I Saw her Again' and as it came to the false start 'I saw her' which Lou Adler had decided to leave in the track on one of the choruses, he immediately remarked, 'It's a mistake, isn't it?' 'Yeah,' Denny explained, 'but we left it in 'cause it sounded good.' 'Yeah, we've done that a lot,' replied McCartney. 'Where?' asked Denny, immediately intrigued as to where this could possibly have happened on a Beatles record. 'You don't know, do you?' laughed McCartney. 'Tell me where,' Denny asked again. 'Uhuh,' said McCartney. 'If you can't hear them, there are no mistakes.'

By the time dawn rose, the Mamas and the Papas, and Cass in particular, felt more and more comfortable around their new friends, and Harrison extended his welcome by offering them the use of his car and driver for the rest of their stay. London had lived up to every one of the group's expectations.

Back in LA after the trip to London, Cass was glad to have had some respite from the dramas of the previous few months and relieved to have day-to-day life in the group back on a more even footing. It was not to last long.

John was by this time missing Michelle severely and began talking to her to see if they might be reconciled. As far as he was concerned he had told Gibson that her position in the group was permanent, whether he and Michelle got back together or not, and that was the way he intended it. But Michelle had other ideas and the possibility of regaining her rock star status was much more tempting than having to return to her problematic marriage. Eventually John realised that if he wanted his wife back, he would have to relent and let her back in the group. He also knew that Cass and Denny would almost certainly have mixed feelings about this. On the one hand, Michelle's presence would reopen the not-so-old wounds, but on the other, having their friend back would be reassuringly simple and comfortable. As undisputed leader of the group, it was John's call and eventually he gave in to Michelle.

As far as Cass and Denny were concerned, they were, like John, almost glad to have Michelle back. Cass also hoped that Michelle's return would herald a new contentment in John and consequently a smoother life for all of them. 'They were *really* happy to have Michelle back,' says Lou Adler. 'John was pretty much a pain during that time she wasn't there, being very much in love with her, and *everyone* was happy she was back. Really.' At the back of Cass's mind, she also still nurtured a small hope that with John and Michelle back together as man and wife, Denny's attentions – and affections – might once again turn to her, this time in perhaps a more romantic vein. On both counts she would be wrong.

*

As soon as Michelle was reinstated in the band, the group returned to the studio to put the finishing touches on their second album: *The Mamas and the Papas – Cass, John, Michelle, Dennie*. The album was almost finished but Michelle came back just in time to record a final couple of tracks. There remains some debate over whether Michelle's voice was re-recorded over Gibson's on the songs she had sung in Michelle's absence and over whose voice appeared on the final recording. Gibson believes her voice is still on many of the tracks, and while others insist that everything was re-recorded with Michelle, Michelle herself admits to having no idea whose voice was on the final cut. The truth is that their voices were essentially similar in pitch, and once the songs were layered with the three other voices and a wealth of backing tracks, overdubbing and strings, it became very difficult to tell. The original album cover shot with Michelle was meanwhile reinstated before any copies were shipped out and the only place the Jill Gibson version of the picture was ever seen was on summer billboards trailblazing the album's imminent arrival.

Since the phenomenal success of the band's debut album, Dunhill were eager to release a follow-up as quickly as possible, and unlike today's situation where artists rarely release albums with less than twelve months between one and the other, at this point it was still common for groups to release as many as two or three in one year. This meant that in between promotional trips and gigs, not to mention both personal and personnel issues, there was very little time for John to write new material. To make matters worse, even when he had written something new, nobody was over-keen to come together to rehearse and record it. With material in short supply, a solution was found in the form of some tracks the group had already recorded for an ABC television special celebrating the music of Rodgers and Hart. At the time, it was quite usual for successful pop groups to perform such family entertainment fare (a year later the Supremes even recorded an entire album of Rodgers and Hart covers) and Cass, in particular, needed very little persuasion. Adler had decided that rather than having the group sing alongside a variety-style orchestral accompaniment, the band's sound should be in keeping with their records. He and Bones Howe had therefore pre-recorded instrumental backing tracks with the Wrecking Crew at Western Recorders so that the group could sing live over them in the TV studio. One of these – 'My Heart Stood Still', was subsequently used on the group's new album whilst another, 'Sing for

Your Supper', would provide Cass with one of her most memorable lead vocals and would surface on the following album. Another track, 'Glad to Be Unhappy' was also recorded, and although it was never included on any of the subsequent albums, it would later surface on numerous compilations. With its theme of unrequited love, the song would come to be seen by some, particularly Denny, as a rather more accurate reflection of the band's story than 'Creeque Alley'. While many of John's lyrics expressed his own personal situation with Michelle, the lyrics to 'Glad to Be Unhappy' could just as easily have been written with the Mamas and the Papas in mind. '"Unrequited love's a bore,"' sang Denny and John in the chorus, whilst on the TV show, ABC's camera homed in on Cass, looking directly at Denny as she sang the response '"And I've got it pretty bad."'

But for the time being, the shortage of new material gave Cass the opportunity to bring in another song of her choice – Martha and the Vandellas' 'Dancing in the Street'. The song had been a favourite of Cass's for some time and was clearly a natural for her to sing. She was the only one of the group who could realistically have even attempted challenging Martha Reeves's original, but it was a song that they all loved, particularly Cass and Denny, and its exuberance was hard to resist. Whenever the four of them were singing together, their problems seemed to evaporate and at the end of the track you can hear Cass and Denny ad-libbing to each other in Mugwump speak, sounding as carefree as the Mugwumps they had once been.

In between marital strife, personnel changes, power struggles and unrequited love aplenty, the recording of the album had been far from straightforward. Although there were clear highpoints such as 'I Saw Her Again', 'Dancing in the Street', the Lambert, Hendricks and Ross-influenced 'Once Was a Time I Thought' and the up-tempo party twang of 'I Can't Wait', the sheer verve and euphoria of their debut had already been tempered by the conflict within the group. But this would do little to dent their fans' enthusiasm.

The Jill Gibson episode had clearly had little effect on the public who had ordered more than half a million advance copies of the album before its release – the highest advance orders for a record since Elvis and the Beatles. It was the most eagerly awaited record of the year, and the new single, 'I Saw Her Again' became the major hit of the summer.

*

Cass and the group's fame seemed to be escalating on an almost daily basis. They had their own private table at the Whisky A Go Go – the hippest music venue in LA – and limos waiting on cue. Cass's new-found wealth also meant that the days of sleeping on Jim Hendricks's floor were well and truly over. She had now moved into what she would later come to think of as the ultimate celebrity pad, 'It was *so* Hollywood!' she remembered. At the top of Summit Ridge Drive in Beverley Hills, Cass's new home had previously belonged to Natalie Wood and looked out to the still undeveloped LA mountains on one side and Beverly Hills below on the other. The main room of the house was a huge A-frame living room which Cass had kitted out with a hammock hanging from the rafters and two gargantuan Voice of the Theatre mahogany-cased speakers. There was also a grand fireplace, but the ultimate showpiece was a waterfall running through the middle of the house into the swimming pool outside.

Now that she had a beautiful house to entertain from, Cass could resume the unofficial salon she had held in Greenwich Village. Almost immediately she became the undisputed queen of the LA rock and roll social scene, and virtually any musician or actor of note who happened to be passing through town would almost inevitably end up being taken to Cass's. Her house was now a regular stop-off on the celebrity circuit, guaranteed to provide a fascinating and stimulating mix of aspiring and established talent.

Cass had always loved meeting new people, particularly if they happened to be British, and on any given day at the house, you could run into a party scene comprising actor David Hemmings, Donovan, who at this point had just scored hits on both sides of the Atlantic with 'Catch the Wind' and 'Sunshine Superman', as well as several if not all of the Hollies. 'There was no doubt that Gertrude Stein had come back to life,' remembers Graham Nash. 'She was *brilliant* and she *loved* friends and she loved to get high with us all. She was *the queen*!'

The teenage Donovan, meanwhile, had debuted in LA at the Trip on Sunset Strip and all four Mamas and Papas were in the celebrity-filled crowd, but Donovan remembers Cass being the 'most vocal fan in the audience'. Donovan subsequently became good friends with everyone in the group, but particularly remembers Cass's warmth. 'Cass made this eighteen-year-old boy welcome in America and she treated me like a sister in a time of overwhelming fame for me,' Donovan remembered in an email from his home in Ireland. He subsequently immortalised his affection for her in his paean to the psychedelic life – 'Fat Angel'.

Cass had also become close friends with the Hollies' Graham Nash and soon not only he but the rest of the group was staying on her floor. (Cass subsequently introduced them to photographer Guy Webster who shot the cover for their American *Stop! Stop! Stop!* album in her living room.) 'I had *all* of the Hollies living at my house – sleeping on the floor because they didn't have any money 'cause they hadn't had any hits, and we had a great time,' Cass later told the BBC's Brian Matthew. The Hollies had, in fact, had several major hits by this time and Nash remembers the reason for their staying on Cass's floor rather differently. 'It was more . . . paralysis!' Nash tells me on the phone from LA after a year's worth of protracted emails. 'Whenever you went over to Cass's house, you got so bloody loaded that, *sure*, you ended up crashing over there. We saw the sun come up *many* times!'

Cass had also continued her friendship with the Beatles. A few months after their meeting in London, the group came to America for what would become their final tour, and they passed through LA to play Dodger Stadium before heading off to San Francisco for their final show at Candlestick Park. As soon as Cass heard even a murmur that the group was arriving, she couldn't wait to see them. Luckily she now had a hotline to her idols as the Byrds had enlisted the services of ex-Beatles press officer Derek Taylor. 'It would be like the underground, whispering, pssst,' remembers Denny. '"Stay by the phone!" She'd be waiting for a call from Crosby who's waiting for a call from Taylor who'd say, "OK, they're coming in from the airport, they're gonna be up at such and such." We had to *wait* till they got to the house from the airport to go over. 'Cause Cass is going, "Let's go *now*, let's go now." "They're not *there* yet!" I'd say. "They're coming in from the *airport*." But she'd be, "Let's go – let's be *waiting* for them!" And then she'd come by my place, beeping the horn – "Let's go, let's go!" Tearing through the hills! I'd say, "We're gonna get *killed*!" And I don't know where we went but the Beatles'd be there. Then that was it – she'd just disappear into the house and heeeey, she'd be having a great time. There'd be a big party going on in the living room and Lennon'd come out whispering, "Come here," and we'd all go up the backstairs and smoke dope up in his bedroom and then go back down and mingle with folks. They wouldn't smoke down in front of people.'

The fact that Cass could now legitimately count the Beatles amongst her friends and acquaintances was the pinnacle of her glory. This was, after all, the ultimate cachet – not only was she wildly famous herself, but she was friends with none other than the Beatles, still without doubt the most famous group in the world. There might be others, particularly in Hollywood, who shared her fame but not everyone could claim the Beatles as friends, and she would soon come to consolidate that friendship further.

In November 1966 'Words of Love', backed with 'Dancing in the Street' (both featuring Cass on lead vocal) was released as a single, and within a month it had reached number five in the *Billboard* charts. If any reminder were necessary, the single only seemed to reinforce Cass's position as the undisputed focus of the group. By the end of the year, however, Cass and indeed the rest of the band were more than ready for some time to themselves. But rather than being able to take time out and enjoy their wealth and fame, the rock and roll merry-go-round was too fast to stop, and almost as soon as they had arrived back from England they were due, yet again, in the studio. Although they had only just released their second album, the group was contractually obliged to deliver a further two albums the following year – an unrealistically pressured schedule by today's standards and not much more comfortable in 1966, but having no choice the band braced themselves for another round of sessions back at Western Recorders. It was not something any of them were looking forward to, but Cass would soon bring some news which would surprise them all.

17

Deliver

If the internal conflict in the Mamas and Papas had seemed at odds with the hippie ideals the group seemed to portray, the contrast would become even more stark as 1966 turned into 1967 – the year which would become immortalised as the summer of love.

The atmosphere in the studio for their second album had been fraught, but by the time it came to recording their third, relations between the four of them had become positively toxic. The clashes between Cass and John had reached epic proportions, Denny was distraught at having to endure Michelle and John's renewed attempts to revive their marriage and, for each of them, the memory of their recent traumas loomed amongst them like recurring spectres. When a journalist asked Cass about rumours that they were going to make a film à la *A Hard Day's Night* or *Help*, she replied that they were. 'We'd like to remake *Virginia Woolf*,' she said, referring to *Who's Afraid of Virginia Woolf* – the notorious Richard Burton and Elizabeth Taylor snipefest. The animosity between the four of them had gradually drained the recording process of its fun and excitement and each session became almost an ordeal to be endured. But then Cass got some news which suddenly cast everything in a different light. She was pregnant.

When her doctor told her, she was as surprised as he was. Apparently, the chances of a woman of her size conceiving were minimal and having become pregnant this once, it was unlikely ever to occur again. This left no question in Cass's mind that she would have the baby. She was still, at least on paper, a married woman as her marriage to Jim Hendricks had never been dissolved. The reality, however, was that she was single and pregnant. By the end of the twentieth century, such a situation would no longer be considered unusual or socially unorthodox; in 1966 it was. It was also far from commonplace. Amongst forward-thinking, free-living hippies it was beginning to happen more often, but as far as the general population of America – or any other Western country for that matter – was concerned, the idea was entirely unacceptable and beyond the pale for decent, civilised folk.

But Cass had never been intimidated by society's rules or expectations. Her success as a performer had given her the financial independence to bring up a child on her own, and even though her romantic life to date had not worked out quite the way she might have wished, she had never let go of the girlhood dream of the perfect home with the picket fence and husband and children. Maybe there would only be one child and the husband might have to come later, but that was OK. Maybe the timing wasn't ideal, but that still didn't matter. The exciting fact was that she was going to be a mother. She was ecstatic. It would bring her a new sense of purpose and a much-needed focus beyond the group. All she had to do now was tell them.

'Guess what?' she said as she bounced into rehearsal the next day, 'I'm pregnant.' John cast her a withering look. 'Fine,' he said. 'When's the abortion?' Flip as this may have sounded, John was in fact deadly serious, as the idea never occurred to him that a woman in the middle of a flourishing pop career and who, furthermore, was not in a regular relationship might even consider having a baby. 'I'm not having an abortion,' Cass told him firmly but cheerfully, expecting a more sympathetic response. 'Give me a break!' replied John before walking out of the studio.

Once Cass had made it clear to the group and everyone else that she fully intended to have her baby, people were naturally eager to know who the father was. Cass's closeness to Denny, in spite of everything that had happened, seemed to make him an obvious contender and over the coming years speculation would extend to several male friends of Cass's, including Jim Hendricks and Graham Nash. John Lennon was even mentioned as a possibility, and Cass would certainly have done nothing to dispel the rumour, unlikely and untrue though it sadly was. But the fact was that Cass wasn't particularly keen to let anybody know the identity of her baby's father. Whenever she was asked, she would remain coy, telling them simply that it was an immaculate conception. The truth was, unsurprisingly, a little more prosaic.

Since Cass had become famous she would occasionally find that, particularly when the group was on tour, young musicians were more than happy to spend the night with a star. Boyfriends and lovers, however short term, were now consequently less hard to come by than in her earlier life. They weren't necessarily the kind of men who Cass would have wanted to have a relationship with as they weren't always her equal either intellectually or in terms of talent, but while John and Michelle did their best to play at wedded bliss and Denny enjoyed the plentiful opportunities available to an attractive male star, Cass was understandably less than happy to spend night after night alone. The high of performing to an adoring crowd of thousands was hard for anyone to come down from and Cass's solution was simply to continue partying after the show and through the night. She had always had a natural talent for creating a party around her and so, whilst the others in the group kept themselves relatively private, within hours of her arrival in any city or town, Cass would have developed an entourage of friends and acquaintances – some old and some new, all more than willing to take advantage of the room-service-fuelled party that would invariably evolve in her room. On nights when she didn't have a room full of people to return to, or on the nights in between gigs, Cass would turn to the sizeable entourage of managers, roadies and session musicians who had by this time become part of the Mamas and Papas' travelling circus. There was now a regular crew of musicians who would play with them for live shows, made up of either the Wrecking Crew or any other session musicians necessary, so it was usually not hard to find fellow partiers, although more often than not, once the party was over, she would again find herself alone.

One night on tour had, however, been a little different. Whilst on the road, Cass had got talking to an attractive curly-blond-haired session musician who'd been playing with the group, and one evening, after ordering in some Chinese food and plenty of drink, the two of them had settled in for the night. It never occurred to Cass that she might become pregnant. She had been told that her size would make it highly unlikely, and she had never thought of this particular musician as anybody other than someone to keep her company for the night. When she discovered she was pregnant, therefore, there was never any thought in her mind that he would be involved in her future or the baby's. She had no interest in forming a relationship with him and didn't imagine he would have any such interest himself. This child was hers and she would have her baby on her own terms.

Faced with Cass's determination, John and the others had no choice but to accept her decision. She had told them she would work right up until the final stages of her pregnancy, so there would be no need to delay finishing the album. And that was what she did, but it wasn't going to be easy. The sessions for the last album had been bad enough with the constant warring with John, but the pressures of having to record as her pregnancy progressed only made matters worse. And the more frustrated and angry Cass became, the more John seemed to home in on her, goading her on, seemingly just waiting for her to collapse under the strain.

The reasons for their disagreements hadn't changed since the last album; they had only become aggravated, not least by Cass's pregnancy and her increasingly well-established popularity. She was also angry that she wasn't writing or singing more lead vocals on the new material, and if she was angry, she made sure people knew it. 'She was *always* complaining,' remembers Lou Adler. 'Somewhere down deep she was like an old Jewish woman – she'd complain about *anything* – the length of the session or the time that it was called. Not artistically, just everything else. She was *crabby* a lot and every time she got that way, John would push her even further. But she was a hard worker. There were nights when we were recording when she was far into the pregnancy and we were pushing her for notes that *probably* were difficult for her to get and she *literally* crawled out of the studio a couple of times. She was pushed to that extent by John and some of it was,' he pauses, 'a masochistic side of him. John had that streak in him. More so [with Cass] than with anyone else in the group.'

While her new-found stardom had given her an edge of confidence when they were recording the last album, she was even more strident now. Having acquired the trappings of wealth – the house and cars, she was going to prove she could flout society's rules by having a child on her own and so, in comparison, John's authority must have seemed relatively insignificant. Any disagreements, however, were usually between the two of them alone, as when Cass was singing lead at a particular session, nobody else would bother coming to the studio.

Amazingly, none of the bitterness which surrounded the recording was evident in the final result and when *The Mamas and the Papas*

Deliver was released a few months later in March 1967, titled in honour of Cass's impending delivery, it became their third million seller and went top five in both the American and British album charts. The next two singles: 'Dedicated to the One I Love' – a Michelle-led cover of the song originally recorded by the Five Royales and more famously by the Shirelles – and 'Creeque Alley' also both went top five.

As a whole, the album contained several memorable tracks including 'Look Through My Window', which had been released as a single earlier and 'Creeque Alley', which, after 'Monday, Monday' and 'California Dreamin'', would become their biggest and most recognisable hit. Written in response to Lou Adler and others' repeated questions as to how the group had started out, the song presented a witty and lyrically convenient, if not entirely accurate, autobiographical version of events. It started off in Greenwich Village where 'Zal and Denny were working for a penny' and took in Cass's supposed medical aspirations with her plans 'to go to Swarthmore'. It also detailed how 'When Denny met Cass he gave her love bumps' and one can only guess how Cass must have felt about having her feelings for Denny exposed in one of their own songs. But as far as Cass was concerned, this revelation would probably have paled in comparison with the song's most prominently repeated punchline: 'No one's getting fat except Mama Cass' – a line which, apart from anything else, certainly helped cement the Mama Cass tag which she would soon come to loathe. But the fact that John had written a line so brazenly and bluntly drawing attention to her size was simply indicative of his attitude to her.

Michelle was shocked when he first sang her the line and couldn't believe he really intended to use it in a lyric, but John defended himself telling her, 'This is art, and we can get away with anything. Particularly the truth.' Whatever Cass may have felt, she didn't let it show. What was more, there was nothing remotely half-hearted about her delivery of that line or any other part of the song; on the contrary, the song is carried almost entirely between her and Denny with John and Michelle's respective harmonies adding the extra notes, but it is Cass's voice which is undoubtedly the strongest overall presence.

The album also contained three Cass leads in the form of the Rodgers and Hart standard 'Sing For Your Supper', brought in from the TV special, and two new compositions of John's: the rather lame

'Boys and Girls Together' and the better 'Did You Ever Want to Cry?' This penultimate track of the album opened with Cass's lead – suitably subdued in keeping with the lyric: 'Did you ever want to cry but you didn't know just why...' again accompanied by Larry Knechtel's honky-tonk piano, with the addition of, in this instance, a psychedelic blues mandolin and some characteristically Four Freshmen-style harmonies at the end. The shortage of strong new material from John was also once again evident. You knew something was amiss when a group who had become internationally famous for their vocal harmonies chose to record not one but two instrumental tracks. The title of one, 'Frustration', was particularly telling.

Since Cass had become pregnant, the ego struggles and conflicts within the group had seemed slightly less important to her and she had spent months eagerly awaiting her child, putting headphones to her stomach in the studio to see if she could hear the baby. She had also decided that her Summit Ridge house would be too small if she was going to have a family, so she had found a new, larger, exquisite Cape Cod-style house on Woodrow Wilson Drive, a small private road off Laurel Canyon, which would remain her home for the rest of her life.

Up until the birth itself, it had been a straightforward pregnancy, and apart from the tiredness she felt after the umpteenth take in the studio, generally she seemed able to carry on with her life exactly as she had before. 'It's almost like sometimes you would forget that she was pregnant,' says Gary Burden, whom Cass had met when she hired him as an architect to help redesign her new house, 'because it didn't really stop her or cause her to change her lifestyle in a great way.' Even Cass's friends used to tease her saying, because of her size, 'How will we ever know you're pregnant, Cass?' But just as Cass didn't let it affect her working life, nor did she see the need to make changes in any other area of her life. Living in the midst of a culture where smoking a joint was at least as normal as having a cup of tea, Cass and her friends believed that they were at the forefront of a new wave of parental practice, and that by approaching parenthood in a way that was radically different from their own upbringings, they could help create a better world for their children. 'Babies of hippies have gotta be different from other babies,' Cass told *Rolling Stone*, 'just by virtue of the fact that they are totally unrestricted. I think that hippies are more enlightened and therefore tend to be a lot freer with their children. Let's put it this way: the kids I went to high school with, well, I've seen their children. My contemporaries are not the people I went to high school and college with: my friends are in the creative forces and their children are different. I've heard that story about kids are high naturally, but I've seen kids that aren't high, kids who've had the high taken out of them.' Cass wanted to try and ensure that her baby did not suffer the isolation she had felt as a child and would not 'have the high taken out of her'. On this basis, there seemed no point in changing her own life just because she was pregnant. 'I took acid five times when I was pregnant,' Cass admitted. 'I don't believe in this chromosomal damage. I think it's all hogwash, a vicious plot by the establishment. I was told all the things I couldn't do when I was pregnant, and I did them all. Because you know instinctively what you can do. I took psychedelics. I didn't feel that I had hurt her in any way. As a matter of fact, it was on an acid trip that I realised I was pregnant – and I was only about three weeks pregnant.'

If Cass had seemed relatively calm about her pregnancy, she was equally serene when it came to the birth itself. She and Burden, despite the fact that he was married, had got into a routine of going out for breakfast almost daily, and over a cup of coffee on the morning of 25 April, she told him that she felt the time was closing in and that they'd better leave for the hospital. With a minimum of fuss, they jumped into her car and set off for the maternity ward.

The birth, however, was less straightforward. Cass's size meant that after long hours of labour, her baby had to be delivered by Caesarean section, which, unlike the current vogue for Caesarean births in some celebrity circles, was something most women in the sixties – whether they were famous, wealthy or otherwise, only had if absolutely necessary. The birth endangered both Cass's and the baby's life, but on 26 April 1967, Cass gave birth to a healthy daughter whom she named Owen Vanessa. Cass had told friends that she had always liked the idea of a girl having a boy's name, and so the baby was named after two close friends – an actor named Owen Orr and Cass's long-standing friend Vanessa.

The difficulty of the birth meant that Cass had to stay in hospital for a month afterwards, but once she had her new baby daughter home, she was entranced by her and, for the time being at least, motherhood seemed to give her life a new focus. Without exception everyone who knew her unfailingly remembers how much Cass doted on Owen. 'She was a great mom,' remembers Gary Burden. 'She instinctively knew how to do that, because she was essentially everybody's mom – I mean it's appropriate that she was in the Mamas and Papas because she was so nurturing and she wouldn't stop, even if it became painful for her. If she thought somebody needed something, she would go out of her way to make sure it happened.' This would prove the case with some of Cass's boyfriends over the coming years, but for the time being, in spite of having had a child, Cass still had a career to attend to and she had never had any intention of giving up one for the other. She had no husband making demands on her to do so, as so many of her generation may have done, and as she had the economic means to pay for help, there was no reason why she should.

She therefore set about hiring a nanny in the form of a seventy-year-old German woman, Mrs Robertson, or Robby as she was known, who had apparently been looking after children for no less than fifty-two years. There was also young Naomi, Cass's housekeeper, who would later become Owen's more long-term nanny, all of which meant that Cass could resume touring and recording and life almost as usual, safe in the knowledge that Owen was being well-looked after.

As far as the public and Cass's fans were concerned, Cass was famous enough to be able to break society's rules and get away with it. The group had just won a Grammy for 'Monday, Monday' and it was as if Cass now existed in a kind of stellar stratosphere where unfeasibly wealthy famous stars lived their lives according to a different set of rules to the mere mortals lingering down below. She could even be coy about the identity of the baby's father and the media were still, on the whole, polite enough not to ask. Although that didn't stop them speculating. 'Cass says Hendricks is not Owen's daddy,' wrote *Esquire* magazine a couple of years later. 'Some people believe that Cass produced the child by sheer willpower. Others hold that the fertilising agent remains a mystery to Cass herself. Reporters for classy magazines don't ask their subjects questions about such matters.'

Whatever conservative society may have thought, Cass's decision to have Owen on her own was in fact perfectly in keeping with the growing backlash against social restriction and confinement which was beginning to define the hippy movement. This was 1967, the year which would become legendary for its 'summer of love' and be seen in years to come as the zenith of the counterculture's attempt to promote peace and love rather than war as a universal axiom. It was the brief moment when, to many, it seemed like everything they hoped for might indeed be possible. The Beatles' *Sergeant Pepper's Lonely Hearts Club Band* album became the soundtrack to the summer, not just in America but throughout the West and once again, Cass found herself not only in tune with the zeitgeist but at its epicentre, creating it as it happened.

Cass's love affair with England had only been heightened by her trip to London the previous year and when Stephen Sanders, her old friend from the Shadows back in Washington, DC, had moved to London at the end of 1966, it seemed the perfect opportunity to set up an English base of her own and so she suggested he find them an apartment to share. Cass could certainly have afforded to rent somewhere on her own, but as Sanders was going to be in London full-time, it made more sense for her to share somewhere with him, as this meant she'd also have company whenever she decided to visit.

Sanders swiftly found them a small house in fashionable Chelsea on Luna Street, a long-since demolished narrow line of terraces which wound from the top end of the King's Road down to the river Thames. The house, which was decorated in what Sanders remembers as 'low hippiedom' soon became, just like Cass's LA home, a regular stop on the social circuit for London's in-crowd. Visitors included John Lennon, Ringo Starr, Brian Jones, Linda Eastman – the future Linda McCartney – scenester and friend of the Stones Stash de Rola – aka Prince Stanislas Klossowski de Rola – film maker and director of *Performance*, Donald Cammell and Beatles aide Neil Aspinall.

After one night's partying, just as day was breaking on Sunday morning, the Beatles arrived on Cass's doorstep. 'It was six in the morning,' remembered Aspinall to Derek Taylor later, 'and we [he and the Beatles] went down the King's Road in cars to see Cass Elliot . . . We had the album with us, finished at last. She had a great sound system. Her flat was in a block of houses, back to back, really close together, and we put the system on a window ledge and the music blasted through the neighbourhood. "We're Sergeant Pepper's Lonely Hearts Club Band . . ." It sounded great. All the windows around us opened and people leaned out, wondering. A lovely spring morning. People were smiling and giving us the thumbs up.' Cass was overjoyed. On another acid-fuelled night, John Lennon ended up drawing on one of the walls in the house and unsurprisingly, once he had left, Cass and Sanders soon had the wall space enshrined.

Cass would come to visit London regularly throughout the rest of her life, but if the launch of *Sergeant Pepper* was one of the landmark moments of the year in London, it was another event in California which would come to symbolise the spirit of the summer. Back in LA, Cass would once again take centre stage as the Mamas and the Papas performed as the headlining act at the Monterey Pop Festival.

Monterey was the first great outdoor music festival and the forerunner of Woodstock some two years later. Over the weekend of 16 June 1967 somewhere between fifty and a hundred thousand people turned up in their hordes to a disused fairground one hundred and fifty miles south of San Francisco near Carmel in northern California. Monterey had previously been the site of a well-respected jazz festival, but this was the first time anyone had thought to hold an event on this scale. The idea was originally the brainchild of Californian scenester and promoter Alan Pariser, but was soon hijacked by John Phillips and Lou Adler who took over organisation of the event on the basis that they had the clout and contacts to pull in a far more impressive and diverse range of artists. This they subsequently did, attracting a now-legendary line-up which included Otis Redding, Jimi Hendrix, the Who, Janis Joplin, Ravi Shankar, Jefferson Airplane, Simon and Garfunkel and, of course, the Mamas and the Papas.

Over twelve-hundred journalists reported Monterey and suddenly the world began to realise that what had previously been considered a relatively small movement, was in fact happening on a much greater scale than anyone had supposed. Otis Redding couldn't believe that the majority of his hippy audience were openly smoking more than cigarettes. 'These fucking hippies man, they're smoking dope like it's *legal* out here. *Everybody's* high,' he commented. And it wasn't just pot they were high on. Owsley Stanley, a kind of hippie wizard alchemist, known as 'the unofficial mayor of San Francisco' and supplier of 'Owsley' acid, wandered the grounds handing out free tabs of 'purple haze' and STP, an even more potent hallucinogen, known for providing a 'three-day trip'. The whole event seemed little short of a cultural revolution.

A banner over the stage proclaimed 'Love, Flowers and Music' and in what amounted to a canny piece of promotion for the festival, John penned a song for his childhood friend and singing partner Scott McKenzie – 'If You're Going to San Francisco (Be Sure to Wear

Flowers in Your Hair)' which although scorned by some as a commercial dilution of the ideals of the time, nevertheless spelt out the flower-power message to the world and its children and became a kind of hippy anthem of its own.

The Mamas and the Papas' role as headliners and co-organisers of the festival seemed to confirm their position as figureheads of the love and peace ethos, but this couldn't have been further from the truth. Cass was irritated by John and Adler's involvement with the festival and saw it as a distraction from valuable touring time, which for Cass, not only provided her with the audiences she adored and who adored her, but also, importantly, her primary source of income; without any touring revenue, Cass only had recording royalties to rely on.

But by the time the start of the festival came along, Cass was as excited as everyone else at the prospect of a giant, three-day musicfest, and, for all its hippy ideals, Monterey was undoubtedly also the must-see event of the summer for the West Coast's in-crowd and rock royalty. Thirty-five years on, Monterey is still remembered by those who were there as a magical, acid-fuelled moment of sunshine wonder and can be seen as such in D. A. Pennebaker's masterful documentary *Monterey Pop*. The film captures not only the artists performing onstage but also the free unconstrained mix of superstars and ordinary but beautiful people in all their technicolour body-painted glory. We glimpse Brian Jones at his most dandyish, wandering the grounds bedecked in stripes and feather boas and we see Cass enraptured as she sits watching Janis Joplin perform her groundbreaking rendition of 'Ball and Chain'.

Cass was naturally curious to see other female performers sing, particularly anyone who, like herself, could be seen to be challenging audiences' preconceptions as to how female performers should look and behave. 'She was ... *absolutely stunned* by Janis Joplin,' remembers Nurit Wilde, Cass's old friend from Toronto and Greenwich Village. 'Because everybody expected Grace Slick to be the queen of the ball, and Janis – I'd *vaguely* heard of her, but I have to say when she sang, she was something else. Everybody was just stunned and she became the queen of Monterey. Cass could not get over it. I think she was a little bit jealous, even though they were *very, very* different singers. But she really was astounded by her.'

Watching the performances with Cass, and by her side throughout the festival, was her new beau – a singer by the name of Leland, or Lee as he was more commonly known, Kiefer. Kiefer was a tall, broad and handsome blond surf god from Florida who'd ended up singing with the Hard Times, a San Diego garage band who, like thousands of others, had come to LA to try their luck and landed a regular gig as house band at the Whisky A Go Go. They had quickly attracted the attention of TV supremo Dick Clark (of *American Bandstand* fame) who swiftly booked them for his new show *Where The Action Is*. Which is where Kiefer had met Cass. Cass was immediately taken by his looks and his easy, laid-back charm and the two of them began dating.

After months of antagonism within the group, Kiefer was just what Cass needed. Originally from Florida and of Dutch parentage, Kiefer was a keen surfer with a sense of fun and adventure which matched Cass's own. Three and a half decades on, time has changed him little and he looks significantly less weathered than many of his contemporaries. Although his still collar-length hair may be a silvery white rather than blond, it doesn't require a great leap of the imagination to see why Cass would have been pleased to be seen with him. As we sit in the gravelled, walled garden of a rock 'n' roll eaterie on LA's Sunset Strip, Kiefer remembers how Cass wholeheartedly embraced the beach life he was part of. 'She really did like to have fun,' says Kiefer. 'In lots of ways. She was basically fearless about trying anything new. And for a girl that was as heavy as she was, she was *active*. Once she wanted to scuba dive. Well, if you put seventy-five pounds of gear on a woman who weighs more than two-hundred and fifty – ha! – it's a whole new science of how to get in and out of the water! But she was fearless! And she was good! God, she loved it and you couldn't get her out of the water! Because it was something new and exciting and she liked things like that. She was definitely in the top ten percent of fearless females and I really liked that about her. She'd get real excited and she was always like: "Let's go do it!"' he laughs. '"Enough talk, I got it, I got it – let's go do it!"'

Similarly if Kiefer wanted to go surfing, Cass was equally game but rather than attempting to surf herself, would sit propped up in her bright red Cadillac convertible waving to her boys out in the water. 'She was *so great*,' says Gary Burden, 'and she'd be the one, like the surfer chick, sitting on the beach while we were all riding waves, you know? That was how she was. She was a welcome addition any place she was. Just for her spirit, for her heart.'

Kiefer also had a canny way with the mechanics of a motor car and had built Cass what was swiftly becoming the de rigueur celebrity must-have of the moment – a dune buggy, which he describes as one of 'those triangular little birdcage frame cars with an engine inside that you have on desert runs'. It was, he says, 'one of the very first ones, with a shortened body and a motor inside – an 1835cc, and when it was souped up, boy the whole thing would scream. It had hand steering brakes and the whole thing with the aircraft safety belts and everything 'cause we needed to stay in the car 'cause we drove the hell out of that thing.' The pair of them would while away hours gleefully tearing around the then undeveloped Hollywood hills. 'There were gigantic flat areas down in between the hills,' Kiefer explains, 'and so we dirt climbed and we just had the greatest time!'

After days on the beach or driving through the dust, Monterey seemed almost like a culmination of the optimism of that summer. Cass and Kiefer stayed a few miles along the Pacific coast at Big Sur, in a suite at the Highlands Inn – a small romantic hotel with big open fireplaces and views straight out to the ocean. It seemed perfectly in keeping with the mood of the festival. 'It was a brand new feeling,' remembers Kiefer, 'and it was all the way to the burn. And everyone had it. It was a couple of days of absolute beautiful camaraderie. There are just no words. Motorcycle policemen running around with their bikes covered in flowers with thirty foot strings of pink and white balloons off the back of their bikes. We stayed up for the whole thing and we didn't miss anything. Ravi Shankar's performance was *incredible*, but we liked 'em *all*! All the performances by everyone were *super*charged. It was amazing. There were no fights, no murders, no deaths, no bludgeonings, you know what I mean? No dwarves ran away with the ring! No human sacrifice,' he laughs. 'It was just totally friendly. And *she* went to see everybody – we went there to *play*! Not play music but to see people. We were having a *great time* because everyone was just so elevated at the time for that festival – it was just one of those things that only happens once. You know they say "Peace and love – everything's OK"? That was *it*. I never saw it before or after.'

The party continued in between performances as Cass held court in the backstage tent, surrounded by her friends, most of whom were performing at some point or other. David Crosby was onstage introducing the Electric Flag, the psychedelic San Francisco blues band on whose second album, *A Long Time Comin'*, Cass had sung backing vocals earlier in the summer. She had become friends with guitarist Mike Bloomfield and bassist Harvey Brooks, whom she would work with later on, and she had also met the Who in London and struck up an intense friendship with drummer Keith Moon. 'They were *great* together,' remembers Gary Burden, ''cause it was all just fun! He was *completely* nuts and it was all just . . . *woo woo*. She was the kind of person who could make Keith Moon be cool, you know? I remember them being very, very funny together.'

After two days of seeing virtually everyone else perform, Cass had to prepare herself for her own performance as the Mamas and the Papas were the closing act of the festival. Everybody was nervous, as somehow it was as if everyone realised that in years to come this show would be remembered above and beyond most others. Cass and the rest of the group also had particular reason to worry as, with John and Michelle busy organising the festival, the group hadn't sung together for nearly three months. As their hour approached, however, lack of rehearsal was the least of their worries. Denny had been as uninterested in the festival as Cass had initially been and he had spent the previous three months back in the Virgin Islands. Two hours before they were due onstage, Denny was still nowhere to be seen. Cass and Michelle passed the time swapping gossip and jokes with Jimi Hendrix backstage, wondering whether they would in fact be performing as, with only one hour to go, there was still no sign of their male lead. Forty-five minutes before they were due onstage, Denny arrived, just in time to catch the Who destroying most of the stage and Hendrix setting his guitar alight. Things had changed since their Hollywood Bowl gig when no one had known who Hendrix was or cared. Anyone would have had a hard time following him and the Mamas and Papas were no exception.

The combination of nerves and lack of rehearsals subsequently led to a decidedly lacklustre performance. The group sang flat throughout much of the set, but no one else seemed to notice much or mind. 'It was *not* their best,' remembers Kiefer, 'because everyone was so *nervous*. But it was so incredible that it didn't matter – their best had nothing to do with it! It was being there and doing it and being part of that thing that was important. That was what made everybody nervous, not performing.'

The Mamas and Papas' performance may have paled in comparison to the spectacles created by the Who and Hendrix, but they were nevertheless figureheads for their generation and they looked the part. Cass had been battling with John since the start over their stage wear as she had always wanted to fulfil her movie-star dreams by dressing as glamorously as possible. But John had always refused, insisting that as hippies, neither she nor Michelle should wear make-up, and when Cass would occasionally try to wear a small hairpiece in an attempt at feminine glamour, he would invariably insist she remove it. Now, however, he had finally relented and after months relegated to the dressing-down hippie aesthetic, she and Michelle were allowed to embrace the newly fashionable 'rich hippie' look. The satins and silks school of dressing-up-box chic had by this time been made hip by the Beatles, not least on their *Sergeant Pepper* album sleeve, and so Cass was now free to choose the most sumptuous fabrics for what would swiftly become her trademark billowing, luxurious kaftans. She and Michelle had, along with Mia Farrow and a few other hipper stars, discovered Profile du Monde, a Hollywood boutique where the shop's proprietor Toni would make them capes, jackets and hipster trousers from the most exquisite Indian sari silks. 'Cass was finally loving it,' says Michelle. 'We spent hundreds of thousands of dollars at Profile du Monde. Cass and I would tell Toni that we needed something the following day and she'd say "Just come in and pick out a sari. She had Cass's measurements – big and flowing.'

As far as outward appearances were concerned at least, the Mamas and the Papas were the embodiment of the peace and love ethos of the festival. Their music may not have been political or part of the growing anti-war movement which was an intrinsic part of the counterculture, but America's hippies with their long hair, beads, sandals and headbands embraced the group and worshipped Cass as their ultimate Earth Mother.

Just as Monterey seemed to have been the culmination of everything that had been happening socially and musically, for Cass it also seemed to clarify in her mind how far matters had deteriorated since she had joined the group. Owen's birth had made her reassess her priorities and she no longer saw the band and John's taunts as the overriding force in her life. The emotional turmoil within the group and her own increasing popularity had already distanced her from them socially. Gradually, over the last few months, she had developed her own friends, and her own life outside the band had now been confirmed by

Owen's birth. 'She was real happy when she finally had her little family,' says Michelle. 'It did make her feel like she didn't need us any more. But by then we were starting very much to go our own separate ways anyway.'

Within a year, Cass would have decided to leave the group and pursue a solo career, but for the time being there were more gigs to play and one final group expedition to London.

18

'I think my character has been besmirched'

After a Mamas and Papas show in New York one evening, some wealthy, sophisticated, one-time sorority girls from Forest Park came backstage with their husbands. These were the people who had snubbed Cass when they were teenagers, but in the light of her fame, were clearly keen to milk their connection for all it was worth. One of them, Mimi Seligman, greeted Cass like a long lost soulmate. She should have known better. 'You didn't know me then,' Cass told the stunned woman, 'and I don't know you now!' Cass had by no means forgotten the way the sorority girls had ostracised her and, despite the passage of time, she had no intention of forgiving. In the years to come, she would delight in telling friends this story again and again, revelling in the glory of being able to inflict a bite of revenge, however small.

Cass may have found stardom, but she was still desperate to prove herself to everyone who had ever mocked or turned their nose up at her, and she clung to her fame like a protective mantle that could shield her from the cold. More so than Denny, John or Michelle, Cass seemed to luxuriate in every inch of her fame. John and Michelle may have had a lavish Bel Air mansion, and Denny's home was similarly palatial, but those around her seemed to intuit that fame was somehow necessary to Cass in a way that it was not to the others. 'I think Cass had more of a desire to be a star than any of them,' says Lou Adler. 'John and Denny were wrapped up in the music and were *always* worried about it and I think, with Cass, you could tell that she wanted to be a star. She liked everything about it. I never felt *either* from Michelle. I didn't feel that she was dedicated to the music or that she was *not* dedicated or that she wanted to be a star; she was a part of the group. Cass was caught up in the trappings of it.'

Becoming so attached to her fame was inevitably precarious. Fame itself is notoriously fickle and the effort of maintaining it can be exhausting. But more than that, fame has never been too concerned with privacy and can bring the world's attention at the least convenient of times. As Cass would soon find out.

Cass desperately needed to prove herself a success in every aspect of her life. She had done so professionally but she also needed to do so on a personal level. For Cass's generation, regardless of the fact that she had a career, a woman was not considered a real success unless she had a man, preferably an attractive one, and in this respect Lee Kiefer fitted the bill perfectly.

Kiefer had by this time moved into Woodrow Wilson Drive, and during the brief periods when Cass wasn't recording or on the road, she tried to enjoy a relatively normal domestic life. Nestled between Laurel and Nichols Canyons the house, although larger than Summit Ridge, was small by rock star standards but beautifully situated with views of its idyllic landscaped gardens and the canyons beyond. With its neatly trimmed lawns, artichokes, passion flowers and Victorian roses nuzzling against the grand stone cottage exterior, *Esquire* later described the house as something 'Bo-Peep might have designed for herself if she had ever struck it rich.' The inside, meanwhile, was a more relaxed affair, which, the magazine added, 'belied its pastoral exterior by closely resembling an East Village crash pad'. The spacious living room was dominated by a large leather hippo, and on either side of the fireplace the bare plaster walls were covered in graffiti and autographs from Cass's friends – famous or otherwise. Some visitors were shocked that Cass should allow people to write freely on her walls but others saw it as the showbiz tradition that it was; Cass was simply bringing a sliver of Broadway life into her home.

Completing the domestic idyll with Kiefer and baby Owen were also the nanny and a small menagerie of eccentric animals whom Cass adored. There was Al – a corpulent, short-haired mongrel grey cat with six toes on his left foot, and Dolly, the enormous shaggy English sheepdog she had inherited from Denny, which, according to Kiefer, 'slobbered on everything within a hundred yards of it', but none of this bothered Cass.

Days would start late with Cass sleeping or luxuriating in bed well into the morning. But Cass's bedroom was much more than merely somewhere to sleep. Whilst in the twenty-first century, modern appliances are commonly found in bedrooms of even the most average home, in the late sixties this was far from the case, and Cass's range of facilities was indicative of her rock star status. Cass had arranged the expansive room in such a manner that there was really very little reason to leave. If the outside of the house seemed fit for Bo-Peep, the bedroom had clearly been dreamt up for Scheherazade reincarnated as a couch potato. Dominating the room was a vast, four-poster bed, ornately carved with birds of paradise, thin elephants and exotic vegetation and draped in lustrous gold velvet. At its foot was a TV, a telephone and a small fridge with cold drinks and snacks. What more could an indolent rock star want?

While Cass was in bed in the mornings, Kiefer would take out the rubbish and feed Dolly, or help put iodine on Al if he was wounded after a fight with a coyote up in the canyon. Then, when Cass eventually surfaced, they would breakfast either at the Jewish deli nearby or at Duke's at the Tropicana, a restaurant and motel with a swimming pool on Santa Monica Boulevard. Back at the house later on in the day there was almost inevitably some friend or other who would drop by and afternoons would usually be spent by the pool.

But whilst Cass's friends were more than happy to spend their days at the house, few of them approved of Kiefer. They were suspicious of the fact that a good-looking young man, who could easily have his choice of girlfriends, would suddenly choose to attach himself to someone who, in spite of her wit, talent and charm, was still resolutely beyond the norms of what was considered the conventionally attractive form for a woman. Particularly when the woman in question was famous and relatively wealthy. 'I believe the word parasite was mentioned earlier,' says David Crosby, when I bring up Kiefer's name, before going on to tell me that he's reminded of a sucker fish, primarily because he was 'a person of lesser stature attaching themselves to a person of means'. 'Maybe I'm being unkind,' he continues, 'but he was certainly not her peer in any sense of the word.' Crosby's view was shared by most of Cass's male friends, but her female friends, including Michelle and her sister Leah, saw the relationship slightly differently. Leah had, like everyone else, initially been suspicious of Kiefer's motives, but soon recognised that the relationship was not as straightforward as the starkly black and white scenario some portrayed. 'I know that Leland was a *true* friend of Cass's,' says Leah, 'and I really felt like he was one of those people who really truly, truly *liked* her, loved her, appreciated her. And that's not only to say he wasn't an opportunist or this or that, but that I think Cass made Leland feel *great*. I think he found in Cass the qualities of someone where you can get the adoration which only your woman or your lover can give you but he was also unbelievably attracted to her mind and her music. I think he just really respected her and wanted to hear what she had to say, was interested in her opinion and of course Cass *enjoyed* that and enjoyed it coming from this guy who she thought was *adorable*. He was a cutie-pie.'

Thirty-five years on, Kiefer himself talks of Cass with notable gallantry and clearly genuine affection and is at pains to present her in the best possible light. He also explains that even at the time, both he and Cass were well aware of people's opinions, but had no intention of letting gossip affect them. 'Of course people said, "Oh, she's got a new toy," says Kiefer, 'and they would say to me, "What are you doing with *her*?" But we never paid attention to *any* of that. We just laughed it off and gave it almost no thought at all, because we were having too much fun.'

Cass was indeed having fun. From her point of view, there were clearly two great things about Lee Kiefer: one was that he was a joy to be around and with his 'let's build a dune buggy and ride it through the sand' approach to life, he appealed to her sense of fun. The second was that he was also indisputably the perfect trophy boyfriend. Kiefer was a Californian surf god par excellence and it is hardly surprising that someone with as much to prove as Cass clearly revelled in the kudos of being seen with him. Just as she had done with Marc Strange in Greenwich Village, Cass paraded Kiefer around, taking him to restaurants, nightclub openings and film premieres. She had never been short of attractive male friends to accompany her on the town, but even with recent new friendships such as Graham Nash or comedian Tommy Smothers (of hip comedy duo the Smothers Brothers), they had never been more than friends. While she nursed crushes on them, she would have to sit and listen as they invariably poured out their hearts to her with the details of their own respective love affairs, which only served to make Cass ever-more conscious of her own single status. With Kiefer on her arm things were different and she was almost combusting with pride. No one could fail to notice the constant stream of tactile gestures and caresses between them, leaving no doubt in anyone's mind that this man was her lover as well as her friend.

In the months before Monterey, Cass had begun to distance herself almost entirely from John, Michelle and Denny, so that they were only ever together either onstage or in the studio. Even before she had become pregnant, it was an understandable move. Michelle's return to the band had brought with it an increasingly messy open relationship between her and John, which didn't seem to be pleasing either of them, particularly not John whose enthusiasm for drug experimentation was increasing by the day. Denny, meanwhile, although still unshakeably close to Cass at heart, had developed his own entourage of friends, acquaintances and hangers-on and had made it his mission to slowly but surely 'drink Michelle out of his life'.

After Monterey, there were still, however, more gigs booked for the summer, the first of which had been arranged for 13 July at New York's famous Carnegie Hall. This particular show would later be thought of by many as Cass's finest moment, and when it came to her solos the audience were spellbound. 'When she sat on the apron of the stage to sing "I Call Your Name",' reported *Esquire*, 'the house went wild. You would have thought Judy Garland had just told them a love secret.'

The group then returned to California to play the Hollywood Bowl and the show would come to be seen as their swansong. Opening for them was an as yet relatively unknown (in America) guitarist by the name of Jimi Hendrix, but the show was nevertheless the calendar event of the week. The audience were ecstatic, and John and Michelle hosted a no-holds-barred after-show party at Bel Air featuring the cream of Hollywood's A-list from Steve McQueen, Warren Beatty, Jack Nicholson and Marlon Brando to Sonny and Cher and Joe Cocker. Cass, meanwhile, was already on friendly terms with all of them and spent the evening surrounded by gushing admirers.

After the gigs, the group was due, yet again, to begin recording, this time for their fourth album – *The Papas & the Mamas*. However gruelling the thought of returning to the studio with John may have been for Cass, it also meant new record royalties, which she now badly needed in order not only to maintain the luxurious lifestyle she had become accustomed to, but also to support her new baby.

The idea of having to work together in the studio didn't appeal to any of them. 'They were all very frustrated with each other, because no one would come together and perform,' remembers Mike Sarne, the British pop star who had scored a lone hit with 'Come Outside' and, having subsequently gone into film-making, had relocated to LA and become a close friend and party pal of John's. 'The loyalties kept shifting around, you know? One would be friends with one and then three days later they'd gang up and they'd be friends with the other one and then they'd be gossiping about each other. And they were always on the phone to each other telling stories and there was no coherent mind – that should have been John's but John was trying to be friends with everybody. It was rather painful to watch.'

In theory the whole recording process should have been more relaxed as John had recently built a fully equipped studio in the attic of his and Michelle's Bel Air home, and so it was decided they would record there, rather than Western Recorders. But whereas having the time constraints of a commercial studio might have forced the group into some kind of action, the freedom of having their own recording facility was potentially disastrous. On the occasions when they did all come together, the four of them would head up through the sliding panel at the top of the stairs into the studio in the early evening and John would begin going over the arrangements he'd prepared. By ten o'clock they'd start the tape rolling and somewhere around midnight they might start getting something they could use. They'd then carry on for a few hours, fuelled by Crown Royal, pot and a few lines of whatever drugs were around until about 4 a.m. by which time no one was feeling too productive and the session would wind down.

Unsurprisingly perhaps, nobody, least of all John, was pleased with the results. Halfway through their previous album – *Deliver*, engineer Bones Howe had quit in protest at the long and frequently unsociable hours the group's sessions were forcing him to keep, and so the band had lost a key component in their recording success. Ex-road manager, and boyfriend of Michelle's sister Russell, Peter Pilafian had therefore been brought in as a substitute on the basis that he had helped build the studio and, having been around the band, would know enough about the recording process to make things work. Eventually, the album would credit the engineering to 'F-Troop' – the name of an American TV series in which an army cavalry unit did everything wrong and committed constant blunders. It was a situation which, with hindsight, Adler remembers as entirely untenable. 'It was a total nightmare. John wasn't writing as much as he had been and drugs were a big problem. Peter Pilafian, who was the road manager, the violin player, was everything else, but he *wasn't* an engineer – he was doing the engineering. And *I* was doing part of it and *I* was *definitely* not an engineer. On top of that, the studio wasn't working well so things kept going wrong, like we'd get a vocal but it wouldn't get recorded or we couldn't find the tapes. *Plus*, I *hated it* – I hated the studio being in their house. When we finally got something going Michelle would decide that she was gonna cook for everybody. So we'd stop the session in order to have these big meals – *hours* it might have taken! Fried chicken and *wine* and wine and wine and wine. By the time we got back, they didn't know *what* song they were doing! It was a *horrible* experience!'

Several sessions later there was little that was usable and John realised that the root of the problem lay not in technical difficulties but in the group's collective morale. 'Everything had just fallen apart,' Pilafian recalls, 'and because of the way they sing, their hearts have to be practically beating together, so psychologically, if they're at odds, it shows in the singing and John knew it.' John called a press conference at the Beverly Wilshire Hotel and announced that the Mamas and the Papas would be 'temporarily breaking up'. 'Only three tracks have been completed,' he continued, 'and we're scrapping the rest for now. We're just grinding the songs out and we're not in any kind of groove. We're beginning to feel phoney as artists.'

In a final attempt to salvage the future of the album, and indeed the group, John decided that what they needed was a change of scene and a break from the relentless touring and recording cycle. They would put recording on hold and go to Europe. Naively perhaps, he thought that if they could all go away together, ideally to somewhere hot, and forget about the day-to-day pressures, they might stand a chance of recapturing the enthusiasm and optimism they had felt in the Virgin Islands. John suggested Majorca, which at this point in the sixties was still relatively unknown, but was rapidly becoming the jet set's latest play pad. Paris was also discussed, and during an appearance on the *Ed Sullivan Show*, the group told Sullivan – and thereby most of America, that they were due to sail to Europe on the luxury SS *France* in two days' time. The shipping line for the *France* had no record of any bookings for the group but as the world had now been informed that the band would be travelling with them, they had no choice but to find three first-class cabins at twenty-four-hours' notice.

The *France*'s first port of call in Europe was Southampton, England. Dunhill planned a brief stay in London and scheduled a gig at the prestigious Royal Albert Hall. Cass was of course delighted to be travelling to London, and in such style. She arranged to leave baby Owen with her mother while she was away and took Lee Kiefer along with her on the journey – although this was unreported at the time. Cass certainly also hoped that Kiefer's presence alongside her might act as protection against John's jeers, but once again she was proved wrong.

John and Denny, like most of Cass's other male friends, had little time for Kiefer and were scornful of what they saw as his servile and obsequious stance towards Cass. Even all these decades on, Denny's attitude is no less charitable and seems to combine the protectiveness of a brother with the disdain, resentment and envy of a jealous lover. 'We called him Lee the loser,' he recalls. 'He was a schmuck. *Anybody* in that situation, coming in there and not being the *man*, letting her be the man. A masculine man wouldn't have done that. She was like, "You do what I tell you and you come and do what I want when I want it, but right now, just go away." "Would you get me some water?"' he says in a mock Cass voice. '"Honey, would you do that?" She didn't *love* him. It was just something to take along on a trip.'

But as far as Cass was concerned, none of these issues were going to spoil what was promising to be a glory-filled adventure. Throughout the trip, the ship's staff and passengers gushed and fawned over the group as though they were genuine royalty and broke into applause each night as they arrived for dinner at the captain's table. As first-class passengers they were even allocated their own wine stewards, but wine was simply an added bonus at this point. Before boarding the ship in Boston, they had sent a roadie off to Harvard Square to score them a pound of grass for the crossing. As they cruised past Cape Cod that night they ordered in champagne and held a party in their staterooms to celebrate the arrival of their new supplies. If they were going to be cooped up together for a week at sea, at least they wouldn't be short of diversions and they proceeded to spend the journey smoking, drinking, reading and sunning themselves on deck.

With Kiefer at her side and a permanent bevy of staff to answer her every whim, Cass revelled in the attention and loved the excuse to dress for dinner each night. Having to fit in with the ship's menus, however, was not always ideal. Since Owen's birth, Cass had been determined to lose weight and had undergone a gruelling five months during which she had fasted four days a week. John's continuing jibes made sure Cass had no shortage of incentive. 'You should have your own record label, Cass,' was one of John's favourites. 'Fat Records. Then the record label's ads could read "Another obese release from Fat."'

'For five months,' Cass later explained, 'I fasted from Monday to Thursday eating nothing and drinking only water, plus an occasional glass of orange juice. On Fridays, Saturdays and Sundays I limited myself to one evening meal of steak and a green vegetable. Sometimes I'd also allow myself a half cup of cottage cheese in the morning and that was it.' Cass had lost seventy pounds but although she had now finished the fasting period, she was still restricting herself to a thousand calories a day – two poached eggs for breakfast, no lunch and high protein dinners of grilled fish or steak and vegetables. The elaborate cuisine on the SS *France* was therefore unlikely to fit in with her plans. 'That was my worst experience,' she said. 'The meals were incredible nine-course affairs. When it came to desserts of crêpes suzettes and cherries jubilee, I almost lost my mind. Once in a while, I'd break my diet and feel terribly guilty.'

But as the journey progressed, food was to be the least of her problems. Halfway through the journey, just as everyone was sitting down to watch a screening of *Dr Zhivago* in the ship's theatre, a storm started up and the projector began to throw warped images of Julie Christie and Omar Sharif around the room. 'We've lost one of the stabilisers,' announced a crew member, 'and we might lose the other, so we're in for a pretty rough night. Would all the passengers kindly return to their rooms, put on their life jackets and await further instructions.'

Cass was convinced that she was about to die and became hysterical as she frantically tried to grapple with the life jacket in her cabin. John, Michelle, Denny and Lee heard screams coming from within and braved the corridors as the liner began to sway from side to side, slamming them up against the walls. When they arrived, Cass was crying and looked whiter than death. 'Leave this to me,' said Denny, as he calmly grabbed another life jacket off the wall and secured it to the first one with an intricate nautical knot and got Cass safely dressed for impending disaster. Once they were all similarly strapped in, they decided to smoke as much grass as possible, just in case they went down, but they all passed out first. The next day they awoke to find themselves once again in calm waters.

If Cass felt as though she had had a near-death experience during the storm, there was worse to come. On 5 October, as the ship sailed into Southampton dock, its seventeen hundred passengers began to disembark. But for some reason unknown to the group, they were held back. Eventually, they were told that police were waiting with a warrant for Cass's arrest and that they were coming on board the ship to search them first.

Neither Cass nor any of the others had the slightest idea what the arrest might be for. The only thing they could think of was the grass they had bought in Boston, but it seemed unlikely that anyone would have known about it and waited till they arrived in England to arrest them. And why Cass rather than anyone else? Whatever the arrest was for, they realised they needed to somehow dispose of the grass and as Cass had stuffed it loosely into her bra as a means of transporting it down the corridors, John quickly told her to run to the ladies' room to ditch it and pretend she was being sick. 'Honey,' she told him, 'I don't have to pretend.'

As Customs and Immigration officials began to board the boat, Michelle ran to help Cass, only to find her in tears, desperately trying to eliminate hundreds of tiny strands of grass which had floated to the surface of the toilet bowl and despite repeated flushing were stubbornly refusing to sink. Eventually, just as officials were beginning to pound on the door, demanding they come out, they managed to scoop it out and hide the damp clumps around the cistern.

As the four of them walked the gangway off the ship, Cass could see Lou Adler and his friend Andrew Loog Oldham, the Stones' maverick manager, waiting for them in Oldham's Rolls-Royce, which was parked alongside the quay. Oldham looked impeccable in an immaculate white linen suit, and, according to Kiefer, 'looked like he'd probably been looking impeccable for about three days'.

The police officer who had informed Cass she was under arrest had refused to produce a warrant and so John and the others suggested that Cass get in Oldham's Rolls-Royce with the rest of them. The police had other ideas, however, and a tug of war ensued as no less than six hefty police officers grabbed one of Cass's arms and tried to pull her out of the car, while John, Denny, Michelle, Lou Adler and Oldham tried to pull her back in by the other. 'It was a *very* comical scene,' remembers Adler. Michelle screamed at them to let her go, but by this time Cass had been handcuffed and, without further explanation, dragged away to a Southampton police station before being driven to London's Scotland Yard.

On arrival in London, Cass was charged, strip-searched and told she would be detained overnight. Bail was not available, she was told, because the police were acting on a civil warrant with no bail clause. Her crime? An unpaid hotel bill some six months earlier at Queen's Gate Terrace – a five-star apartment suite run by the Embassy Hotel, from which they claimed she had also stolen two blankets and a hotel room key, worth approximately ten guineas at the time.

By the following morning, the press were in feeding-frenzy mode as Denny, John, Michelle and Scott McKenzie, who had now joined them in London, picketed the police station brandishing 'FREE MAMA CASS' posters. A cursory trial was quickly held the following day, and when Cass appeared, flanked by constables on either side, despite her ordeal, she refused to show her distress and instead milked the situation for all it was worth, 'Your London police are wonderful,' she told the press, 'but there just weren't enough blankets in my cell last night. Believe me, one blanket doesn't go far around this chick!'

The trial itself, meanwhile, was a hasty affair. No evidence was offered by the prosecution and the charge against her was dismissed. Cass was swiftly acquitted and the magistrate, Mr Seymour Collins, described the case as 'an unfortunate set of circumstances', before assuring Cass that 'you leave this court without any stain on your character'. As Cass walked down the steps of the courtroom with John, Denny and Michelle, a policeman handed her back the handbag which they had confiscated the day before. 'Got any cookies?' John asked her. Cass opened her bag to find that the hash cookies she had brought from America were still there and the four of them were promptly captured on the world's newsreels striding down the steps munching their way into a dope-fuelled haze.

Despite its swift resolution, the whole incident seemed bizarre. The police's sledgehammer tactics seemed unnecessarily severe over such a minor and inconsequential offence and the heavy-handedness of Cass's arrest and subsequent treatment were widely considered shocking. But Cass's case was simply one of a growing number of high-profile rock star arrests to grab headlines that year. Most famously, Mick Jagger, Keith Richards and their art-dealer friend Robert Fraser had been arrested at Redlands, Richards's country home, for possession of very small quantities of drugs. The case had become such a national cause celèbre that *The Times* had penned the now legendary leader 'Who Breaks a Butterfly on a Wheel', in which it denounced the establishment's treatment of the group, saying they were being used as scapegoats for the defiance and non-conformism of their generation. Almost as much fuss had similarly been caused by raids on Donovan and the Jimi Hendrix Experience, whose drummer Mitch Mitchell told the press he was sure, 'The Stones and ourselves must be among the most searched groups in the country.'

By the time it came to Cass's case, despite the furore caused by the Stones scenario, the establishment's assault on the rock community seemed to be continuing unabated. It did not go unnoticed. Cass's arrest raised questions in the House of Commons and protests from the National Council for Civil Liberties. 'Is it one law for everyone – and another for pop people?' asked the *Melody Maker* similarly. 'The *Melody Maker* is astonished that a member of the music profession – and particularly a visitor from another country – was treated in this manner. It wonders if it happened because Cass was a pop star.'

For all Cass's ballsiness she was understandably shocked at the episode. It was also ironic that as the group member who had exulted most in her success, she should suffer such public humiliation; she would certainly have felt the ignominy of her arrest more acutely than someone less emotionally dependent on their public image. Cass may have made light of the incident initially, but she was clearly mortified and told journalists that she thought her character had been 'besmirched'. When asked if she intended to take legal action in response to her treatment, she told the press, 'Just now I don't want to get involved in litigation. Basically I am extremely tired at the moment. I didn't sleep at all in that cell and the decision will have to be left until later . . . But my sense of fair play is roused and the question must be considered. I have been wronged and you know that old story about hell hath no fury like a woman scorned . . .'

Cass never did take legal action, but seven years later when she played the London Palladium she was evidently still anxious to clear her name. 'I'm going to tell you all the truth about the time I got arrested here in England,' she told the audience. 'I was living in a service flat in London and when the time came to leave, I took two sheets with me. I liked 'em, so I took 'em. We've all done something like that at some time, haven't we? So anyway, I forgot all about it and returned to America. The next time I came over . . . I was confronted by the police and arrested for the theft of the sheets. It was very humiliating. Well I was put in about four different jails and I was stripped each time. I don't know where they thought I was hiding the blankets. . . . It was no joke. I was going to admit the whole thing but I was so angry at my treatment, I told them of course I didn't steal the blankets. I was a big star and I had lots of money and I didn't need to do that sort of thing. And you know what? I got away with it. But now you all know the truth.'

Or some of the truth. The reality of the situation was that despite the police's seeming enthusiasm for arresting musicians, in Cass's case, any misdemeanours on her part with blankets or otherwise were not really their concern. They were more interested in the whereabouts of Cass's boyfriend on this fateful earlier visit – not Lee Kiefer, but her old flame from Washington, DC, Pic Dawson.

Since he had lived with her while she was playing the Shadows, Dawson had kept in touch with Cass and they had remained friends and sometime lovers, albeit on an extremely loose and occasional basis. Dawson still nursed dreams of becoming an actor and now that Cass was a celebrity with a string of potentially useful contacts, and also lived in LA, the nerve-centre of the film industry, Dawson lost no time in resuming their affair. His visits were usually short, sharp and intense and each one served just long enough to reawaken Cass's feelings for him. After a few weeks, or even a few days, he would once again disappear with little explanation, but the irregularity of his appearances only seemed to render him more intriguing and fascinating. Dawson had a substantial inheritance and allowance from his wealthy family and so, compared with most struggling actors, was relatively comfortable financially, but even during his days in DC and New York, he had, like many others, supplemented his income with small-time dope dealing. However, while Cass's performing career had progressed dramatically, Dawson's had not, and instead he had developed his drug-dealing activities which had by now escalated onto a more serious, international scale. He was therefore wanted by Interpol, and the British police were keen to question him on what they believed to be an international drug-smuggling operation.

Cass later told Michelle that Dawson had been the sole subject of the British police's questioning. 'Where was he?' they wanted to know. 'Where might they find him?' And 'Was she aware that he was money laundering? And travelling on a diplomatic passport?' It is unlikely that Cass knew any of these details as Dawson was invariably vague about his dealings or activities, and so, after hours of questioning, she had finally managed to persuade the authorities that although Dawson may have been staying with her on her last visit, she had absolutely no knowledge of his whereabouts. As far as the unpaid hotel bill was concerned, the matter was simple. She had given money to Dawson specifically to pay it and left, safe in the belief that the account had been settled. To anybody who knew Dawson, this was more than plausible.

Cass's arrest had temporarily overshadowed the future of the group. The Albert Hall show had already been cancelled, as none of them were in the mood to perform following Cass's arrest. Privately neither the group nor Adler were convinced that they were really ready for such a high-profile show, and a brief press conference had been held announcing the cancellation. The press were also keen to know the group's plans. Had the arrest spoiled the group's holiday adventure in Europe? they wanted to know. 'It's spoiled it to date, certainly,' Cass told them. 'But I'm hoping it'll get better now. We're staying on over the weekend and will do a few clubs and go to a few restaurants before flying to Majorca next week.'

Cass had never needed any encouragement to enjoy London, and as the Royal Gardens Hotel, where they were staying, was next to London's expansive Hyde Park, she and Kiefer spent lazy mornings over jugs of coffee and joints before strolling into the park to feed the ducks on the Serpentine. Afternoons would then often be spent shopping for Kiefer. Just as she had done with Jim Hendricks and Denny beforehand, Cass loved dressing her 'boys' and took great pride in kitting him out in velvet suits from Dandy Fashions and snakeskin boots, topped off with a newly fashionable perm. In the evenings they'd visit friends like Terence Stamp – who duly introduced them to the delights of Spotted Dick (made according to his own mother's recipe, he explained), or attending showbiz parties. Cass's new friends the Beatles invited them to the premiere of *How I Won the War* – a major celebrity event as the film featured John Lennon in his first non-Beatles acting role. The group not only invited Cass but loaned her their Princess limousine, and afterwards they all went on to a party at Cilla Black's house, which Kiefer remembers as 'one of those – oh *God*, everyone-was-there parties', even though there were less than fifty select guests, who Ringo proceeded to entertain by flashing the electric lights on his smart new bow tie.

The parties seemed endless. To celebrate Cass's acquittal, the group held a party of their own at the Royal Gardens, attended by the upper-echelons of London's rock royalty, including the Rolling Stones, who by this time, via a close friendship between Lou Adler and Andrew Loog Oldham, had got to know the group. Jagger had become, and would remain, particularly close to John, but they were nevertheless all friends. During Cass's earlier visits to London she had got to know Brian Jones in particular, and Stones producer Jimmy Miller had taken her to Olympic studios in Barnes to sit in on the recording of *Ruby Tuesday*. Cass was therefore well acquainted with the group, and during the course of the party, Jagger came over to talk. As he was clearly in a position to sympathise with her recent ordeal, he enquired about the trial. Cass dished out every detail of the story, but while she was talking, John came over. As far as he was concerned, his relationship with Jagger and the Stones was yet another source of competition between Cass and himself. The way he saw it, Cass had the Beatles, but he had the Stones. There was no way she could be allowed to boast both groups as her friends. The Stones were his.

John listened for a moment while Cass related the episode in characteristically colourful fashion. Then he interrupted: 'Mick, she's got it all wrong,' he told him dismissively, 'that's not how it was at all!' Having endured a night in a prison cell and a humiliating trial, this was about as much as Cass could stand. 'Fuck You!' she screamed at John, before storming out of the room. It was not simply that John had put her down in front of a genuine British rock god, Cass was also exhausted by his petty spite and constant need for one-upmanship. Despite their history of mutual antagonism, at a basic level, Cass not only respected John's talent enormously but recognised how important a role his songwriting ability had played in making her the star she now was. When she had sung at Carnegie Hall, she had introduced John as 'the man without whose help I'd still be making beer commercials' and apart from gratitude, when he wasn't attacking her, she was as taken in by his charm as everyone else. She was therefore stung by his need to belittle her and a few minutes later, she was pounding on the door of Denny's hotel room. Denny had already left the party earlier, feeling rather the worse for wear, and was awoken by the clamour of Cass kicking at his door screaming 'Fuck him! I can't take any more of this shit! That's it! You're on your own from now on! I quit!'

Denny was convinced this was nothing more than yet another of the endless fights between Cass and John and was certain the whole episode would have blown over in the morning. But this time was different. To add to the group's dramas, Michelle had at this point decided that she was in love with Lou Adler and had gone up to the hotel room he was sharing with Jill Gibson to tell him so. Adler's response had been simply to dip his head in an ice bucket and although Michelle similarly informed John, neither he nor Adler took the whole business too seriously and certainly didn't consider it a threat to the group. Cass, however, by this time, had had more than enough of the dramas, internal and external. People within the industry at home had been telling her for some time now that, as the most popular member of the group, she would have no problem launching a solo career. Until now she had always resisted, appreciating the relative security of the group and recognising John's value as a hit songwriter. Now suddenly, in the light of recent events, these arguments were beginning to seem increasingly irrelevant.

Before any official announcement regarding these latest developments could be made, Cass told the *Melody Maker* of the group's split herself. In a story headlined 'Mama's and Papa's Concert Cancelled – Group Split Up', on 21 October 1967, Cass explained the situation in the typically diplomatic wordage used so often in such situations before and since: 'We thought that this trip would give the group some stimulation,' she said, 'but this has not been so.' She then added that the group felt they were just repeating themselves and had done all they could.

19

Sweet dreams till sunbeams find you

With the emergence of the counterculture and the hippie movement the widespread use of pot and LSD had become so commonplace that comment was more likely to be raised by their absence than their presence. Heroin on the other hand was still considered a no-go zone, associated primarily with debilitated junkies and down-and-outs who would probably steal your life's possessions and anything else in sight. Similarly, in musical terms it was still also thought of as the preserve of jazz musicians and not something that occupied a significant place in white rock culture.

But this view didn't take into account the rock star heroin user. Whilst the old cliché of the jazz musician addict, nodding out, instrument in hand, still prevailed, the reality was that there had always been a subculture of heroin users in the music business who saw the drug as simply an extension of what every other drug had to offer: namely escapism. John had always been particularly partial to experimenting with any mind-altering substance available, and later in the seventies and eighties would develop a serious heroin habit. Cass, meanwhile, although never quite so zealous in her embrace of drugs as John, had by this time similarly become an avid devotee of most drugs available. Including heroin.

Although she had achieved success and fame with the Mamas and the Papas, the dissatisfaction with her self-image and difficulty in finding a genuinely loving, long-term romantic relationship meant that her long-standing unhappiness had far from dispersed. Although her daughter Owen was a source of great happiness, if anything, her life seemed more fraught and complex than it had ever been; with the attainment of success, the stakes had been raised and the pressure to remain successful was now still greater. Any anxieties she felt were also inevitably heightened and accentuated by the cumulative effects of long-term drug use, and so heroin undoubtedly appealed as a sure-fire anaesthetic to emotional pain.

Heroin was the ultimate painkiller and could therefore be viewed, in the short-term at least, as the solution to life's problems. Taken in small doses, it could initially seem no more than a soothing, numbing high, and given that most rock stars would not be facing the financial constraints which might lead many junkies to rob, lie and steal, the whole business could be seen as perfectly manageable and indeed civilised, albeit in a strictly underground manner.

This idea was something Cass shared with her old friend David Crosby, who, like John Phillips, would later go on to some notoriety as one of rock's more far-gone drug casualties. In contrast Crosby now lives a seemingly clean and tranquil life with his wife and adored young son in the remote plains of Northern California. 'We did heroin together a lot,' Crosby tells me as he reclines on a sunbed on his ranch estate high in the mountainous wilds of the region. As we talk, looking out to the panoramic vista of landscape and sky ahead, only the sound of our voices and the gentle music of wind chimes interrupt the acres of silence around us. 'Heroin's sort of like the "Everything's OK" pill,' he explains. '"Hey, your house is on fire! Yeah . . ."' he whispers in an exaggeratedly laid-back tone. '"Your leg's broken! Uh huhhhhh. Hey, you're desperately unhappy!" "I know but I can't feel it." Hhhfffhh.' He snorts derisively. 'Doesn't work, you know? It works for the moment, but in the long run it just makes it worse.'

Crosby talks with the benefit of hindsight and the extensive and painful knowledge which nobody, least of all he and Cass, had in 1968. At that point in the sixties, the only iconic heroes to have died young had lost their lives in car or plane crashes like James Dean or Buddy Holly; nobody had yet been found in a hotel room, dead before their mid-thirties. 'We didn't really know,' says Crosby. 'We thought we were indestructible. We were young, you know – we were gonna live forever. That's the nature of young people. Feel like they're bullet proof.'

It has been claimed that Crosby had introduced Cass to heroin, but this is something he firmly denies, adding that she had started using it some time before he had. Cass herself told close friends that Pic

Dawson, who himself died of a heroin overdose in the eighties, had introduced her to the drug by mixing it with alcohol. She told bass player Harvey Brooks, that she 'didn't see it coming', suggesting she was unaware that Dawson had laced her drink with heroin, but the origins of Cass's introduction to the drug now make little difference. The fact is that Dawson was known to be a heroin user himself and he clearly had an inordinate amount of influence over Cass. Consequently, their shared drug use quickly became central to their relationship.

Heroin would also prove to be another attraction of Cass's favourite city – London. Whilst heroin use was resolutely underground on both sides of the Atlantic, in Britain it was more easily available than in America. 'The Brits decided at a certain point that heroin was a medical problem,' explains Crosby, 'and if you registered with them as an addict, they would supply you with pharmaceutically pure heroin and slowly decrease it, to try and take you off it. Which on the face of it is a pretty sensible thing, but of course, as soon as any of us heard the words "pharmaceutical heroin" we bought a ticket to England!' he laughs.

Drugs would have a seismic impact on Cass's life, both professionally and personally, but paradoxically, these problems would run in tandem with some of the most successful moments in her career.

Although Cass had been living with Lee Kiefer, the hippie free love ethos now meant that monogamy was not only passé but decidedly unhip, allowing everyone free reign to sleep with whosoever they wished whenever it felt right – often within hours, if not minutes of meeting. It was not something that ever really came naturally to Cass, but it did mean that while she continued living with Kiefer, she could maintain an on-off loose liaison with Dawson, whenever he appeared on her doorstep.

Whatever Cass's relationship with Kiefer may have brought her, she still retained strong feelings for Dawson and, with the exception of Denny, he was clearly the man who meant most to her in her adult life. She adored him, and whenever he arrived seemed unable to resist indulging his every whim, whether it was paying for acting lessons, buying him clothes, motorbikes or drugs. 'She was *obsessed* with him,' remembers Kiefer, 'and she was in *love* with him. Whenever he walked in the door, she just turned into a torso, totally and completely helpless and they obviously had something – I don't know what it was, but whatever it was, it was strong.'

Cass's relationship with Dawson was complex and mutually addictive at every level. Like most smart women, Cass found intelligence in a man at least as compelling as good looks, and if someone had both she was doubly captivated. She had always gravitated to people with above-average intelligence, and when bored would entertain herself by playing gentle mind games with those around her. In Dawson, however, she had more than met her equal. 'Pic was the ultimate mind-game player,' remembers Vanessa Ware (ex-Hendricks), 'he was a mind-*fucker*, if you will, and he was *good* at that, but he was also *cute* and had sex appeal in a kind of bad boy James Dean kind of way, although he was much more devious than James Dean. He was more like Rasputin, controlling people. He had this devil in him, but that also made him very attractive.'

Equally importantly, Dawson, unlike so many other men in Cass's life, was not only charming, intelligent and fascinating in his own right, but was happy to be her lover as well as her friend. Cass and Dawson's shared heroin use further fuelled the bond between them and, as her dealer he had an extra hold, but Cass was also attracted to the danger, excitement and sheer unpredictability of his erratic behaviour. Even David Crosby, who could hardly be considered a stranger to walking on the wild side, remembers Dawson as '*way* more than "kind of" crazy' with 'a talent for excess – of *all* kinds, but most particularly drugs'.

Having succeeded in evading Interpol and any other relevant authorities, Dawson would arrive out of the blue only to spend two intensely high and wild days with Cass before disappearing again for months at a time – on missions which were invariably shrouded in secrecy. 'He was hard to hold,' remembers Vanessa. 'He was *elusive* and that got Cass even *more* intrigued because you couldn't control Pic. He might tell you he loved you one minute and the next thing he'd be off with somebody else. It was definitely all about himself and he played on Cass's emotions and took advantage of the fact that she was so wacky for him.'

However much Cass may have enjoyed the diversion of a psychological chess match, she was defenceless when it came to Dawson. His ability to play the little-boy-lost also appealed to the nurturing, mothering side of her nature. 'Pic thought he was Butch Cassidy,' says

Caroline Cox-Simon, Cass's friend from the Shadows days, who would remain friends with both her and Pic for the rest of their lives. 'He wanted to let his hair grow long and be dressed in those clothes and shirts and stuff. He had that fantasy and at some point the actor in him got caught up in the gangster part but he really *wasn't* that at all, but that's what he wanted to be. But everybody was living out their fantasy in that way and they'd be pirates or whatever. I remember he and David Crosby had this game that wherever they saw each other – whether it was the fanciest restaurant in the world or on the street or a dive or in somebody's apartment, they did this imaginary quick draw with guns and they had to do an elaborate death scene: falling against tables and oohing and aahing and crashing like an old-fashioned Western kind of thing. No matter where they were they had to follow through on that. It was that kind of crazy, wacky thing.'

Whilst Cass could obviously see that Dawson was far from ideal boyfriend material, she could also see that, perhaps predictably, he was not all bad. He seemed torn between the expectations of his upper crust East Coast background and the temptation to live a freer, more unshackled daredevil life and this internal struggle inevitably impacted on his relationship with Cass, drawing him towards her for the warmth and security that she offered, whilst at the same time leading him to shy away from the more regular, stable intimacy that she would have liked. 'There was a very sweet side to him that was like the little boy,' continues Caroline Cox-Simon. 'He felt bad about hurting his family, about not having a stable *scene*: you know, not having a woman and children and things like that. There was a part of him that wanted all of that, but there was this other part that just wouldn't back off. He had no discipline; he just lived at the height of his fantasy and he could afford to do it.'

But whatever personal conflicts Dawson may have battled, he also manipulated Cass's drug dependence and love for him to his greatest possible advantage. She had promised to get him an entree into the film world as an actor, and friends remember him trailing her around town, determined not to let go until he had found a similar level of stardom to hers. They also recall him often seeming more of a friend, chauffeur and 'fellow junkie' than a lover. Dawson himself would later tellingly describe Cass as 'a beautiful person whose naïveté makes her susceptible to being taken advantage of by unscrupulous individuals'. But those who knew him also firmly believe that, despite his behaviour, he did have feelings for Cass. Apart from the reflected glory from Cass's star status and financial gain, Dawson's association with Cass also seems to have given him a sense of self-worth and importance which he probably rarely found elsewhere. 'You wanted to be with Cass because she made you feel very *important*,' remembers Vanessa. 'Because he was the dealer, he had a lot of people exalting him but I think, with her, he became a bigger person.'

But even if Dawson did indeed have some genuine feelings for her, his behaviour towards her nevertheless edged her onto a rollercoaster of hope, excitement and heartbreak, which at some level was no doubt as addictive as the drugs they both used. When she was at her lowest, she would sometimes confide in Eric 'the Doctor' Hord who had played guitar with the Mamas and the Papas since their time in the Virgin Islands and was still close to them all. 'She used to cry a lot,' says Hord. 'And I'd say, "Well, *this* guy isn't doing you any good, so you better find someone new in your life, because he's no good for you." But then she'd do that thing like a girl turns her head away in sort of a repose like, "Well, I still love him", and blah, blah, blah but she won't actually say it, she'll just look that way.'

There had been brief moments when it had become obvious, even to Cass, that she was being taken advantage of. Despite being the principal recipient of a trust fund, Dawson's free-form drugs habit often meant that even this supply was sometimes exhausted and he would often tap Cass for money. Cass had always had an overly generous nature, but if she was not forthcoming, he had no qualms about taking whatever he needed. 'Pic was the worst thing that ever happened to Cass,' says Lee Kiefer, 'because he's the one that continued the problem of heroin and kept bringing those satellites around her. He would come and steal from her and ask her for money and she would give it to him. I guarantee that to be the truth because he stole *my* things. I took them back.'

At one point, while Cass had been pregnant, she had lost patience and told Dawson to leave, but he had simply refused. Cass had therefore decided that if he would not leave, she would have to go herself, and drove over to Denny's house on nearby Appian Way. She still felt that Denny was the closest friend she could turn to and he took her in without hesitation. Perhaps, at some level, Cass hoped that in the light of her distress, despite her pregnant state, Denny might be prompted to provide some comforting affection, but Denny was more than occupied romantically with a seemingly endless supply of women at his beck and call, day and night. Dawson, meanwhile, lost no time in following Cass, arriving at Denny's and insisting that he see her. '*He* comes over to my place like some fucking bird-dog,' remembers Denny. 'I told him to get *out*! Go *away*! And he went, but then she *followed* him. Go figure. If I'd taken her down the hall and put her in my own big bed and said, "Baby baby there," he probably wouldn't have even fucking showed up.' Pregnant, and with only the most basic support from Denny, it is little surprise that Cass's resistance was low. A week later, however, Dawson had once again left LA. Within days, the FBI were on Denny's doorstep investigating his whereabouts.

Cass had been entirely serious about wanting to leave the Mamas and the Papas, but it soon emerged that, according to their agreement with Dunhill, they were contractually obliged to finish the album they had started recording.

They therefore returned to John's Bel Air studio. By this time, they were all aware of Cass's heroin use – Cass had at one point offered some to Denny, but he had been violently ill after trying it and never attempted it again. Cass may have been alone in using heroin, but the others were equally immersed in their own drugs of choice and the prevailing mood meant that nobody was likely to comment or criticise anyone else's choices. 'It was a drug culture,' says Peter Pilafian, 'so for anyone to get critical of another person's use of chemicals was kind of out of line – it just wasn't done. Everybody was taking drugs of various kinds and it was just part of the world, part of the ambience. I don't think anyone *liked* heroin, but it was part of the available chemistry.'

Nor did Cass behave in what may now be considered the typically dependent and often desperate manner of the stereotypical heroin addict. Whilst it may have been known that she was using the drug, she rarely let it affect her professionally. 'Cass wasn't an addict,' believes Gary Burden. 'She was not somebody who had a dependency that she had to service every day. No way! She was too powerful and had too much class and too much sense of her duties to have given in that way. She might have missed a rehearsal or she might have been late or frustrated people because she wouldn't do exactly what they expected her to do, but I don't think that she was, in *my* recollection, ever incapacitated.'

As far as the group was concerned, drug issues were only one of a range of problems. The trip to Europe, far from proving the restorative experience that John had hoped, had been a disaster in virtually every respect. Cass was even more disenchanted with the group than she had been before and she would later comment to *Rolling Stone* that she didn't understand the resulting album and that recording it had been an 'arduous task'. This was clearly an understatement.

The rifts within the group were deeper than ever and so it is hardly surprising that the entire tone of the album was desperately sombre in comparison to the dazzling euphoria of their first recordings. The songs were a clear reflection of John's disenchantment with success: '"Sitting in our mansion / guarded by expansion / questioning our motives and our means / wondering why this isn't like the dream"' they sang in 'Mansions', while his rapidly disintegrating relationship with Michelle was the subject of 'Rooms': 'Mornings we would wake up / just to taste our love again / Afraid of some break up before the day could end ... Why can't we seem to get along?' 'Meditation Mama', meanwhile, rather than being about either Michelle or Cass, was in fact written about Mia Farrow, with whom John had been conducting an intense affair.

One song, 'For the Love of Ivy', had taken a whole month to record and once the album was released, just in case there was any doubt as to the tensions within the group, they left in a false start in the middle of the Cass-led 'Midnight Voyage' in which the strain between Cass and John is audible. 'You're late coming in,' John tells Cass. 'I . . . was *right* with you,' she replies in a tone which bears no argument, 'Sorry, *my* mistake,' says John.

The album, eventually titled *The Papas and the Mamas*, did nevertheless contain two exceptional tracks, one being the single 'Twelve Thirty (Young Girls Are Coming to the Canyon)', which was released in advance of the album. Although it only briefly scraped the top twenty in America and its release passed virtually unnoticed in Britain, 'Twelve Thirty' was the last truly great, and inexplicably forgotten, Mamas and Papas single. It was a deceptively smooth combination of two songs John had originally written some time before: the first in New York (where the clock across the street 'always said 12.30') and the second during their first year in California, when John and Denny had been sharing an apartment and young girls aplenty had indeed been coming to the Canyon. It also featured a series of masterful

Mozartian piano solos by Larry Knechtel which helped weld the songs together seamlessly and the single would prove to be the group's final taste of an almost-hit as the Mamas and the Papas.

The album's other memorable track would, more importantly for Cass, prove a turning point in her career. 'Dream a Little Dream of Me' had been a hit for Frankie Laine in the fifties, but had originally been written by songwriter Favian André – a friend of Michelle's father in Mexico City. Michelle had consequently known the song since childhood and the four of them had often sung it in rehearsals. Cass suggested to John they include it on the album. It was an obvious song for her, particularly given her love of old-school standards, and John was immediately keen. John himself, however, would later claim that he had in fact had to persuade her to sing it. He said she had hated it, complaining that it sounded dated and camp. 'I had to make her whistle at the end and do the "ba dah-dahs",' wrote John in his autobiography. 'She rolled her eyes and shook her head. "*Really* corny, you know," she kvetched. "Next we'll be in blackface. Get out the burned corks."'

Sadly neither Lou Adler nor Peter Pilafian, who were the only other people present in the studio when Cass cut the track, remember much about the recording. In terms of Cass's thoughts about the song, Adler was never particularly close to Cass and the constant disputes between her and John often seem to have obscured whatever she was really feeling. 'You never knew which way she was going,' says Adler, 'you never knew who she wanted to *be* at that time, if she wanted to be Barbra Streisand – and Barbra Streisand would *never* sing a song that way, or whoever, and so it's hard to get into her head. But she had fun with it! Once she started to sing, there's personality all over that vocal and it was ideal for her.' There was indeed personality all over it, and despite her initial misgivings, Cass had clearly wanted to make it her own. 'I tried to sing it like it was 1943,' she later told *Melody Maker*, 'and somebody had just come in and said, "Here's a new song." I tried to sing it as if it were the first time.' Cass clearly succeeded, bringing a warmth and tenderness to the song which were unmistakably hers alone and her recording of the song has since become the definitive version.

The Papas and the Mamas presented by the Mamas and the Papas was released in April of 1968, followed by the single 'Safe in My Garden', but Robert Kennedy was assassinated that same week and the sombreness of the nation's mood combined with the darkness of the record did not spell hit by any means. Dunhill were by this time becoming acutely aware that the Mamas and Papas' star not only seemed to have faded but seemed to be on a downward plunge towards obscurity. The individual members' lives were in varying states of disarray, John's ability to write a hit record seemed to be in severe decline and it was obvious to anyone around them that the group's time was effectively over. The mood of the country had also begun to change since the peace and love high of the previous summer: America's youth were becoming more politicised as the anti-war movement against America's continued involvement in Vietnam gained momentum, and although the group's new songs reflected this disillusionment, the group itself seemed to have out-grown their teenage fans whilst failing to attract the older, more discerning listeners. Instead of the Mamas and the Papas, these older fans were by this time listening to what were considered the more grown-up sounds of Jimi Hendrix, the Jefferson Airplane, the Band and the Grateful Dead.

Dunhill, however, were of course keen to keep hold of their investment if at all possible and realised that the group did still contain one potential hit-maker. They also realised that, despite his songwriting ability, this wasn't John. Like everyone else, they were aware that Cass was the most sought-after member of the group and it was almost her popularity alone which had sustained the public's interest over the past few months. From their point of view the way forward was clear: Cass would be promoted as a solo artist and if there was a track on the album which could be issued as a single and billed as Mama Cass, then that's what they would do.

For Cass, the prospect of finally leaving the group was both exciting and daunting. On the one hand venturing out on her own without John's protective governing arm and Denny and Michelle's bolstering presence was frightening; on the other, the chance to be free of John's controlling and undermining ways and enjoy the affection which she knew the public felt for her was too good an offer to refuse. Particularly as those around her, including the group's manager Bobby Roberts, had been telling her she should strike out alone for some time. There must also have been at least a little feeling of vindication on Cass's part towards John at the thought of making a success on her own.

Cass also had another reason to be even more disillusioned with the group than she had been before – if that were possible. In spite of everything that had happened, Cass had never stopped loving Denny. The first bloom of her romance with Lee Kiefer had initially led her to think she no longer needed him, but since Pic Dawson's re-emergence in her life, her relationship with Kiefer had dwindled to friendship alone and given the highly unreliable nature of her involvement with Dawson, she once again began to look towards Denny as her ultimate partner and soulmate.

In spite of her own drug issues, it was still painful for her to see Denny's drinking escalate to an epic scale. At the time, excessive drinking was considered far more dangerous and antisocial than drug use. Alcohol somehow seemed irreparably connected to their parents' generation and so was therefore, by association, uncool. Drugs, on the other hand, still seemed hip and modern. But aside from the social stigma that drink carried, Cass could also see that Denny's effective absence from his own life had begun to spawn a whole new set of issues. It is often easier to see other people's problems than your own, and Cass could see Denny's with sparkling clarity. By this point his drinking had made him oblivious to the financial and legal aspects of his life to the extent that he was gradually allowing himself to be swindled out of most of the money he had earnt; he also stood to lose his home. He badly needed help, and Cass's rescuing instincts immediately kicked in, just as they had done with Dawson. 'It was always sort of like he was injured,' remembers Caroline Cox-Simon. 'He was wounded, so for Cass, it became a matter of taking care of him more than, "Oh, I still have the fantasy that we're gonna get together."'

With the (misplaced) idealism that often goes hand-in-hand with drug use, Cass believed that by allying herself to Denny, they could bring each other the friendship they both so badly needed and somehow or other provide the solution to each other's problems. In the light of her own issues, this seems optimistic at best, but Cass was almost certainly unaware of the severity of her own problems. What she did know was that in spite of Denny's eagerness to sample the excesses of the rock star life, at heart he was still the nice boy from Novia Scotia whom she had first fallen for in Greenwich Village. He may have proved unreliable in many ways, but beneath the celebrity ephemera, he still shared her decency and warmth. He had also never lost the capacity to make her laugh, and perhaps most importantly, she knew he loved her. Did it really matter therefore that they had never been lovers? Cass believed not.

One evening she drove over to Denny's house on Appian Way, arriving unannounced, to find him, as usual, surrounded by a dense fog of empty Crown Royal bottles and hangers on. Cass managed to take him aside so they could talk in private and confronted him with the fact that his life was disintegrating around him. She knew he wasn't getting the royalties he was owed and this was only a fraction of his problems. 'Dennis, get your head out of your ass,' she told him. 'You're getting *fucked* and you don't care? You're going to get screwed, man. You're gonna lose your house. You'll lose everything.' Then she whispered softly, 'Come on, let me take care of you. *I* could make you happy. If you marry me, I can make you happy.'

This was the first time Cass had ever told Denny how she really felt about him. Even though he had known for years, ever since she had played 'their tune' – the theme from *Peyton Place* – in the snow on her rooftop in Gramercy Park, he had known, but this was the first time it had ever been articulated. 'I knew she loved me,' says Denny, 'and I loved her too, but not like she wanted me to. She did weigh three-hundred pounds and I wasn't man enough to deal with that, so I made some stupid joke. She left and something was lost forever.'

Denny's rebuttal left no doubt in Cass's mind that she had to leave the group. 'She'd have stuck it out if *I'd* have been . . . you know . . . with my head on straight,' says Denny sombrely. 'If I had seen the *value* of the relationship. But you don't look at *value* of relationship, you're being led around by your dick. Sorry to be so *graphic*, dear, but that's about the way it was. What do you do? Your brain is out to lunch.' He breathes a heavy sigh and pauses before adding, 'You first have to achieve the human condition, before you can rise above it. And we're trying to achieve it.'

In the wake of Denny's rejection, Cass took the route she often did when life was not so good at home: she went to London. Even though it was still bitterly cold in England, Cass welcomed the change and lost no time in heading straight for the party circuit. As well as British friends like Keith Moon, there were usually also one or two of her American friends there at the same time and on this occasion that included, amongst others, ex-Greenwich Village folkster Shawn Phillips. Philips had had considerable success writing and collaborating with Donovan on his hits, as well as releasing several reasonably successful solo albums of his own. He also had a publishing deal in London with Beatles publisher Dick James. Phillips, however, was unhappy with his career's seemingly slow progress and sympathised with Cass's own anxieties. They soon found themselves offering each other consolation and embarked on a brief affair. The pair immersed themselves in the London scene, spending evenings at fashionable clubs like the Scotch of St James and the Speakeasy, drinking, smoking grass and sampling the new arrival on the London streets – Mandrax or 'mandies' as they were popularly known. Marketed in America as Quaaludes, they were similar to barbiturates in their hypnosedative effect, whilst at the same time being milder and less soporific.

Cass had managed to come off heroin at this point, but these softer options still offered a welcome release from reality. 'She was not at *all* happy about the way things were,' Phillips tells me down the phone from Johannesburg where he is now a certified fire fighter. 'When we *weren't* stoned, or something like that, she could get quite depressed. And a lot of the ebullience I would say was more of a protective front. Because she wasn't all that happy. She was definitely unhappy that the Mamas and Papas were declining, because as long as I had known Cass, she had always worked *with* people, so I think she was a little frightened that she was going to try and work solo.' Cass also explained that the other reason for her unhappiness was her disappointment over Denny. Just as she had to others in the past, she gave Phillips the distinct impression that she and Denny had been lovers. 'The way *she* was talking about it,' continues Phillips, 'yes, they *had* had a fully fledged relationship and I remember her being quite unhappy that that wasn't happening.' In Cass's own mind, her relationship with Denny had clearly been very real in every sense and, unable to rationalise why it had failed, she blamed herself. 'What did I do wrong?' she asked Phillips, hoping for a male perspective on the situation and some kind of answer.

Cass welcomed Phillips's company but she also admired and to a certain extent envied what she saw as his ability to bale out from the music industry altogether. Before his visit to London, Phillips had escaped temporarily to the small Italian town of Positano and spent time living there. It was an idea that Cass found immensely appealing. 'I remember we were laying one night and she said something about the fact that she liked the outlook I had on life,' says Phillips, 'the way I was not *involved*. Because at that time in Italy, I was just totally cut off from *everything*, living in Positano with twelve hundred people!'

Phillips's company only offered temporary consolation, however. There was never any question that the relationship would continue beyond this brief fortnight in London as they both had their own lives and careers to return to. 'It was clear to both of us that we had two different agendas,' says Phillips. 'I had my problems and she had hers, but she made me feel like I was a comfort to her and it was the same for me.'

By the time Cass returned to LA, if she was apprehensive about working alone, there was little sign of it. In June 1968 'Dream a Little Dream of Me' was released in America under the name Mama Cass with the Mamas and the Papas, while in the UK it was simply Mama Cass. As if to shout her independence from the rooftops – or billboards – the poster for the single featured Cass lying on her stomach, naked in a bed of daisies, feet dangling coquettishly in the air and a crown of flowers in her hair. She looked for all the world like some kind of life-affirming cross between a San Francisco flower child, a *Playboy* centrefold and Mae West. The picture had first appeared as a double-spread in the short-lived but cult *Cheetah* magazine and it caused uproar. Even in the supposedly permissive LA rock world, many, in the still essentially chauvinistic, male-dominated culture, were shocked that a woman of Cass's dimensions should do such a thing. But Cass had never been one to kowtow to anyone's dictates of what she could or couldn't do and she was not the only one flaunting her nakedness.

Nudity had by this time become part of the 'let-it-all-hang-out' hippie ethos, and many embraced the idea in their homes, whilst stage shows like *Hair* and *Oh! Calcutta!* brought the trend to the stage. Similarly John Lennon and Yoko Ono, the Jimi Hendrix Experience and the Soft Machine all featured nudity on their album sleeves that year, all of which caused similar levels of scandal. Cass, however, couldn't have been less concerned. Nor were any of her friends in the least shocked or surprised. 'At that point nothing really surprised you about Cass,' says Michelle, 'and it wasn't in bad taste. She also had a butterfly tattooed to her ass and I'd never heard of a woman getting a tattoo. It was just another *thing* that Cass would do. A tattoo? Why would you do that? She said, "Oh, I *love* it! Everyone loves it!" She was a first and she was innovative and she was always stepping over the line and pushing the envelope and she just did not want to be conventional in any way. Whatever her past conventions might have been, she had left them behind.'

Cass's sheer bravado simply endeared her to her fans still further. 'Dream a Little Dream of Me' sold over a million copies and peaked at number twelve during a twelve-week run in the American charts. In contrast to the relative failure of the group's recent singles, the song became not only the biggest hit Cass would ever have but also her personal signature for the rest of her career.

John, of course, was far from happy with the situation but was unable to do anything about it. But John, like Denny and Michelle, had also realised for some time that the group's demise was inevitable. The friction amongst the four of them had threatened their existence almost from the start, and as Cass's discontentment with the group grew, her personal popularity increased. It was therefore little surprise that she had decided to leave.

In the course of little more than two years, the Mamas and the Papas had created a body of work, the best of which still sounds fresh more than three decades later and continues to attract new fans. Like all great pop, their finest songs are both of their time and yet utterly timeless. The group had also spawned a host of imitators in the form of the short-lived Californian 'sunshine pop' strain which continued throughout the latter years of the sixties in groups like Spanky and Our Gang (featuring Cass's friend Spanky McFarlane who would later sing Cass's part in John's 1980s incarnation of the group), the Association and the Sunshine Company. But most importantly for Cass, the group had brought her the fame she had wanted for so long.

In spite of the problems she faced personally, either with drugs or the continuing disappointments of her personal life, Cass had also proved that she could be a success as a solo artist. Now, all she had to do was prove she could hold on to that success, alone.

20

'In the words of my friends'

'In all honesty there are very few songs on the Mamas and Papas albums that I'm really proud to listen to,' Cass told *Rolling Stone* on the release of her debut solo album. 'I don't have the records in my house. Not because I'm a snob. I just don't feel like listening to them. If somebody comes over and says, "Will you play that for me?" what I do is run over to the record player and play "Shake it up, Baby" [clearly referring to "Twist and Shout"] or something, because it offends me. But I don't think I'll take my new album off. It's the first thing I've ever done I can listen to objectively. I can listen to the vocals and the orchestra and everything and not be chained just to my own voice in a playback.' Cass would later return to the records she had made with the Mamas and the Papas and view them more charitably, but in the initial aftermath of their break up, she wanted to distance herself from them in every way possible. She also had a new album of her own which seemed much more appealing.

In the light of Cass's phenomenal hit with the 'Dream a Little Dream of Me' single, Dunhill were eager to capitalize on its success and within weeks had booked her into the studio to record an album of her own to follow. As far as the public was concerned, there had already been talk of the Mamas and the Papas splitting up on their return from England, so despite the fact that they had subsequently recorded another album, with the release of Cass's solo single, the group's split seemed confirmed. No major announcement was made this time; Cass had simply left the group and there was some vague talk that the remaining Mama and Papas might record as a trio.

When it came to choosing a producer for her first album without the group, Cass wanted this to reflect her breakaway as much as everything else. She respected Lou Adler's production talent, but she wanted this new record to sound different and to express her own identity. In theory Cass was experienced enough to have produced the album herself and could have simply brought in arrangers and engineers to take care of the rest, but she was astute enough to realise that she needed someone who could take an impartial overview and steer the project. 'I didn't have the objectivity,' she told *Rolling Stone*, 'I didn't want to hire a staff of people and say, "OK, you write the strings, you write the horns, you write the arrangements, and you play the guitar." I wanted one person that I could work with and really communicate with, who could understand me and my music and what I wanted to say.'

The man she chose for the task was John Simon, who had recently produced Big Brother and The Holding Company's *Cheap Thrills* and the Band's *Music from Big Pink* as well as Simon and Garfunkel and Leonard Cohen. Simon was still only in his late twenties, and, although with his work for these artists he had helped shape some of the newest, loosest-sounding work of the time, he in fact came from a strictly orthodox East Coast musical background. He had been a star jazz musician at Princeton before going on to work at Columbia Records where his perfect pitch had gained him notoriety as someone who couldn't abide musicians playing out of tune.

Cass's friend Alan Pariser had brought Simon over to Woodrow Wilson Drive for dinner one evening and she had liked him immediately, particularly his sense of humour. 'I thought he was silly,' she said, 'and I thought here's somebody I can really work with because I'm basically the silliest person I know.' She had loved *Music for the Big Pink* – although she admitted that when Pariser had first played it to her, she 'was too out of it to listen to it' and it had made no impression whatsoever, but after listening to some of his other work, Cass asked him if he might have time to produce her album. Simon did have time and for the next three weeks, they hung out and talked, swam in the pool and played with baby Owen.

Although Simon had produced various other successful artists, none of them were yet quite as famous as Cass and the Mamas and Papas and he was therefore slightly in awe of her star status. But Cass immediately put him at ease. However much her fame may have meant to her and might have affected her attitude towards John Phillips, it had never manifested itself in airs and graces with people she liked.

On the contrary. 'You felt very comfortable with Cass,' says Simon. 'When you meet somebody that you've just seen pictures of on an album cover and they turn out to be somebody that is just very outgoing and friendly and wants to be your friend and wants you to be *their* friend and is very chatty and funny and not at all snooty, it makes an impression. At one point I had a dune buggy and Cass and I were speeding down Beverly Hills to one of these private clubs that she had access to because she was such a big star and we got stopped by a cop. I was driving and of course when they saw Mama Cass, they said, "Fine, go ahead, no ticket, but be careful." So we went to the club and there's Peter Lawford shooting pool. This was very impressive to me – I was this East Coast, New England boy with no contact with stars, but because of her fame, she had all this access. And she was very easy with it. She was such a good link between normal people and stardom, you know? She wore her mantle very well.'

Once they began to choose material, Cass had a clear idea of the direction she wanted the album to take. Whilst she had always appreciated John Phillips's songwriting ability, she had also become aware that some of her own songwriter friends were developing new songs which suddenly felt more contemporary and reflected the less pop-oriented styles which had recently gained currency. Now that she was on her own, she was keen to move on. 'I had a concept for the album,' she said, 'I wanted to do songs that had been written by people I knew, but had never been able to sing because John wrote most of the Mamas and Papas material: David Crosby, Graham Nash, John Sebastian. I thought I'd call the album "In the words of my friends" but we found we needed broader material.'

Apart from anything else, Cass's approach also seems to have been an entirely practical solution to the question of finding material. Without John Phillips providing new songs, sourcing new material was always going to be a challenge and would remain an issue throughout the rest of her career. In this instance, Cass's friends provided an easy solution; if the likes of John Sebastian and Graham Nash were on hand with songs they were more than willing to give her – 'The Room Nobody Lives In' and 'Burn Your Hatred' respectively (no Crosby song ever surfaced on the album), these were an obvious starting point. There were also two songs from her ex-Modern Folk Quartet friend from the folk days, Cyrus Faryar, but the need for 'broader' material, however, meant that she and Simon eventually chose additional songs by other contemporary writers such as Leonard Cohen, whose *Songs From a Room* album had recently propelled him to cult fame. Cass recorded 'You Know Who I Am' as well as 'What Was I Thinking Of?' by her sister Leah, who was at this point just starting out as a songwriter. It was an act of great generosity. '*I* was like a totally unformed, *baby* songwriter,' says Leah, 'age eighteen, and she's putting my songs on her solo record you know? I listen to them now and I go, "Uh oh!"' she laughs. 'But she was just so *dear*. She was like my biggest fan, my biggest supporter of my songwriting. More than anybody in my life, she made me feel that she was proud of me and my songwriting. Even after I got married, she was the only person in my life that if I said "Cass, I wrote a new song, do you wanna hear it?" She would go, "*Yes*." Immediately!'

When it came to going into the studio, Cass and Simon got together a group of musicians including Cass's friends Sebastian, Stephen Stills and Cyrus Faryar as well as top-level session players: bassist Harvey Brooks and drummer Jim Gordon. In sharp contrast to the arduous, long drawn-out sessions for the last Mamas and Papas album, *Dream A Little Dream of Me* – as the album was eventually titled, was recorded in no more than ten days. Instead of painstakingly recording each track individually, the entire album was recorded almost live and Cass could rediscover the fun of creating a performance in the studio.

It must also have been enormously exciting for Cass to have a new working collaborator with whom there was no history, no emotional baggage and, because of her relative star status, no question of anything less than respect. In contrast to the constant wrangling which had gone on between Cass and John in the studio, suddenly, with someone else at the helm, the whole recording process seemed amazingly easy, enjoyable and unproblematic. Similarly, while John Phillips and Lou Adler had found that Cass's disagreements with them made her 'difficult' to work with, Simon found her quite the opposite. 'She was easy with everything and hardly objected to anything. After she'd picked the songs and we settled on the musicians, she was just happy to show up and sing and she didn't take any more of an active role than that.' From Simon's point of view, having recently worked with Janis Joplin, Cass was also a welcome respite. 'Janis Joplin was like a tornado,' remembers Simon, 'and Cass Elliot was a calm sea. I mean *totally* different. They both had their gifts but as far as working with them,

Janis was just a flying disaster and Cass was as mellow as you could possibly be. Mellow as melted ice cream. She was just so easy.'

The mellowness Simon remembers undoubtedly has an air of chemically induced tranquillity, but whatever difficulties Cass may have been experiencing in her personal life, either with Pic Dawson or in terms of her drug use, she nearly always managed to keep the practical aspects of her life functioning reasonably smoothly. She certainly didn't let any of it interfere with her recording. 'She sort of shepherded this album,' says Simon, 'because she had something in mind. It was *her* idea to do this album – I didn't come to *her* and say, "Let's do an album," and she had a daughter and she looked after her and she had a household and a housekeeper to come in, so she was the matriarch in this house. She didn't abandon her responsibilities.'

Musically the album was a dramatic departure from the melancholy pop romanticism of John Phillips's songwriting. The fact that it was titled after Cass's single might have suggested that this was a commercial album, full of similarly memorable and indeed accessible songs, but this was not the case. John Sebastian and Graham Nash had undeniable pedigree as songwriters but these particular songs didn't by any means represent their best work and certainly not their most commercial. Simon's production was also looser, freer and more experimental than anything the Mamas and Papas had ever released and came complete with a host of incidental 'real' sounds from police sirens and explosions to a woman's sobbing and crowd and animal noises. The album opened with a rainstorm leading into 'Dream a Little Dream of Me', but the song had not been re-recorded; in a kind of sixties version of a remix, Simon simply added the storm sounds to the beginning of the original track before similarly tagging a bunch of party revellers whistling onto the song's finale as the track segued into the next. The album was recorded more than a year after both the Beatles' *Sergeant Pepper's Lonely Hearts Club Band* and the Beach Boys' *Pet Sounds* – both of which had famously used these devices, but Simon denies that either were an influence. 'I never heard *Pet Sounds* until much later,' he says. 'Of course, I heard *Sergeant Pepper* but I had done some stuff before that which was so far out that I was not about to stick to the three seconds between bands all the time.'

This simpler, looser, quirkier style was what Cass had wanted though. She felt that the new album really represented what she was about in terms of the material and style. She hadn't always agreed with the lush style of production on the last Mamas and Papas album and said she thought the music sounded 'so over-produced'. 'It should be so simple,' said Cass. 'Simplicity is the answer to everything and when art becomes work, it is no longer art.'

It must also have been a thrill for her to lead an entire album on her own. Although she had always had a few lead tracks on each Mamas and Papas album, for the most part, their studio time consisted of working towards blending their four voices together; now Cass had the freedom to use her own voice however she wished. 'I guess it's a lot lower key than a lot of screaming and yelling I did with the Mamas and Papas,' she told *Rolling Stone*, describing the new album. 'It's not nearly as intense vocally. I think it's intense emotionally.'

Cass desperately needed the album to be a success, particularly in the eyes of her peers. When *Rolling Stone* asked if she was pleased with the album, she told them that David Crosby had said 'about a dozen times' that 'it took him further than he'd meant to go'. She said she thought this was 'such a groovy compliment', because she believed it was more important what other people thought of it. But when Cass said 'other people', she wasn't necessarily referring to her record company. Dunhill were, in fact, less than thrilled with the album. By backing Cass as a solo artist, they had hoped to repeat the enormous commercial success of the Mamas and the Papas and Cass's first solo single. When they heard this new album, however, they did little to hide their disappointment. 'I played it to the president of Dunhill Records,' Cass told *Melody Maker*. 'He just sat there and I was crushed. They played it to the promotion men and they just sat there too but I knew that there were some fine and beautiful songs on it. There are things in it which they didn't like – sound effects for instance, [but] I'm extremely proud of the album. There are maybe two or three songs on it that I'm not crazy about, but that album is me. It took me a long time to collect the songs.'

Dunhill saw little chance of the album appealing to a mainstream audience. The only people who might be interested in it, they believed, were hippies, and they consequently set about promoting it in the appropriate underground media. There was indeed some logic to this method. The newly termed 'rock music' – meaning anything that had moved away from the pure pop of the earlier sixties (and therefore included Cass's new album), may still have been in its infancy in terms of broad scale popularity, but it was the engine room of the counter-culture as championed by the recently launched and already influential *Rolling Stone* magazine. *Rolling Stone* was the first magazine to treat rock seriously enough to devote detailed analysis to it and consider its stars worthy of lengthy, in-depth interviews. The *Rolling Stone* interview was already considered a high-profile and prestigious accolade and, with the release of her debut LP, Cass was the first woman to be its subject. Cass was delighted to have the opportunity to speak out on a range of issues from music to politics and her approach to life, but in terms of promoting her album, Cass believed Dunhill were taking too narrow a view. 'I don't feel [the album] was promoted properly,' she told *Melody Maker*. 'It was advertised in all the underground press and I don't think that was right. I told them if they spent half of what they spent in the *Free Press* on an advert in *Playboy* they would have had a hit.'

This is debatable as the finished album was rather a hotchpotch of musical styles, encompassing the Stax-style blues of 'What Was I Thinking Of?', the bluegrass country of 'Jane, The Insane Dog Lady' and the rousing gospel treatment of 'You Know Who I Am' along the way, but the album nevertheless sold over a hundred and fifty thousand copies and yielded a small hit in the form of its one and only single: 'California Earthquake'.

Although short of a melodic hook, the song reflected the concerns of many Californians. Other aspects of the song's lyric also echoed Cass's interest in history and sense of adventure, not to mention some of the more romantic, undoubtedly dope-fuelled notions of the time. 'The second verse says: "'Atlantis will rise / Sunset Boulevard will fall . . .'",' Cass told *Rolling Stone*, 'And what could be more timely than that? It's where it's at. David Crosby's boat is anchored about sixty miles from where this temple is supposed to have risen in the Atlantic. This was reported in the *New York Times*. Brandon de Wilde's wife Susan called the *New York Times* to verify it, and they did. Apparently a temple has been spotted protruding two feet above the surface of the sea in very well-sailed waters, near Bimini off the coast of Florida. And it's supposedly Atlantis. So I said to David, "Let's go, man; let's see." Because I pride myself on being an old soul and I would say that I'd know if it's Atlantis. Maybe it's not Atlantis. Maybe it's Miami Beach. But let's go see anyway.'

*

While Cass had been recording the album, life at Woodrow Wilson Drive had become even more chaotic than before. Now that Cass's younger sister and brother had left home, her mother Bess had moved to LA from Washington, DC and had been staying at the house for spells of anything between a few weeks and a few months. As had her brother Joseph, sister Leah and cousin Ralfee. But as well as these family visits, there were also still constant comings and goings from a seemingly never-ending stream of friends, colleagues, sometime boyfriends, visiting rock stars, acquaintances and friends of friends. Cass seemed to like it that way. 'Cass was like the Chelsea Hotel or something,' remembers John Sebastian, 'You'd check in there immediately when you got to LA and in many cases Cass would say, "Oh God, Simon and Mariejke [of hip rock 'n' roll design combo the Fool] just left, the guest room is open, come on in, stay with me."'

On any given day, the house seemed almost like a split-screen movie with half a dozen different scenarios taking place simultaneously in different parts of the house. In the garden, Owen might be playing in her Wendy house with the nanny and some toddler friends and there would be people sunbathing by the pool, whilst inside the house the living room might be filled with another crowd of types – frequently described as nefarious, rolling joints, throwing the I Ching and strumming the odd guitar.

Cass was certainly aware that many of them were simply there to take advantage of her hospitality. Her house was widely known for offering a steady supply of good food and drugs in the comfort of extremely pleasant surroundings, but Cass generally had too many other more pressing concerns to give it too much thought; she had her own personal life and needed to earn money to support her daughter. 'I think Cass was very vulnerable to having people suck off of her,' says Leah, 'to live off of the wealth that she had in one way or another. I feel like there were a lot of people around who, had she been paying attention, she probably wouldn't have let into her life, you know? These people would basically bring Cass drugs but their whole idea was to stay at the house and mooch off of her.'

The hangers on and drug-heavy crowd still seemed to invariably centre around Pic Dawson and another new friend of his and Cass's by the name of Billy Doyle. Doyle would later be described by *Esquire* as a 'stockbroker from Toronto', although this was by no means the full story. Dark-haired and dark-eyed, with porcelain perfect pale skin and rather fetchingly flushed cheeks, Doyle was indeed Canadian, of Irish extraction, and had previously worked in finance, but by the time he was living in LA, most people knew him as a tough-guy with a penchant, like Dawson, for living life quite some way past what most people called the edge. Cass's friend Dave Mason remembers Doyle as 'Darth Vader' and 'a human being I'd rather forget ever existed'. There were various rumours circulating that he had killed a man – although there's no evidence to support this – Doyle himself seems to have actively encouraged them as, rather than putting anyone off, they seem to have only rendered him more exciting and interesting. Cass certainly thought so and she soon began an affair with him.

As with Dawson, Cass was clearly attracted to a man who seemed to bring danger and excitement into her life. Like so many other jaded stars, before and since, having strived for fame in the hope that it would fill some kind of void in her life, Cass found that once she had attained it, the emptiness seemed to return only too quickly. Disillusioned, with less to achieve and more to lose, she found herself desperately looking around for something to recreate the natural high which comes with the first flush of success. Drugs, alcohol or sex – or indeed all three – had traditionally been common sources for most in her situation, and Cass's fame had made these relatively easy to obtain, but she still yearned for long-term romantic love. She was unlikely to find it with Doyle, however, as he seemed as improbable a candidate as Dawson to provide the kind of affection and support she needed, but Cass was clearly enthralled. The frisson of a liaison with someone so louche must have seemed like some kind of consolation for the absence of something more substantial and, just as with Dawson, Cass was keen to see the best in him and consequently paid less attention to his more obvious flaws. 'Billy just seemed like he was one of those people who aren't bad seeds,' says Leah, 'but they're just spoilt and petulant and selfish and self-centred, but they're also really *cute* so women are attracted to them.' Even aside from the evident physical attraction, Cass clearly had an instinctive attraction to men who were invariably unreliable and unlikely to offer her the support and love she needed. Some might question why a woman of her intelligence should repeatedly fall into the same trap, but the rules of attraction have never been governed by rational intelligence. Even apart from the sense of ennui induced by her fame, Cass's predilection for dangerous or erratic men and indeed her own need for the stimulus of an artificial high may well have stemmed from an unconscious need to recreate the instability of her early life. What is familiar, at some level always feels comfortable, even if it is not always in our best interest.

From Cass's point of view, Doyle, meanwhile, despite his macho bravado, seemed to be offering her commitment in the way that neither Pic Dawson nor Denny ever had and Cass would later announce widely that she and Doyle were engaged to be married, although no marriage would ever materialise.

The laissez-faire free-love ethos of the time also meant that Cass's new relationship with Doyle posed no threat to her continuing on/off involvement with Dawson. Dawson himself had made no secret of the fact that he had recently had an affair with Cass's friend Nurit Wilde, but, in spite of the hurt Cass clearly felt, to have expressed any resentment would have meant committing the cardinal sin of appearing 'uptight'. For all its supposed freedom, by 1968, if you wanted to be considered hip, there was just as much pressure to conform to the polygamous free-loving ideals of hippiedom as there had been in the fifties to do the safely-buttoned-up reverse. But Cass soon saw, or at least said she saw, the advantages of being able to maintain liaisons with both Doyle and Dawson simultaneously and was soon proclaiming the virtues of the new free-loving life. 'Of course it's possible to love more than one man,' she told London's *Evening News* in 1974. 'Women are only monogamous because we're told we should be. I'm not. The trouble is that women have been programmed by parents and movies and books and songs to believe this false morality that makes us believe there's only one Mr Right for us, and that if we lose him we should all dress in widow's weeds . . . I've certainly loved more than one man at a time,' she continued, 'I'm independent and value my freedom to live and love as I want more than anything else in the world.'

But whatever pleasure Cass may have derived from her relationships with Doyle and Dawson, both men also brought with them a characteristically unsavoury retinue which seemed to shadow Cass's every move, and although most of her close friends were aware of the harm this was causing her, they generally felt powerless to help. 'I was aware of this struggle to find what she could do after the Mamas and Papas,' says John Sebastian who stayed at Woodrow Wilson Drive with Cass during this period, 'and I did understand that one of the encumbrances of doing all of this was that this group of people were constantly around. I felt that in many ways they were in the way and that they weren't helping her do what she needed to do.' 'There was a period where I just felt like it was impossible to reach her because you had to reach through all this clutter of hangers on.'

Cass, like most of her contemporaries, believed that she genuinely had an opportunity to create a new life and a new way of living and this, coupled with her ability to look for the best in people, often led her to keep her home more open than others. 'She could *be* cynical,' says Sebastian, 'but she could also really be that dreamer. She could see the good in a lot of people who weren't all the way good and I think that that stood in her way occasionally where all of a sudden she'd be involved with a bunch of amphetamine heads who were suddenly living in the house.'

Cass's fame and status as a rock star inevitably brought with it a posse of would-be hangers on, ready to offer whatever services they might be able to provide in exchange for becoming part of the entourage and catching some stardust along the way. Very few stars were immune to the scenario, but Cass's openness and need for affection made her even more vulnerable, and those close to her were often concerned. 'I'd certainly say that I felt that I could have been a better friend during that period,' says Sebastian heavy heartedly, 'that I could have dug in a little bit harder and said, "Wait, you know, this isn't you." I guess the only context that I would be able to do it in most of the time was in the studio, and that *was* a setting in which I was able to kind of take her under *my* elbow and say, "Come on, hun, we're gonna have some fun in the studio. And now is when these other bozos – they don't *have* anything to contribute so they're not getting any closer." Unfortunately in some cases they were round the other side of the glass, but they couldn't get in once we started work.'

Leah, meanwhile, attempted to tackle what she saw as the source of Cass's problems and talked to Pic Dawson. 'At the point where I saw my sister really out of it and stoned and figured out where it came from,' says Leah, 'I do remember I had a big confrontation with Pic where I told him that he needed to get those people out and keep heroin out of the house and that if I found out that that *wasn't* happening, that I was gonna call the cops. We had this *huge* screaming fight. It was just really unpleasant and he even threatened to harm me. He said he was gonna come back and cut up my face with a razor. He was just over the top 'cause basically I had said the magic words "I'm gonna call the cops", and that just wasn't something you said to somebody back then. So I think that helped for a little while but Cass and I had some kind of confrontation about it and she was the one who came and told me that I'd really pissed Pic off and she was worried that he was gonna make good on his threat.'

During Dawson's absences, Cass had tried to overcome her heroin habit and checked into a rehab clinic more than once. After her first stay, her mother, Bess, who couldn't help but be aware of what was going on, had helped nurse her through the difficult adjustment period afterwards, but by the next time, her mother was no longer at the house. Cass knew that going back to Woodrow Wilson Drive would inevitably undo the work she had just spent time and money trying to achieve, so she phoned Denny instead. Although the scenario at Denny's was hardly clean living, it seemed more so than her own home and she thought that if she went and stayed with him for a short while, it would allow her time to ease herself into a new drug-free regime. She called him from the clinic but his friend Bobby Simone answered the phone and told her Denny was apparently comatose in an unshakeable sleep. Simone therefore drove to the clinic to fetch her but, having been unable to talk to Denny, took her back to Woodrow Wilson Drive.

Alongside Cass's mother, Lee Kiefer had also tried to help Cass, but had eventually become frustrated with the impossibility of the situation and, although they were still friends and would remain so, he was now no longer living at the house. 'I had really had enough of it,' says Kiefer. 'Just not being able to stop people from getting her loaded. The heroin – I couldn't *do* anything to protect her. If I left for thirty seconds, there was a rat in the feed bin. Just like this,' he says snapping his fingers. 'If I left her alone for five hours, there'd be somebody over there trying to give her something she didn't need. There was no way I could protect her from that, so I just felt helpless and it became too much for me. She had to stop the heroin. She had a grip on everything else. It was just the heroin – that and Pic Dawson.'

'California Earthquake' was a minor success as a single and the *Dream a Little Dream of Me* album did moderately well, but without the additional income from songwriting royalties, Cass still badly needed to play live as this was much more financially profitable. Since the

Mamas and the Papas had started earning rock-star money, Cass had got used to living the superstar lifestyle and she had no intention of losing it, especially now she had a daughter to support. As she had always enjoyed singing to an audience, playing live was the obvious next move. Bobby Roberts, who had been the Mamas and the Papas' manager at Dunhill, and had continued managing Cass now that she was working solo, promptly set about booking her some dates. Cass had had no thoughts about where she should play, but Roberts devised a plan which was a surprise not only to Cass, but to everyone else.

Roberts had arranged for Cass to headline for three weeks at Caesars Palace, Las Vegas in October of that year and had secured her a record-breaking fee of forty thousand dollars a week (today the equivalent of well over a million). It was an astounding idea. At this point, Vegas was solely the preserve of top-calibre old-school entertainers. It was home to the Rat Pack, and no pop or rock star had ever even considered playing there – Elvis would not debut there till the following summer. So the whole notion of Cass, Queen of the Hippies, playing Vegas seemed entirely revolutionary and was accordingly considered bizarre, not to say foolish, by many. 'In that day Las Vegas was a joke,' explains her friend Gary Burden. 'No serious musician would ever have considered playing in Las Vegas. It was just totally outside of the world that most people in rock and roll had lived in. I don't think people would understand now because everybody plays Vegas now, but in those days it really wasn't like that, and she really was the first person *I* knew from rock and roll who played there.'

Cass knew the idea was incongruous but she had never been afraid to try something new and the lure of such an astronomical fee not only sweetened the plan considerably but, for someone with Cass's financial difficulties, proved hard to resist. Besides, at least a part of her heart had always been in traditional showbiz anyway, much more so than most of her contemporaries, so if anyone was going to try and bring a taste of the counterculture to the land of glitz and more glitz, then surely Cass was the ideal person to do it.

Nonetheless, Cass was determined not to lose credibility within the rock world which had become her home. She may have started out with dreams of singing on Broadway, but via Tim Rose and the folk boom and John Phillips's folk-rock pop songs, it was the world of rock and pop that had become her professional home. As far as her fans were concerned, she was Mama Cass, the ultimate hippie earth goddess and so if she was going to play Vegas, she would have to do it her way.

Cass's plan therefore was to 'knock 'em dead' with a technicolour hippie extravaganza. She wanted to 'bring music and entertainment and relaxation and highness and everything else to Vegas', she said. 'I don't think it's ever been done there.' She was right. It hadn't. But she thought the traditional types of Vegas acts were desperately passé, as she explained to *Rolling Stone*: 'Harry Belafonte was opening there the night I visited,' she told them, 'and his opening number was "Rock Island Line". I sat there and I thought: He's great, but it's gotta be twenty-five years behind what's happening.' In contrast, she wanted her act to turn Vegas on to the psychedelic experience. 'I'm gonna float my band above the stage on an inflatable helium-filled set,' she said. 'When the curtains open, I want them to go, "WHAT???" I met the bosses of the hotel and I caught these owners looking at me as if they were saying, "What the hell is she gonna do?" And I thought to myself: "You just wait . . . you have no idea . . . I'm gonna blow your brains out."'

21

'This show will blow their minds'

Cass's Vegas show was indeed memorable, albeit not quite in the way she would have wished. In order to create the groundbreaking spectacle she intended, considerable planning was needed and a suitably colourful cast of experts was brought in to help. Arranger Jimmie Haskell would adapt the songs, a psychedelic lighting expert was to be flown in from San Francisco and a script was to be written – at a cost of no less than ten thousand dollars (the equivalent of at least five times that amount today), by Smothers Brothers writer Mason Williams (who would later score an international hit himself with 'Classical Gas'). Cass was also to be backed by not only a specifically created small band but also Caesars Palace's twenty-piece house orchestra. And just in case the show risked being dull, along with the production supervisor and a female backing trio, Cass signed up a quartet of be-sequinned singing Mexicans – Los Hermanos Castro, whom she had seen on television.

Cass thought the whole project was immensely exciting. Not only was she going to be breaking new ground and headlining an act in her own right, but for the first time in her career it was the power of her name alone which had the capacity to command these lottery-winning fees. Over the last year, Cass had begun to accrue debts as she continued a Hollywood lifestyle without the income to support it, but now, all these concerns would be at an end. By the time her three weeks at Caesars Palace were over, Cass would have earned enough money to make her financially secure for some time. But for now, it was time to celebrate.

At Tiffany, Cass had a few small trinkets put aside – pending her

Vegas salary cheque: a five-thousand dollar watch and a twelve-hundred dollar pair of earrings. But the grand prize Cass decided to treat herself to was a made-to-measure sable coat. 'Ever since I was eight years old,' she later told *Esquire*, 'there has never been a time when I didn't want a sable coat. I never wanted a mink – I just wanted a sable coat. It was probably some popular song at the time . . . It was just so *soft* and groovy.'

Gradually, however, once the initial excitement wore off, the reality that Cass had a show to prepare began to filter through. This was to be Cass's first solo performance since she had been a relatively unknown artist singing standards at the Shadows in 1965. Although, she had obviously wanted to succeed then, the pressure was in no way comparable now. In the space of the mere three years that had passed since, Cass had become internationally famous and the queen of LA rock royalty. No one was going to miss her debut this time. Cass therefore needed to prove to them all that she could indeed be a success on her own, without John Phillips, without Tim Rose, without anyone. And that she, Cass Elliot, not 'Mama Cass', was now a star in her own right. She had insisted that she was to be billed as Cass Elliot and Caesars Palace had agreed. People invariably still referred to her as 'Mama' Cass, but the moniker had already begun to grate as it seemed to associate her with the group she had just left, whilst at the same time alluding to her size in a manner which she couldn't help feeling was less than complimentary. 'I'm not that brash image I associate with Mama,' she said, 'I get all dressed up to go to dinner with a fella and as I get out of the car some idiot comes up and says, "Hi, Mama." You must admit it's a bit undignified. In my mind it's a combination of being bawdy, vulgar and unladylike. To me it sounds like, "Hi, Mama, what's your price?"' The only person who was allowed to call her 'Mama', she said, was her daughter, and to further disassociate herself from the Mama tag, Cass set about resuming the drastic four-days-a-week fasting plan she had started following Owen's birth. It was her weight, she was sure, that was keeping her locked into her identity as a Mama.

The whole issue of her weight had always been complex and the reasons for her now having decided to try so hard to lose it were equally so. Eighteen-month Owen, she told *Newsweek*, was one of the main reasons driving her. She said that she was dieting to spare

Courtesy of Henry Diltz

Cass takes little Owen for a ride.

Courtesy of Jerry Schatzberg

Luxuriating in the daisies to promote *Dream a Little Dream of Me*.

Cass shares a joke with Jimi Hendrix and Michelle backstage at the Hollywood Bowl.

Courtesy of Henry Diltz

Pic Dawson, lounging in Cass's garden, LA.

Ladies and Gentlemen of the Canyon.
Left to right: Pic Dawson, Eric Clapton, Joni Mitchell,
David Crosby, Gary and Annette Burden, Cass,
and little Amy Burden lolling in the grass.

Courtesy of Richard Barton Campbell Collection

With (Baron) Donald Von Wiedenman, 1971.

Hollywood-diva style for the cover of the Cass Elliot solo album.

Courtesy of BMG

Author's private collection

With Sammy Davis Jnr on his ABC TV show.

At the Playboy Club with George Caldwell, July 1974.

Courtesy of *Daily Express*

Dream a Little Dream of Me:
Cass on stage in London.

the feelings of her daughter and that she didn't want her coming home saying, "Mommy, Mommy the other girls say you're fat."'

Her weight had also long been an issue with both Denny and Pic Dawson. Denny had told her straight out that although he loved her, he couldn't deal with the weight, while Pic Dawson, despite being her on/off lover, had always cited her size as the reason he couldn't commit to her. 'Pic's essential conflict,' believes Leah, 'was that he felt that if he was with her and she was fat, then he would be tempted to cheat on her and he didn't want to do that. So that was what I gathered was the reason why they weren't together really.' Given Dawson's highly erratic lifestyle and frequently shoddy treatment of Cass, the likelihood of him having committed to her, whatever her weight, seems slight at best.

Cass believed that by losing weight she would magically acquire the ideal relationship she craved, but this was in fact one of the great ironies of her life. Had she been slim, and therefore more conventionally attractive, the combination of more obvious physical allure with her intelligence and wit may well have proved daunting for many. Cass was also now famous in her own right and few men, particularly those whom she was most often drawn to, would have been prepared for a relationship in which they would almost certainly have been overshadowed by their partner's success. This is still the case three decades on and was even more so during Cass's lifetime, but Cass nevertheless remained insistent on losing weight and now had the added incentive of her forthcoming solo debut.

As the weeks went by, Cass's initial thrill and excitement began to be replaced by nerves. And the nerves by dread. Gradually her health, aggravated by the severe dieting, began to suffer. As the opening drew nearer, Cass fell prone to repeated stomach cramps and attacks of nausea and resorted to spending days and weeks confined to her bedroom. But even when she wasn't languishing in bed, Cass seemed to be developing a fatalistic attitude to her solo debut. After the first run through with the band, Cass failed to appear at any of the subsequent rehearsals. Even though the band's leader, bass player Harvey Brooks, was by this time staying at Woodrow Wilson Drive with her, when the time came to go and rehearse, she would tell him to go on ahead, saying, 'I'll *meet* you there.' She invariably never arrived. 'Cass, we've got this big show coming up,' he told her, 'the only person that's not at rehearsal is you. How are we gonna make this happen?' 'It'll *happen*,' she insisted. 'It'll *happen*. I'll *get* you.'

A Vegas show was without question the least organic type of show known to man. On the contrary, these were probably the most polished shows in the history of the entertaining world. Even Frank Sinatra had been known to baulk at the prospect of opening there, demanding weeks of minutely honed rehearsals in which every vocal nuance, pause, joke, smile and gesture was rigidly planned out in microscopic detail and rehearsed ad nauseam. There was no remote possibility of anyone ever wavering from the script. As Cass's opening night approached, however, Cass had still not managed to stage a full run through of her show. 'When I hear my music, it will all come together,' she insisted.

Cass was scheduled to have three days of rehearsals in the Circus Maximus auditorium at Caesars Palace before her three-week run began on the Monday night, and so on Saturday 13 October 1968 she flew out to Vegas with Harvey Brooks and the band. From the start, it was clear that Cass and her crew were not a natural fit with the hotel's regular clientele. Cass arrived at the vast, neoclassical temple of kitsch wearing her sable coat, Polaroid shades and white cable-stitch knee socks, and with her crew made her way through the forest of fake white stucco, marble, red carpets and decorously urinating cherubs. In the foyer, meanwhile, hordes of hopeful gamblers, converged in front of individual slot machine shrines bearing paper cups filled with coins and, oblivious to Cass's arrival, carried on.

She had brought Owen and the nanny with her too as she had had it written into her Vegas contract that her baby would travel with her. The Caesars Palace management had agreed that she would have daily time to spend with her as Cass had realised that otherwise she would never see her at all. 'An hour a day I put her on my lap and she plays organ,' said Cass. 'She plays harmonica, she's very rhythmical; she dances all the time.'

When Cass finally appeared for a run through to 'shake the bugs out of the show' that Saturday afternoon, the rehearsal did not go smoothly. Cass was by this time complaining of a severely sore throat and only stayed long enough to go through a medley with the Castro Brothers, before debating with Brooks as to whether she should rest her voice and miss further rehearsals or rehearse and just hope she would have recovered by opening night. They decided on a compromise and Cass returned to her room to rest till the following day, drinking tea with lemon and honey to nurse her voice.

Even during her days with the Big 3, Cass had repeatedly lost her voice, usually just before a high-profile TV appearance. These problems nearly always coincided with a show that was particularly important and when the main vocal responsibility fell to her. When she was with the Mamas and the Papas, as there were always four of them to carry the show, the problem rarely seems to have occurred, but now that the onus was once again on her alone, her nerves were once again causing havoc.

As far as the public at the casino were concerned, Cass was her usual gregarious self. After the afternoon run through, Cass wandered into the Noshorium – the hotel coffee shop– and made lifelong fans of the waitresses, signing autographs and chatting. 'My little girl just *loves* you,' one of them told her. 'She even has your record. Plays it *all* the time. I think it's nearly wore out.' 'Buy her a new one,' Cass replied.

Cass skipped the Sunday rehearsal in the hope that the rest would help revive her voice, but by Monday, there was still little improvement. On Monday afternoon she put in a brief appearance at the final run through and stayed just long enough to mark out her positions for the lighting director, check sound levels with the battered honky-tonk piano which had just arrived by special shipment from LA and discard what was left of her ten-thousand dollar script. Her crew were beginning to be concerned, but Cass remained confident. 'Honesty is all you need,' she told them. 'This show will blow their minds.'

As Cass's opening hour approached, the 950-seater Circus Maximus began to fill up and a buzz of anticipation began to ricochet through the hotel corridors. Jimi Hendrix was already in the audience and Peter Lawford and Sammy Davis Jnr were reported to be arriving at any moment. Inside Cass's dressing room, in spite of celebrity well-wishing in the form of a basket of flowers from Joan Baez, a bouquet from Mia Farrow and a used sledgehammer from Tommy Smothers, the atmosphere was less buoyant. Cass had developed a raging fever and her voice had deteriorated to the point that when she tried to sing, nothing came out. What was more, she told friends her vocal chords had been haemorrhaging. As Cass sat shivering and sweating in her dressing room, huddled inside her sable coat (despite the 100 degrees heat), Bobby Roberts wondered what to do. Friends of Cass's urged him to cancel the show as she was clearly in no state to perform, but Roberts insisted it was too late to pull out and that Cass would have to go on. Pic Dawson was with Cass in the dressing room along with Billy Doyle – who by this time was referring to himself as Cass's fiancé and who, according to John Phillips, had brought along a gargantuan slab of Iranian hash with the words GIFT OF GOD stamped on it in Farsi. Doyle and Dawson's solution to Cass's predicament seems to have been to encourage her to simply blot out whatever the problem was. John remembered that 'they had been chipping on one large wedge of the block' and now, for Cass, even the idea of concentration was ambitious. If she had been ill before, she was now stupefied and virtually comatose.

By the time Cass walked out on stage, the combination of feverishness, a drastically diminished voice, chronic nerves and drug-fuelled blur meant that her natural wit and comic timing were less than a distant memory. At this point, it was no longer a question of whether a disaster was likely to happen, but simply of when.

Despite the proliferation of Cass's celebrity friends near the front of the auditorium, the Vegas audience was also a different animal to the free-spirited, anything-goes hippies Cass had generally performed to with the Mamas and the Papas. The Circus Maximus regulars were hard-nosed gamblers more accustomed to brassy but slick displays of female flesh and feathers. An outsize hippy with a cracked voice was not by any means their style.

The result was predictably catastrophic. 'The reception was lukewarm when Cass walked onto the stage in her psychedelic silk muumuu,' wrote *Rolling Stone*. 'Her hairdo was awry and she showed the effects of just having been awakened from a fifteen-hour sleep. Flatly and uncertainly she began her set with "Dancing in the Street", "Rubber Band" and "Walk on By" assisted by a girl trio. Then she forgot the name of the next song.'

Cass's lack of mental clarity no doubt also contributed to the misjudged decision to regale the Vegas audience with tales of her disenchantment with the Mamas and Papas. 'She didn't know we were in the audience,' remembers Michelle who had a ringside seat with John, 'and she was just badmouthing the group up and down that stage! Saying how much she hated the Mamas and the Papas, hated being in the group, and don't call me "Mama" any more! She said she hated the music. She hated being under John's thumb. It was like she'd washed her hands of it,' says Michelle as she slaps the palms of her hands in a clean sweep. This was not what the audience wanted to hear. The Mamas and the Papas had made Cass famous and her fans were inevitably fans of the group. However much Cass had wanted to prove that she could be a success in her own right, without the group, the fact was that she had as yet only released one solo album which had yielded only one minor hit, so it was unsurprising therefore that audiences would still want to hear the group's hits. 'They wanted to hear her sing "California Dreamin'",' continues Michelle, 'they wanted to hear her sing "Monday, Monday", songs that she never even sang the leads on.'

But Cass's choice of repertoire was the least of her worries. For the rest of the set, Cass proceeded to miss her cues, fluff whatever lines she had managed to learn and forget her lyrics. In her billowing chiffon, she just seemed lost. There was none of the warmth and wit that Mamas and Papas audiences had come to love her for and she seemed a ghost of her usual self. To her friends and fans, used to her sparkling repartee, it seemed like a stranger had usurped her and taken her place.

Harvey Brooks was, meanwhile, painfully aware that she was also singing half a tone flat in virtually every number. 'She went for stuff and the voice just *wasn't there* – it was just shot. And when that starts to happen, your confidence goes away. *Plus* I literally think that she couldn't really hear that well, that she had some kind of sinus thing, part of that whole thing was a kind of virusy bronchitis that comes when your immune system breaks down. And the thing *about* it is she was too messed up with herself to have the confidence to get past it, to be the trouper that she needed to be.'

As the set finally ended, an encore had been expected, but the lack of rapturous applause or ovation seemed to render the whole idea superfluous. Cass returned to the stage and made a short, apologetic speech, saying that she'd wanted to be in show business since she was four. 'This is the big time,' she told them. 'Here it is. If I ever perform again I'll remember this. I don't even know the songs yet, this is the first night and it will get better.' At that point, there was some half-hearted applause before Cass sang 'Dream a Little Dream of Me' and left the stage.

But the ordeal was not quite over. Cass still had another show to perform as the Vegas deal was two shows per night. To make matters worse, as she came offstage, someone told Cass that the billing on the marquee had been changed at the last minute and that instead of proclaiming CASS ELLIOT in proud neon, the Caesars Palace management had switched it to MAMA CASS.

In her dressing room afterwards, the act booker for Caesars Palace made a vain attempt at flattering Cass and propping her up for the next show with compliments. 'They *loved* you,' he told her twice. '*Look*,' he said, '*Newsweek*, the LA papers – they're all out there tonight. You should have heard them after the show! One of them said you were the greatest entertainer of the decade.' But although Cass may have lost her voice and concentration, her mind was clearly still more than intact. 'Is that what they said?' she asked him softly. 'I wonder what they would have said if I'd been good.' Then she apologised. 'I'm sorry, Dave,' she told him. 'I really have a pretty voice, when I'm not sick.' By the second show, Cass's voice had weakened still further and despite her attempts at revving the audience up, encouraging them to 'Come On, Come *On!*', no one was impressed and this time the walkouts made no attempt at subtlety and continued noisily throughout the show.

The following day, Cass was flown back to Los Angeles and taken straight to hospital for a tonsillectomy. The rest of the engagement was cancelled. As Cass lay in her hospital bed in Beverley Hills, friends tried to hide the reviews from her. 'Like some great ocean liner embarking on an ill-fated maiden voyage,' wrote *Newsweek*, 'Mama Cass slid down the ways and sank to the bottom . . .' Even the *Los Angeles Free Press* described the show as 'an embarrassing drag', calling the production 'second rate Ed Sullivan'. Cass's voice was 'out of shape', they said while noting that 'disaster' was the word most often heard throughout the night.

Having hoped for so much, Vegas for Cass had turned into a disaster of epic proportions. Not only had her grand solo debut been an unmitigated failure, but she was now expected to try and somehow explain it all away. This was not going to be easy, even for someone as inventive as Cass. 'I have been trying to struggle up when my planets have been pulling me down,' she offered *Newsweek* shortly afterwards. But a few months later, although still devastated, she was already managing to send herself up to *Esquire*. 'I consider myself second only to [Yippie] Paul Krassner,' she told them, 'in tying totally unrelated facts together to form a conspiracy [but] I'm convinced that I'm the helpless victim of a terrible plot. For weeks somebody has been slipping something into my Chemex coffee pot to cause damage to my pipes at the worst possible time.' She then quipped that she'd like her tonsils to be bronzed and made into earrings, so she could wear them onstage and have 'everything out front'. A few year's later, however, she was clearly looking at the episode more prosaically and indeed honestly. 'I don't think there's a word in English to describe that disaster,' she admitted. 'A group is united. You have someone to share failure with.'

It was this very issue of having had to bear such a high-profile launch alone which had clearly been at the root of her anxiety prior to the show and had been a determining factor as she sought an escape from the pressure. Barry McGuire had remained a good friend of Cass's since he had first introduced her and the group to Lou Adler and was well aware of the anxieties she felt about carrying the show alone. 'She was having a lot of problems with thinking that she wasn't good enough to stand on her own,' says McGuire. 'It's OK working by yourself, but it's not nearly as much fun as having somebody up there to feed and laugh with, to look in the eyes and perform with. And I think that Cass was that way. When she got by herself and the whole load of the show was on her, I think it was very frightening for her. She got scared and started leaning more and more towards mind-altering chemicals to feel differently. Janis [Joplin] was that way. She came to see me do *Hair* (the hippie stage musical) and afterwards we were out together and she said, "How do you do the show straight? How can you not get loaded? Unless I'm absolutely obliterated I can't go out there and sing. I just get terrified." And I think Cassie experienced some of that. 'Cause she would get so loaded that she couldn't perform.'

McGuire is not alone in his belief that drugs played a central role in Cass's Vegas debacle. Within hours of the show, the LA rumour mill had kicked in with its customary rocket-fuelled capacity for expansion, and even thirty-five years on virtually everyone who knew her at the time seems to remember it being the de rigueur topic of conversation throughout the town, from the rock-star hideouts of the Canyons to the clubs and dives of Sunset Strip. The most common assumption was that she had simply miscalculated her drug intake before the show and had been stupefied by substances, most probably heroin.

Cass would later tell boyfriend Donald von Wiedenman that she had indeed shot up with heroin before going onstage and those with her at the time had little doubt that this was what had happened. 'I *really* think she got sabotaged by Pic Dawson,' believes Harvey Brooks. 'Not necessarily on purpose. People would do things that *really* didn't make any sense. There was a lot of *non*sensical things, very self-destructive things they would do to themselves and to others and think it was OK. But that was really *such* a crazy time. I think with Cass, there was just *so* much stuff around the house, and the constant desire to be just *numb*. I think she just numbed herself out. If I *talked* to her about the gig, she was *very* enthusiastic. So it just didn't make any sense, and then something would come *over* her and stop her from doing what she needed to do. It would be some kind of argument with either Pic or with Billy, like her trying to make up her mind over which one was manoeuvring her and it really cut *into* what she was trying to do.'

Even without bringing drugs into the equation, Cass's history showed a pattern of somehow managing to sabotage her own performances exactly at the time when she most needed to be a success. Having to prove herself a viable solo star in somewhere as unfamiliar and demanding as Vegas was simply too much.

But although Cass may have been aware of this pattern, it doesn't necessarily seem to have been something she was willing to confront. When it came to rationalising Vegas, even to herself, Cass doesn't seem to have moved far beyond her quips about conspiracy theories to the press. The practice of analysis, therapy and self-awareness which would become so widespread over the next few decades, particularly in California was not yet commonplace, and Cass seems to have been determined to lay the blame for whatever had gone wrong in her life elsewhere. Hearing of the Vegas fiasco, Tim Rose visited Cass shortly afterwards and talked to her about what had happened. 'She seemed to have set up this pattern in her life,' said Tim, 'where she had to assess blame for everything and it was always *them*. She never seemed to look in the mirror and say, "Maybe it was me. If you had gone and *rehearsed* with the band that were *delighted* to see you be successful;

if you just did *your* part, maybe you'd give yourself a fucking chance." Well, she didn't see it that way.'

Whoever Cass blamed, she soon plunged into depression. Over the months of fraught dieting prior to the show, Cass had lost a hundred pounds and was slimmer than she had ever been in her adult life, but despite having lost so much, she was still large and hardly anybody had noticed. With the depression came apathy and this seems to have extended to the almost twenty-four-hour 'scene' which was generally taking place in her living room. Faced with a crisis, she did what she had so often done in times of stress and turned to food for comfort, as Tim saw when he visited. 'In spite of my own insanity,' said Tim, 'I knew her friends were *really* bonzo dogs, so at least I was a little tie to some kind of sanity. So I went over to the house and in the sitting room it was all dark. It was the middle of the afternoon! The curtains were drawn and the TV was on and there were people getting high in there and I'm thinking, "Oh God, how do you fucking *live* like this?" And I'm in the business! And I said that to her and it was depressing for *me*. We sat in the kitchen and she said, "Do you fancy a piece of pie?" And I said, "No, no thanks, Cass." She said, "Do you mind if *I* have a piece?" By the time we finished talking, she had finished the apple pie.'

When *Esquire* reporter William Kloman came to Woodrow Wilson Drive to interview her a few months later, he found her similarly depleted, curling up on her four-poster bed and crying over the fact that she would have to return her treasured sable coat, as without the Vegas fee, she could no longer afford to pay for it. Instead of landing Cass the windfall she had hoped for, Vegas had instead proved excessively expensive. Estimates of Cass's production costs ran as high as ninety thousand dollars, ten thousand of which had already been spent on the discarded Mason Williams script. Meanwhile, singers, musicians, sound men and lighting men were all demanding to be paid.

Cass was also painfully aware of the impact the Vegas fiasco could have on her career. 'I'm very worried about my reputation in this business,' she explained, 'of always being on time and doing my job, and the whole thing. Now it's all *balown* man, I don't care what anybody tells me about how many people are on my side.' Cass may have tried to reapportion blame for what had gone on, but she also nevertheless felt guilty for disappointing those who had believed in her and supported her. ‘I want people to understand what went down in Las Vegas,’ she said, ‘and be forgiving. I don’t want to have this tremendous guilt that I’ve let everybody down.’

The spectre of her Vegas ordeal would resonate in Cass’s mind for the rest of her life and it would take her some time to overcome her dread of repeating the debacle and prove herself capable of successfully performing live. But in the meantime, Cass was fortunate to have supportive friends, and the pivotal role she would play in the musical and social scene around her would have a lasting impact.

22

Ladies and gentlemen of the Canyon

'Music happens in my house and that pleases me,' Cass told *Rolling Stone*. 'If you come over to my house, and you see Eric Clapton and David Crosby and Steve Stills playing guitar together and Buddy Miles walks in, it's not because I got out my Local 47 book and called up and said let's get a bunch of musicians together.' (Local 47 being the LA branch of the AFM – the American equivalent of the Musicians' Union.) 'My house is a very free house,' she continued, as the magazine insisted that she was the undisputed Queen of Los Angeles Pop Society. 'It's not a crash pad and people don't come without calling. But on an afternoon, especially on weekends, I always get a lot of delicatessen food in, because I know David is going to come over for a swim and things are going to happen. Joni Mitchell has written many songs sitting in my living room. Christmas day when we were all having dinner, she was writing songs.'

Whilst Woodrow Wilson Drive was often a magnet for some of LA's less salubrious characters, Cass also regularly played host to many of her trusted legitimate musician friends. The house had consequently become a kind of second home for friends like David Crosby, Graham Nash, Stephen Stills, Joni Mitchell, Gram Parsons and John Sebastian – all of whom were already seen as rock royalty, and although Cass may have downplayed her role in creating this environment, the fact was that she was not only warm and welcoming, but also had a large, comfortable house which was generally full of interesting people, good food and good drugs. 'That was a fascinating house,' remembers Crosby, 'and I spent a *great* deal of time there. She had probably the nicest house of any of us and there was plenty of room and she was a person that liked having people come over because she was lonesome.'

Despite having close friends, a daughter and a steady supply of visitors, Cass still lacked the companionship and emotional support of a partner. Whatever traumas had occurred with the Mamas and the Papas, Cass had nevertheless felt the security of being part of a group; now that she was on her own professionally as well as personally, her loneliness was much more acute. But Cass rarely allowed people to see the inner unhappiness she so often felt. On the contrary, to most, she was simply the ultimate, welcoming hostess. 'She was *fun*!' says Crosby. 'It was *fun* to go to Cass's, because there would be interesting people there, you would meet other musicians, other artists and stuff and it was a fascinating scene. I *loved* hanging out with her and a lot of really beautiful times happened there. I remember an afternoon when I took Clapton up there and he and I and Joni [Mitchell] and Cass sat around on the lawn playing guitar, talking with each other and just playing tunes. Another day I took Jimmy Page. Cass was very sociable and easy to meet and to talk to and *funny*, so people took to her. Some of the rest of us were a little odder and a little harder to get to know, so she was accessible and she was a person that people coming over from England into the California scene would key on and then from her, they would make other acquaintances. I know *anybody* that was visiting in town that I knew, if they were interesting, I would *always* take them up to Cass's.'

The fluidity of having a permanently open house where most of society's earlier rules had been eschewed provided the perfect framework for Cass to build her own kind of unofficial family around her. In communes across America, many were doing the same, and in the absence of the romantic love and commitment she craved, this at least provided camaraderie, affection and companionship. There was also a general sense of excitement at the discovery of this new, freer life, both musically and socially.

Cass had been used to this kind of freedom since her days in Greenwich Village, but in LA, being able to enjoy fame, money and success in the company of your equally successful friends was something new for them all. 'It was an *extraordinary* time and we were right in the middle of it,' Graham Nash tells me in an accent caught somewhere in the Atlantic, midway between Manchester and Los Angeles. 'And Cass was one of the centres of that society. Unquestionably. This was all so *new* to us in a way! Yes, we knew what rock and roll was, *yes* we knew what success was, but there was something happening in '67 and '68 in Los Angeles that was societally a very interesting slice of time – a lot of people living in Laurel Canyon, a lot of interaction walking over to people's houses with a new song, then you eat something and going out to the studio because so and so's recording and hanging out after that and going to Cantor's for breakfast at three in the morning and going on from that. I mean *constantly* and *fascinating* people . . . *wonderful peaceful* times. We were *friends* and we would talk for *hours*. We'd be smoking heavily and talking and a *lot* of *incredible* music being made. We all knew that it was special. I mean it couldn't have *been* any more perfect: *great* music, *beautiful* women, the *best* dope!'

All of these things were generally to be found at Woodrow Wilson Drive. As well as good food. Cass's visits to epicurean delis like Nate and Al's in Beverly Hills also meant that she had a better supply of food than her friends. There would be fresh bread, bagels and specialist cheeses as well as all kinds of other delicious surprises. 'She was a gourmet and a gourmand at the same time,' says Crosby. 'She would eat very well and a *lot*. She just *loved* good food and she had Cadbury's to make hot chocolate with and she'd make it with cream instead of milk. She was excessive in *all* things.'

A visit to Cass's therefore became a regular part of a day in the Canyons. Crosby and co would pull up in the driveway, honk a horn and beep and yell until Cass peeped her head out of the tiny hexagonal window in the bedroom to see who it was. '*Will* you stop making all that noise!' she'd call out. 'Hey, what are you doing, you lazy slob, get out of bed!' they'd reply, before settling into the garden by the pool. 'We would hang out,' remembers Crosby, 'smoke a joint, laugh, talk, dish other people, all the standard stuff,' he smiles, 'and with *her*, it was fun. We'd go over there and mooch food, mooch drugs, hang out, play, say, "What do you think of *this*?" And we'd sing her something.'

To Cass and her friends, it seemed that having overhauled the old social structures, their new way of living would prove a permanent replacement and nothing could change this. Sadly they would be proved wrong.

Cass's pool was to form the backdrop to many a memorable afternoon at the house. As Cass knew, Crosby particularly enjoyed the water, although his swimming occasionally took on more of a free-form, not to say, static style. 'I took an experimental psychedelic – STP, one time up there,' remembers Crosby, 'and wound up in her pool, clamped onto the side, sort of like a mollusc onto a rock, 'cause I'd found the hot water outlet and I was sure that was God! Ha ha! I was clamped onto it to keep warm just watching these red clouds go really fast – *red clouds going really fast!*' he whispers slowly. 'Several *hours* later they remembered that I wasn't there and they started looking for me and found me in the pool, clamped onto the side. Whheeeeew! *Very* high.'

Cass would prove significant in Crosby's life as she had also been responsible for introducing him to Graham Nash – just as she had brought John Sebastian and Zal Yanovsky together back in Greenwich Village. 'One of the great things that Cass did in her life was turning me onto Graham,' says Crosby, ''cause he's certainly one of the best friends I've ever had in my life. He's a *fantastically* nice human being. And he *loved* her. *Very* much. But that first meeting, she just said, "This is my friend Graham." *I* had no idea. I didn't know about the Hollies. I had only ever heard them on the radio and wasn't all that impressed. I thought their stuff was pretty *pop* but I could hear that there was this guy in there who was without question one of the best harmony singers in the world. 'Cause that's what *I* did. That was my job and I heard this guy doing it better than me and I went, "Oh my Gaaaaawd, how did he *doooooo* that?" But at the time I didn't know who he was so I just rolled a joint of this weed that the English had not encountered yet and got him *stupefied*! Got her stupefied too. And then we had a *very* nice afternoon. Later on she told me who he was.'

More than three and a half decades on, in spite of the stupefying weed, Nash likewise has a vivid recollection of the afternoon. 'First of all he was rolling the most completely perfect joints I had ever seen,' says Nash. 'They looked like cigarettes, they were just *beautiful* and he could do that while never taking his eyes off your eyes. He was doing this *completely* automatically – it was kind of fascinating to watch, and I have that image in my mind to this day. Him in a striped T-shirt with a shoebox-lid full of dope separated into seeds and the stems and the grass itself. It was amazing! And he and I just hit it off.'

Cass also sensed that the pair might be compatible on a musical as well as personal basis and her poolside would famously become the scene of the first three-part harmonies by Crosby, Stills and Nash. The story has oft been told how Crosby and Stills were sitting around singing 'You Don't Have to Cry' (which would later feature on Crosby, Stills and Nash's eponymously titled debut album) in two-part harmony, accompanied only by Stills's acoustic guitar, when Nash listened intently and asked them to repeat the song. After singing it a second time, Nash asked them to repeat it again, listening even more closely. When they'd finished, he asked them if they'd sing it one final time and as they did, Nash added in his third harmony and rock history was made. This episode has since become the subject of some debate: whilst Stills firmly believes it happened at Cass's, Crosby and Nash maintain it took place in Joni Mitchell's kitchen, but wherever it did indeed take place, there is no doubt that the genesis of the trio's coming together evolved with Cass's firm encouragement. Cass was good friends with all three of them and not only knew their voices but also knew that Nash was disgruntled with life in the Hollies, whilst both Crosby and Stills had recently parted company with the Byrds and Buffalo Springfield respectively. 'I think it was very subtle,' says Nash. 'I think she really *knew* what *I* was capable of doing and knew that Crosby and Stephen were in between bands, as they say, so I think she knew *instinctively* that we would get on as *people*. Also I *think* because of who she is and her sense of harmony and history, she knew that certain voices would be very interesting when put together. So I do give Cass a great deal of credit – that's why we dedicated the box set to her.'

A few months later producer Paul Rothschild took Crosby, Stills and Nash into a studio to record their first album. Having been so closely involved in the group's formation, Cass was insistent that she was present on the record itself. 'She said, "If you guys don't let me sing, you can't come to my house any more!" remembers Crosby, "I won't feed you any more." She was kiddin' around but she *wanted* to sing on the record and she is the *only* other human being that sang on the first Crosby, Stills and Nash record. She was the only one that we would let do it, because she was *that* close to us.' To this day, the trio are often reluctant to point out exactly where Cass's vocals feature on the album, but if you listen closely to *Pre-Road Downs*, you can hear Cass singing, "Be sure to hide the roaches."'

Singing on your friends' albums was a much more common practice at this point than it would be in today's climate where groups are often considerably more protective and competitive about their work and expensive studio time is much more closely guarded. In the late sixties the atmosphere was much more open and relaxed and just as John Lennon and Paul McCartney had sung on the Rolling Stones' 'We Love You', whilst Mick Jagger and Keith Richards had returned the compliment on 'All You Need is Love', Cass had similarly sung backing vocals on albums by her friends the Electric Flag and Cyrus Faryar. But even without guesting on friends' records, going to each other's studios to listen to new work seemed as natural as singing itself. 'Back then, that was one of the most fun things you could do,' says Crosby. 'Finish something like "Suite: Judy Blue Eyes" and then invite your friends over. "Come over to the studio – I've got something to play you . . ." And they'd sit down and you'd give them a joint of that stupendous weed and then play that for them. And they'd sit there and turn to jello. It was really fun! Cass was also somebody that you wanted to hear good stuff 'cause she would *know*. She knew the difference because she was a good musician vocally herself.'

Cass had by this time become particularly close to both Crosby and Nash in a manner not unlike the relationship she still maintained with John Sebastian, which, whilst it remained platonic, was at the same time, often ambiguously romantic. This was the same pattern of relationships which had begun with Tim Rose, Jim Hendricks and Denny. Cass seemed to inspire genuine love and adoration in them all, but whilst she almost certainly would have welcomed a more physical intimacy with at least one if not all of them, as had been the case before, that never seemed to be on offer, although Sebastian claims that in his case it was more a question of timing than anything else. '*I* would have certainly been a vague middle person [i.e. someone who was both a co-musician and lover],' says Sebastian, 'had it not been that I was married to a nice Jewish Russian girl and Cass was a traditionalist in many ways and was not the kind of person who would interfere with that. But it was the kind of relationship that had I not been otherwise occupied . . . *I* certainly would have been in the line there to be,' he pauses, 'a little more intimate with her, but it was a matter of timing. And her good taste about those kind of things.'

David Crosby similarly tells me that, '*I* could have loved her [because] inside, she was very beautiful. Very.' With Graham Nash, meanwhile, rumours had circulated almost since the beginning of their friendship that they were in fact lovers. Even to the extent that there was speculation that Nash might be Owen's father. The tales had no doubt been fuelled at least in part by the fact that Spanky McFarlane of Spanky and Our Gang had found Cass and Nash in bed together at a hotel in Chicago when the Mamas and Papas and Hollies were both playing there. Nash, however, remembers Chicago primarily as the occasion Cass turned him onto acid for the first time. 'It was a magical experience!' says Nash, before elaborating that, 'Cass and I were never lovers but we were the *deepest* of friends.' The perceived ambiguity of their relationship was nevertheless unsurprising. 'It *was* romantic,' continues Nash, 'It just wasn't sexual. You could *only* be romantic with Cass. She brought that out in *everybody, all* her male friends – we all *courted* Cass, we all paid homage to Cass. That's who she *was*. She loved flowers, she loved surprises, she loved all the things that *all* women love and she had a *lot* of male friends that would take care of her. We would do *anything* for her.'

These somewhat ambiguous affections were certainly due in part to the fact that Cass was not considered conventionally desirable. Whatever her friends may say to the contrary, there seems little doubt that had she conformed to fashion's dictates and been slim, her friends would have lost no time in becoming more intimately involved with her. Instead she became a fellow partier, and, more significantly, their trusted friend and confidante, just as they became hers. For all the romance and affection with which she was treated, at some perhaps almost unconscious level, Cass's asexuality, in their eyes, rendered her a combination of surrogate mother, counsellor and honorary male. 'Cass was always *there* when you had something you were going through – *always*,' explains Nash. 'Everybody trusted her on a very deep level because Cass would never fuck you over. She would always give you a straight opinion and there was *nobody* that knew women's issues as much as Cass. I think within her life she had been through so many traumas about her weight, about whether she was *pretty*, whether she'd be successful, whether she was gonna attain her dreams. She'd been through life on a very deep level and was *really wise* in the ways of people.'

Cass's position as a woman at the heart of this male-dominated rock community was virtually unparalleled. With the exception of Joni Mitchell, whose talent as a musician elevated her beyond the status of merely Crosby or Nash's girlfriend, Cass was virtually alone in terms of the respect and affection in which she was held within this insular group. Although the hippie ethos aimed to throw off the constraints and restrictions of the previous generation, the feminist movement was still in its infancy, and correspondingly the rock community was not only male dominated but still resolutely chauvinistic in its outlook. The fact therefore that Cass was held in such deep trust and esteem was that much more remarkable.

Socially Cass's success had never been in doubt. In the light of her Vegas disaster, however, Dunhill Records were keen to get her back in the studio as soon as possible. Her fears that the episode might affect her future career were not at all unfounded and Dunhill realised that a rescue operation was necessary. Whatever artistic ideas Cass may have had of her own, what she needed, Dunhill insisted, were some hits, and so this time they would take charge of the album. They intended to ensure that this album was commercial and, unlike its predecessor, contained more than one track which radio stations would be happy to play.

Lou Adler had by this time parted company with Dunhill amidst some acrimony and in the light of his departure, twenty-five-year-old songwriter and musician Steve Barri had been appointed head of A&R and assigned charge of Cass's album. His brief was clear: make sure it contains some hits. Barri had been part of Dunhill's in-house songwriting team, and alongside his writing partner Phil (P. F) Sloan had been responsible for 'You Baby', the Turtles' hit which the Mamas and Papas had recorded on their first album, and Barry McGuire's 'Eve of Destruction' amongst others. Barri had also already signed Steppenwolf and Three Dog Night and would later go on to sign Steely Dan to ABC, but at this time he was primarily associated with what had become known as bubblegum music – the recent strain of infectious pop tunes usually sung by manufactured groups such as the 1910 Fruitgum Company, the Lemon Pipers and, most famously, the Monkees, aimed primarily at the teen market.

The original plan was that Barri would select some suitable material for Cass and then hire a producer to record it with her, but once Cass had sat down with him and gone through the songs, she felt that rather than bringing in someone new, it would be simpler to have Barri produce the album himself. Cass therefore returned to Western Recorders and Barri brought in his regular session players including Wrecking Crew rhythm section: Hal Blaine, Joe Osborn and Larry Knechtel. Dunhill's decision to involve Barri would prove a canny one as the album, and subsequent sessions he produced for Cass, would yield her biggest solo hits and some of the best and most enduring recording of her career.

Although Barri was much straighter than the producers and musicians Cass had worked with in the past and was not part of the hip LA music scene, he and Cass nevertheless got along very well. They both loved comedy, particularly Peter Sellers, and during the sessions, Cass would mimic classic sketches, recreating voices and accents and reducing the entire studio to tears of laughter. Barri was also Jewish and Cass would joke with him, letting him call her Naomi or Cohen, while they shared reminiscences of their Jewish upbringings. 'Sometimes it would be, "Hey, Cohen, you're not getting it right today,"' Barri tells me at his smart suburban Encino home in LA, 'stuff like that. And I seem to remember Cass using that line from *Funny Girl*, "Hello, Gorgeous . . ." and she would do it in a very funny way. We were always kidding around like that. She told me some lines I guess she had heard when she was younger which I still laugh at to this day. She said that when her mother wanted to take a nap she would "cop a drimmel", so that became like a running gag through a lot of the sessions. I would say, "That's getting a little lazy, it sounds like you're getting ready to cop a drimmel on it," and we would just crack up laughing. Then all the musicians started to pick up on a lot of those Jewish expressions we used. It was quite funny.'

Now that going into the studio no longer involved the personal issues that had invariably flared up with John, Denny and Michelle, Cass was adept at keeping her home life and whatever problems she had with Pic Dawson or otherwise out of the studio. 'When I was around her,' says Barri, 'I know that she was always having some kind of problems. There was a *lot* of stuff going on in her life and she would come to the studio and say, "I'm having a shitty day," or something like that, but once we got working and started getting into the music, it was always very positive, very up and she was just really a great person to work with. She was just very professional, so even though you knew about the lifestyle she was living outside of the studio and the problems and the heartbreak and all that stuff, in the studio when she was on, I only knew "Naomi" that came in to sing. She was just such a lively, warm, funny person to be with.'

In terms of material, Barri had used his extensive songwriter contacts and approached some of the best classic Brill Building writers of the time, including legendary partners Barry Mann and Cynthia Weill who provided 'It's Getting Better'. This track, as well as 'One Way Ticket' and 'Make Your Own Kind of Music', which Barri also subsequently produced for Cass, lyrically expressed a desire to move on from a time or situation of trouble and forge your own way to a better life. The songs may have had the infectious – and indeed bubblegum-style sound of daytime radio pop but often spoke of defiance in the face of adversity; escape and survival on your own terms. The album's 'Easy Come, Easy Go' similarly was a case in point with its singalong, foot-tapping, jauntiness belying the lyrics of its chorus: 'He wasn't kind, I wasn't smart / I lost my mind and fell apart / I have to find myself in time, now I can start all over again.' Likewise, when Cass sang '"One way ticket, take me anywhere / Northbound, southbound I don't even care / I know the grass is greener there,"' in 'One Way Ticket', the yearning in her voice left absolutely no doubt in your mind that she meant every word. The songs sounded like they'd been written for Cass. The fact is that they hadn't.

They were all songs which had already been composed but which Barri had cleverly realised would suit Cass perfectly. 'I looked for songs with lyrics that I thought she could really relate to,' says Barri. 'Like "Make Your Own Kind of Music". I felt like, These songs are great – they're pop songs but they also really kind of say something that I feel she would like to say. And when she heard them, she would immediately get it. She said, "Yeah, I love it, this is saying something," or whatever. She always felt that if she didn't write it, she wanted to at least have the song express something that she felt.'

Cass clearly related to the lyrics of Laura Nyro's plaintive 'He's a Runner', which she also included on the album ('He's a runner / and he'll run away / soon there'll be no man / Woman ain't been born who can make you stay / woman get away while you can.') alongside another song of her sister Leah's – 'Who's To Blame'. Barri had, meanwhile, also tried to encourage Cass to write some new material herself. 'The *best* way to make your own kind of music is to make your own kind of music!' he would tell her, 'You know – *write* it! You know all the *best* people. Maybe John Sebastian – you can get with him and write a song, *anybody*.' 'Yeah,' Cass would reply, telling him that she was going to get together with somebody or other, but somehow nothing ever materialised.

As Cass had spent so long surrounded by exceptionally talented writers, not only in the form of John Phillips but also her friends

Sebastian, Nash, Crosby and Stills, she may well have been daunted by the prospect of trying her hand again and wary of failure. When *Melody Maker* later questioned her on the subject, she said, 'I haven't written anything for years. I used to when I first started singing with a group called the Mugwumps, but my songs weren't really very good.' The journalist replied that he was sure she was simply being modest, but Cass insisted that no, she was being 'dead accurate'.

Cass would in fact later form one further writing collaboration, but for the time being she was reliant on Barri's choices. In subsequent years she would claim to dislike the tracks she had recorded with him, considering them insufficiently sophisticated for what she felt capable of. 'Musically, it's not quite what I want to be doing,' she said. 'It doesn't satisfy me. It's a good recording for what it is, but you wouldn't exactly call it social commentary and musically it's not very complicated. If music is what I am meant to do then there should be a little more in it to satisfy me. Bubblegum music is very pleasant to listen to, and maybe that is what I am supposed to be doing. But it's like they say about Chinese food – half an hour after tasting it you are hungry again.' Given that Cass was at this point listening to Cream, Jimi Hendrix and Dylan's *John Wesley Harding* album (which she said 'turned me on'), this was perhaps unsurprising.

The album's title: *Bubblegum, Lemonade and . . . Something for Mama* meanwhile reflected the style of some of its tracks, and Cass's view of it certainly echoed the opinion held at the time by many. In terms of musical credibility, bubblegum was scorned by serious musicians. As the sixties progressed, the boundaries of what could be considered musically hip had changed. In the wake of rock bands such as the Jefferson Airplane, the Grateful Dead, the Band, Big Brother and The Holding Company, as well as the arrival of *Rolling Stone* magazine, rock bands and rock music were taken much more seriously and considered to have meaning and social importance way beyond the chart fare of the fifties and early sixties. Songwriting was now seen as an earnest artistic endeavour and a form of self-expression rather than simply a fast track to wealth and fame. In contrast to the denser, heavier sounds of its hipper contemporaries, bubblegum was perceived as overly commercial throwaway nonsense, generally devoid of artistic integrity. Most people, including Cass, had underestimated the unshakeable power of an infectious melody. It did not occur to them that, in years to come, these records would be seen as classic pop songs – both timeless and of their time, when many of their more worthy contemporaries would be long forgotten.

Barri meanwhile has little recollection of Cass expressing discontentment with the songs at the time. 'People's opinions change as years go on,' he says, 'but when we were making those records, I never had any problem with her not liking the songs and, in fact, some of them, like "Make Your Own Kind of Music" and "It's Getting Better", she really *loved* when she first heard them because we never recorded anything that she didn't want to do. "Move in a Little Closer, Baby" was one she wasn't really *too* thrilled about. That one was not one of her favourites, but she loved "It's Getting Better" 'cause she felt it was kind of positive.'

Barri's need to provide as many sure-fire hits as possible didn't leave much room for artistic experimentation, even had he felt so inclined, but he felt that the lighter pop fare he had chosen also reflected Cass's natural exuberance and warmth. '*My* way of thinking was that I wanted to capture who she was and what she was to me when *I* met her, which was this real fun-loving, positive kind of person that I couldn't imagine anybody meeting and not *loving*. And so, that's why I felt like I don't wanna make it too heavy or whatever, just keep it up and positive and that way when she goes out there and she's on a talk show or whatever, she can be who she is and just let that warmth come out, let that humour come out. And that way it would work best.'

Barri clearly achieved his aim and whilst the album reflected his own pop sensibility, with its jaunty brass augmenting the driving rhythm of the Wrecking Crew, like her best Mamas and Papas tracks, the upbeat nature of much of the album's music not only brought out Cass's humour but also highlighted the poignancy of her voice. More than twenty-five years later, British playwright Jonathan Harvey would use the songs she recorded with Barri, alongside her Mamas and Papas' hits, as the music to his play (and subsequent film) *Beautiful Thing* which featured a young girl who dreamed of being Cass, singing along to her records into a hairbrush in front of the mirror. The soundtrack was a hit and the 'Bubblegum' songs remain Cass's most popular solo work.

'Move in a Little Closer, Baby' (Cass's cover of the little-remembered Harmony Grass hit) and 'It's Getting Better' were both released as singles in advance of the album in spring 1969, and both were hits, with the latter staying in the top forty even longer than 'California Dreamin'.' In June, to coincide with the release of the album itself, Cass hosted her first TV Special – *The Mama Cass Television Program* for ABC. Cass had always felt at ease on TV, bantering easily with Ed Sullivan, and the studios recognised her as a natural TV host. At this point, at the end of the sixties, both in America and Europe, a typical Saturday night's family viewing was essentially a variety show, hosted by either a musical or comedy personality, with various star guests. In shows hosted by the likes of Tom Jones, Dinah Shore, Lulu and Cliff Richard, the standard format would include a few solo numbers by the hosting star, performances by the visiting act, at least one duet between them both and a comedy sketch, usually also featuring the host. ABC therefore considered *The Mama Cass Television Program* a pilot on the basis that if the show was successful, they would commission a full series.

For Cass, doing TV work meant that instead of having to go out on the road, she could earn good money whilst staying in LA with Owen. Having her own series would therefore be ideal. Cass also believed that if a series was commissioned, it might also pave the way for a film career, both in front of and behind the camera. 'It's the next step if the television show goes to a series,' she told *Melody Maker*. 'I know a lot of people say they want to go into films, but I'd like to go into it from a production angle.'

The show, however, was not well received. In spite of guest appearances from Cass's friends John Sebastian, Joni Mitchell and Mary Travers (ex of Peter, Paul and Mary), as well as comedian Buddy Hackett and *Mission Impossible* stars Martin Landau and Barbara Bain, Cass, faced with the pressure of carrying the show alone, appeared slightly nervous and unsure of herself throughout. The script had not helped matters either. Originally written in part by Cass's friend, writer Carl Gottlieb (at the time a successful comedy writer for the Smothers Brothers, and who would later go on to win an Oscar for his script for *Jaws*), most of Gottlieb's material had been thrown out by the producers who were old school variety types and didn't understand the hipper, more contemporary material which would have worked so well for Cass. 'They were totally out of touch with Cass's sense of humour,' says Gottlieb. 'We would write sketch after sketch that would have been great for her to do and every one of them was shot down by the producers who basically took all their Phyllis Diller ugly-girl jokes out of the trunk and put together a special for Cass, rejecting all our material.' Consequently, although three and a half decades on, the show is charming to watch, at the time it was not considered slick and pacy enough for the standards of the day. On the contrary, the show was panned by the *New York Times*, although their reviewer seems unlikely to have appreciated the show under any circumstances. Joni Mitchell was a folk singer who 'would be much more effective if she invested in a few lessons in voice projection and elocution', he wrote, while he considered Cass's voice 'pleasant enough', before adding that it 'lacked colour and sophistication'.

In contrast to the TV show, the *Bubblegum* album was a hit, but Cass's enjoyment of its success was to be short-lived. On 9 August 1969 Cass's friend actress Sharon Tate and three of her friends were all savagely murdered at the house Tate and her husband Roman Polanski had been renting on Cielo Drive, just minutes away from Woodrow Wilson. The bodies were riddled with no less than one hundred and two stab wounds and were found surrounded by vast reservoirs of blood. Cass had known not only Sharon but all three of the other victims: celebrity hairdresser Jay Sebring, Woytek Frykowski, an old schoolfriend of Polanski's, and Frykowski's girlfriend Abigail Folger, heiress to the Folger coffee fortune. The openness of Hollywood society at the time had led to a previously unprecedented crossover between the film and rock communities; if you were successful and hip in either one or the other or at least good friends with someone who was, you were just as likely to end up at a film star's house for the evening as a rock star's. Cass's prominence in the upper echelons of the LA social scene therefore meant she was part of a community which as well as rock stars such as Crosby, Nash, Stills, Eric Clapton plus assorted Beatles and Stones also included Warren Beatty, Roger Vadim and Jane Fonda, Roman Polanski and Sharon Tate, Mike Sarne, Dennis Hopper and Peter Fonda.

With the benefit of hindsight some have claimed that in the months prior to the murders that summer there was an atmosphere of doom and foreboding in the air. In national terms, the optimism and idealism of 1967's 'summer of love' had unquestionably dissipated. Although the anti-war movement had gained momentum as the war in Vietnam continued, the belief that the counterculture could genuinely effect change in the establishment was beginning to dwindle rapidly. Both Martin

Luther King and Democratic Senator Robert Kennedy had been assassinated, while the 1968 Democratic Convention saw anti-war protestors being viciously clubbed by the police in bloody scenes which dominated the nation's TV screens. But whatever may have been happening at a broader, national level, the atmosphere within Hollywood's more privileged enclaves had changed little. 'There may have been a few little spats and tiffs between people that summer,' remembers Mike Sarne, 'but that happens in every community. My feeling is that everyone was on their best behaviour that summer. The murders were like the Twin Towers – it came absolutely out of the blue. And it wasn't that there was a brooding intense feeling beforehand. It was a shock!'

Although Cass's experience of the Hollywood idyll may have always been tempered by her own personal unhappiness, the spirit of hippie optimism nevertheless bred an innocence and naïveté amongst many of them, including Cass, which meant that they had felt safe opening their homes to people who were often strangers. The murders therefore certainly came as just as much of a surprise to her. 'It scared the hell out of her,' remembers Lee Kiefer. 'It scared the hell out of all of us, 'cause it was happening right next to us and it pretty much shook up the whole Hollywood scene.'

In the immediate aftermath of the horrific murders, nobody had any idea who might have committed such violence, nor what their motive might have been. It would be months before the truth was discovered and in the meantime an atmosphere of panic, fear and paranoia swept through the Canyons. The openness and sense of trust that had previously existed, particularly at Cass's, was immediately replaced with suspicion and concern. With the very real-seeming possibility that the murderer or murderers might strike again, most of the previously peace-loving musicians and actors lost no time in rushing out to equip themselves with some sort of protection whether it was a handgun, a rifle or a guard dog. As the police began what would turn into months of extensive investigation, they began questioning virtually everyone who had known the victims and, in the absence of a clear motive, almost anyone was open to suspicion. 'Weeks went by when no one knew what had happened,' recalls Mike Sarne. 'And the police interviewed *absolutely* everybody – a few times. My phone was tapped. And so from then on there was an *immense* feeling of paranoia with everyone having their own little pet theories.'

Having regularly played host to some of the less decorous characters on the scene, Cass was subjected to particularly intensive questioning by the police. Apart from having known the victims – which half of Hollywood society could equally have laid claim to – Cass was further implicated by association. When the bodies of the victims had been discovered, the police had found the words 'PIG' blurrily scrawled on the wall of the house in blood. John Phillips had informed the police of the widely circulating theory that what had been written was in fact 'PIC' – in reference to Pic Dawson. Some believed this could directly point to his guilt. Both Dawson and Billy Doyle were known to have been regular guests at Cielo Drive during the summer and as Dawson was already well known to the police, Cass was once again called in to account for his whereabouts. For all his bravado, Dawson, however, seemed unlikely to have carried out a series of murders of this ferocity. Besides, Cass had no idea where Dawson was, and if she had, it is similarly unlikely she would have told the police.

The other major rumour ricocheting through the Hollywood Hills, which is still cited by many, all these years on, concerned Billy Doyle. It was known at the time that Folger and Frykowski had a penchant for cruising Sunset Strip and bringing home young men. After drugging them, they would tie them up and film them. Some weeks before the murders, as the tale goes, they had a spectacular falling out with Doyle over a business deal gone sour and decided to exact revenge not only by doing what they usually did to their pick-ups but by flogging him in front of an invited audience. They apparently recorded this on film. The story then goes that when Doyle realised what had happened, he was, according to Monkee Peter Tork, who was living in the Canyons at the time, 'murderous'. Raging, Doyle insisted he would kill Folger and Frykowski. Wary that he might carry out his threat, a similarly macho friend chained him to a tree in Cass's garden to calm him down, before hauling him onto a plane out of the country. In the light of Doyle's oft-repeated claims that he had killed a man and his overall hardcore machismo stance, it is easy to understand how an episode like this might have been considered sufficient motive for him to have committed the murders. 'If they were gonna do that to Billy,' says Tork, 'they *wanted* to die! That was death-provoking. It was a murderously dangerous thing to do!'

Eventually, after months of rumour and speculation, both Doyle and Dawson were cleared of suspicion and Charles Manson, a thirty-five-year-old ex-convict, fraudster, pimp and conman with a Jesus fixation, and his 'family' of (mostly young and female) followers were revealed as the murderers. Manson had a talent for attracting the young and dispossessed and somehow managed to almost brainwash his acolytes into accompanying him on his nihilistic quest for supposed salvation and power through murder. Manson and his crew had been frequent visitors to Cass's house, taking advantage, like so many others, of the plentiful food, drugs and generally laid-back, hospitable atmosphere. But Cass was not the only one who had played host to him and his acolytes, unaware of what would ensue. Although in the aftermath of the murders, few would admit to any link, many prominent figures in the LA rock community had not only socialised with Manson and his 'family' – particularly his harem of young women, who made themselves readily available to anyone interested – but developed closer associations with them. As Neil Young later remembered, 'A lot of pretty well-known musicians around LA knew Manson, though they'd probably deny it now. The girls were always around too. They'd be right there on the couch with me, singing a song.' The Beach Boys' Dennis Wilson in particular had welcomed them into his life and taken steps towards helping Manson in his attempts to obtain a record deal and his subsequent failure to do so was at one point considered a motive for the murders. But prior to that, Manson and co would have seemed like no more than yet another of LA's umpteen crews of nomadic hippies, sitting around smoking, playing the odd guitar and hanging out at other people's houses. There would have been nothing noticeable to differentiate them from any other similar group and the open-house atmosphere at Woodrow Wilson meant that it was easy for them to wander in and hang out.

Because of Cass's connections to the case, meanwhile, when it finally came to court, she was subpoenaed as a witness, as was John Phillips, who was also a good friend of Polanski and Dennis Wilson. The police had found sheet music to the Mamas and Papas' 'Straight Shooter' propped up on the music-holder of the baby-grand piano in the living room of Cielo Drive when the bodies had been found, which seemed to link Phillips to the case. Eventually, as the true facts came to light, Cass and John were both cleared of any involvement.

The insouciant freedom of the earlier days by Cass's pool was irrevocably tarnished but Woodrow Wilson Drive would continue to be the backdrop for many more easy-living days yet.

Dunhill Records had, meanwhile, been proved right in their choice of Steve Barri as a producer for Cass and, in the light of the *Bubblegum* album's success, Dunhill sent her straight back into Western Recorders with him to record some new tracks, including 'New World Coming' and 'One Way Ticket', the latter of which would later be released as a single. But whilst creating badly needed hits for Cass, her work with Barri had also created a gulf between her undisputed position as matriarch of LA rock society and the inherent hipness which went with it; suddenly the music that she was making seemed at odds with her irredeemably fashionable social status.

Cass would address this chasm with her next album, but for the time being there were other projects, and indeed people, to occupy her.

23

Baroness Cass

'I was just a kid from England with a bag and a guitar,' Dave Mason tells me down the phone from California. 'And now for something completely different! It was Alice in Wonderland. Or Alice in Blunderland – I'm not sure!' he laughs. 'And Cass had a big heart. She was great! She was cool and she was *into* shit but she had a brain up there in her head and she had a great sense of humour.'

During the course of the summer, Cass's friend Gram Parsons had introduced her to Mason, who had just recently arrived from England. Mason had previously been in Traffic and had written their hit 'Hole in My Shoe', but had now left the band and scored international success with his debut solo album *Alone Together*. He was young and attractive, and significantly, as far as Cass was concerned, English. Cass and he liked each other from the start. Just as she had done with Donovan and Eric Clapton before, Cass immediately made him feel at home in LA.

In the course of the inevitable sessions sitting around the house at Woodrow Wilson with Mason playing his guitar and singing and Cass adding in harmonies, an idea began to emerge that they might work together professionally. Cass was still disenchanted with the predominantly pop sound of the records she had been making with Steve Barri, feeling they lacked musical credibility, and this was also the era of the supergroup. At the tail end of the sixties, leaving the group in which you had become famous had almost become a musical fashion statement. This then needed to be closely followed by the formation of a (super)group with a bunch of your similarly disenfranchised rock-star friends. Crosby, Stills and Nash were a case in point, as were Cream and Blind Faith in Britain. The idea that Cass might be able to legitimately work with a British musician with a blues and rock background, whilst admittedly unusual, therefore didn't seem quite as unlikely at it might have done otherwise.

Cass had been fantasising about working with some of her more musically respected friends for some time, but despite her own star status, most of her ideas seemed a little improbable. 'A group I wanted to put together was Graham Nash and David Crosby but Stevie Stills somehow got involved,' Cass told *Melody Maker*. 'Can you imagine a group like that and with Paul McCartney? I'd love to record with Paul – we match tones, but he's got no reason to record with me.' For Cass, working with other artists of this kind also would have solved the problem of finding material. The previous year she had even hoped Paul McCartney and John Lennon might have a song for her, as around this time McCartney had provided material for Mary Hopkin and he and Lennon had previously given songs to other groups, so the idea didn't seem particularly far-fetched. In the absence of any of this, however, Mason would be a singing partner and songwriter with musical credibility by the caseload.

Having made two solo albums by this time, Cass also realised that she missed the camaraderie of working with other people. Compared with the stresses of working with the Mamas and the Papas, Mason seemed like a walk on the beach. 'I hate to use the word "joyous",' she told *Rolling Stone* the following year, 'but that's it. It's nice to make music ... period, but it's groovier with other people. That's where music started, people getting together and just doing *aaaah* and that's why I like it.' She believed that working with Mason encouraged her to stretch her voice in a way that all John Phillips's cajoling and bullying would never have achieved. 'I sing better with David because he's so good,' she continued. 'You want to do better. I'm singing notes I never sang with the Mamas and the Papas. I used to say "That's too high; I can't sustain it." Now I'm singing higher and higher ... He's made it very easy for me to say, "Here I am, and I sing rock and roll." That was something I never had the courage to do before.'

Aside from the fact that Cass loved his songs and enjoyed his company, the fact that Mason was far from unattractive undoubtedly also played a part. 'She must have had a crush on him,' says Michelle Phillips. 'If she didn't want to fuck him, she wouldn't have been spending all that time with him, *believe* me!' she laughs. As far as Mason was concerned, meanwhile, the situation seems to have been the same as it so often was with Cass's male friends. He liked her very much, but the idea of romance hadn't occurred to him. 'In all honesty, it never crossed my mind,' he laughs. 'So I have no idea. But then I am a bit of a ditz that way! I'm the kind of guy that unless some woman's physically throwing herself over me, I really don't have a clue!'

Once again, the closeness of their friendship was clearly evident to the *Rolling Stone* journalist who interviewed them about the project: 'She and Mason, together,' wrote the magazine, 'talk in a kind of verbal shorthand, one taking an idea from the other's mind to finish half-completed sentences. Two heads and one mind, it appears, although they hardly look like a soul couple.'

The album they eventually recorded seemed to evolve naturally from their friendship. Mason already had some songs left over from his solo album and when they needed some more, for the first time since her writing partnership with Jim Hendricks in the Mugwumps, Cass felt secure enough to work with him and contribute to the writing process. She wrote lyrics to his music for 'Something to Make You Happy' and did the same for bass player Bryan Garufalo's 'Here We Go Again'. Her writing had understandably moved on from the more innocent style of the Mugwumps but both songs dealt with the demise of a love affair and the hard-won wisdom gained as a result. '"I learned a lot from you / All you allowed me to / I saw the truth behind the lies,"' she sang in 'Here We Go Again'. '"But there's one thing that I know / I won't be so sad next time you go."' If these sentiments sounded suspiciously close to the feelings she must have had for Pic Dawson, the lines: 'It comes from the heart this love that I offer you / Don't try and cage it like a wild beast' from 'Something to Make You Happy' seemed similarly resonant of what must surely been his argument to her on more than one occasion.

The resulting album, entitled simply *Dave Mason and Cass Elliot* was essentially a Mason album with Cass providing guest harmonies as she only sang lead on these two tracks and dueted with Mason on a few others. Musically, the album is very much of its time, falling into the standard early-seventies guitar, piano and drums, laid-back country-rock harmony sound, as popularised by their friends Crosby, Stills and Nash, albeit with a bluesier edge. Although it may have fulfilled Cass's wish for musical credibility, the album, however, did little to showcase her voice and would prove to be neither Cass's nor Mason's best work.

Cass seemed excited about the project nevertheless and to promote the album, she and Mason went on the *Tonight Show* and the *Andy Williams Show* and finally debuted the new superduo at Santa Monica Civic Hall before heading to New York's Filmore East. Neither of the shows were particularly well received and although Cass and Mason had told the press that the project would be loose but ongoing, this would be the only time they would record, or indeed perform, together.

Whilst working with Dave Mason, Cass had spent time with him in London and when their gigs in America were over she headed back to the English capital.

She had had to give up the flat she had shared with Stephen Sanders but had subsequently rented various London apartments including a mews house in London's Queensgate near Hyde Park, where house guests included David Crosby and Ken Kesey. She had also got to know a young American journalist by the name of Donald von Wiedenman. They had first met when Cass had gone to London in the spring of 1969 to promote her single 'Move in a Little Closer' and von Wiedenman had come to interview her one rainy day in March.

Cass's British record company had arranged for her to stay in Elizabeth Taylor's regular suite at the Dorchester Hotel and lined up a virtually uninterrupted string of interviews for the afternoon. Cass was well practised at giving the press the upbeat, witty Cass persona they wanted, but she was still nevertheless relieved when she was told that von Wiedenman would be her final interview of the day. She also clearly liked what she saw. Von Wiedenman was a twenty-six-year-old American who had been living and working in London for the past few years, freelancing for various publications including the *Daily Telegraph*'s colour supplement and *Playboy*. He was tall and slim, handsome, sophisticated and debonair and cut a dash on London's celebrity circuit in his customary cape while a broad-brimmed felt hat crowned his shoulder-length auburn hair. He had recently interviewed film directors Bryan Forbes and Joseph Losey for the *Telegraph* and the paper had now commissioned him to go and meet Cass. He would subsequently come to play a significant role in Cass's life, but his journalistic career would waver and in the eighties and nineties he would become better known in some circles as the founder of Stable Entertainment, an adult film production company, specialising in bisexual films. Von Wiedenman talked to me at his LA apartment, which also doubled as Stable Entertainment's offices, high up in the leafy, undulating streets of the Hollywood hills. Von Wiedenman is still lean, charismatic and urbane, although his hair is now close-cropped and the only sign of his flamboyant earlier self is the large, framed photograph of him, hatted and caped in the sixties, which sits on a side table. There is also little evidence on show of his new career; the only hints are his Stable Entertainment business card which features a neighing stallion's head as its logo and the large airbrushed Pierre et Gilles-style painting hanging on the wall opposite the sofa. The subject is a realistically painted figure whose upper half is a winged cherub, whilst from the waist down visitors are greeted at eye level by a fully detailed naked male torso.

Talking to von Wiedenman, it is not hard to see why Cass might have been charmed by him. On the day they first met, she was also relaxed, knowing that her interviews were almost over for the day and gradually she began to peel off the Mama Cass persona, layer by layer. 'The first thing she did after we started talking,' remembers von Wiedenman, 'was ask me to turn off the tape recorder. Which I did. And she just suddenly changed before my eyes and lit up a joint. She offered me a glass of wine and I ended up spending about an hour with her, just talking and taking the occasional notes but basically trying to make it just sort of a conversation.' When the interview was over, Cass told von Wiedenman she had to go to a rehearsal at the *Tom Jones Show*. She said she didn't know anybody there and her assistant couldn't go with her so did he want to accompany her? Von Wiedenman accepted.

During their interview Cass had felt comfortable enough with von Wiedenman to let him see her disaffection with her life and the rather despondent mood she was in, but as soon as it was time for them to leave the hotel suite, she was once again 'Mama' Cass and he was struck by the speed with which she could switch on her public alter ego. 'Cass was really two people,' he says. 'She was one of these people that really *was* . . . you know the English expression Dr Footlights? If someone's sick and they're an actor and they go out in front of the footlights, suddenly they're cured and they can entertain. Well, it's sort of like that because she was depressed and kind of in a funky mood but as soon as she was in front of her public – which was outside the door of that hotel room, she was a *star*. She had on a short denim dress which was sort of ordinary but then all she did was put on a pair of big sunglasses and a fur coat over her shoulder and walk through the lobby of the Dorchester *dragging* the fur coat! And it was such a cliché and so perfect,' he laughs. 'It was just wonderful! And I thought this is gonna be a lot of fun! And so we get in the car and we're getting *very* high and smoking more pot and I'm thinking how's she gonna possibly rehearse and feeling like I'm glad we got most of the interview over with at the Dorchester.'

Cass was not only taken with von Wiedenman but also loved the fact that early on in their interview he had confessed that he really didn't know much about her and asked if her publicist might be able to send him some biographical details. As much as she loved her fame, this was a novelty for Cass. But she had also clearly been impressed by von Wiedenman in other ways and lost no time in letting him know. 'As soon as we got in the limo, I realised she was *flirting* with me,' he continues, 'and then when they had her sing 'Dream a Little Dream of Me' in rehearsal, she sang the whole song to *me*,' he laughs. 'It was embarrassing on one hand because everyone was looking at me but also very *flattering*. It was very sweet of her. I was so taken aback by the fact that someone this famous would do this to me and this was not my ideal of the blonde blue-eyed woman I'd been taught to want for my wife, but at the same time I was *tremendously* attracted to her.'

Once they were back in the limousine, von Wiedenman asked Cass if she'd like to have dinner with him. Cass didn't have to think twice. They went to the newly opened Playboy club, which at the time, far from being in any way sleazy, was considered one of London's major celebrity nightspots. Cass was immediately given one of the best tables in a suitably intimate dark corner and the pair spent the evening chatting and getting better acquainted. Afterwards von Wiedenman took Cass back to the Dorchester and said goodnight.

Cass had planned to stay in London for a while longer after she had filmed the *Tom Jones Show*, saying that, in spite of the chilly March weather, like many resident Californians, she enjoyed the cold. She also wanted some more time to socialise. There was a party at the Dorchester in her honour, attended by the usual throng of British and American celebrities including Tom Jones, who came flanked by numerous bodyguards, Roman Polanski, Phyllis Diller and Lionel Bart. Socialising also included seeing more of von Wiedenman. They went out a couple of times and on the final night, von Wiedenman invited Cass to his apartment overlooking the canal in Little Venice. 'We just had a wonderful time,' he recalls. 'It was the sixties and we dropped some acid,' he laughs, 'and we made love in front of the fireplace on a white fur rug. It was just every possible cliché you can think of and it was *perfect*!'

Although Cass thought Donald was rather wonderful, she didn't necessarily think of him as someone with whom she was likely to form a lasting relationship as, apart from any other considerations, the logistics made this unlikely, but when she went home to LA for the summer they kept in touch. Von Wiedenman began writing to her. 'Her press was that she was *everything*,' he tells me. 'She was an earth goddess, she was a wife, a mother, she was a Madonna, girlfriend – all these things, and she was. She was the good things of every single woman I had ever met in one person. She was just a spectacular human being and when she left I missed her immediately. I mean I didn't think I was in love with her – I didn't think she was in love with me, we just had a great time together.' Cass loved receiving his long, poetic letters but had little time for letter writing herself and would instead phone him in London, and when she arrived back some months later, she soon thought of him again.

On this visit Cass was staying at the Chelsea home of Ian Quarrier, a sometime actor and man about town who Cass had got to know through the London scene. Quarrier had recently played the vampire in Roman Polanski's *Fearless Vampire Killers* and had also cropped up interviewing the Rolling Stones in Jean Luc Godard's documentary about the group *1 + 1* aka *Sympathy for the Devil*, but he was primarily known as a somewhat louche scenester and party-giver with a yen for even wilder experimentation than most. Cass was therefore not the only guest at the house. Others included Polanski and George Lazenby, but although Cass was used to living in the midst of a round-the-clock party, the scene at Quarrier's proved too much, even for her, and she got straight on the phone to von Wiedenman – who it would later emerge, knew Quarrier himself. 'Cass called me in a panic,' he remembers, 'and said, "You got to get me out of here. This place is a *zoo*!" And I knew Ian independently of Cass, and it was.' Cass asked von Wiedenman to come to the house and fetch her. By the time he arrived, she already had her bags packed. 'Can I come and stay with you?' she asked. 'Well, sure,' replied von Wiedenman, 'Absolutely. It'll be *great*.'

That same night, Cass had been invited to the premiere of *The*

Magic Christian, the ill-fated new film starring Ringo Starr and Raquel Welch, and she and von Wiedenman set out to the Odeon Kensington in their hippie finery. In the limousine they decided to drop some acid and have a smoke. '*Everything* was done on drugs,' says von Wiedenman. 'It was just the thing to do. It wasn't secretive – I mean everybody knew everybody was stoned. Especially in the music business. So we were smoking hash in the car and when we got to the premiere, there were a lot of press and they were anticipating Cass's arrival, so she waited till the last minute. She wanted to drive around the block and talk and catch up and make up for lost time and it *was* really nice to see her, but then when we got to the premiere, the driver opened the door and this *enormous* cloud of smoke came out of the door,' he laughs. 'Cass got out and everybody just applauded. It really was a wonderful entrance!'

The Magic Christian has not aged well and was not much better when it was first premiered so Cass and von Wiedenman left before the end of the film and decided instead to go out dancing at the recently opened celebrity niterie Tramp. 'She was a *fantastic* dancer,' remembers Donald. 'I mean you'd think someone of that size would not be a great dancer but she was light on her feet and was just *floating* on the dance floor – she was just great. And then the acid really started to kick in and we went outside and we were running around the streets and chasing each other and we just had a wonderful time!'

The next time they saw each other, von Wiedenman suggested that Cass come and stay at his holiday home near St Tropez in the south of France. Cass had not really travelled far in Europe beyond England and she had never been to the south of France, which at this point in 1970 was still considered the height of exclusive jet-set chic, having been made famous a few years earlier by Brigitte Bardot. The idea of going to stay there with her dashing new boyfriend, and equally importantly, being able to tell all her friends she was doing so, was too tempting to refuse. 'She said she wanted to go because she wanted to tell everybody that she and her boyfriend went to the Riviera and laid on the beach and got a suntan,' says von Wiedenman. But once Cass arrived in the south of France the reality was, perhaps inevitably, somewhat less straightforward. Cass flew to Nice and von Wiedenman met her at the airport in his rather fabulous but minuscule 1954 MGTF convertible sports car. 'It was a tiny little car,' von Wiedenman remembers, 'so when Cass saw it, she said, "I'll just never fit in that!" She was *so* self-conscious about her weight and she made such a big *deal* out of it when *I* would never have *thought* that. I mean if she hadn't said that, that would never have crossed my mind that she was gonna have a problem sitting in that car. Because even though she was heavy, she was small. She was only a little over five foot tall. Julia Phillips said that two minutes after you meet Cass, you forget that she's fat. And you do,' he continues, lapsing into the present tense as her friends often do when talking about her. 'There's such an inner quality about her and she's so funny that it's not even an issue. You don't think of her as a heavy person.'

The hazards of the journey from the airport notwithstanding, the house itself was the epitome of the romantic French rural idyll – an exquisite two-hundred-year-old stone olive mill with its original machinery in the living room and a stream running behind the house. St Tropez itself, meanwhile, was celebrity central. Brigitte Bardot still had a house there and, almost without exception, the women on the beach and in the town's chic bars and cafes were rich and impossibly slim. But this was not going to stop Cass going to the beach. She would simply do things her way. Whilst the twig-thin Riviera beauties paraded topless on the beach, Cass draped herself in an outsize hat, Hawaiian shirt and sarong.

But however uncomfortable Cass may have been on the beach, when it came to going out at night, she would suddenly emerge once more as 'Mama Cass' in an exquisite kaftan, with her hair brushed and just the faintest glow of suntan on her face. 'It was like she was throwing little bits of rock and roll gingerbread behind her and everyone was following her,' remembers von Wiedenman. Cass was instantly recognised and, even amidst so many other celebrities, she drew the most attention, and she loved it. She and Donald fantasised about leaving their respective homes and settling down for a life of domestic tranquillity on the French Riviera with Owen. 'When you walked out in front of the house,' remembers von Wiedenman, 'all you could see were the olive trees and the mountains surrounding it and she stood out there and held her arms out and said "I would love to live out here and Owen would love it so much," and as she said this – and I'm not making this up, this flock of birds took off into the sky and it was like this omen. And we both looked at each other and we thought, We're gonna be *so* happy here together, and she *wanted* that and she wanted to have her daughter and a husband and she wanted a simple life. She thought.' Cass imagined this might be her rustic French version of the white picket-fence idyll she had always dreamt of. But it seemed unlikely to ever go beyond being the fantasy that it clearly was. When the fortnight was over, Donald returned home to London and Cass to her life in LA.

At home in California the 'family' of close friends which Cass had developed around her had gradually dispersed. Crosby, Stills and Nash had released their debut album to phenomenal critical and commercial success, and were now, as Crosby himself reminds me, 'the biggest band in America' and so were almost constantly on the road touring or in the studio recording. The early seventies were also a time when many musicians and others who had embraced the hippie ideals and freedom of the sixties decided to take those ideas further and move out of the cities to explore a less urban way of life. John Sebastian had moved east to Sag Harbour, while Gary Burden had left for Colorado, and, in the wake of the Manson trials, Billy Doyle had returned to Canada whilst Pic Dawson had, for the time being, moved back east.

Cass had therefore found herself with a new circle of friends. She had become particularly close to Leon Bing, a gorgeous, raven-haired Californian model who had recently been on the cover of *Time* magazine. Cass had met her at a baby shower for Cher who lived nearby and the two became friends immediately. Bing was intelligent, sophisticated and highly cultured and she and Cass found a shared love of books, Broadway musicals and old movies. 'She was very well-read and a big reader,' remembers Bing, now a respected journalist and author. 'She had – I won't say catholic tastes, but certainly an eclectic taste: biographies, history, good novels. We would recommend books to each other quite often because I'm a voracious reader. I remember it was *The French Lieutenant's Woman* that I think I read first and just wouldn't even answer the phone and so I said to her, "Get ready to turn off your phones and read."'

Bing also had a small daughter who was roughly the same age as Owen and so she and Cass would often take their children to Playland children's park together. Even their car licence plates were now companions. Cass had arranged to have the name of the Egyptian goddess 'Isis' on her Cadillac convertible (which she nicknamed 'the Jew Canoe') and Leon similarly put 'Osiris' – Isis's male companion god – on hers. When they didn't have the children with them, the two of them would drive off for the afternoon, singing Broadway hits or folk songs in the car before settling down in front of a film. 'We *loved* matinees,' says Bing. 'We just thought it was so decadent, *so* fabulous and we'd have such a good time,' she laughs. 'We saw *The Godfather* together. Oh *God* we loved it! That was the one that we just couldn't wait to huff our asses to and we saw *The Conformist* – stuff like that.' Just as she had done in the past for Michelle and Leah, Cass also loved shopping for Leon and buying her the kind of clothes that she would have liked to be able to wear herself. 'She was incredibly thoughtful,' says Bing. '*Really* thoughtful. She would see something that she would know I'd like and she would get it for me because it reminded her of me. She was a thoughtful person and *fun*. I *miss* her.'

Cass had also become good friends with Beach Boy Bruce Johnston, Keith Allison – the Paul McCartney lookalike lead singer with Paul Revere and the Raiders, Monkees manager David Pearl and an attractive young actor friend of theirs by the name of Donny Wayne Johnson – later to become better known as simply Don Johnson. Another close friend was Jack Nicholson, with whom she shared a love of sports and basketball in particular. 'She *loved* sport,' remembers Bing. 'She and Jack Nicholson would always arrange to watch football together or at least talk on the phone during games. We knew that there was a kind of bond between them based on a mutual love of basketball but I think Jack also liked Cass because she was smart and he could speak to her on subjects *other* than just, "You were so good in *Five Easy Pieces*."'

Cass's friendship with Nicholson seemed to exist on a purely private basis, whereas Leon Bing, Keith Allison, Don Johnson and Bruce Johnston were often to be found at Woodrow Wilson Drive or at Bing's spacious home drinking vintage wine and enjoying what Johnston remembers as 'artsy discussions' along with other visiting friends such as actress Tuesday Weld and Rod Stewart. Sunday afternoons in particular were Cass's favourite time to invite her friends to gather on her enormous four-poster divan to watch the American films of the nineteen thirties which she loved. Leisurely afternoons were spent lolling around watching Clark Gable and Claudette Colbert in classics such as Frank Capra's *It Happened One Night*, while Cass raved about the divine clothes and recited the dialogue virtually word for word.

But despite the affection she felt from her friends, Cass still craved the individual romantic love and attention that was missing from her life. Although there was never a shortage of new men for her to fantasise about or develop crushes on, there seemed nothing tangible on the horizon, so she was more than a little stunned when Donald von Wiedenman phoned her with a proposal. 'I wanna get married,' he told her. Cass was confused and slightly bewildered. 'To who?' she asked. 'To *you*,' he replied. 'Will you marry me?' Cass was now even more confused.

'I have to think about this,' Cass told him and hung up. Two minutes later, she had made up her mind. 'Yes, I'd love to,' she shrieked, 'it'd be great! Come over *here*.' 'Great,' said von Wiedenman.

The only two people Cass had ever really wanted to settle down with were Denny and Pic Dawson. Denny had already turned her down and made it clear that this was never going to happen and with Dawson, although she had continued to hope against all odds, she was at heart realistic enough to realise that settled domesticity was unlikely. Marrying Donald on the other hand would give her the opportunity to provide a regular family environment for Owen and also, perhaps equally importantly, the chance to fulfil the unspoken pressure she felt from her mother to lead a more conventional life. Bess, like most mothers, wanted the best for her daughter but also wanted something more stable than the erratic, volatile existence which had for so long become her norm. For a woman approaching thirty, being single and pursuing a career was still seen as a highly unconventional life choice, and, even though it may never have been said, Cass couldn't help feeling that in some fundamental way she had disappointed her mother by failing to achieve what was supposed to be every 'normal' woman's goal. Marrying Donald was therefore an attractive proposition in many ways. There was also the question of a title. Von Wiedenman's family had been American for the last two generations but they were originally Austrian and technically speaking, although the title had been defunct for many years, Donald was a baron. Marrying him would therefore make Cass a baroness. It was simply too tempting to resist.

In the past, Cass had always been disappointed when her crushes on good-looking men such as Tommy Smothers, Dave Mason and more recently Keith Allison, had not evolved into anything more than friendship. But at some unconscious level, these crushes possibly enabled Cass to enjoy the initial glow of romance without the more emotionally threatening reality of a fully fledged relationship. Donald, however, had proved one of the few exceptions, and even though she had flirted with him she had been as surprised as everyone else when he responded. Her friends were inevitably sceptical of his motives, but for Cass, the temptation to believe that von Wiedenman might offer a genuine chance of happiness was an irresistible draw. She was also certainly not the first person or the last to find herself led by her emotions, rather than her mind. 'She was so smitten and seemed so thrilled with him,' remembers Keith Allison. 'When she got in those things with somebody, she was real girlish, like a schoolgirl crush kind of thing and all her intellect went out the window.'

Conveniently, Cass had finally divorced Jim Hendricks a year earlier and she had clearly seen the court appearance as just another performance and relished every minute of it. Arriving in her sable coat and beige boots, she told the court that her husband was jealous of her fame and that he would 'yell and scream and throw tantrums and stalk out of the apartment'. Anyone who knew of Cass's continuing friendship with the genial and mild-mannered Hendricks would have got the joke. The court, meanwhile, granted her the divorce without contest.

Rather than an elaborate showbiz wedding, Cass decided to have a small, quiet ceremony at the house. Only Cass's mother, Owen, Donald's well-heeled parents and Leon Bing, who was the maid of honour, attended. Cass wore a glamorous black Biba dress, which Donald had brought her from London, while he wore a handmade trouser suit of skin-tight shiny white leather, complete with fringed jacket which Cass had bought him as a wedding present. Donald's wedding present to Cass was a pair of lovebirds in a cage.

Mr and Mrs von Wiedenman had not envisaged their son marrying someone quite so unconventional, but they nevertheless hosted a brief reception afterwards at their home at Woodland Hills before the newly wed couple headed out to Palm Springs for a short honeymoon. Donald had been friendly with Elizabeth Taylor and Richard Burton and had arranged for them to stay in the home of John Leigh, Taylor's private secretary. The luxurious villa had its own pool and, as it was frequently used by Taylor herself, also came fully equipped with its own supplies, of every kind. Under the bathroom sink Cass and Donald found a pharmacy's worth of bottles containing pills of every conceivable description. Afternoons would therefore often be spent floating in the pool on Seconal (which Donald remembers as Cass's favourite) and, amazingly, the pair of them neither drowned nor burnt themselves to death in the sun. This would set the tone for most of their time together. 'We were just high!' says von Wiedenman. 'We were high for most of our marriage.'

Once they returned to LA, the honeymoon continued. 'We spent a *lot* of time in bed,' von Wiedenman continues, 'doing what people do in bed and watching a lot of TV. Since she was friends with Cher and the *Sonny and Cher Show* was on, we watched that and all this TV I'd never seen because I'd been in England for six years, so I was just like mesmerised and Cass loved being the teacher.' They were rarely disturbed unless it was by Al the cat who would come in through the small porthole window above the bed and leave a dead bird on their pillow like some kind of warrior's memento. Just as Lee Kiefer had done beforehand, Donald also fulfilled the role of man-about-the-house and made himself useful running errands and picking up food or dry cleaning in the mornings while Cass slept in. Later on in the day friends would invariably come over so Cass and Donald were rarely alone. If they were, they would either go out to restaurants or stay home playing backgammon. And then there were the parties.

Cass would occasionally host parties at the house or sometimes, as was the vogue in Hollywood at the time, she would rent an empty Beverly Hills mansion, as she did on one occasion when the Stones were in town and she wanted to throw a party in their honour. The party was black tie and the A-list guests mingled around the lavish gardens and pool or helped themselves to prawn cocktail from a three-foot-high ice sculpture of the liner *Queen Mary*. Cass loved an occasion to dress up and, regardless of how many glamorous stars or starlets may have been in attendance, was invariably the centre of attention. 'When she came into a room,' remembers Keith Allison, 'she made an *entrance*, like Jean Harlow or a grande dame. She would time it. She *always* waited and waited till everybody was in full swing and then she would make an entrance.'

Cass had also always had a flair for managing to surround herself with attractive men and at one party for Donald's birthday, she seemed to have outdone herself. Walking into a room she found 'Donny' Johnson, Jack Nicholson and Ryan O'Neal holding a smiling contest to see who could light up the room the most brightly. 'Honest to God,' remembers Donald, 'these three had the greatest smiles – it was like you could turn out the lights and see them!' he laughs.

It all seemed wonderful to Cass. '*You* know what it's like when you first meet someone and you fall in love,' says von Wiedenman. '*Anything* you do is fun, so except for the stuff that caused her unhappiness outside of our relationship, we had a really wonderful first couple of months.' The 'stuff that caused her unhappiness' was Cass's resumed use of hard drugs. Cass had managed to come off heroin twice, but, since meeting Donald, had recently succumbed once again. The problem, aside from continuing, intermittent visits by Pic Dawson, was aggravated by the fact that she had recently given refuge to Carmen Paz – an old friend from the Shadows. Since their folk days, Paz had been involved in two major car accidents and been rendered paraplegic. Homeless and confined to a wheelchair or a hospital bed, Paz had nowhere to go and Cass, out of sympathy, had taken her in and installed her in the empty attic-style 'room nobody lives in' above her garage. But in spite of being on a respirator and having a full-time nurse, Paz was nevertheless managing to deal drugs. Cass was aware of this but felt sorry for her, and, knowing she had no other means of earning a living, allowed her to continue running her self-styled cottage industry from the house.

For the time being Cass turned a blind eye to the obvious illegality of the operation, but what was equally dangerous to Cass was the constant proximity of hard drugs only yards away from her own bedroom. For someone with a history of drug issues, it was a no-win situation. 'Cass would disappear for several hours,' says von Wiedenman, 'and you know, *I* didn't want to hang out with Carmen and Cass reliving old times, but eventually I would be up there more often and I would notice that Cass would talk to Carmen for a couple of minutes and then sit in a corner and nod off for like four hours. Cass was doing heroin and Carmen was doing cocaine.'

Whilst Cass confined her drug use to Carmen's room, keeping it well-hidden from most in the house, particularly Owen, it nevertheless inevitably began to distance her from Donald, aggravating and intensifying any problems which had been lying dormant. Although Donald was more than happy to explore uppers, downers and psychedelics, he, like Lee Kiefer before him, had always steered clear of heroin. 'When we'd do drugs together,' he continues, 'the *same* drugs, like smoking the pot or the acid, *then* we'd have the best time, we'd have fun and it would be a way of celebrating being together. But when she did heroin, we never did it together because I didn't do it and she was in another place – I couldn't get to her, couldn't have fun with her.

The drug that Cass did shut her out from the world; she just withdrew completely and she'd sit in a corner being stoned and not being high.'

Apart from heroin, after years of prescription drug use, Cass had also developed a dependency on the barbiturate Nembutal, which she had long used as a tranquillizer and sleeping pill. In recent months Cass's use had stepped up dramatically with the assistance of a collection of frequently unscrupulous doctors who would happily prescribe anything for a fee which, although expensive, was easily within Cass's reach. Donald was aware of this – and indeed often visited the doctors for prescriptions himself, but he didn't believe the situation was in any way dangerous. He was shocked therefore to wake up one morning and find Cass unconscious beside him. 'Cass OD'd in her sleep on Nembutal,' he tells me in a matter of fact tone, 'and you know?' he adds, 'I don't know whether she accidentally OD'd or on purpose OD'd but she took enough so that she was in a coma and I couldn't wake her up.' Von Wiedenman called the paramedics who wanted to take Cass to hospital immediately. Cass's mother Bess had also arrived, however, by this time and was insistent that they treat her at home to avoid any scandal. Once doctors finally arrived at the house, they told Donald and Bess that Cass would recover but that as she was still in a critical condition she would need full-time professional care, for the time being at least. 'This was like three weeks into the marriage,' says von Wiedenman, 'and we're still technically on our honeymoon and we have full-time round the clock nurses *at home* waking her up every hour at night and looking into her eyes to make sure she doesn't have a petit mal seizure or a *grand* mal seizure because that's what happens when you come off Nembutal. They were weaning her off of it, giving her less and less every day, because if they took her off right away she could easily die! It was a nightmare!'

Although Cass seemed to have initially found some kind of contentment with Donald, the Nembutal and the heroin were clearly still an escape from the other continuing pressures in her life. Despite having had reasonable success with some of her recent solo singles, financially she was still far from comfortable. Cass had continued to spend extravagantly – both on herself and her friends – and couldn't imagine curbing the luxury of her rock-star lifestyle. She also had a young daughter to support, and gradually she had plummeted further and further into debt. Cass had disregarded warnings from her accountants but when the IRS arrived at the entrance to the house and started hammering a notice to her gates saying that the house would be confiscated in lieu of unpaid taxes, Cass could ignore the matter no longer. An agreement was reached and Cass was allowed to pay the money she owed in instalments but she was also put on a strict weekly allowance by her business manager Dottie Ross and was forced to give up her credit cards.

Ross was put in charge of Cass's finances and paying her bills, while Cass herself was limited to three-hundred dollars per week spending money. In theory the plan should have alleviated Cass's problems considerably, but the reality was a little different. 'Cass had three-hundred dollars a week,' remembers Donald, 'and her idea was that if anything got charged to the business manager, she wasn't really *paying* for it. She was only paying for it if it came out of the three-hundred dollars. So we would send out for food and she would charge it to her house account which got billed to her business manager. Or *I* would pay for it. But as long as she didn't have to touch that three-hundred dollars, she wasn't spending any money! Or that's what she thought!' he laughs. 'We ate out a *lot*. We would go out a lot because she had house accounts at a lot of restaurants. I *liked* going out to eat and I knew she did. It was fun. But she never had any money though and so I paid for pretty much everything the whole time we were married.'

Donald's financial contribution to the relationship is heavily debated by Cass's friends, but whoever was paying the bills, Cass refused to accept that she simply could no longer afford the lifestyle she wanted. At Thanksgiving, she had decided to invite some friends over for lunch and wanted to cater for them in a style befitting her star status. She therefore headed straight to Saks Fifth Avenue, and despite having neither credit cards nor cash, Saks immediately offered to open an account. Cass promptly arrived home with a case of sterling silver cutlery and twelve settings of finest Limoges china. 'I blew the budget!' she told her friend Allison Caine, insisting that she come over and see it. 'It was very hot that day,' remembers Caine, 'and Owen was running around in her little undies, with blondie white hair and Cass had bought this whole *shipment* of Limoges. *Fabulous!* We were unwrapping it and it went on forever – gravy boats and soup tureens and *everything*. She bought the *entire* collection.'

Cass had recognised her inability to handle a budget for some time and often joked about it, but this awareness had made little difference.

When Owen was first born, Cass had seen a smart, but murderously expensive pram in Macy's department store and even at that point, had been short of accessible funds with which to pay for it, so she had called her old boyfriend from American University Alan Pollock in San Francisco. A few days later he had arranged to have the pram shipped to Woodrow Wilson Drive, saying they would settle the account at some later date.

Cass's main source of income, other than recording, was from playing live, but even without the anxiety of having to perform again in the wake of Vegas, she was reluctant to go on the road as it would have meant leaving Owen for weeks or even months at a time. Another opportunity for well-paid work was, meanwhile, available in the form of TV appearances. Cass's off the cuff wit made her an ideal guest and although her own show had not been a success, she was still constantly invited to appear on other celebrities' shows. Over the next few years she would appear repeatedly on shows hosted by Tom Jones, Andy Williams, Julie Andrews, Carol Burnett, Mike Douglas, Dinah Shore and Ed Sullivan, as well as numerous others including the *Tonight Show*, the *Smothers Brothers Comedy Hour* and *Hollywood Palace*.

Appearing in these shows meant that Cass could earn good money without having to leave Los Angeles, and therefore Owen, as most of the TV studios were only a ten-minute drive from her front door. But TV also had its drawbacks. Cass missed the warmth and interaction of a live audience, but more importantly she had no control over the scripts. A central part of most shows were the comedy sketches and these invariably focused on her weight, taking every opportunity to cast her as the butt of the joke. One skit on the Carol Burnett show featured Cass and Burnett as neighbours.

'You know something, Stella?' says Cass. 'That fire escape gets more rickety every day.'

'Hey, can I ask you something, Betsy?' comes back Burnett. 'How come you don't use the stairway?'

'I'm not allowed. It's in my lease!' replies Cass as the canned laughter kicks in. 'What are you gonna have for dinner tonight,' continues Burnett to Cass, 'chicken, roast or ham?' 'Yeah,' replies Cass, to still louder audience cheers. Without exception, this was the tone of every appearance Cass made on the show. Others were little better. Even Dean Martin introduced her onto his *Comedy Hour* with the lines: 'Cass Elliot is a truly great entertainer and I love that gal. I wouldn't say she's fat, but from the front she looks like Carol O'Connor from behind!' The studio audience guffawed with laughter.

Cass would smile and laugh in the studios, but she was understandably devastated by the humiliation and would be in tears by the end of the show. She needed the work, however, and she also realized that her size had come to define her in the public's mind and being overweight had become an irrevocable part of her stage persona. She dearly wanted to lose weight, but she now had to contend with the fact that were she to come down to what was considered a more normal size, the public might no longer consider her 'Mama Cass', and might in turn lose interest.

Some months before, in early 1970, Cass had been in London once again, this time to record the theme song to a new film which manager Bobby Roberts and his new partner Hal Landers were producing called *Monte Walsh* – a European-style Western starring Lee Marvin and Jeanne Moreau. Cass went into the studio with British composer John Barry to record 'The Good Times Are Comin'' – the film's exquisitely plaintive title song with poignant lyrics written by Burt Bacharach's long-time collaborator Hal David. The song would provide one of Cass's finest moments, proving what she could achieve given writers of Barry and David's calibre.

Musically the song was much more stripped down and melancholy than Cass's earlier Steve Barri productions, but as with several of the songs he had found for her, the lyrics spoke of determination and survival in the face of adversity but took their own knowing stance on looking forward to better times. They could easily have been written with Cass in mind and the way she sang them, there was no question that she had lived every word. 'The good times are comin' / When they come I'll be there / With my both feet firmly planted in mid air / . . . I'm not about to come unhinged / When everything goes wrong / A fact is something to be faced / But not for very long.' Cass did indeed believe the good times were coming, as she had always done. '"There's gonna be a place for us, a place where we belong,"' she sang and it was this very belief which had always spurred her on. Some good times were in fact not far off, but before they could happen she would have to make an unexpected visit to her musical past.

24

Power to the people

By the summer of 1971, the Mamas and the Papas had been officially defunct for some three years, but owing to a contractual anomaly with Dunhill, all four of them were due back in the studio together one final time.

Since the group had broken up, Dunhill had been fiendishly repackaging their material in a desperate attempt to coax every last egg from their golden goose. There had been no less than three compilations: *Farewell to the First Golden Era*; *Golden Era Volume 2* and *16 of their Greatest Hits*, an anthology including session talk and interviews, a re-released version of *If You Can Believe Your Eyes and Ears* and the widely castigated and indeed substandard Monterey live album. Dunhill was at this point in the process of being sold to major label ABC, but all four of them had now received a letter saying they would be individually sued for two hundred and fifty thousand dollars unless they delivered a final album. The idea seemed insane.

While Cass had been busy forging a solo career for herself, Denny had tried to do the same, although his attempts were hampered by his determination to drink away his sorrows and his fortune, only taking time out briefly, under obligation to Dunhill, to record a nostalgic country rock solo album *Whatcha Gonna Do*. Michelle had finally divorced John and had since married Dennis Hopper – although this lasted only six days. She had also done some backing singing for Leonard Cohen and was taking acting lessons, in between looking after daughter Chynna and spending time with her new beau – Cass's friend Jack Nicholson. John, meanwhile, had been busy pursuing a short-lived film-making project with his friend, director Mike Sarne. In typically sixties, drug-fuelled fashion, their plan was to make a film based on the lives of Byron and Shelley, featuring what now seems like a fantasy cast of Jimi Hendrix, Bianca Jagger and Genevieve Waite, John's new wife. He had also written some of the songs that would eventually surface on his *Wolfking of LA* album and had begun to make solo appearances, playing acoustically at LA clubs like the Troubadour. The thought of recording a new Mamas and Papas album was hardly inspirational to any of them.

If the second, third and fourth albums had lacked the initial spark and insouciance of their debut, this reunion bore only the flimsiest resemblance to the carefree innocence they had once represented. They looked different too and Henry Diltz's cover shot showed the once relatively clean-cut John and Denny sporting a look which seemed to take the early seventies fashion for wildman-style facial hair to its furthest limits and somehow seemed to highlight their malaise.

The atmosphere during the sessions could not have been further from the closeness they had originally known. Michelle brought Jack Nicholson along to the studio, while Cass would often bring Donald, who inspired the same scepticism in John and Denny as Lee Kiefer and her other boyfriends in the past. But Cass was now a star in her own right, so the dynamics had changed and one day, Cass couldn't help but take great delight in John's horror when Donald arrived at the studio wearing an almost identical white leather trouser suit to the one John was wearing. John, it emerged, had recently commissioned the almost identical suit and wore it into the studio firmly believing that he was the only man in LA to be sporting something so impeccably hip. 'It was the funniest thing,' remembers Denny. 'It was like two women, I swear to God! We're wearing the same thing! John took the pants off and wouldn't wear them 'cause he said Cass bought those pants and I'm not gonna wear anything that she thinks is cool.'

But Cass's fragile health meant that she still didn't always have the upper hand. In the wake of her recent scare, she came to sessions accompanied by a uniformed nurse paid to monitor her and check her blood pressure as she sat, hour after mind-numbing hour, knitting and reading in the control booth. John would later recall having to ask the nurse's permission in order to even talk to Cass. Just as he was getting to the vocal part he wanted her to sing, the nurse would take her blood pressure and tell him, 'She can't sing any more.' Nurse Regina was consequently considered such an integral part of the sessions, she was credited on the sleeve for 'Medical Aid'.

The four of them were rarely in the studio together and the tracks were mostly dubbed, one vocal at a time. John had decided that as well as writing the songs, he would produce the album itself and it was only his painstaking hours of splicing tape together that created some kind of illusion of supposedly live harmony. The result was perhaps better than might have been expected, although Cass's voice was much less prominent than on their earlier recordings – possibly due to her frail health. The album bore little resemblance to the lush, harmonised optimism of the previous albums but instead sounded very much of its time. With its laid-back, early seventies funk feel and its soft close harmonies, the overall sound was not unlike one of the better film soundtracks of the day and as such is worthy of reappraisal.

Cass, however, later admitted to BBC Radio 1's Brian Matthew that she thought *People Like Us* was '*dreadful*', before elaborating that although 'the songs were great', she didn't like the mix of the album or the instrumentation and laid the blame clearly with John. 'Of course, as was John's wont,' she said, 'he had total control over everything that was done, and nobody else could say anything.'

But at some level Cass had perhaps enjoyed being able to share the responsibility for the album and have some kind of companionship in the studio, however arduous. When *People Like Us* was initially released, although she was certainly fulfilling her record company duty by enthusing about it to the press, there was also an element of truth to her comments. 'To make music with other people is really a beautiful thing,' she told *Rolling Stone*. 'I don't play an instrument, so I don't know how it feels to sit down and jam. What we do is perhaps a little more restricted than jamming because we work out the parts and everything, but the high, I'm sure, is the same, if not better, because you know what the potential is – where it can take you.'

The album, meanwhile, was neither a critical nor commercial success. It may have fared better had it been issued under a different name as by 1971 the very idea of the Mamas and the Papas seemed hopelessly outdated. Its only single 'Step Out' might have been more aptly named Out of Step and merely grazed the top eighty before vanishing without trace.

In the light of Cass's solo career, *People Like Us*'s lack of commercial success hardly seemed relevant to Cass. She was more interested in where her own career could take her next as the completion of this last Mamas and Papas album meant that her contract with Dunhill was finally due for renewal. But for the meantime she had problems closer to home as her relationship with Donald was slowly but surely beginning to unravel.

The initial thrill of new romance had soon worn off. Although Cass had been captivated with Donald and the excitement of being a baroness – albeit in name alone – what had seemed tenable when they were alone in London or the south of France soon seemed less so in the context of her life in LA. The gradual realisation that their relationship might not, after all, be the long-term success she would have liked, coupled with the mood swings brought about by dieting and drugs, prescription or otherwise, soon manifested itself in continuous friction between them, often over the smaller details of their domestic life. The two of them had had a constant battle over the temperature in the house as Cass preferred it much cooler than Donald. It was something which often proved a problem with others and Cass had consequently installed locks over the air-conditioning controls to avoid them being tampered with. Donald, however, had a key and one morning, while Cass was asleep, adjusted the controls to turn the system down and went off to do some errands, forgetting to readjust the controls before he left. He returned to find Cass in a rage. 'She was *so* mad, she was just *seething*,' remembers von Wiedenman. 'She had *smashed* the air-conditioner case with a hammer *and* she had taken this Mickey Mouse watch which she had bought for me as a welcome to California present and smashed it with the hammer as well. I said, "Cass, you didn't have to do that – you could have waited till I got back." And then she pulled the "this is my house" thing, which everybody always does at some point about their house, or their car, or their shoes that you borrow or whatever and I said, "This is not worth fighting about, this really isn't." Because previously the fights always used to be joke fights, it was never sort of a serious fight and that's when I realised that things were getting to her that shouldn't be getting to her. And that's when Carmen was at her peak and Cass was most high.'

A few months later Donald again pointed out to Cass, as had several others, that, apart from the damage it was doing to her personally, housing Carmen's illegal operations was a serious risk to her own career. 'Cass, if nothing else, this is just not *cool*,' he told her.

'We're gonna get busted. And *she's* not gonna be in the news – *you* are.' Whether Cass finally took heed of Donald's advice or not, a few days later, Paz was gone.

Even without Paz's shadowy presence in the house, Cass's relationship with Donald seemed to be drawing to its end. Since moving to LA, Donald's journalistic career had reached a hiatus and so, presumably in an attempt to provide him with an official role, Cass suggested he become involved in managing her career. At this point, at the cusp of the seventies, the idea of a woman being more successful and famous than her male partner still sat uneasily in most people's minds. The manager route therefore offered a tried and tested solution whereby the man could still be seen to be taking an important and dominant role in the relationship. Donald, however, was unenthusiastic and was keen for them to return to their original idea of moving to the south of France and starting a new and quieter life there. For a time, Cass liked the idea, thinking she could escape and return a year later as the slim, new Baroness Cass, but once she faced the reality of the idea, she realised just what life would be like in a sleepy French village where, if you didn't speak French, as Cass didn't, you had to point if you wanted to buy even a loaf of bread. Heading to France would have completed the girlhood dream she still nurtured of living the perfect happy-ever-after nuclear family fairy tale. It would likewise have fulfilled the obligation she felt to her mother to live up to her expectations, but Cass also knew that giving up the superstar life she had worked so hard to achieve and still badly needed for her own sense of self-esteem, was unrealistic. 'The only way she got any validation,' says von Wiedenman, 'was through performing and being famous. And even though she got a tremendous amount of validation through me, it just wasn't enough.'

Cass had recently started seeing a psychotherapist, and along with coming to terms with her drug problems she was also becoming more aware of her own needs. But rather than explain to Donald herself, Cass took the unusual step of asking her therapist to tell him on her behalf. 'She asked me to go see her shrink,' remembers von Wiedenman. 'She said *she* couldn't tell me but she said, "My shrink'll tell you." So I go to see her shrink and she says, "Basically, Cass cannot give up all of this for the love of just one person and she knows that and I know that and she can't tell you that." And I said, "Well, you know, I kind of figured that out, but I thought that it's not the applause per se that she likes, it's not like she needs a live audience, it's the attention and it seemed to me that her husband could give her the attention she needs." And she says, "No, she says she really can't. You really can't. No matter who it is, it's not you. It's just that one person can't give her the attention she needs."'

Although there was clearly more than an element of truth to this, Cass may also have used this as a convenient excuse to bring a marriage that wasn't working to a close. None of her friends had liked Donald from the start and although much of their scepticism was due to seeing a good-looking man with no visible employment with someone of Cass's celebrity, his manner also aroused suspicion. 'He was syrupy sweet,' recalls Keith Allison. 'There was just something that didn't ring true – like it was phoney. We just thought *this* guy can't be for real – he's *acting*! He was trying *so* hard. It was like, "Oh, my dear, I've brought you *this*, oh my *love*, I've brought you *roses* today!" Like, give me a fucking break! That's not who *we are*. Everybody *loves* that but it's just how he *did* it. He tried so hard that it was obvious to us that it wasn't real. All of us that were friends with her – we were *so* sceptical. He was a young, blond-haired, *slim*, nice-looking guy and we're looking, like, what does he *want*? So he has a title. He doesn't *have* a cent and we felt like he was living off her and he was thrilled to death at the star value that she carried and we had very little hope for any future. We were only concerned about her being heartbroken in the end, when and if he dumped her. She was so smitten and seemed so thrilled with him and was thrilled to death about being married to a baron but she was also emotionally very fragile. As tough as she was intellectually, she was *obviously* fragile and had all these neuroses and she was *sick* a lot.'

As it turned out, Donald didn't dump Cass, but given von Wiedenman's subsequent sexual orientation, the likelihood of a long-term relationship seems slight, to say the least. They were divorced early the following year (citing 'irreconcilable differences'), but they would remain friends for the rest of her life.

This didn't make the demise of the relationship any easier for Cass though and, despite her sessions with the therapist, she still succumbed to an enveloping depression. In the wake of their break up and the realisation that she was on her own again, Cass would spend days in her room lolling on the four-poster with the blinds drawn.

Most people didn't see her at these times, but occasionally close friends would come by and find her languishing upstairs with her nails bitten and her hair uncombed, surrouned by dishes of leftover food, not having left the room for a week. Then someone like Leon would come in and lift the blinds and begin to clear up.

Cass felt that she was primarily to blame for the relationship's demise. She felt that her fame, her lifestyle and her propensity for excess made traditional domesticity difficult to attain and inevitably alienated people with less excessive tastes themselves. 'Cass was an extravagant person,' says songwriter John Bettis who became close to Cass around this time. 'I don't mean in the material sense. When Cass did *anything*, she did it to eleven. And she was aware, because she was a bright lady, that most people didn't. It was a trial for people to be involved with someone like that and although I think on one hand she was glad she had it, on the other, she knew it came at a hell of a price.'

Cass was also not alone in some of the problems she faced and her situation was symptomatic of many of her generation who were now on the cusp of their thirties. The idealism of the mid sixties had evaporated and the country's mood had changed dramatically. A man had been killed at the Altamont pop festival, the Beatles had split up amongst bitterness and acrimony, and Jimi Hendrix, Janis Joplin and Jim Morrison had all recently died drug-related deaths. Added to the political assassinations, the general sense of malaise seemed as all-pervasive as the optimism of the previous era. 'People forget now how dark it was from '69 to '76,' says Bettis. 'America was *not* a happy place. Far from it. No matter where you turned, whether it was the gas crisis, whether it was the rampant drug problems everybody had, whether it was the fact that we had opened up a Pandora's box with free love and relationships to where there *wasn't* any fixed point any more. By the time we got to 1969 everybody between the ages of twenty and twenty-eight was a drug addict. Everybody had been through two or three failed relationships of living with somebody, because we were all kids who didn't know what the fuck we were doing. And by the time you got to 1970 you were exhausted and you were sure that if you could just find another drug you'd be OK!' He laughs. 'And then *suddenly* it was all dark.'

While Cass's personal life may have been a source of continued unhappiness, her career, meanwhile, seemed to finally be showing signs of offering her the artistic freedom she had craved. Since her contract with Dunhill had now finally expired, Bobby Roberts had negotiated her a new million-dollar four-album deal with RCA. The label would allow her to explore a more sophisticated, less pop-oriented musical direction, and producer Lewis Merenstein was brought in to begin work on a new album.

Merenstein had made his name as an engineer working with some of the most revered names in jazz, from Charlie Parker to Thelonius Monk and Dizzy Gillespie. He would later achieve greater fame as the producer of Van Morrison's *Astral Weeks* and *Moondance* albums, but at this point he was keen to bring his jazz experience to a different genre. Only a few years older than Cass and from a similar background in Baltimore, Merenstein and Cass developed an instant rapport as soon as they met at RCA's New York offices. 'We didn't know each other very well but I guess at some level we did,' Merenstein tells me, 'because as we walked out of the president's office, there was this five-foot plastic dog in the reception area that was like a replica of the RCA trademark dog, and Cass and I both looked at each other and simultaneously, without saying a word, she picked up one of the dog's ears and I picked up the other and we started down the hall with it. We got in the elevator and I said, "What are we *doing*?" and she was so funny,' he says. 'She said she was gonna hold the dog up for ransom. *God* it was funny! Then the guard downstairs said, "Where are you going with that?" and she said, "Don't you know who I am? I'm Cass Elliot." He said, "OK," so we put it in the trunk of the limo – that's the only place it would fit, and we went back to the Waldorf where she was staying and she said she was going to write letters of ransom and take it back to LA on the plane. Well, we weren't in her room five minutes with the dog when the phone rang and it was Bobby [Roberts] rather irate because it was her first meeting with RCA since signing this major deal and we'd pulled a stunt, so to speak. They were pretty upset, but it worked out OK because RCA sent people over to bring it back and it gave us a chance to have a nice chat together and we became sort of friends that had pulled off this caper together. I felt we were kindred spirits after that.'

Cass was keen that this new album would finally distance her from the lush, harmonised, pop sound of the Mamas and the Papas and her solo Dunhill recordings. 'Cass didn't want to do anything that sounded like anything she had done with the Mamas and Papas,' explains Merenstein, 'so we intentionally didn't use background singers on many of the songs. This was her opportunity to be Cass Elliot – not Mama Cass – and she was enormously proud of it because she was given the freedom to just sing herself and not be put into a sound. That's why the album was called *Cass Elliot* – it was her. It was her all the way.'

Jazz legend Benny Golson was also brought in as arranger and to differentiate the record as much as possible from her past, Cass chose material of a more mature, serious nature such as Judee Sill's 'Jesus Was a Crossmaker' and two Randy Newman songs: 'I'll Be Home' and 'I Think It's Gonna Rain Today'. Cass also decided to record her friend Bruce Johnston's 'Disney Girls' and persuaded both him and Beach Boy Carl Wilson into the studio to play and sing on it. Cass had always loved the Beach Boys. She was friendly with Brian and Dennis Wilson and loved 'Good Vibrations' so much that when the song was nominated for the Grammy for 'Best Single' against 'Monday, Monday', she had swapped her own nomination plaque with Johnston's for 'Good Vibrations' and promptly hung it on the wall at Woodrow Wilson Drive.

Cass's interpretation of 'Disney Girls' would prove one of her most memorable recordings, and although the song has been covered by numerous artists from Jack Jones to Art Garfunkel, Cass's version has become a favourite not only of her fans but of Johnston himself. 'She probably has the *best* version of it,' Johnston tells me, 'just in terms of being the actress turning time back, going back to when she was fifteen. I was in the studio when she did the vocals and in her head she started reacting to the lyrics and she just put the personality in it. It's about going back to simpler times because I think anybody in any era wants to peel back time because life does give you a lot of cholesterol and in these times, here in the twenty-first century, so many of us spend our dream time thinking about getting back into high school, you know? No mortgage, no job, *nothing* – just go to high school and learn something and have fun, and Cass realised that that was what the song was about and she started making herself younger in the performance. That's when I realised that she *probably* could have been a working actress like Bette Midler or something just because of her *read* of it. It was *great*!'

Cass, as she had done in the past, was keen to record most of her vocals in one or two takes as live performances rather than the cut and paste multi-track method which was becoming more and more popular, and most of the time the sessions went well. But there were some days when her despondency surfaced and she would come to the studio, pleading depression. 'She was going through a hard time,' remembers Merenstein, 'and we were recording one day at RCA with the whole orchestra in the studio and she came in and lay down on the couch in the office, depressed, saying she just couldn't do it. She was very dramatic, you know – filled with drama! But it was also genuine, and at that time Talk Radio was very big, where you phoned in your problems, and suddenly she had called in and was sitting on the phone talking about her marriage. I said, "Cass, all of the people are here to perform, you've *got to* do it. RCA'll really be upset – it'll cost a fortune." Then I said to her, "I tell you what – I'll call the Union and I'll get somebody who can sing in your key and we'll do the tracks and we'll overdub." I actually got the Union on the phone and said, "I need somebody that sounds like Cass Elliot." She popped up out of that couch like a flash and looked like she was going to whack me. She said, "Oh no, you don't. What are you doing? Get off the phone! I'll do it! I'll do it!" And she showed up and performed like a real trouper. She always did, even if it was in the last minute. She always knew what she was supposed to do.'

The romantic nature of many of the songs was especially poignant to Cass in the light of her recent break-up with Donald and she told him she was dedicating the album to him and her therapist. She said the songs conveyed all the things she wanted to be but couldn't and, as a final gesture, she wore the Biba dress he had given her for the black-and-white cover photo. This was Cass's chance to emulate the screen divas of the thirties she had always idolised and the photo was shot by legendary Hollywood photographer George Hurrell in the style of Greta Garbo and the other stars he had photographed decades earlier.

Cass saw this album as her chance to prove herself artistically but by the time the album was released in February 1972, the public's perception of her had changed and the fact that she had become such a regular fixture of mainstream TV worked against her when it came to recording less populist material. Cass had chosen the Randy Newman and Judee Sill songs because she wanted to realign herself with contemporary adult music, but the mundane, deeply unhip 'let-me-show-you-how-to-bake-a-pizza' cosiness of some of her TV appearances had already cost her credibility and alienated her from much of her counterculture audience who now wanted 'authentic', serious AOR singer-songwriters. Cass had chosen the songs themselves primarily for their lyrics. 'I'm much more word-oriented than a lot of singers I know,' Cass later told the BBC, 'I think that's mainly because I don't write my own material. So when I hear a song, the first thing I listen to is the lyrics . . . it has to be something I would *feel* or say.' This was entirely understandable but the result sometimes meant that Cass's choice of songs were not the most musically accessible and the rest of her career would in fact be a case of a great voice in search of a song.

The *Cass Elliot* album, meanwhile, also included covers of older standards from the early sixties such as 'Baby I'm Yours', the gorgeously yearning 'I'll Be There' and 'All in the Game' – presumably aimed at appealing to her more mainstream fans, but these instead provided a slightly incongruous mix, and the attempt to please two audiences at once consequently pleased neither.

Two singles were released from the album: 'Baby I'm Yours' – to coincide with the album's release in February – and the beautifully tender, nostalgic 'That Song'. Both Cass and Lewis Merenstein had wanted 'That Song' to be the first single as it had been specially written for Cass by backing vocalist Bill Dean and with its 'Dream a Little Dream of Me'-style mixture of romance, whimsy and poignancy was undoubtedly one of the stand-out tracks on the album. When Cass had first heard its lyrics of lost love and how 'that song – that old song . . . starts me cryin' again', there had indeed been tears in her eyes, and she had clutched the demo tape to her chest refusing to let Merenstein take it away, but when it came to releasing the singles, both she and Merenstein had been over-ruled by RCA who insisted that 'Baby I'm Yours' be issued first. As it turned out, neither made any dent on the charts. Unless you were a singer-songwriter à la Carly Simon, Carole King, Judy Collins or Joni Mitchell, the early seventies were one of the worst periods in musical history to be a solo female artist and for the white chart-topping songstresses of the sixties, almost without exception, these years would prove the leanest of their careers. Apart from Cher's 'Gypsies, Tramps and Thieves', the careers of Sandie Shaw, Lulu, Petula Clark and Cilla Black had all been more or less relegated to pop's attic, where, as far as most of the public seemed to be concerned, they would gather dust for at least the next decade. Dusty Springfield, meanwhile, whom Cass had always admired, had the tremendous good fortune to be guided by Jerry Wexler to record her seminal *Dusty in Memphis* album, but although this would be revered as a classic of its kind in decades to come, at the time, she too was considered out of sync with current trends and would only begin to re-emerge into the charts with the advent of disco in the late seventies. Cass, meanwhile, was to have no such options and one can only guess what she might have created given the input, guidance and direction of someone with as much vision as Wexler.

Although the *Cass Elliot* album was not a hit, Cass still felt artistically validated by it herself and saw it as the start of a new, more independent musical direction. It also marked the beginning of a less self-destructive phase in her life. In September of 1971 Cass had turned thirty, and perhaps spurred on by the sobering reality of reaching this significant age marker as well as the disintegration of her marriage to Donald, she had set about taking stock of her life. With the assistance of her therapist, she now seemed to be coming to terms with some of the childhood issues which had governed her weight and subsequent drug use. 'She was doing five-days-a-week, heavy, intensive psychotherapy,' remembers Leah, 'and she was clean and sober and she'd lost a bunch of weight so she was no longer doing diet stuff. She was mentally and physically in the best shape she'd ever been in. She'd been playing tennis, she was really active and she was just in a *great* place.'

Having begun to confront her own demons, this new phase in Cass's life also motivated her to become more involved in improving the world around her. Alongside Frank Zappa, Eric Burdon and Grace Slick she had already lent her support to an organisation which had particular relevance to her own history: the Do-It-Now Foundation, an educational and therapeutic facility providing a twenty-four-hour free clinic aimed at preventing the spread of methedrine 'speed' among eleven, twelve and thirteen year olds in America.

But drug issues aside, Cass had also begun to become more actively involved in politics. Her generation had gradually become more politicised as the sixties progressed, and throughout the decade there had been a belief amongst young people that, perhaps for the first time, activism and political involvement on the part of ordinary people could affect change.

The greatest factor in motivating people to protest had been the escalation of the Vietnam war. Between July 1965 and December 1967 alone a greater weight of bombs had been dropped on Vietnam than the Allies had dropped on Europe in the entire Second World War and there would ultimately be fifty-eight thousand Americans killed and over two million Vietnamese. A Gallup Poll taken in 1968 had shown that, even by then, no less than 52 per cent of the American population thought the war was a mistake and burning of draft cards had almost become commonplace.

The protest movement had gained significant momentum, and mass demonstrations and marches had become a regular fixture of the end of the decade. Cass was impressed by the sentiments of her activist friends, Abbie Hoffman and Paul Krassner – leading protagonists of the recently formed 'Youth International Party' or 'Yippies', whose media savvy credo was that people should 'do whatever the fuck they want' and whose political pranks, such as burning money on Wall Street and appearing naked in church, were rapidly gaining them cause célèbre status as the youth movement's foremost spokesmen. But although she agreed with their beliefs, such antics were not Cass's style; instead she had joined in the now legendary epic march on the Pentagon in 1967, along with a hundred thousand others.

Cass was, however, disillusioned by her experience there as she had seen the inaccuracy with which its attendance was reported in the media. 'I was at the march on the Pentagon, right in the front taking pictures, just being there to find out what was happening,' she told *Rolling Stone* the following year, 'and I was knocked down and stepped on. I don't want to do that again. It didn't accomplish anything. Everything that happened in the newspapers was just lies. There were a hundred thousand people there, not fifteen thousand. And it was very orderly, very well organised. They just did not tell the truth.'

Feeling that this kind of organised protest was futile, by 1972 Cass therefore sought a different way of provoking change and playing a more proactive role in achieving it. 'I never got involved in politics in my life before,' she said, 'I used to think I lived in an awful country; I hated watching it being badly run. Then one day I suddenly thought, look, this is my country. Why should I stand aside and not try to make it good?' As someone who was in the public eye, she believed she should use her fame in a constructive and beneficial way. 'I think everybody who has a brain should get involved in politics,' she told

Rolling Stone. 'Working within. Not criticising it from the outside. Become an active participant, no matter how feeble you think the effort is. I saw in the Democratic Convention in Chicago that there were more people interested in what I was interested in than I believed possible. It made me want to work. It made me feel my opinion and ideas were not futile, that there would be room in an organised movement of politics for me to voice myself. If you are in a position of influence, you should do something about it. Not necessarily inflict your opinion on other people, but if you really think you're right, you should tell it.'

Becoming a parent had increased Cass's concern and heightened her awareness of politics and the need to make a better life for the next generation: 'I've always been so apathetic,' she said. 'I figured OK, maybe the world is going to fall down around me. [But] now I feel, and maybe that's motherhood too, [that] I want to make the world a better world. My child is going to be living, with God's help, long after I'm gone and I would like her to know that it's going to be a nice place for her to live in. And it's my job and the job of all of us to make it happen now, so that we don't dump the mess into our kids' laps that we are fighting with now . . . I don't want to have to turn around when she's twenty and say, "I'm sorry about the way things are in the world." . . . She's going to be around for a long while . . . and so am I.'

With these ideas in mind, Cass began actively lending her support to democratic Senator George McGovern in his run for the 1972 presidential election against Republican Richard Nixon that year. The South Dakotan McGovern, was, despite being fifty years old, known as the 'peace candidate' or the 'longhair' and the central premise of his campaign was his pledge to withdraw American troops from Vietnam, end the war and extend amnesty to those who had illegally evaded the draft. All of which Cass wholeheartedly agreed with. 'He's a fine American,' she told the *Guardian*, '[and] he cares about America. He cares about the people who aren't working, about creating jobs, and alleviating the tremendous economic pressure that we're under with inflation and the rise in the cost of living and the lowering of the dollar. I'd feel very comfortable and not so frightened about the future of the United States if he were president.'

Cass also demonstrated an awareness of how America was perceived by the rest of the world, which was, and often still is, far from commonplace. 'It's difficult for many Americans,' she acknowledged, 'especially those who've never travelled abroad, to realise the contempt with which America is often regarded overseas. The more I travel, the more I meet people and I become aware of what is going on in the world, I begin to think, well, wait a minute, we think we're so bloody great and so damned fabulous but we're really not doing a whole helluva lot: what we're doing is barbaric, in fact, in many countries.'

She then continued to expand on America's foreign policy with views that are no less apposite three decades on: 'It seems that America handles its foreign policy in one of two ways: we either bomb them out or buy them out. It's just bombs or bucks. This is supposed to be the age of reason, so there's just gotta be another way. There are a lot of us "liberals" who are concerned about what is going on and who would like to see America not pouring so much money into a war we can't win . . . even *that* is silly "a war we can't win". Does that mean that if we win, it makes it more worthwhile? What can you win? Thirteen more feet to drive your ambulances on?'

Cass spent a significant part of the year campaigning on McGovern's behalf, either at rallies or high profile fundraising functions. 'I give you one of the great talents in America today: Mama Cass,' the compere would announce as a drum roll heralded her arrival on the rally stage. 'I'm for McGovern,' she would tell them, once the crowd's cheers had died down, 'because he speaks *directly* to the issues I care about, especially that war in Vietnam, and with McGovern in the White House we won't *have* any more war in Vietnam because he'll terminate the one we do have.' She would then explain why she believed this was a particularly important election and why it was imperative that people voted and persuaded their friends to do the same. Cass had always been a natural public speaker, but in order to be fully prepared she brought with her a stack of small index cards so that if, during question-time, she was asked how the senator stood on a particular issue, all she had to do was flick through the cards until she found an appropriate quote.

Her easy way with a crowd also made her the perfect campaigner, as McGovern himself tells me down a crackling phone line from Montana where he now lives. 'She was very good at rousing the crowd,' he remembers. 'She was *so* well known that she always got a good reception wherever we presented her. I remember one night we did a series of receptions in private homes in Manchester, New Hampshire. I think I did eight of them in one evening and each house was jammed to the rooftops and she and Shirley MacLaine would go ahead of me and entertain the crowd till I arrived. It was just a nice interlude in an otherwise heavy political programme. I had a reputation for being a liberal but when people would see prominent Hollywood stars and entertainers, it kind of changed the image a little. And Cass's name was a household word in every part of the United States. Everyone from ten year olds to hundred year olds liked her, so it really helped explain why we ran strongly in that rather conservative setting.'

As well as the rallies, Cass also got involved in a wide range of other campaigning activities. She took part in a play with Jane Fonda at a high-profile Madison Square Garden fundraiser staged by Rose Kennedy and went on TV talk shows elaborating on the senator's policies. There were also fundraising concerts by Simon and Garfunkel – who reformed for the occasion, Peter, Paul and Mary and most famously the 'Four for McGovern' concert organised by Warren Beatty at Los Angeles' eighteen-thousand-seater Forum. The 'Four' were Carole King (who had just released *Tapestry*), James Taylor, Quincy Jones and Cass's old nemesis Barbra Streisand. On the main floor, where guests had paid a hundred dollars per seat, Cass spent the evening working as a celebrity usher alongside Burt Lancaster, Jack Nicholson, Goldie Hawn, Gene Hackman, Jon Voight and Carly Simon.

Afterwards, there was an informal reception backstage for the artists, and for the first and only time, Cass had an opportunity to sit down with McGovern himself and talk. She would later proudly describe this as one of her greatest moments, but she clearly also made an impression on McGovern, as he remembers, even all these years on. 'I was very impressed with her,' he recalls. 'She was a very intelligent and well-motivated person. She talked about the campaign and said she was *for* me primarily because of my opposition to the war and that she felt very strongly about that.' As far as the public were concerned, Cass's political involvement further heightened her image as a forward-thinking, intelligent woman, and her social concern seemed to wave a banner for independent-minded women the world over.

This was also a time when musicians had become more and more politicised and politically outspoken. Previously pop musicians had been actively discouraged from expressing opinions on anything more controversial than their favourite colour, and politics in music had been consigned to the dusty annals of the folk boom with Pete Seeger, the Weavers and Bob Dylan in his early protest-singing incarnation. But things had begun to change as the sixties had progressed. As early as 1967 Paul McCartney had begun to mention the Vietnam war on British TV and by late 1971 John Lennon had released 'Power to the People' and included 'I Don't Want to be a Soldier' on his *Imagine* album, as well as, of course, staging his politically motivated bed-ins with Yoko Ono, whilst Marvin Gaye had captured the feelings of so many with 'What's Goin' On'. In the wake of the Vietnam war, young people in particular had, meanwhile, become disillusioned with conventional politics and begun to look to musicians and leaders of the counterculture to articulate their own concerns and beliefs. As a result musicians' social standing had become elevated far beyond that of mere entertainers, and suddenly the Beatles, the Stones, Bob Dylan, Leonard Cohen and Marvin Gaye became revered as prophets and spokespeople for their generation. Cass's role in McGovern's campaign therefore carried more weight and impact than it might have done either before or since.

But whereas many musicians' political activities were short-lived, Cass nursed more long-term ambitions. 'I think that I would like to be a senator or something in twenty years,' she told TV's Mike Douglas. 'But I have a lot of feelings about things. I know the way I would like to see things for this country and when I talk to people, everybody wants pretty much the same thing: peace, enough jobs, no poverty and good education. And I've learned a lot. When you travel around you really do get to feel – not to be cliché – the pulse of the country and what people want. I'm concerned, and it's no good to be unconcerned and just sit there.'

In spite of Cass's and many other celebrities' efforts on McGovern's behalf, when it came to the Presidential election, it seemed that as far as the majority of the American electorate were concerned, he was considered too radical and detrimentally connected in more reactionary minds with 'the three As: acid, amnesty and abortion'. He won only 38 per cent of the nation's vote and Richard Nixon began his second term in the White House.

Cass certainly shared in McGovern's disappointment and defeat, and although the Vietnam war ended in January of the following year, she was nevertheless frustrated by the seeming futility of her efforts on

McGovern's behalf. The ability to affect change, which had been such a central sixties belief, seemed, like most of the accompanying sixties optimism, to be simply yet another lost cause.

But whilst Cass's activities on behalf of McGovern may not have had a vast impact on the general public, they had not escaped the attention of the FBI, who clearly considered Cass worthy of monitoring. It would later emerge that they had in fact been keeping a file on her since her days in the Mugwumps, presumably due to her associations with at least one drug dealer. In 1972 their sources revealed that she was of 'the hippie generation', had allegedly smoked marijuana, was 'very independent' and, most dangerously of all, had 'a mind of her own'.

Cass was presumably unaware of this. In the meantime, she had further recording obligations to RCA, but before those would happen, there would be an unexpected encounter with Denny.

25

'Don't call me Mama any more'

'I don't suppose I'll be in the business in ten years' time,' Cass told the *Guardian* in 1972. 'There's too much pressure, so when it gets to be too much, I'll quit, call it a day, and perhaps work behind the wool counter in Harrods.'

Cass had recently taken up crocheting and explained to the newspaper that her life was indeed now extremely tranquil. 'I'm very quiet,' she said. 'I don't drink, and I'm not very pop-oriented ... Being encompassed in pop music was not something that I sought after. I'll be thirty-one in September – a difficult age for what people think I should be doing.'

Cass's recent campaign activity for George McGovern was indicative of the restlessness she felt about her future. Her new-found optimism had led her to readdress her career and the feasibility of continuing as a singer in the years to come. Along with her recent thoughts of a political career, she also began to look towards acting and television work as another possibility.

With the exception of the sketches on shows like Carol Burnett's, she had always enjoyed working on screen and had made a special guest appearance in the 1970 children's film *Pufnstuf* – a proto-Muppet-style hippie witch musical starring child actor and *Oliver* star, Jack Wild. When the Mamas and the Papas had first become famous, Cass had also filmed a couple of screen tests for an Andy Warhol film, supposedly to be titled *The New Beauty* in which Cass would be surrounded by 'beautiful boys'. Cass had not particularly enjoyed the tests though, describing them as a 'Zen experience' and the project never materialised. 'All the other Warhol girls are so silent,' said Cass. 'If there's one thing I'm not, it's silent. Even when I'm standing still, I'm not silent. (Warhol) didn't even talk to me. He sent someone over to tell me to sit in a chair and not smile or be affected by anything. It totally spaced me out.'

More recently, however, there had been talk of TV situation comedies, while film companies had likewise begun to approach her with offers of scripts, and this now seemed a more likely future for her than either pop or rock 'n' roll. Cass also liked the idea of producing other artists and had made some tentative in-roads, producing a single for torch singer Roberta Sherwood as well as a single and album for 3's A Crowd, a talented Canadian folk-rock combo she had discovered in Toronto and introduced to Dunhill. Due to her own recording commitments however, although she remained credited as producer on the records, particularly those of 3's A Crowd, Steve Barri had essentially produced them himself.

Cass was still keen to become more involved in producing, if the right opportunity arose, but for the time being she just wanted to bring as much variety into her life as possible. 'I've done quite a lot of things,' she later told the BBC, 'And in order to keep it interesting for *me*, I can't be exclusively a recording artist or a cabaret performer or a television artist . . . As long as I can keep doing diversified things, I'll keep interested in my career. Because I *need* the challenge of doing new things.'

Cass felt that she had reached a turning point in her career, but the uncertainty of her future would soon precipitate the return of her older concerns.

Cass was due to record a follow-up to *Cass Elliot*, but instead of returning to RCA's LA studios, which Cass had found overly large and not unlike 'a small airplane hangar', she decided that this time she'd like to record in London. Lewis Merenstein would produce again, but Cass wanted to get away from LA, to see her English friends and take advantage of the relative intimacy of London's Trident Studios which at the time was regularly churning out hits by Elton John, Harry Nilsson and many others. She also wanted to explore the different sound she felt might be possible in Britain.

British session musicians and studio engineers were revered as amongst the best in the world and were known for creating a distinctive, slightly tighter sound than the somewhat looser American style. Recording in England was also less expensive than America. Just before she left, she received an unexpected visit.

Since she had recorded *People Like Us*, Cass had seen little of the group with the exception of Michelle. Whereas previously Cass had always been closest to Denny, now that Michelle was no longer with John and they had motherhood in common, they had become close once more, often taking Owen and Chynna out together and sharing a school run with Cher whose daughter was a similar age. Although Cass and Denny hadn't fallen out, they hadn't seen each other for quite some time either. Cass had since been married to Donald and progressed her own career while Denny was still drinking heavily and had acquired a wife and child, almost inadvertently. Cass was therefore surprised to find him and Jim Hendricks standing on her doorstep one afternoon.

The three of them sat by the pool and reminisced about the Mugwump days. Cass was glad to see them both and a few hours later when they left, Denny suggested he come back a little later on. When he returned, armed with a bottle of Green Label Jack Daniels, the two of them flopped onto Cass's four-poster bed and settled in for an evening in front of the TV.

Denny's earlier refusal to marry Cass had finally convinced her that even though she still loved him and he clearly cared deeply for her there was no likelihood of their having a future together. They chatted about what was going on in their lives and careers and Denny suggested a musical collaboration between the two of them, along the lines of her Dave Mason album. Cass was stunned. 'You wanna get together *now*?' she asked. The irony was, of course, that years earlier, after the Mugwumps had split up and before they had formed the Mamas and the Papas, Cass had wanted desperately to sing with Denny. She had spent months, if not years, fantasising about the possibility, but now that seemed several lifetimes ago and too much had happened since. Denny tried suggesting that they bring in Jim Hendricks to sing with them, just like old times, but this made little difference. 'She just said, "No," remembers Denny. 'Not, "Let's talk about it," or anything. Just, "No."'

Cass was committed to recording for RCA, so even had she wanted to, there was no room in her schedule to begin a new project. It was perhaps something she might have reconsidered at a later date, but in the meantime, this was not going to stop them enjoying the evening.

Once they were together, drinking, chatting and laughing, they felt as close as they ever had. Cass had perhaps wanted Denny too much in the past and now that she had stopped hoping, indeed perhaps because she had stopped hoping, she finally got what she had dreamed of for so many years and Denny spent the night with her at Woodrow Wilson Drive. In the morning, Cass prepared croissants and blueberries for breakfast. There was nothing to say and no plans to make. Denny had a wife and child, and in Cass's mind, the night's events probably seemed more like a conclusion to an earlier part of her life than a beginning. As soon as they had had breakfast, Cass got ready to leave for London.

In June of 1972 Cass spent two months at London's Trident Studios recording the album which would become *The Road Is No Place for a Lady* – titled after a song of Leah's. There were songs by her friends Jimmy Webb and Paul Williams, but apart from the high-drama, emotional sweep of the strings-fuelled opening number – 'If You're Gonna Break Another Heart', which was released as a single, the album did not really contain any stand-out tracks. Although the warmth of Cass's voice lifts what is often mediocre material, she was once again let down by the lack of quality songs and there was little opportunity to really explore her voice to its best advantage.

The production today sounds very much of its time, featuring the piano-heavy rhythm section that was so much a feature of early seventies records of this kind, but the album was also dogged by technical problems and the American release was delayed due to a fault in the mixing stage at Trident. Even without these hitches, it is unlikely that either 'If You're Gonna Break Another Heart' or the follow-up single 'Does Anybody Love You?' the album's other strongest song, would have had any impact on the charts, falling neither into the singer/songwriter genre, the country rock of the Eagles, which was now dominating the American charts, nor the early glam-rock of British bands like Mott the Hoople.

Cass realised she needed to take her career in a new direction and began to feel that perhaps she needed to move away from rock and pop altogether. 'I've changed *quite* a bit musically,' she told the Skitch & Co US Army Reserve radio programme in 1973. 'I was looking for a home for myself in rock music, whereas, all along I had known that I really never had a rock background. I like classical music, I like jazz and I like what people now call middle-of-the-road music . . . With the

Mamas and the Papas I was really firmly entrenched in rock music and when I left, I sort of guess I expected to stay there, but I didn't have the material and I really didn't have the inclination. So, I had to look for a place for myself to find out what kind of music I wanted to make.'

In order to find out, Cass decided the first step was to hire a new manager. She had been managed by Bobby Roberts since she had first signed to Dunhill with the Mamas and Papas and so it made sense to make a clean break from her past with the group and start afresh. Enter Allan Carr. Remembered by some as a more rotund, shorter, bitchier Elton John-type, Carr, who died in 1999, had camp as his middle name and both his feet were unshakably rooted in the sequinned land of what Cass called 'big-time showbiz'. He held some of the best and biggest parties in LA, and in the showbiz world, he was unquestionably the manager of the moment. He would later go on to produce the stage musical of *Grease* and the Broadway hit *La Cage Aux Folles* and had already looked after Peter Sellers, Herb Alpert, Tony Curtis and Hollywood actress Ann Margaret – one of the highest-paid Vegas stars of the day.

As far as Carr was concerned there was no question as to what direction Cass should take. It seemed clear that her days as a rock or pop star were over, and as she didn't write her own material but nevertheless needed to maintain her career and profile whilst earning as much money as possible, the cabaret circuit and Las Vegas seemed the obvious, and perhaps only, route. The same had been suggested to Dusty Springfield, whose career seemed to have reached a similar impasse, but interestingly, and indeed wisely, Springfield had refused. Cass, meanwhile, recognised the need to try something new and earn money, and as she had always naturally veered towards showbiz herself, was willing to be guided by Carr.

An idea was therefore hatched that Cass would prepare a musical cabaret-style revue to take on the road across America. To ensure that there were no repeats of the previous Vegas episode, however, Carr put together a team of top-class professionals including musical director Marvin Laird and choreographer and director Walter Painter to create a slick, flawless show.

This time there would be no singing Mexicans and Cass would carry the show alone, with the exception of two male dancers who would double as backing singers and serve as sidekicks throughout the act. Musically, apart from a Mamas and Papas medley, including, naturally, 'Dream a Little Dream of Me', the show consisted mainly of old standards such as the Tallulah Bankhead classic 'I'll Be Seeing You' and 'Only Make Believe'. There was also the odd contemporary song such as Paul McCartney's 'My Love' – a personal favourite of Cass's – and a couple of specially written new songs including 'Don't Call Me Mama Anymore', which would provide the title for the show. Cass had been attempting to lose the 'Mama' moniker since she had left the Mamas and the Papas, but it seemed irredeemably lodged around her neck, like a cheap sign pointing downwards towards her weight. 'I know people work all their lives for instant recognition,' she told the *New York Post*, 'but for the things I want to do, like act, do films, maybe a Broadway play, I think I should have a last name. When Michelle made *Dillinger* nobody billed her as Mama Michelle. So why should I be hung with it?'

Even apart from her name, very little about the show bore any resemblance to anything she had ever done with the Mamas and Papas; this was showbiz in the oldest sense of the word. One of the centre pieces of the act was a soft-shoe version of 'Only Make Believe' in which Cass strutted along with a cane in between her two co-dancers. 'That was the high point that I remember in the act,' says Walter Painter. 'She was *so* charming in it. She would put her hand on one of their thighs and he would get nervous and she would get nervous and they would "make believe I love you" and it was just a sort of twist on the number that hadn't existed before. It was done tongue in cheek and she was *very* funny in it. *Very* good and it had sort of a wow finish and was really received very very well.' Painter also wanted to take advantage of Cass's dancing ability and, having observed how nimbly she could move – indeed, 'better than most', he comments – he choreographed a substantial amount of dancing into the act and although Cass had never really worked in this way before, it came easily and naturally to her. 'She loved it and was *good* at show business,' says Painter. 'You didn't *know* that when she was in the Mamas and Papas. She was just that heavy-set girl on the end, you know? But she was *way* more than that.'

On 9 February 1973 they debuted the show in Pittsburgh to smooth over any unpolished edges, safe in the knowledge that even if things went catastrophically wrong, in Pittsburgh, very few people would ever be likely to know or care. 'We played in Pittsburgh at some, I'll lovingly call it . . . dump,' recalls Painter, 'to break the act in so nobody could see it. *We* wanted it because, who *knew*? She had never done this before and we were a little concerned about what do we *have* here? And it didn't take very long to see that we had something very special.'

It was good to play somewhere so resolutely off the prime circuit as it was not only Painter and the rest of the team who were nervous. Apart from TV shows and the rallies she had attended on behalf of George McGovern, this was to be the first live show Cass had played since Vegas in 1969 and she was understandably anxious. 'I think she was just concerned about getting all the material right at that first venue,' remembers musical director Marvin Laird, 'but once she got the hang of how much an audience loved her on her own and that they didn't *really* need the other three (Mamas and Papas), she loved it.'

Pittsburgh was indeed a success, but Cass still had to build her confidence further before she could brace herself to return to Las Vegas. Cass's anxieties were also aggravated by the knowledge that, in the light of the earlier Vegas scenario, many doubted that she could ever successfully carry a high-profile show alone. 'I think people thought that this was going to be a valiant, but probably unsuccessful effort on the part of yet another rock star who was part of a group and was striking out on her own,' says Laird. 'It was probably *not* going to be met with a great deal of success. I think people just felt that she wasn't going to either *be* strong enough or *feel* strong enough on any one front to hold people's attention for a whole evening. But she proved them wrong.'

Cass did prove them wrong and the shows received unanimously glowing reviews. 'Cass Elliot came ready to take the town by storm,' wrote the *Hollywood Reporter*, 'and take it she does with an utterly charming, entertaining and delicious concoction of hit records, old favourites and great gobs of her own earthy, hit wit and personality.'

After sucessfully playing the Flamingo in Vegas, Cass toured the country with the show, playing casinos and hotel supper clubs in New Jersey, Miami, San Francisco and Dallas, culminating in a two-week run at the famous Chicago cabaret venue, Mr Kelly's. Cass now had a hit show and as she was still contractually required to deliver another album to RCA, Allan Carr decided the obvious solution would be to record a live album of the show.

He therefore brought in big-band jazz producer Jack Daugherty and the album was recorded over a few nights at Mr Kelly's and some days in a nearby studio. The recording included the show's key songs interspersed with snippets of Cass's audience repartee and captures some of her relaxed and light-hearted manner, but although her voice had always been naturally suited to singing standards, the material, once it was laid down on vinyl, sounded more like C-list Broadway or the blander end of MOR (middle of the road). What Cass really needed was an obvious hit and this was something the album clearly lacked. It would once again prove difficult to market, particularly as at this point in the early seventies, very few artists with a view to commerciality, or otherwise for that matter, were recording this kind of material. Whereas since the nineties, some of the world's biggest stars from Rod Stewart to Robbie Williams have all recorded entire albums of standards, in the seventies, with the exception of Bryan Ferry, whose musical credibility allowed him more freedom, this was about as un-rock 'n' roll as you could get.

From Cass's point of view, meanwhile, the live album idea was not something she would naturally have chosen herself. 'This whole thing about doing a live album I have been against,' she told the show's scriptwriter Chet Dowling. 'I think there's nothing more *boring* than a live album unless you're somebody *really* special. I think if you're really important – if you're Marlene Dietrich and you make one performance a year, then you record it. No matter what she sings, no matter whether she falls down, you record it because you just don't know when she's going to do another one.' The remark would prove ironically prescient.

Some months before starting the *Don't Call Me Mama* shows, Cass had met lyricist John Bettis, who at that point had recently scored a global hit with 'Goodbye to Love' for the Carpenters. Bettis would go on to write further hits for them and was unofficially considered a kind of 'third' Carpenter, and as Cass had admired the duo since their emergence in the charts the previous year, she had consequently been delighted to meet him. 'Cass and I hit it off *famously*,' remembers Bettis, who has since gone on to write hits for Madonna ('Crazy For You'), Michael Jackson ('Human Nature') and the Pointer Sisters ('Slow Hand'). 'It was like I already knew her and she already knew me – it was very odd. We laughed at the same things and we liked the same music because she was a little folky and so was I.'

Cass was also thrilled when Bettis arranged an introduction to the Carpenters themselves, and the four of them went for dinner at LA's exclusive L'Auberge restaurant. Over beef Wellington and vintage wine, Cass and Richard and Karen Carpenter seemed to have no shortage of subjects to talk about. 'They got along famously,' remembers Bettis. 'Also Richard and Karen's parents were from Baltimore and so was Cass and so that set 'em off, and then musically and humour-wise it was very clear that the three of them had an enormous amount in common. They made their way through opera and show tunes and popular records and it was an astonishing thing to watch those three superstars singing harmony with each other for about three hours. They were clearly all cut from the same cloth somewhere along the line, the only difference was that Cass was much more of a street person from her days of struggling. And her recreational activities were different than Richard and Karen's!' he laughs. 'Karen sipped at the wine – she really didn't like drinking but Richard was drinking with dinner and Cass and I were ... whatever the *next* stage of inhaling alcohol is beyond drinking!' he laughs. 'I'm sure there's a name for it!'

Cass's new-found sobriety had not lasted that long and although she had come off heroin, drink and some sort of drugs were never too far off the menu. After dinner, Cass invited everyone to Woodrow Wilson Drive for coffee and the four of them made their way up the Canyon in Cass's Cadillac and Richard Carpenter's Ferrari. It soon emerged, with Cass's love of fast cars, that she too had previously owned a Ferrari. 'Cass was telling Richard that she used to shift the gears by tone,' continues Bettis, 'and he was dumbfounded. He said, "I thought I was the only person in the world who ever did that. There's a certain pitch it gets to and you shift the gear and you don't have to look at the tack or anything else." She said, "Absolutely right!"' he laughs. 'And I have a dim memory of us switching cars around so that Cass could play with Richard's car and somehow I led them up there to Cass's.'

Once at the house, Cass envisaged an evening of chemically enhanced musical entertainment, much as she would normally enjoy with any other musician friend, but she had yet to discover that the Carpenters were, in some respects at least, a little different from most of her other musical acquaintances. 'Cass, I think, was expecting to have Richard go to the piano and they'd just bang out songs all night, kind of like she and I did,' says Bettis, 'and in a subtle way, Cass was offering things. One had to be *subtle* then, but as Paul Simon would say: "the hints and allegations were so big you could have dressed 'em in a suit". And Richard knew what he was being offered. I don't think Karen did. She was *awfully* young, she was probably twenty and she didn't have a clue other than she was pretty sure it was something she'd never done! So Richard and Karen had a cup of coffee, made their excuses and went home!' he laughs. 'After that I pushed Karen to get together with Cass, to call her to have lunch or something like that because I thought they'd be good for each other. Karen didn't have the kind of associations, at that point especially, that I felt she could talk to someone who'd understand what she was going through – the stardom aspect of it all, the weirdnesses. But it never materialised. I think Cass was a little too real for Karen in a way. And then Cass always had that undercurrent of kind of self-destruction. Under the surface. Also, once Cass realised who Richard and Karen are, she went, "Ooooh. They really *are* like that. They just happen to be musical geniuses." But Cass and I stayed friends 'cause I was always the crazy one of the three of us.'

Although Bettis never became part of Cass's circle in the way that some of her other friends did, she nevertheless formed a close and intense friendship with him, offering him valuable advice and support as he tried to extricate himself from a draining relationship with a heroin-using girlfriend. Cass also confided in him to a certain extent about some of her own experiences and troubles. Bettis was younger than Cass and less-established in the music industry and therefore looked up to her as someone who was already a major star, but Cass's feelings towards him clearly followed the same pattern as so many of her male relationships. Some years later, Bettis realised that during the early days of their friendship she had been interested in him romantically, but at the time he had not picked up on it and they remained purely platonic friends. This would have been just one of an ongoing string of disappointments for Cass, but the closeness of their friendship meant that when it came to writing a song for her *Don't Call Me Mama* show, Bettis was in a prime position to write something which he felt lyrically expressed Cass's true feelings.

First Bettis needed to ascertain what kind of thing Cass had in mind though. 'What do you want?' he asked her on the phone. 'A fucking hit. What do *you* want?' she replied. 'OK, well I want that too,' said Bettis. Cass, however, knew that Bettis might need a little more information and so they talked for a while till eventually Cass told him, 'Well you know *me*. I need something that's real.'

Cass felt that the song Bettis eventually wrote for her – 'I'm Coming to the Best Part of My Life' (to music by Roger Nichols) – was indeed real for her. '[This song] really expresses the way I feel,' she told the audience at Mr Kelly's and the song's lyrics seemed to reflect her recently found optimism: 'There's nothing I can see to hold me down / I'll be trying till I'm flying / And I'm feeling no pain . . . I finally feel the future's on my side / No more blues songs / Only new songs'.

'I was not surprised at all that she loved it,' says Bettis. 'I did what she wanted me to do – I wrote a song about the inside of her and that song is as accurate a depiction of what was alive and well in Cass Elliot from the time she was three years old as anything I could think of. And that's why she loved it so much. She *knew* that's what it was. Cass always believed that statement – coming to the best part of my life – every day she lived. That's what kept her going. But I drew on an awful lot of what I knew about the positive angels in Cass's character. She was an undefeatable person. She had a lot of . . . stuff that defeats a lot of people because a lot of desperate people cling to Weight-Watchers or whatever but can't find it in themselves to go out and live their lives. But Cass had an indomitable spirit in that way. She knew there were things that she couldn't control about herself, but she wasn't going to let them limit what she did with her life. It was a *remarkable* thing to see. It's like someone winning a worldwide yacht race with a broken mast. You had that feeling about her. But it didn't take away the plaintive quality to her spirit.'

By the time Cass was performing the *Don't Call Me Mama* shows, the resilience Bettis had observed when he had first met her over a year earlier was much less evident. The survivial instinct that he had drawn on for 'Coming to the Best Part of My Life' were certainly still there, but Cass's optimism was beginning to flag. To coincide with the album's release, Cass had recorded a TV special, similarly entitled *Don't Call Me Mama Anymore*, with guest appearances from Dick Van Dyke, Joel Grey (newly famous since the release of *Cabaret* the previous year), Cass's mother Bess and Michelle. The show was not well-received, criticised (as with her earlier TV show) for poor scripting and lucklustre sets.

But despite the album and TV show's lack of success, her stage shows had meanwhile re-established her reputation as a strong, professional performer. Allan Carr therefore began plans for Cass to tour around Europe. The show would be adapted slightly and this would mean a new round of rehearsals, but she was also still constantly being invited onto high-profile TV chat shows and so her schedule was now nearing overload. Cass's new (slightly) healthier lifestyle meant this should not necessarily have been a problem, but her love of a party and the need to unwind from the stresses of a frequently hectic, pressured existence meant that some of the older issues were beginning to re-emerge.

Shortly before the end of Cass's American tour with the *Don't Call Me Mama* shows, Michelle Phillips had come over to Woodrow Wilson Drive one morning to take Owen and Chynna to San Diego Zoo. She found Cass lying on the kitchen floor, having fallen and hurt her knee. The injury was serious enough for Cass to need several days in hospital and meant that although she was just about able to perform the following week, she had to play the final shows at Mr Kelly's using a cane to support her. When asked how her injury had come about, Cass told people that she had simply slipped in her kitchen – a household accident that could, of course, happen to anyone. Many close to her, however, had other thoughts. 'She and I both knew what it was,' says John Bettis. 'I mean, we've all *done* it, you know? She was having a little too much fun one night and made a mis-step probably, but she was just pissed about it and I never did get a straight story.'

When Cass performed on the *Tonight Show* some months later in April 1974 she collapsed backstage and was immediately rushed to hospital once more. This time the story made the press in both America and Europe, accompanied by photographs of Cass on a stretcher with her hair in curlers. 'I tipped over,' Cass told the papers, 'I don't know how else to explain it. I had a very bad headache that day and I hadn't been able to eat anything. Ordinarily, I know, you wouldn't think that was such a hardship for me,' she continued, 'but my blood sugar level dropped or something and I just sort of tipped over and spent four days in the hospital.'

Falling over in one's kitchen could possibly be explained away, but collapsing at the *Tonight Show* was, in media terms at least, on an entirely different scale. The press frenzy was humiliating and only added to Cass's distress. 'I could work all my life to do a good piece of work,' she said, 'and nobody would ever hear about it. But just tip over somewhere where there's a camera and they go click-click-click.'

Cass's explanation of the drops in her blood sugar level were perfectly plausible but those close to her felt the cause was more likely to have been similar to that of her earlier knee injury. Although Cass had in theory stopped using heroin, this by no means meant that she had given up drugs altogether. In the early twenty-first century, heightened awareness of drug and alcohol issues means that most ex-drug users abstain from any mind-altering substances, as, apart from anything else, these would be likely to weaken one's resolve. In the early seventies, however, there was considerably less knowledge or awareness, nor was there the supportive environment Cass would have needed in order to maintain such a stance. 'When Cass cleaned up her act,' remembers Donald von Wiedenman, 'it wasn't like me cleaning up my act and not taking anything. She would use pot to mellow her out when she wasn't doing the other or coming off the other drugs. And certainly she would have had a couple of drinks if she weren't having any drugs.' Cass had always preferred barbiturates or 'downers' rather than a stimulant high, but cocaine use in Hollywood in the early seventies was at its zenith and was hard to avoid, even had she wanted to. A culture of abstinence was virtually non-existent at the time, but Cass nevertheless knew that continued excessive use of barbiturates, alcohol, cocaine and other prescription drugs was far from healthy, particularly given her weight. But Cass, despite the recent spate of drug-related rock-star deaths, like so many others, believed that her drug use was under control. If she didn't, she was clearly not ready to confront the issue.

One of Cass's old friends from Forest Park High School, Chip Silverman, had stayed in touch with her over the years and she would often go out with him and a few other old Baltimore friends whenever she was back east. Silverman, now a PhD addictions consultant who was previously Special Adviser on Drug and Alcohol Abuse to the Governor of Maryland, went to visit Cass in hospital shortly after her fall, and at this point had already begun working in drug rehabilitation. 'I was talking to her a bit about what I was doing in the addiction field,' Silverman remembers, 'and first she told me I couldn't *dare* lecture her. I knew what was going on and I think she was getting a lot of stuff like Dilaudid (a painkiller) that she was persuading the nurses to get for her. But I understood. People take things for a lot of reasons, OK? And I'm sure there was an escape she was looking for that she couldn't find elsewhere. But when I would kind of talk about it with her, I would end up talking circles because she was very *smart*, you know? I know that sooner or later, people are always gonna have to come to me, but it's not gonna be sooner, because until people bottom out, they don't really *wanna* hear from you. And so, with her, I would just say, "You know, you gotta be *careful*." I was explaining to her that it was gonna impact on her performance because there were certain things you knew that would click. I would say, "Hey, look, you don't wanna fuck up in Vegas again, you don't wanna do *this*. It's gonna impact on your voice and your image, you know?" But she really didn't want to hear it. There's not much you can say to people, especially when they're high, and she just didn't wanna *talk* about that. I would start to mention it a little bit, when she'd get into, "Hey, what's *this*?" and then we just would stop.'

During the shows at Mr Kelly's in Chicago, Cass had been backed by various session musicians including Wrecking Crew bassist Joe Osborn and her old friend session drummer Jim Gordon – with whom she had embarked on a brief affair. Some years earlier, Gordon had spent time in England playing with Eric Clapton in Derek and the Dominoes (and co-writing 'Layla') but had since returned to LA with a major heroin habit. By the time he was playing in Chicago with Cass he was on methadone in an attempt to come off heroin, but was still drinking heavily and was also already beginning to be troubled by the 'voices' which would later urge him to kill his mother (for which Gordon is currently serving a life sentence). Spending time with Gordon can therefore hardly have helped any resolve Cass might have had, and Osborn remembers being struck by her capacity to take large quantities of Quaaludes with seemingly little effect.

Similarly, whilst almost all Cass's friends were drug users on a low-key, grass or hash-smoking level, aside from Gordon, there were also several good friends such as Gram Parsons and British musician Graham Bond who were also heroin users. But most significantly, there were still intermittent visits from Pic Dawson, who, despite the fact that Cass now considered him an ex rather than current boyfriend, still felt free to arrive unannounced at any time of the day or night.

Only a few months earlier, Dawson had made one of his more dramatic entrances to Woodrow Wilson. 'Cass and I very often would have a sleepover,' remembers Leon Bing, 'and her bed was just huge so we would spread out a panoply of food and just watch movies and have a good time and laugh. Now I must make clear, Cass and I were not lovers; she was not gay and nor am I – it was very much like a high-school sleep over and we'd maybe blow a little weed. So on one of these nights we were sound asleep (Cass was a heavy sleeper and I'm more of a light sleeper) and I awakened and someone was pulling my arm hard. I looked up and there was a guy with long hair and a beard standing over the bed and he was saying, "Get the fuck out of that bed or I'll kill you." I looked at him again and there was what looked like blood all over the front of his white T-shirt and he yanked me out of the bed.' After trying unsuccessfully to wake Cass, Bing ran downstairs and called a male friend of hers who, in the light of the Manson murders, kept a pistol at home, and he came straight over to the house, armed and ready to use the gun if necessary. But the intruder, it emerged, was Dawson. He had cut his hand while breaking in through the French windows, staining his white T-shirt, and on staggering into the bedroom, in his rather less than clear-headed state, had been convinced that he had found Cass in bed with another man. Cass and Dawson were unreservedly apologetic to Bing the following day, but the impact of having Dawson around her once again, in what was plainly a drug-addled state, can hardly have aided Cass's situation.

In spite of her success with the *Don't Call Me Mama* show, Cass still clearly felt an enormous void in her life. She doted on Owen, but she still lacked the validation of a loving partner and a stable home life. The surrogate 'families' she had created over the years, most recently with Leon Bing and Keith Allison, had now once again dispersed since Bing had started a new relationship and Allison and 'Donny' Johnson were, like Cass herself, busy pursuing their own careers. In the small hours of the morning, either on the road or at home, during the inevitable emotional slump which followed a successful performance, her life would often appear particularly bleak and she would call old friends and lovers, clearly needing someone simply to listen and offer support.

Marc Strange, her old Canadian boyfriend from the Mugwump days, had stayed in touch and would often receive these calls, as would Allan Pollock who she had known when she was briefly a student at American University in Washington, DC. Her calls were nearly always to people she had known in an earlier, more innocent time of her life, and were often to those who, unlike her rock and roll friends, led more ordinary, prosaic lives. On other occasions, her experiences at Forest Park seemed to form the main thrust of the unhappiness she was clearly desperate to escape.

No doubt accentuated by alcohol- and drug-induced depression, the rejection and injustices she had felt as a teenager seemed no less real and painful than they had at the time. 'She just never could get away from the way the girls had treated her at high school,' remembers Silverman. '"I hated this one, hated that one," and she loved it when Mimi Seligman had come back at a Mamas and Papas concert and Ellen had just said, "You didn't know me then and I don't know you *now.*" I'll bet you she told me that story at least a dozen times. She just *loved* it! She was obsessed with how they really didn't *accept* her. Sometimes,' he continues, 'when she'd come into town, she'd be getting high and she'd get maudlin over this stuff, and when she was stoned, she tended to do too much sometimes, you know? She always sort of overdid it and a lot of times some of the guys'd go, "OK, let's get rid of her, we can't hear this shit again!" And maybe we'd leave her somewhere, in a restaurant or even in the car. She wasn't the only one who would get like that, but she would just be incoherent, too smashed and we always felt bad and went back for her, you know? I couldn't deal with the guilt! But I think there's a message there too, when people do that, that I'm gonna do as much of this as I can 'cause I don't wanna remember anything else. Whatever that hurt was, this was a way to deal with it.'

If her days at Forest Park still haunted her in a way, it seemed natural that she would turn to her friend Sharon, the person who had been her closest friend at the time. 'On occasion she would call me,' remembers Sharon, 'and she would say, "I'm in New York, I'm at the Pierre, call me tomorrow at eleven and we'll have brunch and hang out." I said, "Great," and I would call and there would never be any answer and this happened maybe twice. And so I kind of got used to the fact that something was going on and I didn't know what it was, because on the phone she sounded so great and so up and we were gonna get together like old times. I didn't have any expectations and I was just there when she wanted me but I always felt like maybe she didn't want to face me for some reason and I couldn't understand that.' Cass had also called Sharon when she had been scheduled to host Carol Burnett's show for a few weeks over the summer. Although by this time Cass's address book read like a *Who's Who* of the music industry and Hollywood, tellingly, she had looked towards her teenage friend for support, perhaps trying to recreate the relative innocence of her adolescent years. 'I want you to be on with me,' she told her. 'What am *I* gonna do on there?' asked Sharon. 'What we *always* did,' Cass replied. 'You were so funny. You were great. We'll just do skits like when we were kids. It's gonna be great.' Sharon began preparing for the appearance but nothing came of the plan.

At this point in 1974 Cass had appeared on countless TV shows but she was still clearly nervous and anxious at the prospect of having to carry a high-profile TV show alone and, similarly, when she had been asked on the *Tonight Show* some months earlier, she had likewise insisted that Leon Bing appear with her and this had indeed happened.

She would turn to Sharon, however, when she was at her lowest. 'She called when I had moved to Massachusetts,' remembers Sharon, 'and she was really bummed-out and not in great shape and I said, "Why don't you come up and stay with me, just hide away here and just stay with me for a while, relax a little bit?" And she said, "I can't. Everybody knows me. There's no place that I can go." She just didn't see that as a possibility at all. She was too far away from normal life.'

Cass did indeed feel that there was nowhere she could go and felt trapped by her fame. Her celebrity meant that she was instantly recognisable wherever she went and the public were often notoriously immune to her need for privacy; on one occasion a fan had even approached her for an autograph whilst she had been seriously sick in a restaurant.

Cass was therefore clearly reaching out to Sharon, just as she had done to Allan Pollock, Marc Strange and others, and, at some level, she must have realised that what she really needed to do was to step off the showbiz treadmill, take some extended time away from her day-to-day life and distance herself from its more disruptive elements. She needed to not only stop being Mama Cass, but to also stop being Cass Elliot, and instead spend time finding Ellen Cohen. Cass needed to get away, whether it was to Massachusetts or somewhere else, so long as it was far away from the party scenes of LA, New York or London, and she needed to go there for quite some time. As someone who had first been given prescription drugs as a teenager, Cass had now had over fifteen years of daily drug use and would have needed months if not years to fully acclimatise to a non-drug-taking life. But in order to do that, she would also have needed to wean herself off the equally powerful addiction to her own celebrity. But this was perhaps the hardest task of all, because while she bemoaned the lack of privacy which her stardom entailed, with the exception of Owen, her celebrity seemed like her greatest achievement. Whilst several of her friends had bailed out of the maelstrom that was LA in the early seventies, with the exception of Bob Dylan, very few people in her position had had the strength to willingly stand back from the spotlight and risk halting their careers for any considerable time.

Regardless of how low she was feeling, Cass generally managed to convince most around her that she was still feeling buoyant and embracing a cleaner-living lifestyle. There were plans to record another studio album over the next year, but in the meantime, Allan Carr had arranged for her to take the *Don't Call Me Mama* show on tour to England. Cass's British dates would kick off with two weeks at the world-famous London Palladium, arguably the grandest and most old-time showbiz venue in the country. Cass would have the opportunity not just to spend time in the city she loved, but also to perform there for the first time, and to do so on her own terms. She would be the headlining act, not as the Mamas and the Papas, not as Mama Cass, but as Cass Elliot, and this would be her show.

Musical director Marvin Laird and choreographer Walter Painter would both accompany her to London, but Allan Carr also realised that she would need someone to act as tour manager and to this end hired a sometime musician, actor and wannabe scriptwriter by the name of George Caldwell. It was a decision which would have major repercussions for Cass.

26

'Big-time showbiz'

George Caldwell was exactly Cass's type. Half Native American and half German, the thirty-five-year-old Caldwell was tall, dark, lanky and good-looking in a jean-clad, rugged Californian kind of way and usually managed to attract the attention of every woman in the room. He was also assertive and had an air of capability and control. Anyone who knew Cass could almost have singled him out as her type.

Caldwell began his new role handling Cass's last few American dates and, within weeks of meeting her, he was not only her tour manager, but her boyfriend. 'George was just suddenly there,' remembers Marvin Laird, 'and then the next thing I knew Cass and George were a romantic item. Walter and I were thrilled because Cass being that happy meant the performance was going to be real good!' Later it would be discovered that this was something which had similarly occurred to Allan Carr.

There was little time for Caldwell to meet many of Cass's friends before they left for England, but as had been the case with Donald and most of her earlier boyfriends, nobody was impressed. She took him to meet Leon Bing and although it was only a brief meeting, Bing found him obsequious and over-attentive, rushing to light Cass's cigarette before it had even touched her lips. As she puts it, 'Worse than Donald.' Cass, however, seemed genuinely happy and was consequently disappointed at her friend's disapproval. 'When we went into my bedroom,' Leon remembers, 'she said, "You're pulling the same thing. You don't like *anyone*." "I just want you to be careful," I said, but Cass came back with "I was nothing but supportive when you met Mervyn," and blah blah blah. It was just one of those girl conversations.'

Leah's impression of Caldwell was no more favourable than Bing's.

'There was something about his body language and his features,' she says. 'He just seemed real different from anybody that Cass usually hung out around. He also had this macho thing which I think she really *liked*. Even when she thought it was stupid, you know? She was just a sucker for that kind of thing. But that wasn't why I didn't like him. In all fairness to George he never did anything to me – it was just a vibe I got.'

By the time Cass was due to leave for London, she herself had become disillusioned with Caldwell and was loath for him to accompany her on the trip. She was also riled by the realisation that if he came to England he would make more money from the tour than she would herself, as the expense of taking a choreographer, musical director and two dancers to London and providing accommodation throughout the tour meant that Cass had had to borrow money in unsecured personal loans in order to do so. It was not an entirely uncommon situation; in the days before global merchandising deals made touring more profitable, many artists made a financial loss on tour in the hope that the resultant increase in album sales would recompense the investment. But none of this made Cass any happier about the idea of Caldwell coming on tour.

The fact that he had been booked by Carr as tour manager made the situation difficult. For all the robustness of Cass's professional persona, when it came to standing up for herself her resolve would often crumble. 'It seemed to me that she was trying to ease George out of her life,' says Leah, 'because Cass would never *ever* throw anybody out or say, "I'm breaking up." She would just try, and maybe George was a little scary for her and she didn't *wanna* say, "Get out."'

Given that this was Cass's tour, it seems strange that she would not have been in a position to dictate who would or would not be her tour manager. Although she had put her faith in Carr to guide her career forward, she had often disagreed with him over various issues, but in this instance, Carr seems to have won the argument and Cass felt powerless to change the situation.

As ever, she managed to put her best, jovial face on the situation and shortly before she left for London, she went East to upstate New York and visited John Simon who had produced her *Dream a Little Dream of Me* album, and was now married to her old friend from the Shadows, Caroline Cox. The Simons had established the commune-style Lookout Farm, and over the days Cass happened to be there

Simon threw a party in memory of Duke Ellington who had just died. Some of the Simons' friends and neighbours had brought their teenage children along with their musical instruments and so Simon quickly arranged Ellington's 'Mood Indigo' for three horns and Cass, so that she sang lead, while the teenagers on clarinet, trumpet and saxophone played the harmony parts underneath. The party carried on for several days and Cass seemed to be having as much fun as everyone else.

She was pleased to see her old friends and enjoyed the party, but she also had another reason to be happy. Cass had gone to Lookout Farm with Pic Dawson, and whether they were together as friends or lovers, in the light of the recent complications with George Caldwell, Cass would certainly have been glad to be with someone she was close to, regardless of anything that had happened in the past.

To most people who saw her in the weeks before she left for London, she appeared genuinely excited at the prospect of playing the Palladium and had never seemed happier. Nurit Wilde visited her at Woodrow Wilson shortly before she left. 'I just remember how *happy* she was,' remembers Wilde. 'She was just thrilled. They'd been rehearsing and she said that she was going to have dancers behind her, it was gonna be a *show*. And she was so *sweet* that day. Cass could be very cutting – if you got on her *wrong* side, because she was so verbal and so *clever*, she could just cut you to shreds, but she just was so sweet and *so* happy.'

Marvin Laird similarly remembers Cass's positive mood prior to leaving. 'She was *very* excited about it. Even though she was nervous, she felt that there was *everything* for her to gain because it was a place where they had not seen her on her own but they had a great feeling for her based on her Mamas and Papas songs. Also she thought that being in a place that served tea and crumpets everyday was just going to be "swell!".' he says in faux English accent. 'Much more fun than Vegas! I had also worked there many times before that and I had been building up to her what *I* knew about English audiences. I said, "They are gonna *love you*," so she was looking forward to it.'

However optimistic Cass may have appeared to Laird and others, she was also understandably nervous at the rather daunting prospect of headlining at the Palladium. More so than she had perhaps allowed people to know. She had successfully carried the show at a string of venues across America, including the Flamingo in Las Vegas, but none were quite as prestigious, as famous, or as large for that matter, as London's two-thousand capacity Palladium. The Palladium was unquestionably 'showbiz' in a way that the stadia and large arenas she had played with the Mamas and the Papas were not. Built in neoclassical, white stucco grandeur in the centre of London's West End, the Palladium was the epitome of show business glitz in its original top-hat-and-tails, sequin-sparkling form. This was where Frank Sinatra, Sammy Davis Jnr and Liberace had played, and Cass's show was to be followed by Debbie Reynolds.

The closest equivalent Cass had played had been Carnegie Hall in New York with the Mamas and the Papas, and although she had triumphed there, she had not had to play the show alone. Cass was also apprehensive about how the British audiences would react to her decidedly un-rock-'n'-roll-style show. 'The big problem is getting people to accept me doing other things,' she later told the *Daily Mirror*. 'When they see me on stage or on the box they're gonna think I'm gonna burst into "California Dreamin'" or some other song.'

In addition to these concerns, the fact that London was also Cass's second home meant the pressure to succeed was immense. Cass needed something to control her nerves and even today, let alone at that point in the seventies, many doctors would still prescribe some sort of tranquillising medication. In 1974 this would have been a relatively straightforward solution, but Cass seems to have been keen to cover herself for all eventualities. Possibly fearful that her nerves would simply overwhelm her, and also perhaps motivated by her recent encounter with Pic Dawson, Cass approached her old London flatmate and friend Stephen Sanders. 'She was leaving for London,' remembers Sanders, 'and she asked me where she could get some Quaaludes, which kind of made me nervous,' he says sombrely. 'I gave her a few before she left – three, so that she could sleep on the aeroplane, which obviously was not the *exact* reason she wanted them I realised after. She also asked me where she could score some heroin in London and I said I really wouldn't know, 'cause I *didn't* know.'

Cass was close enough to Sanders to have confided in him had she been in real distress, but at the time of her departure, apart from her drug requests, there were no other signs of anxiety. She was either keen to keep up the appearance – to herself as much as everyone else – of optimism, or she was genuinely riding on an albeit paper-thin wave of excitement. 'She seemed very optimistic about her life,' Sanders recalls, 'and everything was going OK. I had no detection of her being despondent or depressed or anything else like that.'

Cass had spent her life masking her true feelings and the contradiction between what she had asked of Sanders and the way she had appeared both to him and so many others was indicative of the growing gulf between her public and private persona.

Having arranged for Owen to stay with her mother Bess, on 10 July 1974 Cass arrived in London. She was met at the airport by RCA's Head of Artist Liaison, Barry Bethell, whose job it was to look after her while she was in England and Bethell soon joined the ever-swelling legions of people who felt that they were Cass's friend and confidant. 'Before we even got back from the airport,' remembers Bethell, 'you felt as though you'd known her for years. It was somebody you could confide in and you'd talk to. It was very difficult not to become friends with her. She *wanted* you to be her friend.'

Another friend of Cass's, Harry Nilsson, had suggested that while she was in London, she stay in the luxurious six-room apartment he kept at Curzon Place in Mayfair, and arranged with Keith Moon – who was currently living there – that he would temporarily move out. The apartment was perfectly situated near Hyde Park in London's West End, and once you had entered the grand Victorian building and made your way up to the fourth floor through the iron folding gates of its old-fashioned lift, you reached room after room decorated in the art deco-inspired chrome and mirrors style of the day. It was also very rock 'n' roll with plush, expansive white sofas and royal-blue tiles and mirrors in the bathroom. Slightly less rock 'n' roll but rather charming nevertheless was the small balcony complete with pot plants and window boxes looking across to the narrow Georgian streets of Shepherd Market nearby.

Cass had spent so much time in London over recent years that she was firmly ensconced in the social scene and had almost as wide an array of London-based friends as she did in Los Angeles. Composer Lionel Bart was a particularly close friend and the two of them would spend hours on the phone commiserating with tales of each other's romantic disasters. 'Lionel Bart *loved* her,' remembers Barry Bethell, 'and they were very, very good telephone friends. They were sympathetic towards each other – he would pour his heart out to her and she'd pour her heart out to him and nobody would get anywhere, but they both felt better because of it.'

Cass also made a point of helping friends and acquaintances of every description. 'She was always wanting to do favours for people,' continues Bethell. 'If anybody was in trouble, she seemed to be more of a mother figure to some of them than anything else, and she never seemed to forget people from previous times when she was over. She always asked me to arrange theatre tickets for people and things like that. "Oh they'd *love* to go and see this. I'll give them a call – you arrange the tickets," – that sort of thing.' Despite having a major performance to contend with, when Bethell's wife Barbara went into hospital to have their first child, Cass still found time to send her an impossibly vast basket of fruit and flowers from Harrods.

Cass seemed radiant. 'I'm in big-time showbiz!' she kept saying, telling people how excited she was to be performing at the Palladium, and almost without exception everyone got the impression that Cass was not only happy but that she seemed to have embraced a clean-living, healthy lifestyle. 'The good thing about Cass,' says Marvin Laird, 'was that she was coming out of that period of her life where she felt like she had to rely on something out*side* of herself to get through the day. When we played the Palladium, she really did love George.'

Despite the earlier friction between them in America, by the time Cass was in London, she once again seemed happy with George Caldwell, and if she wasn't she at least seemed determined to convince everyone, not least herself, that she was. Two days after arriving in London, she was invited onto BBC Radio 1 to choose her 'top twelve' songs. One of the tracks she chose was the Stylistics' then current hit 'You Make Me Feel Brand New', which she told the BBC's Brian Matthew was her favourite song of the moment. 'I really relate to it,' she explained, 'because the past six or seven months in my life, since I've been back on the road doing cabaret . . . I have a very nice friend, [so] I *do* feel the way this song is.'

Cass's evident contentment with Caldwell seemed to confirm in people's minds that her life had unquestionably changed for the better. 'She was in *love* with him,' says Laird, 'and I don't think he was in love with her but he really treated her well and she seemed happier than she'd ever been. And she wasn't using drugs – I *think* she wasn't using drugs; she *might* have been but not noticeably and certainly not like she had in the old days. She *felt* for the first time that she was being validated for being who she was and that people loved what she did. It was OK for her to be Cass Elliot, not Mama Cass. She really was having a great resurgence of her own positive energy at that time and it wasn't about drugs or anything like that.'

Just as she had been in the past, Cass was clearly in love with being in love. Choreographer Walter Painter remembers seeing her with Caldwell picnicking by the Albert Memorial in Hyde Park. 'I have an image in my mind of the two of them sitting on a blanket under the statue having wine and sandwiches. They were in *love*, I guess,' says Painter. 'They had a very big affinity with Queen Victoria and Prince Albert. They sort of saw themselves as those two, not that anybody felt that they were royalty, but they would often go and visit Prince Albert's statue and just hang. They took delight in telling me the story of that relationship and I think they were smitten with the tragedy of it, that Albert died very young and that she loved him dearly to the point where she built the Albert Memorial and they named the Albert Hall and all of that. It was sort of – if something ever happened to us, I would do that for you. That kind of thing.'

For all this 'making believe' that they loved each other, Cass was more than bright enough to realise that Caldwell's feelings were perhaps somewhat less heartfelt than her own. Her impending opening at the Palladium meant that she was the focus of widespread media attention and was featured in virtually every major British newspaper or magazine. Her relationship with Caldwell was almost inevitably therefore the subject of scrutiny as she had been photographed with him on the town. The press were eager to know if Caldwell might become Husband Number Three, particularly as Cass, having technically been married twice, was classed alongside Elizabeth Taylor in the multi-marriage stakes. Her response to the press's speculation contained more than a grain of truth, however. 'I love George more than I've ever loved any other man ever,' she told the *Evening News*, 'but it doesn't mean either of us feel the need to marry one another. At the moment, I love him. I respect him. He respects what I do. But it's not a binding contract. I'm happy as I am. Marriage to me means being trapped. I don't think it is necessary.' Cass was in fact telling the press much more than they perhaps realised. She said she loved and respected George, but that he, in return, respected – rather than loved – not her, but what she did.

Since arriving in London, Caldwell's role had evolved, and while he was billed in the Palladium programme as production manager, he was generally perceived as Cass's tour manager, boyfriend, protector and minder; if you wanted to get near Cass, you generally had to get past Caldwell first. She clearly enjoyed the feeling that she was being looked after and found George's controlling stance reassuring and protective. 'If there was anything she needed,' says Painter, 'the first words out of her mouth were, "Where's George?" She wanted to know where he *was*. He wanted to know where *she* was. They were just . . . connected somehow.'

Marvin Laird, meanwhile, who spent more time around the couple (Painter went back to America shortly after the opening night), remembers their relationship as being more complex. 'He was very supportive of Cass,' remembers Laird, 'and very much one to compliment her and to say, "That sounded really great," or something that was going to buck her up – that was one of his instructions, but it was always a supportive feeling that I got. When we would go out after the show or after rehearsal he always deferred to her. It was not really a kind of holding the chair relationship but he was a gentleman with her, and it didn't seem like it was just star fucking. It really didn't. It was just a very deferential supportive thing that he presented to her and I felt that he was a good influence on her.'

But in spite of Caldwell's support, as the opening night approached, Cass's nerves began to seep through. The throat problems, which had arisen virtually every time she was due to play an important show, surfaced once again, and Cass was prescribed tranquillisers by her private GP, Dr Anthony Greenburgh, to alleviate her nerves and help her sleep. She was also treated by a throat specialist – Dr Scott-Brown – who advised her to rest her voice as much as possible. This was obviously difficult with rehearsals necessary for a major two-week engagement, performing two shows per night, but Cass was clearly in a very different state of mind to her Las Vegas debut, and in spite of her nerves, seemed happy and confident. This time Cass appeared to be genuinely attempting to conserve her voice. Rather than partying every night, she often stayed in the flat, crocheting or reading her book – Solzhenitsyn's *Gulag Archipelago*.

After a few final rehearsals, on 15 July Cass opened at the Palladium. Or at least she did in the second half of the evening. The Palladium was still essentially a variety theatre and it was about as far removed as was possible from the sex and sweat of rock 'n' roll. The show opened with the unironically named 20th Century Steel Band – a bunch of Jamaican musicians who did what their name suggested and played everything from jazz to waltzes on their steel drums. They were followed by the terminally unhip pop rockers Paper Lace, who had inexcusably scored recent hits with 'Billy Don't Be a Hero' and 'The Night Chicago Died'. Next on the bill was a Mario Lanza-style tenor by the name of Joey Loren followed by Irish comedian Tony Cawley, while European ventriloquist George Schlick closed the opening half of the bill.

If there was any doubt in the audience's mind as to what kind of show this was to be, the opening of Cass's own act made it quite clear, and it laid on the showbiz dazzle with several trowels. As the orchestra played the final bars of the overture, a trapdoor opened from below the stage and Cass rose up, Phoenix-like, wearing a diamante-studded denim dress and white knee socks, with a matching denim parasol grandly propped over her shoulder. 'If this is big-time showbiz,' commented the *Observer*, 'she seems to say, let's have the lot. Forests of microphones appear, lights flash all over the place, the stage goes up and down and the orchestra advances across like Armageddon.'

The script, meanwhile, was no less showbiz. Once Cass had chatted with the audience, her two male dancers came on and introduced themselves: 'My name is Joseph Croyle,' sang Joe. 'That's right, it's *Joseph* Croyle – imagine how surprised and pleased my dad was, when the doc came out of the maternity ward to say, "Mr Croyle, it ain't a goyle!" Scott Salmon, the other dancer, then sang: 'My name is Scott Salmon, just like the fish you used to eat Fridays – Scott *Salmon*, I've come a long way, mammy, since you changed my didays!' Perhaps you had to be there.

But whilst elements of the script may not have pushed too hard at the boundaries of contemporary comedy, Cass's own comic talents and ability to handle an audience seemed to more than compensate. 'It was a very *intimate* thing that she created onstage,' remembers Marvin Laird, 'some of it really funny because she just had a wicked sense of humour, but the intimacy that she created, even in a big place like the Palladium, was quite remarkable because she let the audience in. Although she had a pretty voice and a pretty *face*, I think she was disarming to her audiences because they were not expecting to have this nice feeling like they were sitting with their favourite cousin Suzy just having a nice kind of chat. It was not an arty stage act that we did for her but what we tried to have come across was this humanity that *was Cass* and what a real person she was – the Yiddish word is '*haimishe*' [meaning 'homely'] – what a *haimishe* girl she was. A real family girl who'd give the odd recipe out during the show, talking about cooking lunch for her daughter, so she'd take the time onstage to say, "Well, if you really want, this is *my* recipe for a good brisket." That sort of thing and it was all very casual and not planned.

'She'd also begun to develop a real sense of confidence with how she comported herself onstage,' continues Laird, 'and she felt free enough to take off her shoes and just be herself and *kibbitz* [engage] with the audience. She felt *welcomed* onstage so it was remarkable to see her come from that frightened place that I saw her in when we first did Vegas to where she was when we played London, in a very small amount of time.'

In the same way that the audience may have felt like they were sitting with their favourite cousin Suzy, Cass talked to them as if they were indeed a favourite cousin of hers. During the first night show, she spent time telling them of her humiliation at the hands of the British police back in 1967 when she had been arrested at Southampton and seemed at pains to explain her innocence, clearly concerned that her fans might consider her a thief or criminal of some kind. She also wanted them to know how much her life had changed over the last few years.

It was as though she saw her fans as a primary source of love, and fearful that she might risk their disapproval and the withdrawal of their affection, was eager to present herself in the best possible light. 'She'd make the odd casual reference to, "Oh that was back when I didn't even know what my name was!"' recalls Laird, 'or, "I was too stoned to remember that," or whatever and it was all good-natured and self-deprecating but from a really positive point of view. It was not bemoaning the fact that she had trashed her life up a bit,' he laughs.

The audience was full of Cass's London friends, the press and specially invited fans. Cass had a list of twenty of her most devoted English fans, and whenever she came to London she made a point of writing to them in advance and letting them know her performance dates. This time she personally invited them to her show as her guests; the front two rows were reserved for press, but the next two rows were for her fans.

Everyone seemed to adore the show and Cass received a standing ovation at the end of the night. Afterwards, Cass charmed the gaggle of fans huddling by the stage door, chatting to them and signing autographs before heading off in RCA's Rolls-Royce to Crockford's – a smart private casino in Curzon Street, very close to Harry Nilsson's apartment. Over dinner with Caldwell, Painter, Laird and the dancers, Cass seemed genuinely triumphant, both with the show and in Caldwell's company. After dinner they all went on to Tramp and Cass took to the floor with both George and dancer Joe Croyle. When Tramp finally closed several hours later, Cass gathered the group up, which had by this time expanded to include Ann Margaret, Britt Ekland, Sammy Davis Junior, Marianne Faithfull, Ryan O'Neal, David Hemmings and his wife, actress Gayle Hunnicut, Lionel Bart and Harry Nilsson and invited everyone back to Curzon Place to continue the party.

The next day, most of the press reviews were favourable. Despite being out of step with current musical trends, Cass's London dates were still considered a major event. The Mamas and Papas had always been seen as a seminal group in Britain and Cass still had a large residual fan base and audience. The show was a hit and Cass's career now seemed to be taking a new, upward turn. 'There was a *lot* of quote unquote 'contacts', as we say in Hollywood,' remembers Painter, 'meaning a lot of talks about projects, you know? Lots became possible because of the dates she played. I had been around that kind of sizzle before, and the sizzle was *definitely* there.'

Cass was due to record both an appearance on Twiggy's TV show as well as her own BBC TV special, but this was unfortunately cancelled due to a production assistant's strike. The regional tour was, however, still very much on schedule and as news of Cass's Palladium success started to edge its way across the Atlantic, Allan Carr started to receive new offers of film scripts and TV shows for Cass at home in America. Cass had been keen to act for some time and had been sent numerous roles since she had appeared in *Pufnstuf*, but they invariably cast her as what she called 'the girl with the glandular problem in the corner' and she had consequently turned them down. It seemed that a suitable part might now finally have arrived though. Cass had been sent a script with a part she liked and was just waiting to hear whether she would be given the role. 'This one is the part of a *real* person and I'm looking forward to it,' she said. 'I'll know before I leave England.'

Cass seemed excited about all these possibilities. She had asked her London PA Dot McLeod to come back to LA with her after the tour and work for her full-time, and when the London dates were finished, she was planning a short trip to Paris with her English music journalist friend Miranda Ward. She also seemed to be keeping her voice problems at bay with the help of a throat spray called Pig Melba, which Dr Scott-Brown had prescribed as well as her own remedies: orange juice and brandy, both of which she would swig between numbers either from a bottle on the piano or from her booth in the wings of the Palladium.

But aside from these complaints, physically Cass appeared to be healthier than ever. Although she had wanted to have the recently introduced stomach bypass operation (which Allan Carr had recently had to great success), she had been told this would not be possible as she had an ulcer, but she had nevertheless shed over six stone. She was clearly proud of her achievement and regaled journalists with her expertise on vitamins, informing them that part of her success was due to a new diet she had discovered which involved cutting out white foods.

Some of the audience, however, noticed that there were moments when Cass seemed to find the show physically strenuous. 'Excuse me while I stand here and breathe,' she told them as she stepped back from the microphone. This was not necessarily unusual for any performer required to sing and dance her way through a seventy-minute act, but Cass's audience banter also displayed a growing awareness of her health. 'When you get to my age, nasty words like heart attack crop up,' she told them. 'It's really not a very nice prospect so you've got to do something to keep your weight down.' A few days later she told the *Daily Express* that she had been having recurring premonitions of her death.

As the two weeks at the Palladium continued, audiences began to dwindle and by the end of the run, Cass was often playing to a less than full house. By today's standards, selling out two shows a night at a two-thousand capacity, central London venue for two weeks would be a hard task for all but the most global of stars, but the booking was standard at the time. Although she didn't show it, Cass was understandably embarrassed but fortunately, as the opening had been so well attended and well received, most people were unaware of the situation.

Her *Don't Call Me Mama Anymore* album, meanwhile, was not faring too well in the British charts. Despite a lavish launch reception at the roof-garden penthouse suite of RCA's head office in Curzon Street, the fact that the album contained no clear hits or particularly obvious radio options made it difficult to promote. The musical climate was no easier in Britain than it had been in America. Progressive rock was making its stealthy Neanderthal advance on the nation's record collections and suddenly Yes, Genesis and Emerson, Lake and Palmer were capturing the album charts, while the glam-rock sounds of Sweet, Mud, Slade and Suzy Quatro dominated the singles. Mainstream hits were still possible: Charles Aznavour had made the Top Ten with 'She' that month, and Stephanie de Sykes and Leo Sayer had both also recently had Top Twenty hits, despite a serious dearth of credibility in both cases, so it was not impossible. Cass just needed the right material, and realised this herself.

The album had received a caustic review in *Melody Maker* (as had the Palladium show), and in response she had telephoned journalist Kit Galer to tell him she absolutely agreed. 'It's awful,' she said. 'It so turned me off I haven't recorded anything for a year because of it.' Cass may indeed have become disillusioned with some of the material, but this was certainly not the sole reason for the lack of a follow-up, as her touring schedule alone would have made this impossible. If Cass genuinely felt disheartened about her material, however, there was no sign of it during her shows and this simply highlighted yet again the discrepancy between the way she appeared and the way she genuinely felt.

Her dieting was another case in point and it seemed to have similarly come to a halt. While telling the world's press about her non-white food diet, the shopping list she gave to PA Dot McLeod included double cream, single cream, soured cream, white sugar and white bread. Cass, like millions of dieters before her and since, clearly found it easier to retain the necessary resolve when she was feeling happy, but since her opening night, her mood had changed. 'I'm very tense and can't sleep,' Cass wrote in a note to Dot, 'but I'm trying to keep quiet. Please ask [Dr Scott-Brown] for the tranquilisers he spoke to me about . . . Also get new bottle of brandy for tonite [sic]. Love Cass.'

George Caldwell had, meanwhile, maintained his attentiveness to Cass throughout the first part of her Palladium run, but once the show seemed to be running smoothly, he was free to think about his own musical ambitions. He would later go on to play drums and briefly act as producer for British blues man Alexis Korner, but whilst with Cass, he lost no time in putting Dot McLeod to work transcribing Eagles song lyrics so that he could sing them, possibly with a view to working with his friend Lowell George. Caldwell's aspirations also extended to scriptwriting and he similarly spent time dictating two full-length science fiction-style film scripts to Dot, presumably in the hope that via Cass's extensive Hollywood contacts, they might somehow get commissioned.

There were also various rumours about Caldwell's fidelity to Cass, although there's no evidence to prove their validity. One evening when Caldwell had been due to accompany Cass to dinner with singer Sandy Denny, mutual friend Miranda Ward and their respective boyfriends, he called Cass with an excuse at the last minute. Coincidentally both Denny's and Ward's boyfriends similarly seemed to find themselves unavailable and the three women spent the evening lamenting the irony of their shared situation.

Caldwell generally seems to have taken the relationship rather less seriously than Cass. As dancer Joe Croyle remembers: 'People were saying that they were gonna get married or engaged or something, and he just kind of laughed, you know? Like, "Ha!"' he snorts dismissively. 'He'd say, "That's just in the papers," and, 'We're friends," or something. It wasn't like it was a big deal.'

By the end of the Palladium run, Caldwell was sleeping in a separate room at the flat and his waning attention reinforced Cass's earlier anxieties. 'I don't know if people like me for *me* or for what I can get them or do for them,' she told Miranda Ward. 'You know if somebody fancies you, it's because you're *fanciable*.' For all her professional success, Cass's sense of self-worth had clearly plunged once again and she did not believe she might be considered genuinely desirable in her own right. 'What was *un*said and unspoken,' remembers Ward, 'was, "If they fancy me, you've got to work out why. Because I'm not fanciable." And that used to annoy me because most people *didn't* see her as fat.'

Cass had always doubted the depth of Caldwell's feelings for her but just before the final show she heard something that seemed to indicate things might be worse than she had imagined.

Cass would often call friends in California when she arrived home after the shows as the eight-hour time difference meant that whilst it was the early hours of the morning in London, it was still only mid-evening in Los Angeles. She had called Michelle Phillips to tell her how thrilled she had been after the opening night, but she now called Donald von Wiedenman.

'I *think* that Allan Carr is paying George to be my boyfriend,' she told him.

'What do you mean?' he asked.

'Well, I think he hired him as my road manager and told him to keep me happy and make me fall in love with him.'

'Why would you think that?' asked Donald.

'I just overheard a conversation between Allan and someone,' she told him. 'I just feel *so* manipulated. I just wanna *die*.'

Von Wiedenman knew from earlier conversations with Cass that she had not been getting along well with Carr. He would frequently make jibes about the fact that since his own stomach bypass operation he could now eat freely without gaining weight whilst discouraging her from losing any herself, saying it would harm her career as she would no longer be recognizable as 'Mama' Cass. Their relationship had become increasingly strained and Cass's claim therefore did not come as a great surprise. Three decades on, it is virtually impossible to establish the facts as Carr is no longer alive to comment and, despite extensive attempts to track him down, George Caldwell proved untraceable. At the time, despite what he knew about Carr, Donald was uncertain whether there was any truth to the idea and knowing that she still had one final performance left, he did his best to reassure her. 'Just remember,' he told her, 'you don't know *anything* for sure and tomorrow's your last night, so go out there and knock 'em dead.'

When Cass played her final Palladium show on Saturday 27 July there was a full house and it seemed like the audience would never stop cheering. Before she left the theatre for the last time, Cass left a message in lipstick on the dressing-room mirror for her friend Debbie Reynolds who was due to follow her: 'Dear Debbie,' she wrote, 'if they are half as nice to you as they were to me, you will have a great time. Love Cass.'

Cass was fêted across London as a major success. After the show she went to Mick Jagger's thirty-second birthday party in Chelsea. She was thrilled to have been invited and chatted with Rod Stewart, Pete Townshend and other friends until well into Sunday morning when she drifted on to a brunch which singer Georgia Brown had thrown in her honour.

By this time, guests were beginning to notice her blowing her nose and coughing repeatedly. Her voice sounded hoarse and she appeared to be having trouble breathing. She was obviously not well, but she seemed in good spirits and Brown later commented that Cass had been feeling 'very happy'. She was only drinking lightly, but by late afternoon Cass was certainly ready to head back to Curzon Place. She had, after all, performed not one but two shows the previous day and had been partying solidly ever since. She would have been without sleep for at least twenty-four hours by this time, but on Sunday evening another friend, American TV writer Jack Martin, had arranged a cocktail party in her honour and it would have been impolite not to attend. Cass asked Allan Carr how long etiquette required her to stay and put in as brief an appearance as possible before making her excuses. She kissed Martin goodbye, promised to see him soon and told him she'd had a marvellous time at the party. She said she'd never been happier in her life.

When she arrived back to Curzon Place, Joe Croyle was there as his hotel had been overbooked and Cass had invited him to stay at the flat. They chatted for a while and she told Croyle about Jagger's party. She said she hadn't wanted to leave because there had been so many friends there. She seemed contented but said that as she was tired she was going to relax and play her guitar a little before settling into the large king-size bed. It was little surprise she was tired. She may only have been thirty-two years old but playing two shows at the London Palladium before partying so extensively would have been strenuous even for someone a decade younger.

In the morning, as it was Monday, Dot McLeod arrived ready for work, followed by George Caldwell. He wanted to begin making arrangements for the regional tour, but as Cass was asleep, he, McLeod and Croyle sat around watching cricket on TV. Without Cass, there was little they could start doing. 'It was just a waiting sort of a day,' remembers Dot McLeod (now Hendler). 'We weren't really doing anything, because the focus of all of our lives was sleeping, so we were just being quiet.' Nobody questioned Cass's need to sleep as it seemed entirely understandable in the light of her performances over the weekend and her heavy party schedule subsequently. 'Of course she slept during the day,' continues Dot, 'as you *would* if you were doing a 6.15 show and an 8.45, but this was like the sleep you would have after three days of parties and it seemed understandable to me in *that* sense.'

Shortly before midday Dougal Butler, Keith Moon's PA, came by the flat needing to pick up some clothes of Moon's. Caldwell told him Cass was sleeping but that he should go straight into the bedroom nevertheless and get what he needed. Butler walked into the room, saw Cass lying on her side and went straight to the built-in wardrobes behind the bed. He took Moon's clothes and left, without looking back at Cass's face.

By mid afternoon, Cass was still not awake and Caldwell, rather than going in himself, suggested Dot went in to wake her. This amount of sleep seemed excessive even for Cass and, as it was now mid-afternoon, there were things that needed to be done. Dot went into the room and saw Cass still lying unclothed on the bed. 'I'd seen her naked every night during changes for the show,' remembers Dot, 'but I had a strange feeling and I felt very uncomfortable and I realised that something was awfully wrong. There was definitely something in the room and when I touched her, she was cold.'

Dot came back out and told Caldwell and Croyle that something was clearly not right. 'She looks really *funny*,' she told them. 'She's got some stuff coming out of her mouth and looks kind of odd.' 'Well she's either asleep or she's dead,' Caldwell replied blankly, before going into the bedroom to check himself.

When he emerged from the room, he was, as Croyle remembers, 'freaked out'. 'We have a problem, you know?' Caldwell told the others, 'because Cass is dead.'

In the last few hours of her life, having completed the Palladium run, Cass had time to think back over the events of the last few weeks and months. As she had done so often before, she thought of

Denny, and the next day when she was found, Dot also discovered a page of handwritten notes which Cass had left for her to type up. They were liner notes for Denny's new solo album: *Waiting for a Song*, which she had sung backing vocals on, along with Michelle, some months earlier in LA. The page was headed with the words: 'Please use verbatim'. They read as follows:

> Everybody says at one time or another 'oh so and so is a great friend of mine'. Sometimes they're exaggerating a bit and sometimes they're telling the truth. But if loving someone, knowing them for twelve years, singing with them for five or six years and sharing bad times and glorious ones, don't cover the ground of close friendship, the definition of friend escapes me.
>
> But enough about that. That's personal and has nothing to do with the very evident fact that Dennis Gerard Stephen Doherty has one of the great voices and finest musical tastes of our generation. Present company excepted of course.
>
> When I first heard the initial tracks I prostrated myself at his feet on Sunset Boulevard begging to be allowed to sing backgrounds. Another fan of 'The Demon' as we call him, a beautiful young girl by the name of Michelle Phillips also pleaded to be included. With typical Doherty reserve, he flung us into his car and whisked us straight away to the studio where he kept us under lock and key until we got it right. We did.
>
> Most important, he did.
>
> At last Denny's got an album that any exceptional artist would be proud of. And that's what he is – exceptional.
>
> I know most liner notes are supposed to tell the reader where the artist was born, how much he weighed, and whether he was singing from birth. But *I'm* writing this and I said what I wanted except for one thing – he's made a super album – listen and hear for yourself. It was a long time coming – but tell me what things aren't worth waiting for.

Cass had had to wait for most things she had ever wanted in her life, but the knowledge that they would come to her in the end had always spurred her on. At some level she had always known that Denny loved her, just as she had known since she was a teenager that she would be 'the most famous fat girl who ever lived'. She was indeed, but she was also much more.

27

Hollywood Memorial

In the wake of Cass's death an increasingly fantastical array of rumours began to circulate, ranging from a drugs overdose – at the more straightforward end – to assassination plots by the FBI. Thirty years on, people still harbour different theories, but what is certain is that she did not die choking.

Over the hours that followed, nobody was quite sure what to do and so George Caldwell called Allan Carr in Los Angeles for advice. Carr told him not to do anything or tell anyone what had happened, most particularly not the press. Carr couldn't have known the circumstances of Cass's death, but he would certainly have been aware of her earlier drug use and would have considered it as a possible factor. In the light of the relatively recent high-profile deaths of Jimi Hendrix, Jim Morrison and Janis Joplin, as well as Cass's friend Gram Parsons who had died a drugs-related death less than a year earlier, he would have been keen to avoid any scandal. In the early twenty-first century the idea of rock stars dying young in drug-related circumstances is still newsworthy, but no longer has the impact it had in the early seventies. Despite the succession of rock deaths and the ubiquity of drugs in celebrity circles at the time, the very idea of drug use was still considered more shocking by mainstream society. Carr would therefore have hoped, even after Cass's death, to protect her reputation and thereby his own interest by ensuring her records continued to sell.

Carr needed someone who would, if necessary, understand the delicacy of the situation, and with this in mind suggested Caldwell call her GP Dr Greenburgh, who was well-known on London's celebrity circuit as doctor to the stars. Before Greenburgh arrived, Caldwell removed anything that he felt might be seized upon by the police and sensationalised by the press. These included some Temazepam tranquillisers and half a bottle of liquid cocaine. By the time Greenburgh arrived, it was around six o'clock, and within half an hour the press seemed to have got hold of the news. Suddenly there were over a hundred journalists swarming around outside the building, desperate to get the story.

Greenburgh immediately offered a straightforward explanation for Cass's death. His first impression, he told the press, was that it appeared to have been a simple case of asphyxia. 'From what I saw when I got to the flat,' he told the *Daily Express*, 'she appeared to have been eating a ham sandwich and drinking Coca Cola while lying down – a very dangerous thing to do. This would be especially dangerous for someone like Cass who was overweight and who might be prone to having a heart attack. She seemed to have choked on the ham sandwich,' he continued, unwittingly giving rise to the myth which would still be in circulation more than three decades later. Clearly aware that some may have had theories of their own, he added: 'Drugs and drink were not part of her life . . . I gave her some drugs on the opening show two weeks ago, but that was only to help first-night nerves. I realise that there are innuendos in this sort of death about drink and drugs,' he conceded, 'especially drugs, but I have no reason to suspect that Cass was either on drugs, drinking too much or tried to commit suicide . . . She did not need drugs . . . She was so happy and full of life. She was in very good form, very stable and very healthy. A jolly sort of person.' He also added that she had had a chest X-ray in 1970 which indicated her heart was functioning well and was entirely normal.

What Greenburgh had presumably overlooked is the small but highly pertinent detail that the sandwich by Cass's bed had not in fact been touched (as recorded by Inspector Kenneth Humm once the police were called). But Greenburgh's comments were only his initial observations and whilst no doubt made with the best intentions, they could hardly be considered conclusive.

The following day, the Home Office's top pathologist Professor Keith Simpson reported that, having performed an hour-long autopsy, it appeared that Cass had not in fact died from natural causes. The autopsy details were not disclosed but Professor Simpson told the press that he would need to carry out further tests to determine the cause of death. In a further attempt to rule out any suggestions that her death was drug-related Dr Greenburgh then told the press that perhaps

Cass's death might have been caused by heart failure: 'She was a very big lady,' he told the *Daily Telegraph*, 'and I would not rule out the possibility of a heart attack.' Just in case anyone was still harbouring any other ideas, he reiterated, 'There was no reason to assume her death was due in any way to drugs or drink.'

A few days later, however, the results of the inquest were announced. In contrast to Professor Simpson's earlier findings, Coroner Gavin Thurston's verdict recorded that Cass's death was indeed from natural causes, stating on the death certificate that it was a result of 'fatty myocardial degeneration due to obesity'. Professor Simpson then explained to the *Times* that, as a result of her weight, she had, as Dr Greenburgh had suspected, had a heart attack because there was fatty degeneration of the heart muscle fibre. He said he had found nothing blocking her mouth or throat, and the fluid substance on her lips would have come from the lungs in a heart attack. He also added – again – that there was no trace of alcohol or drugs in her blood.

All death is, in some respect, caused by heart failure and Cass's weight could certainly have been a contributing factor. At the time of her death, despite having slimmed considerably the previous year, she still weighed sixteen stone – roughly twice the weight considered appropriate for a woman of her height. It was nevertheless unusual for excess weight to be a cause of death. When the coroner's verdict was announced, medical experts agreed that such an occurrence was highly uncommon. 'It is most unusual for a woman to die in her thirties of a heart attack caused by overweight,' commented Dr Malcolm Carruthers, a leading British heart expert. 'Many girls who weigh double what they should, live perfectly happily to a much greater age.'

Whilst there is no doubt that Professor Simpson's findings were accurate, the absence of any alcohol or drugs, prescription or otherwise, is surely inconclusive, given that within the previous twenty-four hours Cass had not only been seen drinking brandy during her Palladium show but had subsequently stayed out for a further fifteen hours without sleep. The likelihood of anyone, let alone someone of Cass's celebrity stature, attending a non-stop string of parties, including Mick Jagger's, in 1974 without partaking of drugs or alcohol seems implausible at best. Medical opinion, meanwhile, confirms that there are various reasons why any such substances may have remained undetected owing either to the nature of the tests conducted or a time delay between her death and the autopsy.

Cass had a long history of drug use, and despite what may have been her best intentions to remain drug free, the fact that she had asked Stephen Sanders not only for Quaaludes but also where to obtain heroin suggests that the idea of finding at least temporary escape was never too far from her mind. It seems highly unlikely, however, that if she looked to drugs that final evening that she would have seriously intended any dose to be fatal. Consciously, she probably had no wish to die, but she may also have reached a point where she was no longer too careful about living.

For all Cass's surface optimism and bonhomie in the weeks leading up to her death, she often felt less happy when she found herself alone. Even without her anxiety about the situation with Caldwell, the come-down after a two-week performance and a weekend of parties would have been considerable, but highs and lows were not new to Cass. 'The last time I remember seeing her in London,' remembers David Crosby, 'she seemed caught in that cycle of unhappiness and it was sort of manic. She would get *very* happy when she was partying or high or playing music, 'cause she was *immensely* good at it. When she was singing she was happy, because *there* she was the queen. She could sing like nobody's business and when she was doing that, she was elevated. But the party would end and then would come the wee hours of the morning and she'd be by herself and she did *not* like being by herself. That wasn't so good – alone at night, three o'clock in the morning . . . coming down, she'd get the blues *very* badly, I think. And it would always come back to how did she get saddled with weighing three hundred pounds? She wanted to be as pretty as Michelle. She wanted to be loved.'

Despite the official verdict that Cass had died from a naturally induced heart attack as a result of her weight, the evidence would suggest otherwise. When viewed together, her recurring depression and continued drug use, the discrepancies in the findings of the first and second post-mortem examinations, the implausibility of there being no drugs or alcohol in her body and Allan Carr's clear attempts to conceal evidence, all make it virtually impossible to imagine that this was not a drug-related death.

Within days of Cass's death, George Caldwell went to Wales with Miranda Ward to escape the media frenzy, leaving Joe Croyle to stay in the flat and deal with the aftermath. In the weeks and months that followed, despite numerous attempts by Cass's sister Leah and her family to contact Caldwell, he never returned their calls. Miranda Ward gave Caldwell Cass's address book, along with some other personal belongings, in the belief that he would pass them on to her family, but they, like Caldwell himself, were not seen again.

A few days after the inquest, Allan Carr arranged for Cass's body to be flown back to Los Angeles. The funeral was to be a Carr production rivalling the scale of Cass's Palladium shows and the invitation list featured almost every major, and minor, Hollywood player of the time. Even the choice of venue had its own, albeit tarnished, glamour. Situated next door to Paramount Studios, the Hollywood Memorial Cemetery was already the final home of some of Hollywood's most glamorous and notorious characters, including Rudolph Valentino, Tyrone Power and Bugsy Siegel.

On 3 August 1974 more than three hundred friends, colleagues, fans and photographers attempted to clamour their way into what was clearly the showbiz event of the month. But whilst some saw it as a 'love-in' for Cass, others were surprised to find themselves at a gathering more akin to a rock opening than a dignified cremation. 'It was a real zoo,' remembers Stephen Sanders. 'There were just millions of people and reporters and it was just a real media circus. I thought funerals should be somewhat solemn and this was not at all solemn, I can tell you. People were pushing back and forth! None of us could get in and I had to go in with John and Michelle to get near the whole thing.'

Every other guest seemed to be arriving in their own chauffeur-driven limousine, making a grand entrance. Some brought bodyguards who elbowed people aside, jostling through as if they were edging past a velvet rope at a club. Ryan O'Neal, Sammy Davis Jnr, Tuesday Weld and Dudley Moore sent telegrams. Peter Lawford arrived fashionably dressed in a prison-style striped suit, Sonny Bono sported a flowery, embroidered peasant shirt open to the waist, while other guests included Jack Nicholson, Carol Burnett and Helen Reddy, as well as of course, John, Michelle and Denny.

Then there was the scramble for seats as nobody had predicted the vast number of people who would attend. When the memorial chapel finally reached bursting point, those who could not get in sat on metal chairs on the lawn or just bustled around outside craning to get a good view.

Although Cass had not considered herself a practising Jew since her bat mitzvah as a teenager, the service was held according to Orthodox Jewish custom. Her mother Bess, Owen, Leah and her brother Joe were therefore separated from the crowds behind a curtain. Even there, however, they could not help but be aware of the chaos and at one point Joe had to rescue seven-year-old Owen from being trampled by the crowd.

The ceremony itself, meanwhile, was as traditional as possible. Cass lay in an open coffin and after mourners had filed past, a rabbi gave a simple eulogy, although he had never met Cass himself. He talked of her unique personality and her generosity of spirit, saying she had, 'A capacity and a willingness to give of her energy, of her time, of her finances. In fact,' he said, 'someone mentioned to me that she was known as an easy touch.' Finally, he read the lyrics to 'Make Your Own Kind of Music'. He said Cass had been 'a woman with music in her soul'.

As in life, nothing was straightforward about Cass's death. Leah knew that Cass had made a will but somehow it was never found, leading to confusion over the handling of her estate. Not even her burial was straightforward. After the cremation at the Hollywood Memorial Cemetery, Bess arranged for Cass's remains to be moved to the Baltimore Hebrew Congregation Cemetery where they were interred. But in 1991 she moved the ashes back to California to Mount Sinai Memorial Park in Los Angeles where they now remain. They are buried alongside a simple stone on which two musical notes bracket the simple inscription 'Ellen Naomi Cohen – Cass Elliot'.

Epilogue

Cass's death made headlines in almost every newspaper in Britain and was similarly covered in the American press. The news was unanimously greeted with shock, dismay and sadness, but the following week, the results of her inquest were obscured by President Nixon's resignation over the Watergate scandal. Cass's premature death now seemed symptomatic of the instability and turmoil which had been gradually enveloping America. Suddenly everything which had once seemed certain and dependable now appeared as transient as the weather. 'Everyone was traumatised by her death,' says Leah. 'I'm *still* traumatised by it. There was something so *shocking* and untimely about it. I really don't understand it to this day. It was also a real weird time in America and somehow Cass's death seemed to embody a lot of what was really crazy about that time.'

In spite of the chaos and confusion surrounding Cass's death, Owen's life at least regained some stability when Leah took her to live back on the East Coast with her and her husband, drummer Russ Kunkel, and their small son Nathaniel. Cass's loss was nevertheless felt no less profoundly by both her friends and family. 'Cass was a very special person to be loved by,' says Leah. 'When you talked to her, she would look right at you and it wouldn't matter how many people there were in the room, but you felt like you were getting her one hundred per cent, undivided attention, and if she asked questions, you felt like you wanted to *answer* them. You didn't feel like you were being cross-examined but that someone was genuinely interested in you. It was that sort of unconditional thing but I also think that I was really lucky to be her sister because I didn't have to earn that.'

All of Cass's close friends including John Sebastian, David Crosby, Graham Nash and Gary Burden, point out that three decades after her death, they still miss her. 'She's one of those people who never dies,' says Burden. 'She lives in everybody and I can think of her and I feel her presence all the time.'

When Cass and Denny were in the Mugwumps and the group's prospects looked grim, she would often ask, 'If this is where we are now, where will be in five years' time?' In his 2003 stage play, Denny answers her one last time: 'I don't know Cass,' he says, 'but I do know that you have to live with the things you do. The only thing is – you're gone and I miss you.'

When Cass died, many were quick to include her in the category of tragic female artists who had died drug-related deaths such as Janis Joplin, Billie Holliday and Judy Garland, but any comparisons are at best superficial. These deaths are often attributed in part to the frequent irreconcilability of being an artist and a woman in a predominantly male world, but whereas others were arguably often victims of this situation, Cass smoothed a singular path for herself by the sheer power of her voice, intelligence and personality.

Cass rarely allowed herself to be seen as a tragic figure. On the contrary, she seemed determined to survive, and one of the central ironies of her life is that ultimately she did not. Cass had extraordinary resilience and the decades following her death might have proved a more conducive environment in which to overcome her difficulties with drugs. 'Cass would have been in recovery for sure,' believes her friend Allison Caine, 'because we all knew Cass wanted to go along with the rest of us. If Cass had lived, she would have been in the front row of AA, she would have been at Betty Ford, she would have embraced sobriety and all of the new health thing. She would have gotten a nutritionist and had a gym at the house and done all that, because she was a survivor.'

Had she lived, Cass would certainly have diversified her career. She already had plans to begin producing records for other artists and was scheduled to work with an as yet unknown young singer named Roberta Flack who she had championed. But those who knew her, without exception, believe, as she did herself, that her greatest forte lay in her personality and humour and that this would easily have formed the basis of a successful long-running career as a talk-show hostess in the mode of a sharper Cilla Black, Ricki Lake or Oprah Winfrey. 'It was just so obvious,' says Michelle Phillips. 'She knew she definitely would have had her own television talk show. She would have been Oprah before Oprah was Oprah. She would have done movies, she would have done Broadway. She would have been a huge star – even today. Because she maintained her stardom all the time. She was always doing something and she had a lot of things lined up in her mind to do.'

Cass did indeed have a lot of things planned, but it seems unlikely she would have completely relinquished music. The versatility of her voice meant that she could have diversified further musically and she would surely have revelled in the current vogue for old-school musicals such as Cole Porter's *Anything Goes*. 'She could have been a blues singer and she'd have made a marvellous jazz singer,' says producer Lewis Merenstein. 'She had *enormous* emotional expression and sensitivity and she certainly had the vocal ability to sing in any style she wanted to.'

Similarly, while the seventies were a bleak time for many artists who had come to fame in the sixties, with neither disco nor punk appropriate for their styles, the eighties saw them embraced by a new generation of performers; just as Sandie Shaw, Dusty Springfield and Gene Pitney collaborated with the Smiths, the Pet Shop Boys and Marc Almond respectively and went on to have chart hits anew, Cass may certainly have enjoyed a similar musical renaissance. That same decade she would also have had the option to join John Philips's reformed Mamas and Papas, although it is unlikely she would have been so inclined.

But even apart from these possibilities, Cass had also had another idea. She told Tim Rose that she was thinking of writing a book about her time in the Mamas and the Papas.

In the decades since Cass's death, the freedom women have gained to pursue their own careers and live lives to their own design has meant that Cass's professional stance and personal life are no longer considered out of the ordinary, but some of the barriers she had to cross are, if anything, ever more rigidly in place. For all the progress women have made in their battle to be seen as individuals rather than merely objects of desire, attitudes have changed relatively little towards women who do not conform to accepted standards of female attractiveness. On the contrary, since the sixties, the pressure on women to be slim, and thus less present and less forceful, has never been so strong. Eating disorders may now be acknowledged as serious issues on par with drug or alcohol addiction, to be addressed and treated accordingly, but whatever progress may have been made in recognising these problems, the stigma of being overweight remains and Cass's phenomenal success as an international star is ever more relevant.

In the twenty-first century, 'California Dreamin'', 'Monday, Monday' and Cass's own 'Dream a Little Dream of Me' have become international standards, instantly recognised by people of all ages the world over and constantly discovered anew by each successive generation. Contemporary artists as diverse as Boy George, kd lang and Anthony Kiedis of the Red Hot Chili Peppers cite Cass as an influence. 'The greatest white female singer ever,' was how Boy George once described her, while kd lang tells me, 'It's the timbre of her voice and also her attitude and being a big woman like that and being confident. I'm very attracted to that sort of confidence and individuality. She was cool.' Kiedis, meanwhile, is similarly inspired: 'I do love The Mamas and the Papas, and maybe, subconsciously, I'm inspired by them, especially Mama Cass. There have been times when I've been very down and out in my life and the sound of her voice has sort of given me a reason to want to carry on.'

Although to many who knew her, Cass was the constant clown, the party wit who was guaranteed to make you laugh, alongside her warmth and vulnerability, the true sadness of much of her life inevitably surfaced when she sang. More than thirty years after her death, it is this humanity which continues to win over new generations of fans, because in her voice you hear her life.

Cass Elliot's Top 12

On 17 July 1974, less than two weeks before her death, Cass recorded an interview in London for BBC Radio 1's *My Top 12* with Brian Matthew. As the show's name suggests, she was required to choose twelve of her favourite records. These are the tracks she chose, in no particular order of preference, but in the order she played them:

1. Honky Tonk Women *the Rolling Stones*
2. Drive My Car *the Beatles*
3. Come Together *Ike and Tina Turner*
4. Marcie *Joni Mitchell*
5. Polk Salad Annie *Tony Joe White*
6. You're Sixteen *Ringo Starr*
7. King Midas in Reverse *the Hollies*
8. Everybody is a Star *Sly and the Family Stone*
9. You Make Me Feel Brand New *the Stylistics*
10. Maybe I'm Amazed *Paul McCartney*
11. Get Down *Gilbert O'Sullivan*
12. Living in the City *Stevie Wonder*

US and UK discography

THE BIG 3

SINGLES

The Banjo Song / Winkin', Blinkin' and Nod
10/63 FM 3003

Come Away Melinda / Rider
12/63 FM FM-9001

The Banjo Song / Winkin', Blinkin' and Nod
01/64 FM FM-9004

Nora's Dove (Dink's Song) / Grandfather's Clock
05/66 Roulette R-4689

ALBUMS

The Big Three
[The group's name was misspelt as the 'Big Three' rather than Big 3 on nearly all of their releases] 10/63 FM 307 / SFM-307

The Big Three Live at the Recording Studio
06/64 FM 311 / SFM-311

Compilations

A Rootin' Tootin' Hootenanny
One track: 'Come Along' 06/64 FM 310

The World of Folk Music
Various artists LP with exclusive live version of 'Come Along'
1964 FM 319

The Big Three Featuring Cass Elliot
Compilation featuring tracks from both Big 3 albums, issued after the Mamas and Papas' success 03/68 Roulette R/SR 25361

Distant Reflections
By the Big Three featuring Mama Cass 07/82 Accord SN-7180

Troubadours of the Folk Era Vol. 3 – The Groups
One track: 'Rider' CD 04/92 Rhino R2 70264

The Big Three Featuring Mama Cass Elliot, Tim Rose and Jim Hendricks
Reissue of both FM albums CD 10/95 UK Sequel NEMCD 755

The Magic Circle . . . Before the Mamas & the Papas
Three tracks: 'Rider', 'Come Along', and 'I May Be Right'
CD 03/99 Varèse Sarabande VSD 5996

The Big Three Featuring Mama Cass
Reissue of both FM albums CD 10/00 Collectables COL-CD 6216

THE MUGWUMPS

SINGLES

US I'll Remember Tonight / I Don't Wanna Know
09/64 Warner Bros 5471

Searchin' / Here It Is Another Day
04/67 Warner Bros 7018

UK I Don't Wanna Know / I'll Remember Tonight
10/64 Warner Bros WB 144

ALBUMS

US *The Mugwumps: An Historic Recording*
07/67 Warner Bros W/WS 1697

UK *An Historic Recording of the Mugwumps*
05/70 Valiant VS 143

The Magic Circle . . . Before the Mamas & the Papas
Two tracks: 'Searchin'' and 'I'll Remember Tonight'
CD 03/99 Varèse Sarabande VSD 5996

THE MAMAS AND THE PAPAS

SINGLES

US California Dreamin' / Somebody Groovy
12/65 Dunhill 4020

Monday, Monday / Got a Feelin'
03/66 Dunhill 4026

I Saw Her Again / Even If I Could
06/66 Dunhill 4031

Look Through My Window / Once Was a Time I Thought
10/66 Dunhill 4050

Words Of Love / Dancing in the Street
11/66 Dunhill 4057

Dedicated to the One I Love / Free Advice
02/67 Dunhill 4077

Creeque Alley / Did You Ever Want To Cry
04/67 Dunhill 4083

Twelve Thirty (Young Girls are Coming to the Canyon) / Straight Shooter
08/67 Dunhill 4099

Glad To Be Unhappy / Hey Girl
10/67 Dunhill 4107

Dancing Bear / John's Music Box
11/67 Dunhill 4113

Safe in My Garden / Too Late
05/68 Dunhill 4125

Dream a Little Dream of Me / Midnight Voyage
Shown as by Mama Cass with the Mamas and the Papas
06/68 Dunhill 4145

For The Love Of Ivy / Strange Young Girls
07/68 Dunhill/ABC 4150

Do You Wanna Dance / My Girl
10/68 Dunhill/ABC 4171

Backing vocals for Barry McGuire

Child Of Our Times / Upon A Painted Ocean
10/65 Dunhill 4014

This Precious Time / Don't You Wonder Where It's At
12/65 Dunhill 4019

UK California Dreamin' / Somebody Groovy
01/66 RCA 1503

Monday, Monday / Got a Feelin'
05/66 RCA 1516

I Saw Her Again / Even If I Could
07/66 RCA 1533

Look Through My Window / Once There Was a Time I Thought
09/66 RCA 1551

Words of Love / Dancin' in the Street
01/67 RCA 1564

Dedicated to the One I love / Free Advice
03/67 RCA 1576

Creeque Alley / Did You Ever Want to Cry
07/67 RCA 1613

Twelve Thirty (Young Girls Are Coming to the Canyon) / Straight Shooter
09/67 RCA 1630

Glad to be Unhappy / Hey Girl
12/67 RCA 1649

Safe in My Garden / Too Late
06/68 RCA 1710

For the Love of Ivy / Strange Young Girls
09/68 RCA 1744

You Baby / My Girl
02/69 Stateside SS 8009

Go Where you Wanna Go / No Salt on her Tail
09/70 Stateside SS 8058

Shooting Star / No Dough
02/72 Probe PRO 552

EPs

US *If You Can Believe Your Eyes and Ears*
01/66 Dunhill DS-50006

The Mamas & the Papas
09/66 Dunhill DS-50010

The Papas & the Mamas Presented By The Mamas & The Papas
04/68 Dunhill/ABC DS-50031

A Gathering Of Flowers
Interviews with 'Papa John' and 'Mama Cass'
10/70 Dunhill/ABC SPD-13

People Like Us
10/71 ABC 50106/Little LP LLP 167

ALBUMS

US *If You Can Believe Your Eyes and Ears*
01/66 Dunhill D/DS-50006

The Mamas & the Papas – Cass, John, Michelle, Dennie [sic]
08/66 Dunhill D/DS-50010

The Mamas & the Papas Deliver
02/67 Dunhill D/DS-50014

The Papas & the Mamas Presented by the Mamas & the Papas
04/68 Dunhill/ABC DS-50031

People Like Us
10/71 Dunhill/ABC DSX-50106
Reissued 06/89 on CD as MCA Special Markets MCAD-31344.

Backing vocals for Barry McGuire

This Precious Time
12/65 Dunhill D/DS-50005

Compilations

Farewell to the First Golden Era
10/67 Dunhill/ABC DS-50025

Golden Era, Vol. 2
09/68 Dunhill/ABC DS-50038

A Treasury of Great Contemporary Hits
07/69 Dunhill/ABC DS-50057

16 of Their Greatest Hits
09/69 Dunhill/ABC DS-50064

A Gathering of Flowers (The Anthology of the Mamas & the Papas) (2LP)
01/70 Dunhill/ABC DSY-50073

Historical Performances Recorded at the Monterey International Pop Festival
03/71 Dunhill/ABC DSX-50100
Reissued 03/91 on CD as *One Way* / MCA Special Markets MCAD-22033

20 Golden Hits (2LP)
02/73 Dunhill/ABC DSX-50145

California Dreamin'
1973 Pickwick SPC-3357

Monday, Monday
1974 Pickwick SPC-3380

The Mamas & the Papas (2LP)
1975 Pickwick PTP-2076

The ABC Collection
1976 ABC AC-30005

The Mamas And the Papas Greatest Hits (2LP)
1977 Tee Vee Int'l. TA-1006

UK *If You Can Believe Your Eyes and Ears*
01/66 RCA RD 7803

The Mamas & the Papas – Cass, John, Michelle, Dennie [sic]
01/67 RCA RD/SF 7834

The Mamas and The Papas Deliver
06/67 RCA RD/SF 7880

The Papas and the Mamas
09/68 RCA RD/7960

People Like Us
11/71 Probe SPB/1048

Compilations

Golden Era Vol. 2
12/68 Stateside (S)SL 5002

Hits of Gold
04/69 Stateside (S)SL 5007

A Gathering of Flowers
11/70 Probe SPB 1013/4

20 Golden Hits
05/73 Probe GTSP 200

Monday, Monday
01/74 MfP SPR 90025

California Dreamin'
09/74 MfP SPR 90050

Hits of Gold
10/74 ABC ABCL 5003

20 Golden Hits
10/74 ABC ABCD 604

The Best of the Mamas and the Papas
05/77 Arcade ADEP 30

The Mamas and the Papas Complete Anthology
09/04 MCA Universal 982 168 0

SOLO SINGLES

As Mama Cass

US Dream a Little Dream of Me / Midnight Voyage
Shown as by Mama Cass with the Mamas and the Papas
06/68 Dunhill 4145

Dream a Little Dream of Me / Midnight Voyage
06/68 Dunhill ST-75

California Earthquake / Talkin' to Your Toothbrush
10/68 Dunhill/ABC 4166

Move in a Little Closer, Baby / All For Me
B-side non-LP 02/69 Dunhill/ABC 4184

Move in a Little Closer, Baby / I Can Dream, Can't I?
03/69 (Stateside SS 8014)

Move in a Little Closer, Baby / All For Me
03/69 Dunhill/ABC 4195P/ 01318

It's Getting Better / Who's to Blame
05/69 Dunhill/ABC 4195

Make Your Own Kind of Music / Lady Love
10/69 Dunhill/ABC 4214

New World Coming / Blow Me a Kiss
01/70 Dunhill/ABC 4225

A Song That Never Comes (different mix) / I Can Dream, Can't I?
07/70 Dunhill/ABC 4244

Different / If I Could (Main Title) (vocal by Jack Wild)
Promo single from the film *Pufnstuf*
07/70 Capitol SPRO 5047 /45-74532

The Good Times Are Coming / Welcome to the World
11/70 Dunhill/ABC 4253

Don't Let the Good Life Pass You By / A Song That Never Comes
11/70 Dunhill/ABC 4264

UK Dream a Little Dream of Me / Midnight Voyage
6/68 RCA 1726

California Earthquake / Talkin' to your Toothbrush
11/68 Stateside SS 8002

Move in a Little Closer Baby / I Can Dream, Can't I?
03/69 Stateside SS 8014

It's Getting Better / Who's to Blame
7/69 Stateside SS 8021

Make Your Own Kind of Music / Lady Love
11/69 Stateside SS 8031

New World Coming / Blow Me A Kiss
03/70 Stateside SS 8039

A Song That Never Comes / I Can Dream, Can't I?
09/70 Stateside SS 8057

As Cass Elliot and Dave Mason

US Something To Make You Happy / Next To You
01/71 Dunhill/ABC 4266

Too Much Truth, Too Much Love / Walk to the Point
02/71 Dunhill/ABC 4271

UK Something To Make You Happy / Next to You
1970 Probe PRO513

As Cass Elliot

US Baby I'm Yours / Cherries Jubilee
02/72 RCA 74-0644

That Song / When It Doesn't Work Out
04/72 RCA 74-0693

The Costume Ball / The Costume Ball
Promo only release from the film *Doctors Wives*
Dunhill/ABC SPD 15

(If You're Gonna) Break Another Heart / Disney Girls
08/72 RCA 74-0764

Does Anybody Love You / The Road is No Place For a Lady
11/72 RCA 74-0830

I Think a Lot About You (studio version) / Listen to the World
05/73 RCA 74-0957

UK Baby I'm Yours / Cherries Jubilee
09/72 RCA 2179

If You're Gonna Break Another Heart / Don't Call Me Mama Anymore
07/74 RCA LPB 07521

SOLO ALBUMS

As Mama Cass

US *Dream a Little Dream*
10/68 Dunhill/ABC DS-50040

Dream a Little Dream of Me
Promo EP 10/68 Dunhill/ABC LP-DS-50040/7S-LP

Bubblegum, Lemonade and . . . Something For Mama
06/69 Dunhill/ABC DS-50055

Make Your Own Kind of Music
11/69 Dunhill/ABC DS-50071

Pufnstuf (Soundtrack) (one track: 'Different')
07/70 Capitol SW-542

UK *Dream a Little Dream of Me*
12/68 Stateside (S) SSL 5004

Bubblegum, Lemonade and Something for Mama
11/69 Stateside (S) SSL 5014

As Cass Elliot

US *Dave Mason & Cass Elliot*
Reissued 02/89 on CD as MCA MCAD-31340
03/71 Blue Thumb BTS-8825

Cass Elliot
02/72 RCA LSP 4619
Reissued 09/88 on CD as RCA 4619-R-2

The Road is No Place for a Lady
10/72 RCA LSP 4753

Don't Call Me Mama Anymore
09/73 RCA APL1-0303
Reissued 11/00 on CD as *One Way* OW 71000 including three bonus tracks

UK *Dave Mason and Cass Elliot*
1971 Probe SPBA 6529

Cass Elliot
1972 RCA LSP 4619

The Road is No Place for a Lady
1972 RCA SF 8306

Don't Call Me Mama Anymore
7/74 RCA APL1-0303

Compilations

US *Mama's Big Ones*
03/71 Dunhill/ABC DS-50093

Dream a Little Dream of Me
1974 Pickwick SPC-3359

Cass Elliot (2LP)
1975 Pickwick PTP-2075

Dream a Little Dream – The Cass Elliot Collection (CD)
02/97 MCA MCAD-11523

UK *Mama's Big Ones*
10/74 ABC ABCL 5011

Dedicated to the One I Love (CD)
02/02 UK Spectrum 544 625-2

RELATED RECORDINGS

SINGLES

Groovin' Is Easy / Over Lovin' You
By The Electric Flag Cass provides uncredited backing vocals on the A-side
10/67 Columbia 4-44307

Coat Of Colors / Bird Without Wings
By 3's a Crowd Produced by Cass and Steve Barri
12/67 Dunhill 4120

Give To Me Your Love / Thanks
By New Phoenix Produced by Cass
04/68 World Pacific 77884

Let's Get Together / I Don't Wanna Drive You Away
By 3's a Crowd Produced by Cass and Steve Barri
05/68 Dunhill 4131

I Taught Him Everything He Knows / A World I Can't Live In
By Roberta Sherwood Produced by Cass
06/68 Dunhill 4136

Babylon / Precious Time
By The Organ Grinders Produced by Cass
08/69 Smash S-2242

Sit Yourself Down / We Are Not Helpless
By Stephen Stills Backing vocals by Cass Elliot, Rita Coolidge, David Crosby, Graham Nash and John Sebastian
02/71 Atlantic 2790

ALBUMS

Christopher's Movie Matinee
By 3's a Crowd Cass and Steve Barri produced the album
04/68 Dunhill D/DS-50030

A Long Time Comin'
By The Electric Flag Uncredited Cass backing vocals on 'Groovin' Is Easy'
04/68 Columbia CS 9597
Reissued 11/88 on CD as CK Columbia / Sony 9597

Crosby, Stills & Nash
By Crosby, Stills & Nash Uncredited Cass vocals on 'Pre-Road Downs'
05/69 Atlantic SD 8229
Reissued on CD as Atlantic 19117-2

Stephen Stills
By Stephen Stills Cass backing vocals on three tracks: 'Go Back Home', 'Sit Yourself Down' and 'We Are Not Helpless'
11/70 Atlantic SD 7202
Reissued 12/95 on CD as Atlantic 82809-2

Cyrus
By Cyrus Faryar Cass backing vocals
10/71 Elektra EKS-74105
Reissued 08/98 on CD by Japanese Elektra - AMCY-2381

Bob Neuwirth

By Bob Neuwirth   Cass backing vocals

09/74   Asylum 7E-1008

Reissued 10/98 on CD Japanese Asylum AMCY-2902

Replay

By Crosby, Stills & Nash   Cass's vocals on 'Pre-Road Downs' *are* credited on this album

12/80   Atlantic SD 16026

Reissued 12/94 on UK CD as Atlantic 75682679–2

Beautiful Thing: Music From and Inspired By the Motion Picture (soundtrack CD)

10/96   MCA MCAD-60013

With thanks to Richard Barton Campbell and Greg Russo

Bibliography

Barris, Chuck. *The Game Show King: A Confession.* Caroll & Graf, New York, 1993

Breiner, Wini. *Young, White and Miserable: Growing up Female in the 50s.* The University of Chicago Press, 1992

Brend, Mark. *American Troubadors.* Backbeat Books, San Francisco, 2001

Cantwell, Robert. *When We Were Good.* Harvard University Press, 1996

Carne, Judy with Merrill, Bob. *Laughing on the Outside, Crying on the Inside.* Paperjacks, New York, 1986

Crosby, David & Bender, David. *Stand and Be Counted.* Harper San Francisco, 2000

Crosby, David & Gottlieb, Carl. *Long Time Gone.* Doubleday, New York, 1988

Didion, Joan. *The White Album.* Simon & Schuster, New York, 1979

Einarson, John & Furay, Richie. *For What It's Worth: The Story of Buffalo Springfield.* Rogan House, London, 1997

Frame, Pete. *More Rock Family Trees.* Omnibus Press, London, 1998

Gavin, James. *Intimate Nights.* Limelight Editions, New York, 1992

Gitlin, Todd. *The Sixties: Years of Hope, Days of Rage.* Bantam, New York, 1989

Greenwald, Matthew. *Go Where You Wanna Go: The Oral History of the Mamas and the Papas.* Cooper Square Press, New York, 2002

Halasz, Piri. *A Swinger's Guide to London.* Coward McCann, New York, 1997

Hall, Doug. *The Mamas and the Papas: California Dreamin'.* Quarry Press Inc., Kingston, Ontario, 2000

Heale, M. J. *The Sixties in America.* Edinburgh University Press, Edinburgh, 2001

Hoskyns, Barney. *Waiting for the Sun.* Bloomsbury, London, 1997

Johnson, Jon. *Make Your Own Kind of Music: A Career Retrospective of Cass Elliot*. Music Archives Press, Los Angeles, 1987

Laing, Dave, Dallas, Karl, Shelton, Robert & Denselow, Robin. *The Electric Muse: The Story of Folk into Rock*. Eyre Methuen, London, 1975

Lee, Martin A. & Shlain, Bruce. *Acid Dreams, The Complete Social History of LSD: The CIA, the Sixties and Beyond*. Grove Press, New York, 1992

Levy, Shawn. *Ready, Steady, Go!*. Fourth Estate, London, 2002

Lewisohn, Mark. *The Complete Beatles Chronicle*. Pyramid Books, London, 1992

Masters, Brian. *The Swinging Sixties*. Constable, London, 1985

McParland, Stephen. *California Confidential: In Conversation with Kim Fowley*. California Music Books, Australia, 2000

Oldham, Loog Andrew. *2Stoned*. Vintage, London, 2002

Orbach, Susie. *Fat is a Feminist Issue*. Arrow, London, 1998

Phillips, John. *Papa John*. Dolphin Books, New York, 1986

Phillips, Michelle. *California Dreamin'*. Warner Books, New York, 1986

Ruppell Shell, Ellen. *The Hungry Gene: The Science of Fat and the Future of Thin*. Atlantic Books, London, 2002

Sanders, Ed. *The Family*. Nemesis Books, London,1993

Shapiro, Harry. *Graham Bond, the Mighty Shadow*. Guinness Publishing, London, 1992

Shapiro, Harry. *Waiting for the Man: The Story of Drugs and Popular Music*. Helter Skelter Publishing, London, 1999

Silverman, Chip. *Diner Guys*. Birch Lane Press, New York, 1989

Smiley Childs, Marti & March, Jeff. *Echoes of the Sixties*. Billboard Books, New York, 1999

Taylor, Derek. *It was Twenty Years Ago Today*. Simon and Schuster, New York, 1987

Unterberger, Richie. *Eight Miles High*. Backbeat Books, San Francisco, 2003

Unterberger, Richie. *Turn, Turn, Turn*. Backbeat Books, San Francisco, 2002

Webb, Adam. *The Life and Music of Dennis Wilson*. Creation Books, London, 2001

Woliver, Robbie. *Hoot: A Twenty-Five Year History of the Greenwich Village Music Scene*. St Martin's Press, New York, 1994

Zimmer, Dave & Diltz, Henry. *Crosby, Stills & Nash: The Biography*. Da Capo Press, Cambridge, MA, 2000

Index

extracts reading groups
competitions books new
discounts extracts
competitions
books new
events books
extracts
new reading groups
interviews
events extracts
discounts
new books events
events new
discounts extracts discounts
www.panmacmillan.com
extracts events reading groups
competitions books extracts new

Printed in the USA
CPSIA information can be obtained
at www.ICGtesting.com
CBHW031207160324
5470CB00008B/428